RESCUE AS RESISTANCE

How Jewish Organizations
Fought the Holocaust in France

RESCUE AS RESISTANCE

How Jewish Organizations
Fought the Holocaust in France

Lucien Lazare

Translated by Jeffrey M. Green

COLUMBIA UNIVERSITY PRESS
NEW YORK

Columbia University Press
New York   Chichester, West Sussex
Copyright © 1996 Columbia University Press
All rights reserved

Library of Congress Cataloging-in-Publication Data
Lazare, Lucien.
  [Résistance juive en France. English]
  Rescue as resistance : how Jewish organizations fought the
Holocaust in France / Lucien Lazare ; translated by Jeffrey M.
Green.
      p. cm.
  Includes bibliographical references and index.
  ISBN 0-231-10124-4 (cloth : alk. paper)
    1. Jews—Persecutions—France. 2. Holocaust, Jewish (1939-1945)—
France. 3. World War, 1939-1945—Jewish resistance—France.
4. World War, 1939-1945—Jews—Rescue—France. 5. France—Ethnic
relations. I. Title.
DS135.F83L3613   1996
944'.004924—dc20   95-50615
                                                              CIP

Casebound editions of Columbia University Press books are printed on permanent and
durable acid-free paper.
Printed in the United States of America
c 10 9 8 7 6 5 4 3 2 1

The Press gratefully acknowledges the generous assistance of the Florence Gould Foundation
and the French Cultural Services in the publication of this work.

TO JANINE

Contents

༄ঙ৽

༄ঙ৽

Foreword

In contemporary usage, the term *Resistance* is clearly categorized. In France, the Resistance has its National Committee and its medal. Members of the Resistance are known as *maquisards*, or *francs-tireurs*. This vocabulary features the combat waged against the occupiers and their collaborators on French soil by men and women, without regard to ethnic origin, religion, or ideology.

This general definition nevertheless obscures Jewish resistance, but not that of Jewish members of the Resistance, who were in no way different from other members on the level of commitment and action. It obscures, rather, the resistance of those who acted within Jewish resistance movements to wage a battle for survival. At first they did it all alone, and later with the help of other Frenchmen.

These two parallel combats are very different, although the enemy was the same. The chronology, what was at stake, and the operations were essentially very different.

French national resistance began in 1940 with the Occupation, whereas Jewish resistance began as early as 1938, with the rise of external dangers.

The goal of the former was to rid the homeland of the Nazi invaders, while that of the latter was also the struggle to ensure the survival of men, women, and children who were hunted down because they were Jewish.

The strategy of the Resistance was guerrilla warfare, both psychological and military; that of Jewish resistance often gave priority to rescue, by spiriting some people across the borders and by camouflaging most Jews as Aryans in France itself.

As for the operations themselves, for the former they consisted in gaining support by means of the underground press and by infiltrating the government, sabotaging communications, and harassing enemy troops. But the other resistance was devoted to assisting Jews who were deprived of means of subsistence, providing them with false identity papers, finding safe shelters for them, supporting them morally and spiritually, helping prisoners escape, and sometimes by the armed elimination of those who informed on Jews.

The Resistance sought to put an end to French subjugation, which overlapped with one of the major aims of the Allied war effort. The Resistance fought for the liberty and honor of the nation.

The Jews, for their part, were aware that the enemy sought their disappearance, though they did not know how it intended to carry out its wishes. In fact those who had an intuition of the Nazi plan of dehumanization and physical extermination were few.

At first, as the dangers increased, the Jews labored to maintain their spiritual and cultural life. But when the occupiers and their collaborators arrested, concentrated, and deported Jews, this was a brutal break, following which physical survival no longer depended only upon assistance, but also and primarily upon as complete a dissimulation as possible of Jewish identity.

Nevertheless the passion French and immigrant Jews bore for France gave them a powerful desire to associate themselves with the general struggle. They did so within the ranks of the French forces of the interior (FFI, *Forces Françaises de l'Intérieur*) and of the irregulars and partisans (FTTP, *Francs-tireurs et partisans*). Thus the tenacity with which these Jews clung to life was equalled only by that which they displayed in armed combat.

A study tracing the vicissitudes of this particular resistance movement has long been needed. This is the past that Lucien Lazare, a historian but also a witness and participant, has explored in this excellent book.

Acknowledgments

I was asked to write this study by former members of the Jewish resistance in France and by the directors of Yad Vashem in Jerusalem, who made available to me the means necessary for accomplishing the project.

Their goal is to make the battle of the Jews of France under German occupation better known, for this battle has too often been minimized, even hidden from view.

I extend my complete gratitude to them, and in particular to those who permitted me to consult their archival sources: Hadassa Modlinger and Judith Kleiman (Yad Vashem), Claudine Cohen-Naar and Ulrich Hessel (Centre de Documentation Juive Contemporaine in Paris), Marek Web and Fruma Mohrer (Yivo Institute in New York), Menahem Schmelzer (Jewish Theological Seminary in New York), Cardinal Jean-Marie Lustiger and the RP Philippe Ploix (the Maison Diocésaine of Paris), and Alain Michel (Éclaireurs israélites de France in Paris).

In my travels in search of sources for this study, I benefited from the warm hospitality of Charlie and Else Bendheim, Henri and Bella Masliah in New York and Jean-Louis and Micheline Trèves in Paris.

I am grateful to Aron-Lucien Lubin and Abraham Polonski, who made available the archives of the Armée Juive, to Adrien Gensburger and Jean Hirsch, who showed me the logs of the Compagnie Marc Haguenau, as well as to all those who gave me access to their private collections or provided documents: Arlette Abraham, Henri Bulawko, Rachel Chegam, Léon Chertok, Lilette Cohen, Margot Cohn, Rachel Cohn, Ralf Feigelson, Roger Fichtenberg, Ignace Fink, Gaby Shor-Fischer, Denise Gamzon, Marie-Rose Gineste, Sigismond Hirsch, René Kapel, Pierrot Kaufmann, Hillel Kieval, Serge Klarsfeld, Anne-Marie Lambert, Georges Loinger, André and Renée Neher, Jacques Pulver, Emmanuel Racine, Andrée Salomon, Vivette Samuel, Denise Sikierski, Claude Spiero, André Ullmo, Claude Vigée, Denise Weil, Jacqueline Dreyfus-Weil, and Ninon Weyl-Hait. Former resisters have given me their testimony, which is acknowledged in my notes. While I was working, Richard I. Cohen read and annotated my manuscript with zealous attention, and I have benefited from his rich experience. Azaria Shmueli edited the text of this book with scrupulous care.

Alex Derczanski, Annie Kriegel, Robert O. Paxton, and Léon Poliakov offered me plentiful advice with infinite patience. My conversations with Hillel Kieval, Serge Klarsfeld, and Renée Poznanski sharpened my understanding of the sources. My thanks to them all.

The Scientific Director of Yad Vashem, Israel Gutman, guided my steps throughout this study. I remain deeply grateful to him.

I also benefited from the initiative and persistance of my friend Julien Engel. A grant from the Florence Gould Foundation made the English translation possible.

LUCIEN LAZARE

RESCUE AS RESISTANCE

How Jewish Organizations
Fought the Holocaust in France

PART I

THE RISING DANGER

1

⋄⟨❀⟩⋄

France from 1938 to June 1940 and the
Problem of Foreign Nationals

The first transport of Jews deported from France to Auschwitz left the Bourget railway station on March 27, 1942. It consisted mainly of people of foreign nationality.[1] Though the Nazis were not concerned with the such a distinction, the French authorities, whose police force had jurisdiction over the arrest of the Jews destined for deportation, preferred to send away foreigners.

As early as 1938 the French government had begun to apply repressive measures against foreign nationals, whose presence in the country was felt at that time as a threat to national prosperity and security. Aversion toward foreigners only increased as time passed. Hence they were the first target chosen for the anti-Jewish policies of the Vichy regime, beginning in 1940.

An Outburst of Xenophobic and Anti-Semitic Fever

Often receptive to immigration and proud of its traditions of hospitality, France did not as a general rule betray the confidence and hopes of those who sought refuge on its soil. Thus it is necessary to dwell upon the circumstances attending the upsurge of xenophobia and anti-Semitism in France immediately before the war.

Instability and the threat of war in the international arena and domestic political and economic stagnation imbued the French with feelings of unrest and insecurity in 1938–39. Their confidence in republican institutions was shaken. Fear of war was inspired both by a profound desire for peace and by the more or less clear awareness of their country's lack of preparedness. The applause that greeted the Munich agreement of September 1938, despite French commitments to Czechoslovakia, revealed the defeatism pervading public opinion.

Following Franco's victory in Spain in March 1939, France found itself facing totalitarian regimes on three of its continental borders, and the dynamism, military potential, and cohesion of these regimes were attractive. Successively, the war in Ethiopia, the Anschluss, the Sudeten crisis, and the invasion of Czechoslovakia had underscored the incapacity of democratic regimes to resist the barrage of territorial expansion launched by the dictatorships and their policy of force. Those who had believed in the reliability of the agreements negotiated and signed with Nazi Germany now lost their illusions.

Domestically, the combined effects of the economic crisis and the failure of the Popular Front had shaken loyalty to the Third Republic, which was unable to prevent governmental instability, social unrest, economic stagnation, and political and financial scandals. A portion of the public lent a sympathetic ear to those who would challenge a regime that no longer seemed capable of coping with fascist dictatorships and the Soviet Union. Discontent and worry had created a climate favorable to the campaigns waged against the republican regime both by the Communist Party, which favored an alignment on the Stalinist model, and by rightist parties and leagues agitating for a constitution similar to those that had triumphed in Rome, Berlin, or Madrid. The receptivity of large portions of French public opinion to foreign political experiments betrayed a decline in the national pride of a people formerly convinced of their value. Both those nostalgic for the ancien régime and committed republicans had once based their national self-esteem upon belief in French hegemony as a factor in the progress and civilization of the world. Now, instead of placing their own experience in the service of foreign peoples, an increasing number of Frenchmen sought models abroad to resolve their internal crises. In the 1930s it had not been common to compare French demographic and economic statistics with those of other powers. Hence the political leadership paid scant attention to the regressive character of the French situation. Doubtless the French people were aware of the country's demographic decline, leading the governments of the 1920s to call for the immigration of foreign workers, and in 1939 the Family Code was finally instituted to stimulate population growth.

However, they were not aware of the lag in technology and industry. Nearly half of the French population (48.8% in 1931) was still rural, at a time when less than a quarter of the population of other industrialized countries was rural. On the whole, French agriculture continued to use nineteenth-century methods and equipment. Industry, crafts, and communications networks suffered from a very low rate of investment, which paralyzed technological progress and commercial dynamism.

The world economic crisis, which did not affect France until 1931, paradoxically disguised the true causes of the vulnerability of the French economy. Rather than acknowledging that the country had fallen behind in the modernization of plants and equipment, the French explained away unemployment and the decline in purchasing power as the repercussions of the world crisis and by the presence of considerable numbers of immigrants in the country.

Further, the 1930s were marked by an explosion of xenophobic feelings encouraged by the anti-Semitic propaganda of the Nazis. As early as 1920 a significant part of the Parisian press had been infected with anti-Semitic fever. The Bolshevik revolution, the abandonment of France by the Allies during the negotiations at the peace conference, the British mandate in Palestine—all of these were attributed to "Judeo-German intrigues."[2] During the following years, however, there was a decline in anti-Semitism and xenophobia. In 1924 the anti-Semitic newspaper *La Libre Parole* ceased publication.[3] The law of August 10, 1927 generously liberalized the procedures for acquiring French nationality. The Popular Front, having won the elections of 1936, appointed Léon Blum, the most prestigious and widely heeded leader of the left, as President of the Council, despite implacable hatred and attacks directed against him by anti-Semitic circles.

While xenophobic and anti-Semitic passion had become a constant element in French political battles by the time of the Popular Front's electoral victory, nevertheless one segment of public opinion was immune to this contamination. François Goguel[4] has suggested a dual division of contemporary France. Transcending the multiplicity of political parties and spiritual affinities, two antagonistic temperaments split the French population into rather equal parts: those who believe in the established order and those who believe in movement, to adopt Goguel's analysis and terminology. Being a "permanent factor" in the French situation, this division into two camps can be a tool for analyzing political choices. By taking aspirations and irrational tendencies into account, it enables one to explain how the intensity of passion has occasionally overcome the reflexes of democratic discipline.

During the 1930s, France was prone to deep malaise. The unprecedented economic crisis had shaken confidence in the virtues of liberal regimes that had previously given Western democracies prosperity and political hegemony in the world. The challenges presented by the Bolshevik regime and the rapidly expanding fascist dictatorships made it necessary to revise political values and options. Journalists and authors evoked feelings of insecurity and national decadence. Rightist political organizations emphasized the necessity of domestic reform: in 1939 Drieu La Rochelle warned against "the terrible French inadequacy."[5]

The camp of the established order, with its conservative mentality, focussed its fears on the dangers of Bolshevism, denouncing the leaders of the Popular Front as its agents. The conservatives applauded the Munich agreement, viewing the Nazi dictatorship as a bulwark against Bolshevism.[6] "Better Hitler than Blum," became a popular slogan in the late 1930s. Although anti-Semitism had not been manifest during the prior decade, nevertheless it remained as a "residue of antipathy toward the Jews"[7] and reemerged in the context of the passionate climate of crisis. The Stavisky affair[8] brought anti-Semitism to the foreground, and it was "an important catalyst in mobilizing opposition to the Popular Front."[9] Prominent writers such as Bernanos, Brasillach, Céline, and Drieu La Rochelle made their readers familiar with militant anti-Semitism, sometimes expressing themselves with unrestrained violence. In 1939, Jean Giraudoux, the Superintendent of Information in the Daladier government, recommended the creation of a Ministry of Race.[10]

Conversely, those in favor of social progress saw the rise of fascism as endangering France. This camp of movement protested against the Munich agreement.[11] Its mentality was strongly represented in the parties of the left and was the source of its electoral achievements. Called first the Union of the Left and then the Popular Front, the coalition of these parties gained a majority in the Chamber of Deputies in three of the five elections held between the world wars.[12] Nevertheless, the coalition collapsed every time it took power, when interests other than electoral alliances came into play. For in fact the socioeconomic program of the radical socialists was incompatible with that of the socialist and communist parties.[13]

Thus the barrier against fascism raised by the left was neutralized or circumvented. Governmental instability derived from the precariousness of the electoral coalitions exacerbated the feeling of insecurity. Pre-fascist tendencies gained ground, expressed by the new extreme-right parties and aimed at combatting the parliamentary republic.

The Jews, the First Target of Xenophobic Laws Under the Third Republic

The atmosphere thus created favored xenophobic and anti-Semitic feelings. The repeated failures of the parties of movement to remain in power ultimately cleared the way for the opposing camp, that of the established order. The rules of the parliamentary game and democratic discipline ceased to operate. Thus, starting in the spring of 1938, the Daladier government took measures against foreign nationals consistent with the desires of the xenophobic circles. The decree of May 2, 1938 called for the expulsion of foreign nationals without residence or work permits. Those foreigners who were expelled but unable to find another country to accept them would be assigned to live under police surveillance in remote villages. One section of this decree specified the sanctions to be imposed on illegal immigrants caught using false papers, but an appended report denied that it sullied the French tradition of hospitality, since the government only wished "to strike at any foreigner . . . unworthy of our hospitality."[14]

On November 12, 1938 another decree increased the severity of the preceding one by replacing house arrest with detention in "special centers." According to Marrus and Paxton, this text is "the act of founding concentration camps in France."[15] The later decree also simplified the procedure for depriving naturalized citizens of their French nationality if they were "unworthy of the title of French citizen."[16]

Between the promulgation of these two decrees the International Conference on Refugees, convened by President Roosevelt, had been held at Evian in July 1938. The thirty-two participant countries proved quite reluctant to admit the political and racial refugees driven out of Germany and Austria by Nazi terror. The failure of this conference left the victims the choice between acceptance of persecution or the hazards of illegally entering a foreign country. The tragedy entered a more acute phase following the violence committed against Jews throughout Germany after Crystal Night, November 10, 1938, three days after the assassination in Paris of the German diplomat von Rath by a young Jew of Polish origin, Grynszpan.

In France foreigners had become an obsession during the 1930s. At the beginning of the decade they constituted seven percent of the population, approximately three million people. The largest groups were the Poles and the Italians, most of whom had been encouraged to move to France after the First World War, when there was a general shortage of labor in France. After 1931 the economic crisis caused the departure of some foreigners, and despite continued influx into the country, their total had decreased by 500,000 by 1936.

Xenophobia was aroused by unemployment, the decline in industrial production, as well as the instability of the international situation. Hitherto foreigners had been welcomed in the name of French traditions of hospitality. Moreover there had been a need for workers and soldiers in response to the larger population of Germany. Henceforth they were perceived as a burden and a threat to the country's security. Italian refugees fleeing the Fascist regime might constitute a possible source of diplomatic complications with Italy. Similarly, from 1933 on, the arrival of German refugees, including many Jews, was viewed by some Frenchmen as potentially damaging to Franco-German relations. Finally, in January 1939, a total of 400,000 refugees arrived from Spain—escaped members of the International Brigades and Spanish republicans fearing reprisals from Franco—and this sudden influx provoked a repressive reflex in the French authorities. Denounced as formentors of Bolshevik subversion and as enemy infiltrators upon the nation's soil, these refugees were placed in mass detention centers.

For almost ten years the clientele of the rightist parties as well as a growing number of unionized workers, dominated by the specter of unemployment, became accustomed to the idea that the foreigner was the enemy of France. The Jews occupied a growing place in this ideology, disproportionate to their numbers among the immigrants and refugees, and they were singled out as warmongers. Drieu La Rochelle wrote that an invasion of four million foreigners, including one million Jews, had descended upon France.[17] The deputies of the right demanded that the government put a stop to the influx of stateless Jews, the agents of Bolshevism and anarchism.

Because of the absence of data on the illegal entry of some of the Jewish refugees after 1933, the number of foreign Jews in France can merely be estimated. According to Y. Bauer, 55,000 Jewish refugees who had arrived after 1933 were still present in France on the eve of the war.[18] If one adds the 90,000 Jewish immigrants present in 1933,[19] one comes to a total of about 150,000 foreign Jews in 1939, which was 0.35% of the French population and only 6% of the number of foreigners. For the sake of comparison, the number of immigrants who arrived following 1933 was 720,000, of whom 620,000 were political and racial refugees.[20] The repressive measures contained in the decrees of May and November 1938 were not directed explicitly at the Jews. Nevertheless, the political and racial refugees, including a high proportion of Jews, were the first counted among the "undesirable" foreigners. Most of them had entered France illegally and did not possess valid residence permits. Upon the outbreak of the war, they were detained. In the course of Franco-British and Franco-German diplomatic contacts, the Quai d'Orsay made known a plan to settle 10,000 Jewish refugees in New Caledonia or Madagascar, conditional upon the participation of the other member countries of the Evian Committee for Refugees that had been established in London.[21] During the first days of the state of emergency in September 1939 after the outbreak of the war, the police indiscriminately arrested 15,000 "enemy" nationals, mainly German and Austrian refugees. They were detained in the camps at Gurs, le Vernet, and Saint-Cyprien which had been hastily established several months earlier to assemble the refugees from Spain, most of whom had already chosen to be repatriated.

Almost half of those detained in September 1939 were freed during the following three months. But the arrests were resumed in May 1940, this time of entire families. Of the 40,000 civilians detained in camps in the South of France in 1940, 70 percent were Jews.[22]

Thus two-thirds of the victims of the 1938 legislation permitting the authorities to deprive foreigners of their liberty belonged to a community that represented only 6 percent of the total of foreigners in France: the Jews. Certainly texts and official speeches under the Third Republic were free of any anti-Semitic references. Nonetheless the mechanisms established by the policies regarding foreigners were chiefly used against Jews who had been driven out by the Nazis and believed they had found a safe haven in France.

On June 14, 1940, the German army entered Paris. Having become President of the Council, Marshal Pétain demanded the acceptance of the armistice conditions of June 17; then on July 10, he disbanded Parliament. The Third Republic was no more. The most active members of the camp of order had taken power. The portion of the public in favor of the camp of movement accepted the situation born in military defeat. It took refuge in fervent devotion to the Hero of Verdun. On the whole it plunged into a state of prolonged lethargy. Further, the policies regarding foreigners instituted by the decrees of 1938 had not aroused public opinion to the point of making the authorities back down or even hesitate.

These policies could thus be pursued and reinforced without the risk of arousing more criticism than had been the case under the Third Republic. Far from being relegated to the background by the military, political, and economic aspects of the defeat and the Occupation, the problem of foreigners and refugees in France became more acute than ever. The exodus had displaced eight million people who fled to the south, terrorized by the onslaught of the German troops. These included 1.2 million people of various nationalities, fleeing from Holland, Belgium, and Luxembourg. One of the major early concerns of Marshal Pétain's new regime was to repatriate these millions of refugees to the north. The German authorities refused the entry to the territories they had occupied of about 40,000 Jews who had fled from Belgium and the Netherlands.[23] Thirty thousand foreign Jews, who had enlisted in the French army as volunteers, were demobilized[24] and detained or else enrolled in the Foreign Laborers Groups (*Groupes de travailleurs étrangers*, GTE).

These measures did not constitute a new policy but rather the continuation of that which had been instituted two years earlier by the Daladier government. They came into play before the promulgation of repressive anti-Jewish laws and before the French authorities bowed to German pressure or demands. For years foreigners had been perceived as the enemies of France. After the defeat they became the scapegoats, responsible for the country's misfortunes. More than the rest, the foreign Jews lacked consular protection and the possibility of repatriation or emigration, and thus they became the privileged target of repressive administrative measures. Even the tens of thousands who had fought in French uniforms, many of whom had received military honors, were subject to the treatment designed by the Third Republic for foreigners "unworthy of our hospitality."[25]

The centralized structures and traditions of France doubtless affected the behavior of the authorities, leading officials undeviatingly to obey the wishes of the parties of the established order, which had held power since 1938. The passivity and resignation of the French who identified with the humanitarian values of the camp of movement had left the field free for the zealots of xenophobia and anti-Semitism. Among the Jews in France, up to now only the foreigners had been targeted. Still spared, the Jews of French nationality were very soon to become the object of new legislation promoted by the Vichy regime.

2

۞

The Jews in France in 1938–1939

While census data taken in secular and republican France did not indicate the religious affiliation of the respondents, the Vichy government counted the Jews separately as part of its consistent policy of discrimination. Hence information exists today that permits an estimate of the demographic situation of the Jews in 1939 and 1940.

The global figures of the census taken in the summer of 1941 indicate 287,962 Jews.[1] Regarding the Jews who went uncounted, one must be satisfied with data that is verifiable though only approximate, about prisoners of war and people held in detention. The figures are shown in table 2.1

Thus there were approximately 340,000 Jews in France in July 1941. One year earlier, during the weeks following the armistice of June 1940, the Jewish population had included another 10,000 who emigrated before the Vichy census. Hence the number of Jews in France at that time was approximately 350,000.[2]

As for the Jewish population of France in September 1939, when the Second World War began, the earlier total of 350,000 includes 40,000 Jewish refugees from Belgium, Holland, and Luxembourg who arrived in France after the shock of the Nazi invasion in May and June of 1940, as well as 6,500 Jews from Baden and the Palatinate, who had been deported by the Nazis in

Table 2.1

NUMBER OF JEWS IN FRANCE, JULY 1941

Number of Jews Counted in Census	287,962
Prisoners of war	12,000[a]
Detainees in French camps and GTEs	35,000[a]
Those who avoided the census	*5,000[a]*
Total uncounted:	52,000[a]
Total Jews in France:	339,962

[a]Figures are approximate

the southern zone in October 1940. Thus in September 1939 there were approximately 300,000 Jews in France.

The 1941 census data indicate that 60 percent of the Jews were French nationals (of whom about three-fifths were French by birth and two-fifths were naturalized citizens), and 40 percent of the Jews were foreign nationals and stateless. Thus the national origins of the Jewish population of France in 1939 can be divided as shown in table 2.2.

Table 2.2

THE NATIONAL ORIGINS OF THE JEWISH POPULATION OF FRANCE, 1939

Native Jews:	110,000		110,000
Immigrant Jews:	190,000	including	
		naturalized French	
		citizens:	*70,000*
		Total of French Jews:	180,000
		Foreign nationals and	
		stateless:	*120,000*
Total:	300,000		300,000

This population was not homogeneous. Most historians accentuate the division between native and immigrant Jews. Vidal-Naquet emphasizes the cultural oppositions and their political implications: "I belong to . . . a family where patriotism, you might even say French chauvinism, had become a kind of second nature. . . . The immigrants were, in general, rather poorly accepted by their 'coreligionists' of French origin, who viewed them as inciting to anti-Semitism."[3]

One could easily present numerous quotations illustrating the same division, taken from the studies of Poliakov, Scherr, Schwarzfuchs, and Philippe.[4]

Without having the same family experience as Vidal-Naquet, these authors
concur with his conclusions. Nevertheless the situation was not black and
white. "The Jews in France in 1939 did not constitute *one* community or even
two communities (or two subgroups), but rather a *plural* group whose
boundaries are and were truly indefinable."[5] Internal divisions deprived this
group of all homogeneity. Fragmentation and confusion thwarted any effort
at unification. "The community lived on a petty level and was rather little
concerned with its survival," writes Schwarzfuchs.[6] This observation refers to
the conservative management of communal affairs as well as the absence of
projects or initiatives meant to cope with problems directly concerning the
Jews: anti-Semitism, the influx of refugees, and Zionism.

Immigrant Jews from One Generation to Another

Studies of the history of the Jews in France between the two world wars have
explored articles in the press as well as those archives which were accessible;
they also gathered and utilized oral testimony. What is now needed is a
typology that will provide a key for the clear understanding of that turbu-
lent period.[7] Despite the abundance of literature, there are certain blind
spots. Thus no study describes the life of the many *shuln*, small religious
communities of Jewish immigrants, which re-created the liturgical institutions of their places of origin in Paris and in several cities of the east and
north of France.[8] Though they were centers of the communal life for a considerable part of the Jewish immigrants, these *shuln* were nevertheless abandoned by the second generation, who had already been acculturated by their
schools. The sons and daughters of *practicing*, Yiddish-speaking Jews spoke
French and were increasingly less observant of religious prescriptions. The
French cultural model exercised an attractive force sufficient to divide the
first two generations of immigrants, giving rise to radically different views
of commitment to their communities. The majority of the children of
observant Jews abandoned all participation in organized Jewish life, while
others, more political than their parents, were active in Zionist movements,
the collection of funds for Jewish settlement in Palestine, international
Jewish social action, the French Jewish press, and various cultural and athletic organizations frequented by immigrant Jews.[9] They opted for a political response to anti-Semitism, providing a major part of the activists and
militants in the Ligue internationale contre l'antisémitisme (LICA, the
International League Against anti-Semitism), which was founded in 1928.[10]

Weak among native Jews, the immigrant Jews' tendency to organize had
given rise to a profusion of associations, movements, parties, charities, and

publications (Paula Hyman lists the titles of 133 Yiddish dailies published in France between the two world wars).[11] This profusion is both an expression of the vitality of the first generation of immigrants and of its difficulties in identifying with the established community, and it also illustrates its extreme heterogeneity, a major cause of fragmentation on the level of institutions and leadership. Generally speaking the immigrants, arriving in waves of various size, integrated neither within the existing structures of native French Jewish organizations nor within those created by earlier groups of immigrants.

Although efforts at integration had been made, they failed, in part because the leadership circles remained hermetically sealed against the new arrivals.[12] In this respect, France was in no way different from other countries that were open to Jewish immigration, as shown by historical studies of the other Western Jewish communities.[13] Similarly, the rapid acculturation and integration of the second generation to their new surroundings (at first the French Jewish community and later French society itself), along with their identification with their adopted country, ultimately rendered obsolete the organizations of the new immigrants. Everything took place as though a "centrifugal dynamic"[14] were casting the Jews "from the ghetto into the West."[15] By the end of the 1930s, the children and grandchildren of immigrants from the turn of the century sat on consistorial boards and served as rabbis,[16] while others had achieved eminence in the world of the sciences and letters.

The most frequent reflex among the new arrivals was to establish *landsmanshaften*, mutual associations of people from the same area, which advanced money to their members for burial, sickness, and unemployment. There were more than 170 of these in 1939.[17] For the nonobservant, these *landsmanshaften* served as community centers. Many of them contained libraries, cultural circles (mainly offering classes in French), legal assistance specializing in naturalization procedures, a small auxiliary school in Yiddish, and a fund for loans and mutual assistance. The waves of Jewish immigration during the 1920s and 1930s contained a relatively high proportion of political militants, unequally divided among Zionists, Bundists (socialists, mainly Polish, who were radically opposed both to the Communist Party and to Zionism), and communists.

The majority of *landsmanshaften* were affiliated with federative organizations. The *Féderation des sociétés juives de France* (FSJF, the Federation of Jewish Associations of France), founded in 1913, included nearly ninety of them in 1938. The president of the FSJF, Marc Jarblum, a Zionist connected with the directors of the French socialist party, known as La section française de l'Internationale ouvrière (sfio, the French Section of the Workers' International), had given it a Zionist leaning. For their part, in 1938 the communist Jews created the Union des sociétés juives (usj, The Union of Jewish Associations), with which about 50 *landsmanshaften* were affiliated.[18] These two federations indicate a profound need for unity, which was nevertheless counteracted by political rivalry for leadership of the Jewish immigrants as a whole. Let us add that there was some tension between older *landsmanshaften* and the new arrivals, mainly associated with the usj, who reproached the former for being too bourgeois.[19]

Like the observant Jews, the second generation of those identified with the fsjf did not generally adopt their parents' communal identification or political activism. Those who did pursue committed Jewish action, a minority, were affiliated with he same organizations as the children of observant Jews, notably the lica. Hyman notes that the first generation tried to "maintain its judaism," as it had been observed in its country of origin. But its institutions were abandoned by the young people. The auxiliary schools, both religious and secular, were attended by only 1,500 children in 1939, which was less than 10 percent of the school-age children of the immigrants.[20]

This could indicate a degree of inconsistency in the parents' behavior. Although they wished to transmit their heritage of traditions and values, they also wanted to provide their children with the tools necessary for mastering Western culture and gaining economic success. They resolved this contradiction to the detriment of Jewish education.[21]

The Consistory and Youth

On this particular point, they followed the reflexes that had characterized the emancipated Jews of the West since the beginning of the nineteenth century, in the case of France. The participation of native French Jews in communal life was plummeting. The decline of their institutions, their religious associations (known as "*consistoires*," Consistories, a term dating back to the Napoleonic age) accelerated sharply during the 1930s: there was a strong decrease in the number of dues-paying members, in rabbis, in Bar Mitzvah ceremonies, marriages, and burials. Participation in consistorial elections was reduced to insignificant numbers. The auxiliary schools of the consistorial communities had even fewer pupils, both absolutely and relatively, than those of the organization of immigrant Jews.[22]

Nevertheless, some members of the younger generations were active between the two wars, attempting to give a new spirit to French Judaism. In

1919 they founded a youth association, Chema Israël, with educational and religious aims. After rapid development in the capital and in fourteen provincial communities, the association declined with equal rapidity, reducing its activities to the simplest level by the end of the 1930s.[23]

Other young people from Consistorial circles had joined the *Union universelle de la jeunesse juive* (UUJJ, the Universal Union of Jewish Youth), created by immigrants from Salonika. The UUJJ called for a fight against assimilation and addressed all young Jews, whether or not they were believers. It took a position in favor of Zionism, set in motion an education program that included the study of modern Hebrew, and undertook action against anti-Semitism as well as in defense of the rights of national minorities. The Consistory and its rabbis published vigorous critiques of the UUJJ, reproaching it for adopting a secular form of Judaism and for commitment to political action. After a period of exceptional success toward the end of the 1920s, when it served as one of the rare meeting places between young native-born Jews and immigrants, the association began to dwindle, and by 1938 it was moribund.[24]

As critical as it was of the UUJJ, the Consistory was even more radically opposed to the LICA. This was a political organization created in 1928 by immigrant Jews, among its activists were young people from every Jewish milieu, including the native-born. Resolutely activist, the LICA condemned anti-Semitism in political terms, viewing it as a plague driven by the right and the fascists.[25] The Consistory was irritated by its slogans, its mass demonstrations, and its defense groups, which engaged in violent confrontations with the xenophobic fascist grouplets that rampaged in poor, heavily Jewish neighborhoods.[26] The Consistory reacted even more vigorously against the LICA because the militant behavior of some of the young people active in it openly contradicted its motto, "Religion and Fatherland." The attraction of the LICA is explicable in that it equated anti-Semitism with xenophobia and fascism, and the fight against anti-Semitism with the defense of immigrants and with peace.

Another indication that some young people from the Consistorial milieu sought the renewal of French Judaism is provided by the creation in 1923 of the Jewish scouting movement, the *Éclaireurs israélites de France* (EIF). In 1938, when it was showing signs of vitality, it included about 2,500 young people, divided among the Parisian region, Alsace-Lorraine, the Oran region in Algeria, and Tunisia. It recruited members in both affluent and poor neighborhoods and provided a melting pot for both native and immigrant Jews.[27] Open to the observant, the secular, and to Zionists, the EIF had developed in a direction favorable to Zionism and encouraged the study of modern Hebrew. The organization participated in the fight against anti-Semitism led by the LICA, though without affiliating with it entirely.[28] After trying in vain to force the leaders of the Jewish scouts to accept a definition of the movement's aims limited to "the practice of scouting and love of France," the Consistory acquiesced to the choices made by the EIF. Rather than break with their young leaders, mainly the product of the consistorial milieu, it admitted that they served as a counterweight to the Zionist youth movements and a happy alternative to non-Jewish scouting, while at the same time being useful for the acculturation of young immigrants.[29]

The Politicization of the Immigrants

Approximately three-quarters of the Jews, both native-born and immigrant, belonged to the lower-middle or middle class. They were small manufacturers, artisans, merchants, professionals, and officials.[30] A few individuals had achieved fame in the areas of banking, the arts, letters, science, and politics, while almost 25,000 Parisian Jews (as well as small numbers in the east and north of France), recent immigrants, lived in poverty and sometimes misery. Those without residence or employment permits, the distribution of which was severely restricted, had to avoid the inspections of the immigration police and avoided charitable organizations. The state of wage earners, mainly employed by Jews in the clothing, leather, and furniture industry, was less precarious than that of the piece-workers. Numbering about 10,000 in Paris,[31] they worked at home, usually without work permits or union protection, underpaid by the owners of the workshops that placed orders with them.

Nonobservant Jews belonging to that least privileged of categories were very receptive to the message of the left, but the number of activists was small. The three main political options vying for influence among the Jewish immigrants were the Zionists, themselves fragmented into several parties,[32] the communists, organized by the Jewish Intersyndical Section of the *Main-d'oeuvre immigrée* (MOI-yiddish, Immigrant Manual Labor), and the Bundists. Although the numbers of immigrant political activists were small, the cultural circles organized by the parties reached a large public. This was also true of the political press. The circulation of the Yiddish daily *Parizer Haynt*, close to the FSJF and Zionist in orientation, exceeded that of the Communist daily *Naye Presse*.[33] In the provinces Yiddish cultural circles thrived in Lille, Lens, Metz, Nancy, Strasbourg, Mulhouse, Belfort, Lyons, Roanne, Montpellier, and Toulouse.[34] Zionist influence dominated in the centers where Jewish immigrant students were active in running the circles, in Paris, Nancy, Montpellier, and Toulouse.

The directors of the Consistory had an understanding of political interests different from that of the immigrant organizations. The latter demanded the intervention of their representatives against all measures aimed at the immigrants, anti-Semitism, and the expansion of Nazism. A part of the native Jewish youth rebelled against the rule dear to the directors of the consistorial institutions, according to which good citizenship and exemplary patriotism, and above all, "not to call attention to oneself," were the only means suitable for dissipating anti-Semitism. These directors disapproved of the participation of young French Jews in the demonstrations of the LICA and condemned that of the immigrants. This was mainly because the LICA politicized its campaign and accused the French right of promoting anti-Semitism. The Consistory warned "our recently immigrated coreligionists" that "one does not criticize the government of a country where one is demanding hospitality."[35]

The main effort made by consistorial circles in favor of the immigrants and refugees was philanthropic in nature. The Comité de bienfaisance israélite de Paris (CBIP, the Jewish Welfare Committee) was overcome by the influx of refugees from Germany after the rise of the Nazi regime. Thus in 1936 the Consistory took the initiative of creating the *Comité d'assistance aux réfugiés* (CAR, the Committee for Assistance to Refugees). The American Joint Distribution Committee (AJDC, also known as "the Joint"), the well known Jewish relief organization founded in 1912, matched funds raised locally.[36] However, a number of indigent Jews preferred to turn to the mutual assistance organizations promoted and managed by the immigrant Jews.

1938, A Critical Year

In 1938 the Jewish community was put to the test more than ever before. A dizzying succession of events, both international and local, underscored the internal disagreements that prevented the fragmented community from reacting coherently. A brief chronology of the year 1938 contrasts the accelerating emergence of threats to the Jews with the immobility of the Jewish organizations.

March 11: The Anschluss, the forcible annexation of Austria by Nazi Germany, produced an influx of Austrian Jewish refugees. In France the extreme right accused the Jews of trying to force the government to declare war in the name of Jewish interests. The Jewish organizations all acted in their own fashion, without coordination.[37]

March 27: The undersecretary of the Immigration Ministry convened representatives of Jewish philanthropic and mutual assistance organizations and asked them to provide funds to finance the obligatory repatriation of the refugees in Germany. The FSJF, the AJDC, and the HICEM (a Jewish overseas emigration assocation) responded negatively. The delegate of the CBIP proposed Jewish participation in the expenses, in the event that "a more favorable solution" proved impossible, but he was in the minority.[38]

April 20: The national convention of the LICA was held, supported by the leaders of the PCF, the SFIO, and the Radical-Socialists, with the participation of delegates from 200 Jewish immigrant organizations and no official participation of native Jews. The LICA claimed membership of 32,000.[39]

April 21: The Marchandeau law was passed, suppressing publications inciting racial hatred.

April 24: The unity conference sponsored by the communist USJ was held. The FSJF refused to take part, although several dozen associations connected with it were represented. But the leaders of the USJ saw that their popularity was decreasing because of the communist stand against taking in refugees: "No vacancy! France for the French!" wrote L'Humanité.[40]

May 2: A decree was passed expelling foreigners without residence permits or assigning them to supervised residences. No Jewish action was taken on behalf of the racial refugees.

July 6–14: The international conference on refugees was held at Évian. Before the conference L'Univers israélite wrote: "The democracies will never abandon the Jews." After the failure of the conference, the Jewish press organizations remained silent.[41]

September 29–30: The Munich summit conference was held. France and Great Britain submitted to Hitler's annexation of the Czechoslovakian Sudetenland. A new anti-Semitic campaign accused the Jews of pressing the government to make war. The Jewish press attempted to refute these accusations and to reassure its readers. Regarding the distress of the German Jews the Chief Rabbi of Paris, Julien Weill, declared in the pro-Munich, right-wing daily paper, Le Matin: "It is not our place to take, at this moment, any initiative which could in any way harm the efforts presently under way toward Franco-German rapprochement."[42]

October 29–30: The Szbonszyn affair. The Nazi government deported Polish Jews to Poland, but Warsaw forbade the entry of those whose passports had expired. Twelve thousand Jews were stranded at Szbonszyn, in the no man's land, under appalling conditions.[43]

November 7: Hershl Grynszpan, a seventeen-year-old whose parents were among the victims of the tragedy of Szbonszyn, assassinated von Rath, the counselor at the German embassy in Paris.

November 9–10: Crystal Night in Germany. The "rioters," in Nazi uniforms, committed violence against Jews, synagogues, and Jewish businesses under the pretext of punishing them for the assassination of von Rath. The Yiddish press in France called for self-defense. The shock of Crystal Night aroused the solidarity of the Consistory leaders, and, in response, a central refugee committee was established, demanding the admission of 10,000 Jewish children to France and the abolition of the decree of May 2, 1938. The FSJF appealed for order and calm in Jewish neighborhoods.[44]

December 12: A decree was passed authorizing the government to intern "undesirable foreigners" in "special centers" and simplifying the procedure for the suspension of French nationality.

The War

Hard hit by the attitude of the French government, which had remained silent after the barbaric scenes of Szbonszyn and Crystal Night and reinforced its apparatus for the repression of foreigners, the immigrants and refugees withdrew into themselves. The celebrations of the 150th anniversary of the French Revolution in 1939 provided the Jewish press and public speakers with an opportunity to appeal to republican principles and their beneficial effects for the Jews, without explicitly mentioning the fate of the refugees.[45] A few weeks later, on September 1, France was involved in the war: there was a general mobilization and the evacuation of residents of Strasbourg and places near the Maginot Line to Vienne, Charente, Haute-Vienne, Dordogne, and Cher, the departments designated to receive the refugees from Alsace-Lorraine, of whom approximately 15,000 were Jewish. The Jewish immigrant organizations, including MOI-Yiddish (in violation of the policy of neutrality adopted by the PCF under the effect of the German-Soviet pact of August 23, 1939) called for mass conscription in the war against the Nazis. Nearly 40,000 foreign Jews enlisted in the French army in 1939–1940.[46]

Were the Jews of France aware of the unprecedented dimensions of what was at stake in the conflict? With the exception of a few rare individuals, whose voices went unheeded, they displayed the same torpor as the great democratic states, which responded too late to prevent or limit the catastrophe. The Jewish communities of these countries were afflicted with the same shortsightedness. The sluggishness of established institutions and of the ideas that guided them was nowhere shaken by the advent of a barbaric regime in a long civilized country. Although the World Jewish Congress was established in 1936, proclaiming "the inconceivable tragedy" of the Jewish situation,[47] this did not alter the apathy of organized Judaism. Both the paralysis of the League of Nations and the sterility of the International Conference on Refugees in Évian in 1938 were noted with passive resignation.

Being a disharmonious amalgamation of various cultures and traditions, the Jews of France were not united by the feeling that they shared a common destiny. One would seek in vain a leader whose authority inspired the respect if not the adherence of all. The most distinguished people produced by this community acted outside of the Jewish realm. The eminent scholars of the Society of Jewish Studies analyzed Jewish texts like paleographers, and they related to expressions of Jewish life like paleontologists. Among the Jewish authors of France, with the exception of the poets Fleg and Spire, "there were hardly any whose works bore a flame, a dynamic drive," notes Moshe Catane, who points out "the large measure of skepticism" and the lack of inspiration in French Jewish creativity.[48]

Signs of a Future Renewal

Although this description of a Jewish community at the end of its tether and moribund, hardly concerned with its survival, and the plaything of a "centrifugal dynamic," leading its young generations to the loss of identity, is accurate, there were nevertheless notable changes during the 1930s that should be noted.

True, the French Zionist movement had not managed to attract a large number of members and activists. As fragmented as the Jewish community itself, its presence as an organization was marginal. Having limited their definition of Jewish identity to a matter of religion, native Jews were generally resistant to the idea of a Jewish nation and accepted Zionism as at best a charitable project for the benefit of Jews deprived of a fatherland. Nevertheless, one could discern what Paula Hyman has called "an infiltration of Zionism."[49] The future reconciliation between French patriotism and Zionism was declared on April 2, 1937 by Rabbi Jacob Kaplan in a sermon given at the synagogue on rue de la Victoire. According to Kaplan, support for the Jewish national renaissance was "a patriotic French task and a Jewish religious task."[50] The Jewish scouting movement, born in a native

Jewish milieu, was open both to Zionism and to immigrant youth. Among its leaders were fervent advocates of Zionism, who at the same time expressed the multiple dimensions of Jewish identity.[51] Some of the immigrant youth sought to break with the existing institutional structures, which did not inspire their confidence. They spoke in a militant Jewish voice expressed in articles published in their periodicals rejecting assimilation and presenting Zionism as "the only solution of the Jewish problem."[52] These same young people, together with native Jews, led the battle against anti-Semitism in the framework of the LICA.

Another sign of a possible change is that in 1936, when a young teacher, Marc Cohn, established l'école Maimonide, a Jewish high school in the suburbs of Paris. In contrast to other Jewish initiatives, the founders of this school viewed it neither as working toward the acculturation of immigrant youth nor as a philanthropic institution for the benefit of refugees, but rather as an ambitious educational project combining Western culture with the authentic sources of Jewish culture.

An effort to unite the Jewish organizations, more successful than those launched in vain by the leaders of the large Parisian institutions, led to the creation in Strasbourg in 1936 of the Committee for Coordination of Youth (Comité de coordination de la jeunesse juive). Promoted and run by activists from the consistorial community, the committee sought the adherence of all the movements in order to mobilize Jewish youth against the Nazi danger. In December 1938 it addressed an open letter to the Chief Rabbi in Paris, following his declaration in a daily newspaper, Le Matin. The committee wrote that "Jewish youth was convinced that an individual's dignity as a Frenchman could not be purchased at the price of his dignity as a Jew."[53] This reaction expressed the disapproval of some members of the consistorial milieu of the declaration made by the Chief Rabbi of Paris. The activists of Strasbourg organized the efficient absorption of Jewish children and adolescents fleeing from Germany from 1936 on. Good use was later made of this experience under Nazi occupation, when children were saved by the Jewish resistance.[54]

Do these few signs, involving a negligible portion of the Jews of France, merit our attention? They do at least indicate a direction contrary to that taken by the established institutions and reveal a potential for survival within an environment abandoned to discouragement, a desire for unity instead of division, and the offering of Jewish options to the most aware among the young people, who, in general, were slipping into the loss of Jewish identity. Though this potential for survival was embryonic and fragile, it was at that time the only chance for the renewal of Judaism in France.

3

⟨⟨❋⟩⟩

The Uniqueness of Jewish Resistance

From the perspective of the military events of the Second World War, with its huge armies and enormous means of destruction, Jewish resistance seems to be an insignificant episode, hardly worthy of attention. Conversely, the idea of the dynamic reaction of a tiny, unarmed community against the massive aggression of the most formidable military power in history gives that resistance legendary dimensions.

In any event, it has not yet found its place in historiography. It is absent from the patrimony of recollections and myths that constitutes the memory of our contemporaries.

Henri Marrou wrote that "the number of points of view from which one can interrogate the past is practically inexhaustible."[1] This principle helps us to understand the contradictory evaluations pronounced upon various events, but it does not explain the amnesia that has erased Jewish resistance from our memory. Could this be a first, derisory aspect of its uniqueness?

A Battle That Has Been Ignored

An Israeli historian of the Holocaust, Yehuda Bauer, writes: "When all is said and done, any form of Jewish resistance to the Nazis is nothing but a small footnote with respect to what happened in Europe in general and among the Jewish population in particular. But for the Jews, this footnote is of great importance. It indicates the ways through which the renewal and regeneration of the Jewish people were possible."[2]

The enormity and horror of the Final Solution, suddenly revealed in their inexpressible monstrosity after the collapse of Nazi Germany, have justly monopolized thought and attention. With difficulty, the survivors, amputated and mutilated as no people had ever been in history, have regained their breath to live again and reconstruct. For several decades the lasting shock of mourning has combined with the mobilization of energy in service of the will to rebuild and the refusal to twist the blade in the wound—all contributing to the long-standing neglect of Jewish resistance.

The first generation after the war asked how and why six million Jews had let themselves be led like sheep to the slaughter. Though the survivors felt this question to be blasphemous and unfairly implying their guilt, it naturally emerged among young people. Living in the context of Jewish independence and sovereignty reconquered in Israel, they lacked information about the Jewish struggle against the Nazis, with the exception of the hopeless heroism of the Warsaw Ghetto uprising.

Within the more general framework of the history of the Holocaust, this reaction is one illustration among many of the problems presented by efforts to understand this page of history, which remains the most hermetically sealed against human intelligence. "Perhaps . . . posterity will understand all of this even less than we,"[3] despite the advantage brought by the perspective of time. However, coming generations will perhaps ask how so many Jews could have participated in resistance, going so far as to set up rescue networks and armed combat units. During a debate on the historiography of Jewish resistance in France, David Douvette noted that "the proportion of Jewish participation in the war and the Resistance in all its forms is by far the highest, comprising approximately a quarter of the Jewish population capable of action."[4] His quantitative appraisal takes into account regular armies, the Resistance networks, and Jewish resistance as such. Before him, a historian of the Resistance, Henri Michel, who had at first ignored Jewish resistance,[5] later emphasized its "exemplary" character, writing that the Jews "passed, without transition, directly from oppression to war as partisans; and they were not the last to engage in this warfare as partisans, following the example of others and with their approval. Rather, they were among the first, and all alone."[6]

Thus, after a long period of silence, the theme of Jewish resistance has begun to be studied. We are witnessing the gradual and growing awareness of its historical specificity. This is also a result of the development of research concerning the Second World War and of the need to bear witness felt by the survivors, urged by the desire to redeem from oblivion the epic of which they were the heroes. The bibliography of Jewish resistance has been enriched by numerous titles during the past decade. It includes reports,[7] memoirs, testimony,[8] narratives,[9] documents,[10] the collected papers of conferences,[11] and an as yet too modest number of research papers.[12] The present study is the first to treat Jewish resistance in France as a whole.

Rescue: The Specific Vocation of Jewish Resistance

Georges Wellers gave the most categorical expression to the specificity of Jewish resistance when he condemned confusion between "what was done to save the Jewish community from the collective death that had already been set into action ('Jewish resistance') and what was done to save conquered France from Nazi domination, a long-range task ('French resistance')."[13] Rather than use Wellers's terms, we prefer to speak simply of "the Resistance" or of national resistance.

Hillel Kieval seems to have been the first to apply rigorous methodological rules to a definition of "Jewish resistance." According to him, this term means "only those actions which consciously aimed at combating the persecution of Jews and, ultimately, at preventing their deportation and murder."[14] Jacques Adler proposes the same definition, but makes it more selective by eliminating non-clandestine action from the realm of Jewish resistance.[15]

According to this definition, the official actions taken in Vichy by the Consistory have no place in this study. The same would also apply, for example, to the act, which was neither fraudulent nor clandestine, of liberating several hundred Jewish children from internment camps in southern France. Conversely, the participation of Jewish organizations in operations aimed at saving France from Nazi domination would concern only "French resistance." Hence it, too, fails to fit the proposed definition and would have no place here.

Wellers gives a specific list of the characteristics of Jewish resistance: "True Jewish resistance was that which helped Jews hide by finding them a secure hiding place; by forging counterfeit identity papers for them, such as false baptism and birth certificates, and false ration cards; by giving them safe passage over the Swiss or Spanish border, or across the demarcation line; by providing them with a minimum of financial means necessary for their daily, clandestine existence; by ridding them by force of arms of informers and 'Jew-hunters'; by helping and instigating the escape of Jewish detainees; by composing, printing, and circulating news meant to give the persecuted people moral support and arouse sympathy for them among the non-Jewish population. All of these activities involved great risk for the Jews and non-Jews who engaged in them: . . . torture, execution, and deportation."[16]

Weller uses this list as the key to his classification of Jewish organizations, which he divides into three categories:

1. True organizations of Jewish resistance, such as Rue Amelot and the OSE (*Oeuvre de secours aux enfants*, Children's Rescue Network).

2. Jewish organizations exercising a double activity, being at the same time part of the Jewish resistance and also part of the "armed resistance," such as the OJC (*Organisation juive de combat*, Jewish Combat Organization), the MOI-FTP, and the EIF.

3. Organizations that had nothing to do with Jewish resistance other than the fact that many of their members were Jewish, such as the Carmagnole Battalion, the Marcel Langer Brigade, or the Manouchian-Rayman Group, which were units of the communist resistance.[17]

This classification is too narrowly selective, because it tends to underestimate the value of the military option. Among the categories of resistance activities, those such as the underground press and military operations[18] did not enjoy priority within the ensemble of Jewish resistance organizations. Preoccupation with rescue is manifest both on the level of the effort invested and also in the uniqueness of this resistance.

However, the Jewish communists engaged most of their forces in guerrilla operations. This choice maintained the split between them and the other Jewish resistance organizations from 1942 to 1944 and was also a source of malaise among the Jewish communists themselves.[19] The argument persists to this day with regard to the Jewish identity of the Jewish communist organizations. Wellers denies this identity, as does Léon Poliakov, who writes: "The ideology of their resistance was as little Jewish as that of combatants in the ranks of the general French Resistance."[20] The official historiography of the PCF (Parti communiste français, the French Communist Party) also denies this identity. In reference to the term "Jewish resistance," David Diamant writes, "such a term seems inappropriate to us," because "the Jews were obliged to differentiate themselves, since the difference was imposed upon them by the enemy."[21] By defining Jewish identity as a condition obedient to the will of the Nazis and their accomplices, Diamant suggests that the goal of anti-Nazi combat was to abolish that identity as a source of differentiation.

David Douvette denounces this tendency to de-Judaize communist Jewish resistance as the action of a minority among the generations of the children of immigrants, who "sought to break with a past which they regard as alienating." For him, the Jewish identity of Jewish communists of the generation of *Yiddishland* cannot be questioned.[22] Rayski protests against the effort at "dismantling [Jewish resistance] on the level of its historiography." He recalls the participation of Jewish communist organizations in a fully clandestine manner in "efforts aimed at unifying the struggle of the Jews of France and also to lay the foundations of the future community."[23] Finally, Annie Kriegel also opposes to the de-Judaizing of Jewish communist resistance. She suggests a two-stage definition. The first stage would be "Jewish resistance viewed as the Resistance of the Jews," which is not incompatible with "a more demanding definition: Jewish resistance is a Resistance among whose motivations and self-definitions certain targets have priority, the major and most urgent criterion being the safety of Jews."[24] This author thus expresses the ambivalence of the Jewish communist resistance: its leaders felt responsible for the defense of specific Jewish interests, while at the same time behaving as disciplined activists of the PCF. More than once this position trapped them in a dilemma, because the defense of the interests of the PCF by military action took priority over the cause of humanitarian service that Jewish interests represented.

Similarly, until shortly after the end of hostilities, the Western Allies also put off consideration of the humanitarian problems raised by the Nazi plan to exterminate the Jews and the Gypsies. Let us mention two examples:

1. The imperative of military priorities was invoked to explain the refusal to launch an aerial attack against the gas chambers and crematoria of Auschwitz-Birkenau.

2. The U.S. Treasury Department strictly prohibited the transfer to Europe of any sums originating in the United States to avoid the risk of having this money assist the enemy war effort. This policy was detrimental to the philanthropic relief work of American organizations such as the AJDC (American Joint Distribution Committee), the Quakers, or the YMCA, which participated in the rescue of Jews in Europe.[25]

The latter case also illustrates the application of policies favoring the military option over operations to rescue Jews. But in this instance the heads of the noncommunist Jewish resistance organizations did not have to resolve this contradiction themselves. Whereas the communists, subordinate to the orders of the PCF, engaged the better part of their forces in military action, the other organizations decided, completely independently, to concentrate first of all on rescue. Toward the end of 1943 they quickly made the transition to armed combat, together with the networks of national resistance, but they maintained the rescue operations intact.

A Different War

The major respect in which the condition of the Jews in France between 1940 and 1944 was unique concerns the identity of the victims of repression. The only non-Jewish Frenchmen to be persecuted were those who rebelled, resisted, or violated the laws of the occupier or of the Vichy regime. By contrast, all the Jews—men, women, and children, even invalids and helpless patients in the hospitals—were first subjected to a discriminatory and humiliating regime and then marked out for deportation and death. War of a unique and previously unknown type was thus being waged against the Jews.

Insubordination exposed Frenchmen to the rigors of repression. The Jews, however, whether or not they were French, had no hope of escaping the enemy except by committing a long series of infractions: avoiding the census of the Jews, not wearing the yellow star, escaping from a detention camp, camouflaging themselves behind forged identity papers, etc.

If to resist is refusal to submit to the authority of those who wield power and to thwart their will, for every Jew resistance was the only chance of surviving. Whereas, for a non-Jew, to obey the laws and regulations was a way of avoiding risk, the opposite was true for the Jews. There were immense losses among those Jews who respected the law. Conversely, non-Jews who went underground in order to resist were placing themselves in danger. This danger was the same for a Jew who went underground, but it was much less than the danger courted by the law-abiding Jew. Under the Nazi regime and that of Vichy, Jews were on an equal footing with non-Jews only in the underground. Although resistance meant the risk of death for a non-Jew, for a Jew it meant the same risk, but also an additional chance of survival.

These equations did not become clear until very late. One cannot write the history of the Jews during the successive phases of the war on the basis of the conclusions presented above. "To understand historical reality, sometimes it is necessary *not to know the end*," writes Vidal-Naquet,[26] who observed that "we have knowledge that [the Jewish leaders] did not possess in entirety."[27]

On the one hand, the plan for the final extermination of the Jews evolved gradually. Before launching the offensive against the Soviet Union of June 22, 1941, Nazi policy was to force the Jews to emigrate.[28] The beginning of the deportations was kept secret and was unexpected. The Germans spread disinformation and managed to make people believe they were creating an ethnic resettlement of the Jews in Eastern Europe.[29]

On the other hand, one must also bear in mind the general atmosphere reigning in France until the great roundups of July–August 1942 and the first massive deportations, and even until the application of the Service du travail obligatoire (STO, Compulsory Labor Service) law in February 1943. The majority of the French population had reacted to the defeat with resignation. Their strong desire for peace was already evident in the relief with which the Munich agreement of September 1938 had been applauded, and it was also expressed in the fervor surrounding Marshal Pétain.

Like the other occupied countries, France aspired only to "rediscover the lost paradise," an aspiration which Werner Rings has called "the obsession of Europe."[30] The Jews were not immune to the general tendency to accommodate oneself to the bitter aftertaste of defeat. Most of them were reluctant to break the law, for they were convinced that they had to be "in order" to avoid provoking difficulties from the authorities and to guarantee their security. Precariously installed in a world of illusions, in the main they were as little inclined to leave the realm of legality as other Frenchmen. Nevertheless, some scholars have stated that in general the Jews joined the Resistance before other Frenchmen.[31]

Jewish enlistment in the Resistance was different not only because it came earlier than general enlistment, but also in the relative numbers and quality of the people involved. Poliakov notes that the Jew "found himself enrolled almost automatically in underground life, because to flout the laws, to enter the area of illegality, was the best way of surviving."[32] But it's important to note that this observation applies to whole families, including young children and old people. Hence the Jewish organizations found it necessary to try to bring an entire population into the underground. This meant arranging their "Aryanization," finding lodging and means of subsistence, while all of France suffered from shortages in these areas. Jewish resistance operated systematically in this direction beginning in 1943, gradually improving its methods and effectiveness.

French Aid to Jewish Resistance

In Eastern Europe the majority of the population was indifferent, sometimes hostile, to the fate of the Jews. The resistance movements and partisan units there went so far as to take part in the hounding of Jews. In France, by contrast, the Resistance, many members of the clergy, part of the administration, and elements of the population all took risks in actively and effectively participating in the rescue of Jews. Unquestionably the STO was a major cause of the unpopularity of the Vichy regime and of the policy of collaboration, especially since its application in February 1943 coincided with German military setbacks at the Stalingrad front and in Libya. But the fate inflicted upon the Jews also played a role in the notable change of French public opinion that began in the summer of 1942.[33] The public disapproval by some bishops of the persecutions was decisive in bringing many French people to assist in the rescue of Jews, not without flouting the law.

Brotherhood in Arms

On the military level, Jewish resistance mainly operated under orders from the Resistance. It was not successful in attacking those responsible for the deportations. As for freeing deportees by attacking the trains, "this was simply beyond our power, and, in any case, this was an action with unpredictable consequences," testifies Rayski.[34] Nevertheless, the free armed forces of the AJ (*Armée juive*, Jewish army) network operated in Nice, Lyons, and Paris and managed to strike at paid informers on Jews who were used by the Gestapo. It was also the AJ which, after giving them military training, spirited Jewish fighters across the border into Spain so that they could make their way to Palestine and join the Jewish Brigade which had been formed under the British flag. As for the partisan units formed by the Jewish resistance movements, they took part in the operations led by the FTP, the AS (L'Armée secrète, the secret army), and the FFI in order to save France from enemy domination.

The Diversity of Jewish Resistance

The variety of Jewish resistance organizations partially reflected the variety within French Jewry before the war. Raising the issue of the consequences of this fragmentation is merely to pose a rhetorical question. Moreover, the hypothetical existence of a centralized and monolithic organization would hardly have been appropriate to the particular laws of clandestine action, where isolation is an elementary safety measure. Various Jewish milieus, which were very different from each other both socioculturally and politi cally, produced their own resistance network, within which the members found an appropriate framework for action. This diversity did not prevent true coordination in several areas, nor did it interfere with the concerted action of leaders of every tendency. In January 1944 this concerted action produced the charter for a representative organization of all the Jews of France to be set in motion after the Liberation. The men and women who, before the war, had participated in initiatives directed against the general rejection of Jewish identity were among the principal activists in the Jewish resistance. In the dark night of the occupation, they roused the first harbingers of a revival of Jewish studies and growing interest in Zionism. The values that gave the Jewish resisters the spiritual force not to succumb to the physical power mobilized against them carried the seeds of a potential Jewish renewal in France.

The history of Jewish resistance is that of Jewish groups active between 1940 and 1944 organized to sustain the morale of the Jewish population on the religious, spiritual, cultural, and political levels, and to ensure their physical survival by distributing means of subsistence, often clandestinely, by rescuing Jews from internment and deportation, and, finally, by carrying out military operations. Hundreds of the resisters in these networks, mainly young men and women, were subjected to torture, execution, and deportation.[35]

PART II

❧

ORGANIZED JEWISH REACTIONS FROM JUNE 1940 TO JULY 1942

4

❧

Jewish Assistance Organizations

When the troops of the Wehrmacht entered Paris, not a single leader of any organized Jewish group remained in the capital. The rabbinate, the immigrant associations, and the groups of Zionist activists were all deprived of their directors. The leaders had either fled or shared the fate of their regiments: some were taken captive, others escaped to the south of France. Many rabbis who were serving as military chaplains, while most of the leaders of the Jewish Scouting Movement (EIF, *Eclaireurs israélites de France*) had been mobilized in 1939 as reservists. Almost none returned to their posts in Paris before the liberation of the country.

Despite certain discriminations, Jewish prisoners of war were treated like those of other French prisoners of war until the German capitulation. After a brief waiting period, the Jewish leaders who had made their way to the south found themselves targeted by a German ordinance forbidding Jews to cross the demarcation line. They became refugees, dispersed throughout the non-occupied zone. Two exceptions were the Chief Rabbi of Paris, Julien Weill, who returned to his post immediately after the French defeat, and one of the leaders of the EIF, Fernand Musnik, who had been taken prisoner while severely wounded and was repatriated several weeks later in a medical convoy.[1]

Tens of thousands of Parisian Jews had also chosen the route of exodus. Among those who had not fled were the families of prisoners, officials, owners of small stores, artisans, and the most poverty-stricken proletariat. Ignorant of French and of France, of which they knew only a neighborhood to which they had barely become acclimated, the recent immigrants had scarcely budged. The census of Jews taken in the northern zone in October 1940, in response to a German ordinance, revealed a population of 148,024 Jews in Paris.[2]

The first ordinances instituted against the Jews in the northern zone by the occupation authorities, dated September 27, 1940, include taking the census, stamping the word *juif* on identity documents, and the placement of a yellow sign saying *Affaire juive* (Jewish business) in the windows of Jewish-owned stores.[3] These measures struck against a population bewildered by the brutality of events and deprived of its leadership. No directives, not even improvised instructions, were issued to guide the Jews in response to these measures, which were generally accepted with passive and submissive discipline. The leaders of MOI-Yiddish made no comment about the order to take a census of the Jews. They themselves went to be counted.[4] Jewish merchants displayed the obligatory sign. Many of them placed a second sign in their windows, in red, white, and blue, to show their clients and passersby their record of military service and the official honors they had been awarded.[5] A Jewish journalist, Jacques Bielinky, condemned to idleness by the circumstances, patrolled the commercial streets of Paris and recorded in his notebook that several Aryan merchants had placed yellow signs in their windows, having noticed that, far from doing any harm, they attracted customers in their neighborhood.[6]

Although some people, fortified by an imperturbable temperament and with a tendency to courage, managed to display a kind of euphoria,[7] most of the Jews were in disarray. The actions taken to conform to the official regulations helped them convince themselves that, legally speaking, they were beyond reproach. The certainty that they had left no grounds for possible police action against them allowed the Jews who had remained in Paris to overcome their anguish regarding the unknown perils in store for them in the future.

Were there Jews who disobeyed the orders of the occupier and avoided the census and also refrained from having their identity cards stamped? Certainly. Among those whose family names were not specifically Jewish and whose social behavior did not betray Jewish identity, it is likely that some had the presence of mind and courage to make themselves outlaws. But this required not only a long habit of dissimulating Jewish ties but also an exceptional degree of awareness.

Very few people realized that submission to the orders exposed them to more risks than rebellion, and that "every step taken towards legality was a step toward their own destruction."[8] Those who avoided the census now mingled with the Aryan population.

Approximately 180,000 Jews were dispersed in the southern zone, in a region where only 40,000 Jews had lived before the war. In addition to the refugees from the northern zone, from the Departments annexed by the Reich (Moselle, Bas-Rhin, and Haut-Rhin), from Belgium, Holland, and Luxembourg, were entire families deported to the southern zone by Nazi order: 3,000 Alsatian Jews (July 1940), 1,400 German Jews from the northern zone sent by the German police of Bordeaux (August 8, 1940), and 6,500 Jews from the Baden area (October 22, 1940).[9] The French authorities detained all those deported in the latter two convoys in camps at Saint-Cyprien and Gurs, bringing the number of foreign Jews in detention to nearly 40,000.[10] In October 1940, the new arrivals were divided as shown in table 4.1.

The census taken by the Vichy administration in July 1941 counted 129,938 Jews in the southern zone.[11] How great was the proportion of those who evaded the census?[12] The answer is especially difficult to establish, since it is impossible to determine how many crossed the line of demarcation ille-

Table 4.1

FOREIGN JEWS IN FRANCE

Origin	Free Jews	Interned Jews
a) Refugees from the three departments annexed by the Reich and from the northern zone	65,000	
from the Netherlands, Belgium, and Luxembourg	30,000	10,000
b) Deportees from the three departments annexed by the Reich and from Bordeaux	3,000	1,400
from the Baden region		6,500
Other detainees arrested in France		22,000
Totals	98,000	39,900

gally. Hence it is futile to compare the estimate of the population as of October 1940 with the results of the census in the following year. However, a far greater number of Jews moved to the southern zone between 1940 and 1942 than moved in the opposite direction, either to the northern zone or abroad.[13] Before the deportations began in March 1942, the number of Jews in the southern zone constantly increased, for this region was the only refuge for Jews fleeing the northern zone. Although dispersed among several hundred localities, most of them had first sought a safe haven in the large cities. In Marseilles, Lyons, Toulouse, Nice, Grenoble, Limoges, Périgueux, and Montpellier, they formed clusters numbering several thousand people.

Before the application of the first anti-Jewish measure by the new regime, a severe problem arose during the first few days following the debacle of June 1940: thousands of Jews, possessing no resources for their subsistence, were in great distress. Among these, the foreigners were liable to be classified as "superfluous to the national economy," and thus interned in camps. Even more acute was the misery of the detainees, who were deprived of liberty and totally exposed, the pitiful objects of the humiliations and brutality of the corrupt guards, who robbed them of their meager food rations.[14]

The assistance organizations, broken apart by the mass exodus of June 1940, which was accompanied by the dispersion of their leaders and employees, were impossible to locate at first. In Paris, Jewish offices and dispensaries were closed. In the southern zone, the embryonic philanthropic services were set up by religious organizations that were not suited to running them and lacked the means to respond to needs.

Nevertheless it took the Jews only a few weeks once again to shoulder the responsibilities of assistance, both through established bodies, which were reconstituted in the southern zone, and by means of newly emerged organizations.

Helping those in distress was the first action taken by Jewish organizations under German occupation. Their needs grew incessantly in size and urgency, and assistance remained a constant imperative throughout this period. However the repertory of these organizations' activities was far more extensive.

Jewish Coordination and Relief Initiatives

The creation of new structures between 1940 and 1942 refers notably to bodies combining several preexisting organizations, with the aim of coordinating or unifying the relief activity. Two such organizations were created following Jewish initiatives, *le Comité de la rue Amelot* (the Amelot Street Committee) in Paris and *la Commission centrale des organisations juives d'assistance* (the Central Commission of Jewish Relief Organizations) in the southern zone. The groups had only one thing in common: their origin as a reaction to the situation born of the occupation of France. They were both created without a preconceived plan, coordination among the protagonists, foreign pressure on the Jewish community, or a dominant personality or group of leaders; their origins, spontaneous and unprecedented, were unconnected with, and very different from, each other.

Created in October 1940 at Marseilles, the Commission centrale brought together native and immigrant leaders, worked openly, and chose as its primary task the coordination of relief for those interned in camps. Fifteen months later, it had to end its existence after the establishment of the *Union générale des Juifs de France* (UGIF, General Union of French Jews), an administration created by a Vichy law of November 29, 1941. The Comité de la rue Amelot, for its part, arose in June 1940 at Paris, and was always a secret organization. It was composed of immigrant Jews and managed organizations and institutions that had legal status. But its direction remained unknown to the public and the authorities. It survived the establishment of the UGIF as well as the deportation of its principal founders. After its legal activities were dissolved and transferred to the administration of the UGIF, Rue Amelot continued its clandestine work of relief and rescue throughout the northern zone until the Liberation.

Le Comité de la Rue Amelot

Following the German entry into Paris, before the occupying authorities had made the slightest gesture against the Jews, several activists had already begun to discuss ways to respond to eventual anti-Semitic measures. A handful of junior functionaries of the FSJF (*Fédération des sociétés juives de France*, the Federation of French Jewish Organizations) met on June 15, 1940, in the apartment of one of their number, Léo Glaeser. Noting the absence of the leaders of the community and its organizations, as well as the paralysis of all of its institutions, they agreed to reactivate those services of which they had been in charge for years on the local level: a medical-social dispensary, and four public soup kitchens.[15] These decisions were made and immediately implemented, clearly showing that the participants in the meeting were preoccupied by the distress of the Jewish immigrants, who habitually made use of the dispensary and soup kitchens in question. A brief inventory showed that these services lacked the means to function for more than a few days. They possessed a balance of 200,000 francs [then the equivalent of approximately $2,000], while the soup kitchens had only a small stock of provisions remaining. The decision was made to raise money and to make contact with the French directorate of the American Joint Distribution Committee, which had subsidized the FSJF from 1933 on.[16]

The small group of activists who gathered in Léo Glaeser's home believed that the life of the Jews, both individuals and institutions, would sooner or later be controlled by the occupiers of Paris. Being immigrant Jews, they doubted they could count upon aid or protection from the native Jews or the French authorities. After meeting almost daily from June 15 to June 30, they resolved not to submit to German orders that could disrupt or paralyze the organizations of which they had taken charge. In immediate terms this resolution was moot, though it was soon to be put to the test by German ordinances and pressures.

Finally, the participants in these meetings formed a committee made responsible for the management of the dispensary and the soup kitchens, whose legal status posed no problem for the moment. A secretary general was appointed, David Rapoport, and the headquarters were placed in the dispensary called La Mère et l'Enfant (Mother and Child), at 36 rue Amelot.[17] Thus the Amelot Street Committee was born, under the double sign of Jewish social solidarity and resistance to the orders of the occupier.

Was this the birth of a spirit of resistance? Did the men of Rue Amelot lay the foundations for a resistance movement? In fact, in the convulsions of the defeat, and in contrast to many other Frenchmen, the Jews had no difficulty in determining who was the enemy. The Nazis had absolutely freed them of concern as to what camp to choose: The armistice and the offers of collaboration that followed it did not include the Jews, especially not the immigrant Jews. In some ways, the resolution not to submit to Nazi orders, though it was moot when first formulated, was really a statement of fact. The Nazis were waging merciless war against the Jews. Their goal was to eliminate them, not to make them submit.

Certainly no one yet knew how the enemy would operate. Once hostilities between Germany and France had ceased, in fact and in law, and the legal authority was embodied by the administration, police, and courts of a French government, the civilian population, including the Jews, were placed under the authority, even the protection, of the French legal system. When a regime institutes exceptional measures under exceptional circumstances, the spontaneous behavior of almost all the civilians is obedience to orders, for they are convinced that civic discipline is the best protection against the risk of reprisals and arbitrary actions. The same is true of the ordinances signed by the occupation authorities, who most often had them executed by the French administration.

However the men of Rue Amelot were hardly inclined to place themselves under the protection of the legal authorities in a regime that discriminated against the Jews. Coming from Russia or Central Europe, they had fled countries where power was wielded despotically and violently. Republican France had not impeded the free expression of their political opinions within their small Zionist or Bundist groups, where democratic procedures were respected with almost religious fervor. That double experience immunized them against any pernicious illusions regarding cooperation with a totalitarian power. They reacted as activists committed to ideologies that categorically condemned the Nazi dictatorship. The elements of a spirit of resistance were thus potentially in place. Certainly it is excessive to view the creation of the Rue Amelot Committee as the first step in establishing a resistance network. But the principled choice to evade the control of the authorities bore the seeds of violations of the law. Let us recall that we are not discussing individuals but rather social and communal charities. In this instance, managing them on the margins of the law and official regulations sooner or later entailed passage into the underground.

David Rapoport and his co-workers were not yet dreaming of acting under the cloak of secrecy in June 1940. Their project was limited to the private domain. They envisaged no appeal to official organizations responsible for assistance to the indigent. They lacked tools to estimate the size of the budget needed to aid the disinherited. But the constraints of food rationing soon forced them to turn to the government. The strictly private character of their social work could be preserved for only a short time.

Though they showed more foresight than the other Jews who had remained in Paris, the men of Rue Amelot had no inkling of the dilemma involved in carrying out social and communal work. The Germans were planning to establish an obligatory structure of Jewish community, intended mainly to supervise the functioning of the social assistance activities. Their method combined direct action as well as action by intermediary French authorities, depending on whether it was applied in the northern or southern zone. In Paris, SS Lieutenant Theodor Dannecker, charged with organizing an anti-Jewish service within the German police at the Paris headquarters of the Central Security Service (RSHA, *Reichssicherheitshauptamt*), personally orchestrated the appropriation of the Jewish community, beginning in October 1940.[18] Thus, very rapidly, a contradiction arose between the commitment to Jewish social assistance in the face of growing distress, and refusal to bow to the will of Nazi officers. At the Mother and Child dispensary, those in charge sought, not always successfully, to have their own way with the authorities. They were to undergo their apprenticeship in resistance while playing a double game, as their social action developed and branched out in response to the accelerated pace of severe anti-Jewish measures.

In August 1940, Rue Amelot was joined successively by *l'Oeuvre de secours aux enfants* (OSE, the Children's Rescue Network) and ORT (founded in Czarist Russia as *Obshchestvo Rasprostraneniya Truda*, Society for Manual Work).[19] Its dispensary and a medical and social center belonging to the OSE were placed under community management. Jewish physicians graciously extended loans. The American Quakers, who had come to the aid of the OSE even before the war, now lent their assistance to Rue Amelot, first providing supplies of food, clothing, and medicine.

In October 1940 a representative of the socialist Zionist youth movement entered Rue Amelot, which had been formed of Zionist and Bundist activists, and he led several small groups under the aegis of the Marxist pioneering movement, *Ha-Shomer Ha-Za'ir* (Young Guard). The young people used the rooms occupied by the soup kitchen on rue Elzévir, which was run by Rue Amelot, and on Sundays they would go out to the forests on the outskirts of Paris. Their educational, cultural, and athletic program gave a major place to Jewish history and to the study of the pioneering accomplishments of the Zionists in Palestine. Many young people attended assiduously and fervently. Now, the social action of the Amelot Committee had been supplemented by an element composed of young people, whose first activities were on the level of Jewish cultural indoctrination. Belonging to leftist political movements, they constituted a potential for militancy, ready to pass into action. At the end of June 1941, after the outbreak of the Wehrmacht offensive against the USSR, the Jewish communists organized within MOI-Yiddish made contact with the youth leaders of the Amelot Committee, and they began to plan joint action. Within a few months this led to the formation of joint "cells," which were strictly secret. Their first operations were raids against Jewish factories and workshops that were producing equipment for the Wehrmacht. Rapoport was consulted and kept informed regarding cooperation with MOI-Yiddish.[20]

The combination of people with such incompatible ideologies as Zionists, Bundists, and Communists can be explained if one recalls that awareness of the common danger had become so acute as to blur the differences provisionally. However, this was not the case in most of the Jewish communities and settlements in Europe. The differences among the Zionist parties with various leanings as well as that between Zionists and

Jews actively opposing Jewish nationalism could not always be suspended in the face of danger striking all Jews indiscriminately. It has been shown that even during the ultimate revolt, in certain ghettoes of Eastern Europe, partisan loyalty overcame the imperative of making a united front against the enemy.[21]

It would be risky to try to explain the exceptional character of Rue Amelot in uniting the factions. The survivors recall David Rapoport's charisma, his disdain for the satisfactions offered to the vanity of one who wields power, his attachment to the rules of democracy, and, finally, his unconditional self-abnegation toward the accomplishment of his task. Those who were close to him speak freely of his Tolstoyan air. He was a bearded patriarch whose eyes glowed with a soft light. He was short, slightly stooped, feverishly active, irritable, but most often combative and enthusiastic. He fixed his interlocutor with a look that immediately filled him with a sense of security. Though tormented and restless, he was endowed with natural benevolence, giving the impression that he embraced the anguish of those who came to ask him for help. The influence he exerted had the strange power of comforting and consoling people. Professor Henri Baruk, a volunteer with the Rue Amelot teams, has told how he was fascinated to observe Rapoport in an atmosphere of perpetual agitation in the tiny office of the dispensary. One of the activists with the Committee has written of him as "a secular rabbi."[22] In his presence, his colleagues, the emissaries of the ideological factions, became the representatives of a community of disinherited people. Other leaders called for unity and tried to work out formulas for compromise, intended to permit incompatible doctrines to coexist in peace. In Rapoport's case, his personal influence motivated the group.

The Bundists, opposed to cooperation between the Committee and the Communists, considered withdrawing. But the Committee disdained ideological disputes. Concrete problems of the war for Jewish survival were discussed, without regard to the members' affiliations. In contrast to the leaders of the FSJF in the Southern Zone, Rapoport had abandoned all political activity the moment the occupation regime was in place. His charisma probably favored and stimulated the gathering of a large part of the immigrant Jewish community under the aegis of Rue Amelot. Thus, during the first weeks of the occupation in Paris, the Jewish community, deprived of its leaders, produced its own leaders from among its most disinherited elements and those most exposed to danger from the enemy: the Rue Amelot team.

The decision to reopen the medical and social dispensary and the soup kitchens reflected a certain desire to return to normal. It was as if the most important, perhaps the essential thing, was not to let oneself be paralyzed and disturbed by the convulsions and misfortunes of war, but to resume one's daily routines. Previously the disinherited immigrants had needed the assistance provided by the Jewish charity organizations. Nothing had changed in that respect, except that the needs tended to increase. Thus it was necessary to keep the charity organizations in operation.

Only later did the idea take root that the war necessitated a strategy other than simply reestablishing peacetime institutions. In more than one case, a study of the reactions of Jewish organizations in countries invaded by the Nazis shows a tendency to operate according to peacetime norms and routines as soon as the population has adapted to the structure laid down by the edicts of the occupying authorities. Taking account of the circumstances, the increased number of the needy, and the severe gravity of people's distress, the Jewish leaders and their established or improvised institutions generally confronted the war in the first instance by taking stronger action on the social or philanthropic level, providing mutual assistance or benevolence, as well as cultural action, either religious or secular.

The Committee met almost daily during the first two weeks of the occupation. Its agenda included an examination of the technical problems of the functioning of its activities: personnel, supplies, finances. It raised funds, notably among those attending the synagogues frequented by the immigrant Jews, where the poor were also found, and those making use of the soup kitchens and dispensaries.[23] The owners of small and middle-sized businesses were convened at information meetings and asked to make contributions. The Committee managed to renew contact with the Joint, using, among other things, the good offices of the Quakers. Being citizens of a neutral country, the United States of America, whose diplomatic representatives were accredited at Vichy, the Quaker mission possessed passes permitting them to cross the demarcation line between the northern and southern zones. They often carried messages between the Committee in Paris and the Joint services, which had withdrawn to Marseilles. During the first months of the occupation, the Quakers also discretely arranged the transmission of funds from the Joint to the Amelot Committee.[24]

Then David Rapoport invited those responsible for other, similar Jewish charities, which were still paralyzed, to join the Committee. Dr. Minkowski, the only member of the board of the OSE who had remained in Paris very quickly agreed to be coopted and decided to reopen the medical and social dispensary of the OSE.[25] In September 1940, Rapoport proposed to the Chief Rabbi of Paris, Julien Weill, that he unite the native and immigrant communities. His purpose was to stimulate and to reactivate the *Comité de bienfaisance israélite de Paris* (CBIP, the Jewish Welfare Committee of Paris), which belonged to the consistory, and to extend the collection of funds to the native Jewish milieu, under Julien Weill's moral authority. His attempt had no immediate effect. Chronologically it coincided with Lieutenant Dannecker's first efforts to establish a centralized Jewish community for Paris and the Seine region. At that stage, the SS officer was proceeding by exerting pressure on the Paris consistory, so that it would take the initiative in creating a centralized Jewish organization.[26]

On September 22, the press reproduced a German order dated August 28, subjecting all associations to the authorization of the German regime in order to continue their activity. One charity affiliated with Rue Amelot, le Foyer des israélites réfugiés (the Home for Jewish Refugees), which contained a soup kitchen and a hostel for old people, wrote to the secretary general of the Committee: "We must cease our activity unless we receive permission to function."[27]

For the first time the men of Rue Amelot realized they would have to disobey the enemy in order to operate. The charity work was continued. They simply neglected to apply to the authorities for permission to go on. While this action already placed the Committee outside the law, at this stage of the Occupation, no official was yet supervising the activity of associations. The attitude of the Committee thus gave rise to a situation of passive resistance, where the unsubmissive victim of aggression was not, for the moment, punished. Everything took place as though the blow struck by the aggressor had been avoided and had remained without consequences.

In November 1940 Rue Amelot first made contact with the world of detention. The French police imprisoned aliens "of irregular status," generally those without a valid residence permit, in the Tourelles barracks. The severe scarcity of rations served to the detainees was the most pressing problem. Most of the families of the Jewish detainees, about one hundred in number, were absolutely destitute and many of them asked for assistance at Rue Amelot. The Committee obtained permission to have supplementary rations brought daily to the Jewish detainees in the Tourelles barracks.[28] Very soon, during the contacts between the two mess-tin bearers from Amelot and the detainees, plans for escape were laid. The operation itself seemed to be feasible, presenting no major difficulty. However, it was necessary to solve the problem of what was to be done after the escape—how to "regularize" the status of the escapee. Paris would be distinctly inhospitable toward detainees from the Tourelles barracks who chose liberty. In order to protect the escapee from pursuit, he had to be provided with false identity papers and taken across the demarcation line, if possible with his family. The question was not placed on the agenda at the meetings in the

Committee office. A minority there had already proposed the closing of the soup kitchens and the dispensary, following the publication of the August 28 ordinance, in order to avoid subjecting those using them to dangerous risks. Discreetly informed by the two food-bearers, Rapoport decided to act in the greatest of secrecy in order to obtain false identity papers for the potential escapees.

It took only a few weeks to discover and exploit the possibility of obtaining false identity cards for the escapees from the Tourelles barracks, by means of which they could cross over to the Southern Zone.[29] Here the infraction committed went beyond passive failure to obey an order. This was the first experience of active resistance, in order to rescue victims who had already fallen into the hands of the enemy or his auxiliaries.

Having taken this step, the mutual assistance association already had one foot in the underground. During the daytime it continued to distribute aid, meals, clothing, and medical care to those in need, hiding nothing but the origin of the goods. Behind that façade, it resisted the enemy, violated his orders, frustrated his actions, and, in short, developed the structure and mode of action of a resistance movement operating in the shadows.

In David Rapoport's case, the persecution of the Jews was the origin of his humanitarian and social response. In 1918, in his native Ukraine, he had participated in the creation of orphanages that took in thousands of children, the victims of the Petlyura massacres. In 1920, in Warsaw, he had led the Central Committee of the Union of Jewish Refugees. In 1939 at Paris, he had improvised and, under the aegis of the FSJF, had coordinated assistance for indigent families where the fathers had been detained as "enemy aliens."[30]

Then, under the circumstances born of the occupation of France, humanitarian and social action led to resistance. This observation holds true in general of the Jewish charity organizations. They evolved in a manner identical to that of Rue Amelot, which has been described here at length as a prototype. There is a crucial difference between prior circumstances, where Jewish social action sought to cope with exceptional needs and dangers, and the situation of occupied France. That difference is the war. For most Frenchmen, while the armistice did not put an end to the war, at least it ended the hostilities. This was true of those who accepted the armistice, that is, almost the entire population. The Jews, too, reacted as though the hostilities had ended. Their problem, lived subjectively, was to adapt to the status of a discriminated minority as best they could, with the hope that this would be a passing phase. Thus everybody sought to be "in order," with diligence proportionate to awareness of their vulnerability. The minority condition was felt by the Jews as unprecedented in France, who were struck all the harder because they loved France and had placed full confidence in it.

The Central Commission of Jewish Relief Organizations

Even during the phony war, before the German invasion of France, officials of HICEM (a Jewish emigration organization composed of the Hebrew Immigrant Aid and Sheltering Society, JCA, the Jewish Colonization Association, and EMIGDIRECT, a German Jewish emigration association) had listed candidates for emigration in the internment camps.[31] After the debacle and the armistice, the Paris HICEM office had reconstituted itself in Marseilles and sent delegates to the camps in order to renew contact with the detainees. The first actions taken in Vichy offered some cause for optimism. Official policy favored the emigration of foreigners. The head of the HICEM office wrote to the New York headquarters on November 25, 1940, that there was hope for emptying the camps by means of emigration.[32] He requested urgent assistance from the American directorate to obtain immigration visas as well as funds to pay for transportation by sea. The European delegation of HICEM had transferred its headquarters from Paris to Lisbon. Its mission was to obtain transit visas via Spain and Portugal, issued to those possessing immigration visas for countries across the Atlantic. It was also responsible for reserving places on ships, which were reduced in number because of the war. The task of the Marseilles office was to obtain exit visas from France. The bureaucratic complications generously invented by the Vichy regime, to the detriment of its own policy, heaped obstacles in the path of the delivery of visas.[33] By means of tedious work, HICEM helped 6,449 Jews to reach freedom outside of France between the armistice in June 1940 and the end of 1942, which saw the end of legal emigration. Among this number were only a few hundred detainees. Rather than emigration, it was deportation that would empty the camps.

Two years of suffering preceded this fatal conclusion. Many organizations sought to relieve the material distress of the detainees and to give them courage and hope. The alarm was sounded by a young rabbi, René Kapel, stationed in Toulouse in July 1940, waiting for his demobilization. Slightly stooped, thin and elegant in his dress, with a sympathetic look and timid gestures, he was a courteous and attentive man, scrupulous in temperament but subject to vehement outbursts. Informed by his colleague, Rabbi René Hirschler, of the internment of 7,500 German and Austrian Jews who had been evacuated from Belgium in the camp at Saint-Cyprien, near

Perpignan, he went there on August 2, 1940. His captain's uniform opened the doors for him. Overwhelmed by the unbearable sight of the atrocious distress reigning in the camp, he gave an emotional report before the French rabbinical association, which met at Lyons on September 3.[34]

Kapel suggested taking steps to organize emigration, to demand the transfer of the detainees of Saint-Cyprien to less unhealthy camps, and to solicit the aid of French and foreign humanitarian organizations. During September another rabbi, Henri Schilli, improvised for himself the position of chaplain to the camps of Agde and Argelès. At the same time the OSE intervened, the headquarters of which had withdrawn from Paris to Montpellier. Appointed as medical adviser to the OSE, Joseph Weill had a systematic survey made of the situation in the camps in the southern zone.[35] Kapel guided a delegation of the AJDC in Saint-Cyprien. In September he obtained the first contribution of 200,000 francs to purchase warm clothing and blankets for those interned at Saint-Cyprien, Gurs, and Le Vernet. The AJDC had this contribution administered through the good offices of the Quakers, who were also involved in providing assistance to the detainees in the camps at the same time.[36]

In conformity with its traditional methods, the AJDC recommended that the directors of the Jewish organizations unify their action. Its representative in Marseilles, H. Katzki, gained the cooperation of Jarblum, the president of the FSJF, and that of the Chief Rabbi, Hirschler.[37] A provisional commission of Jewish mutual assistance groups met in Marseilles at the end of July 1940, without the participation of the *Comité d'assistance aux réfugiés* (CAR, the Committee for Assistance to Refugees). Being close to the Consistory, the directors of the latter were not yet prepared to share responsibility for assistance on an equal footing with the immigrant Jewish leaders. They suggested associating the FSJF in an advisory capacity. Thwarted on this point, they refused to participate in the unification project. But on September 4, before the rabbinical assembly in Lyons, Hirschler fervently pleaded the cause of uniting the charities. On October 30, 1940, when the Central Commission of Jewish relief organizations met in Marseilles, under the aegis of the Chief Rabbi of France, CAR joined it, along with the other organizations: FSJF, OSE, ORT, AIP (*Association des Israélites pratiquants*, the Association of Observant Jews, connected with Lubavitch), EIF, the Works of the Chief Rabbinate, OASI (*Oeuvre d'assistance sociale israélite*, the Jewish social assistance mission), HICEM, and AJDC. René Hirschler was appointed Secretary General. Would the Commission simply coordinate assistance, as CAR wished, in order to preserve its complete autonomy, or would it centralize it, as Hirschler and the FSJF desired? The AJDC remained neutral regarding the disagreements between CAR and the FSJF, giving a separate allocation to each of the charities associated with the Central Commission.[38] Hence the organizations remained autonomous.

Thus endowed with limited powers, the Commission nevertheless sought to extend assistance to the detainees. The impulse given by the Secretary General and the persuasive power he exerted on his surroundings played a significant role. "He was tall, handsome, distinguished, seductive, charming. Intelligent and well educated, hard working, ingenious, firm in his principles, flexible in everyday life."[39] Although CAR was somewhat tardy in its enthusiasm for action in the camps,[40] Hirschler was supported by the determination of Julien Weill, who organized a team of social workers with activistic tendencies within the OSE. Using the support of understanding government officials, Hirschler obtained the agreement of the camp commanders to place a rabbi in each of them as a chaplain. He made multiple appeals to the Vichy government, requesting measures to ease the extreme distress of the detainees. These officials were also subjected to parallel pleas from various humanitarian organizations such as CIMADE (*Commission intermouvements auprès des évacués*, Intermovement Commission for the Evacuees, a Protestant organization), the SSAE (*Service social d'aide aux émigrants*, Social Service for Assistance to Emigrants), the Quakers, the YMCA, and the Swiss rescue organization, along with the Jewish organizations combined within the Coordination Committee for Assistance in the Camps, headquartered in Nîmes (see chapter 6).[41]

The Nîmes Committee soon obtained the agreement of Vichy for the establishment of resident teams of social workers and doctors in the camps, an idea conceived of by the OSE. It also obtained the transfer of all the detainees of Saint-Cyprien, as had been demanded by Kapel and the HICEM.

The impetus given by the Secretary General of the Central Commission thus brought a relative improvement in the living conditions of the detainees, as well as hope for the liberation of the children. The OSE, the EIF, CIMADE, SSAE, the Quakers, the YMCA, and the Swiss rescue organization created volunteer teams among the detainees, charged with providing social and medical services in the camps. ORT opened vocational training workshops. Hirschler and Weill set to work in an effort to wrest a decision from the officials authorizing the liberation of the children.

The action of the charities united within the Central Commission henceforth took on a new dimension. Assistance efforts began to transmute into rescue operations. The specter of deportation had not yet touched anyone's consciousness. But the atrocity of the regime in the French camps was such that the worst, that is to say, death, lurked to prey upon all those whom nature had not endowed with an exceptionally robust constitution. Indescribable food shortages, exposure to the weather, and the absence of prevention and medical care condemned the detainees to rapid exhaustion. During Kapel's first visit to Saint-Cyprien, on August 2, 1940, a typhus epidemic was raging, and 200 people had been infected.[42] The implacably precise reports submitted to the Nîmes Committee by Julien Weill in December 1940 revealed the imminent ravages of mortality in the camps. It was urgently necessary to dispatch massive food relief, to create sanitary services, and to free the most vulnerable detainees, the children, old people, and pregnant women.[43] So long as there were no deportations, these were the terms in which the Jewish organizations, with the help of their counterparts in the Nîmes Committee, conceived their mission of safeguarding the detainees.

In order to direct and supervise the action of humanitarian organizations, the heads of the French Police created the *Service social des étrangers* (SSE, the Social Service for Foreigners) in January 1941, headed by Gilbert Lesage, a French Quaker activist.[44] As such, before the war he had brought aid to political and racial refugees from Germany and Austria. Lesage was connected with Robert Gamzon, the national commissioner of the EIF, as well as with Hirschler and Weill.[45] The SSE was not a disappointment. It became an indispensable auxiliary of the clandestine Jewish rescue networks with respect to foreign Jews.

The establishment of resident teams in the camps, with the explicit agreement of the regime, thus gave rise to a first sector of semi-underground activity, enjoying the cover of an official organization. This precedent was to inspire the methods of most of the Jewish organizations which, originally being responsible for assistance, were later forced to transform themselves into clandestine rescue networks.

5

⌘

The Youth Movements

The declaration of war, and the resulting mobilization of adults, in September 1939 almost completely paralyzed the now-leaderless youth movements. The sports and cultural clubs of the Communist Jewish youth were included in the prohibitions aimed at the Communist Party and its various dependencies. The evacuation of the areas close to the Maginot Line had dispersed the members of the orthodox religious movements, Jeunesse Mizrahi (Mizrahi Youth) and Yechouroun, which had been active only in the eastern departments of France. The military collapse, the debacle, and the exodus of June 1940 completed the task of completely dislocating the youth movements.

As an organization, however, the EIF, the Jewish scouts, were less vulnerable to the convulsions that traversed France in 1939 and 1940. This was because adult women had taken over for the men who had been mobilized, and it was also because, heralding the movement's future social activities, it had opened centers for the evacuation of children in the Southeast in 1939, and these provided a basis for reorganization after the exodus. The National Commissioner, Robert Gamzon, a communications officer, first sought to reach London , where he hoped to continue fighting in a French uniform. But he soon gave up that project, bowing to the arguments of his colleague on the National Board of the movement, Edouard Simon.[1]

Gamzon finally decided to place himself at the service of the abandoned
and vulnerable Jewish community, devoting himself completely to the
reorganization of the EIF in the southern zone. As early as August 1940 he
had submitted to the National Board, convened at the children's evacuation
center in Moissac, a plan of action conceived to respond to the needs of
entirely new circumstances.

The Study Circles

In every other case, including that of the EIF in Paris, a period of improvised
reactions preceded recovery of equilibrium and restructuring. In Paris the
absence of the directors and the dismantling of community institutions as a
result of the war, the exodus, and the German invasion, had dealt the most
severe blow to the youth movements. However, precisely these circumstances, which had plunged the adults in disarray and ignorance of the
future, aroused among certain young people a powerful need to seek moral
sustenance, directives, and a response against the anti-Semitic aggression
already present in the press and on the radio. This quest was particularly
urgent among the children of immigrants. Some of them had been active in
the Zionist movements, which were the first to recover. Informal meetings
were first held in a hatmaker's workshop on boulevard Sébastopol.

The desire to assist the Jewish population impelled one of the leaders of
these meetings, Henri Bulawko, an activist in *Ha-Shomer Ha-Za'ir* (Young
Guard, in Hebrew, a marxist pioneering movement), to address the Chief
Rabbi of Paris, Julien Weill, who directed him to Rue Amelot.[2] There he was
associated with the social work and charged with assembling the youth.
Beginning in September 1940, young Zionists of various affiliations had
been given the use of a center in the public soup kitchen on Elzévir Street.
Jewish study circles for adolescents, meetings centered on Biblical themes
with songs in Hebrew and Yiddish for children, and political education for
young activists attracted approximately 200 participants. Beginning in the
spring of 1941, Sundays were used for outdoor activities in the suburbs.[3]
This initiative responded in some measure to the needs of the young people
in search of a more authentic image of their people than the perverted one
presented by official propaganda. But neither the community nor the
movements themselves considered a project entailing coherent commitment and action.

The same disarray affected the EIF in Paris, where the local leadership
tried to reconstruct the groups that had been active before the war. In

October 1940 a German ordinance prohibited scouting in the northern zone. But one of the movement's adult leaders, Fernand Musnik, took the first initiative. He decided to circumvent the German order and reconstituted the local groups in Paris under the cover of the charity organizations, without using the scout uniform and emblems. Visits to Paris by a leader of the movement who secretly crossed the demarcation line made it possible to renew contact with the southern zone. Reorganized by Musnik, a very active leadership team ran study circles and leadership training courses, giving major emphasis to Jewish studies: history, literature, and philosophy.[4]

Immediately following the defeat of France, many young Jews reacted by forming study circles. Independent groups emerged simultaneously in Paris, Lyons, Toulouse, Montpellier, Grenoble, Marseilles, Limoges, and Périgueux. There are almost no archival documents on this subject, and in most cases it is not known who took the initiative and who were the first activists.[5] This surge of activity expressed a desire to learn about Judaism and to explore the sources of the people, civilization, and spirituality of their ancestors. Young people who had hitherto lived their Judaism passively, indifferently, or in secret suddenly saw it imposed upon their consciousness in the form of aggression by a powerful enemy. Those who set about studying Jewish values were guided by an intuition urging them to prepare themselves morally in response to the aggression directed against the Jews. They had never been militant. What was more normal than to turn to the activists, the older members of the youth movements, and to ask them questions? Although unprepared, the leaders of the youth movements took over these circles without the least formality. There was no official application, no joining. They functioned without a secretariat or a hierarchy. No one felt the need to publicize or distribute the program of these study circles. For more than one of their participants they served as a school for the training of activists and enriched the members of the youth movements. "The circle was a revelation . . . that changed the opinions and destinies of the participants," wrote a Jewish resistant of the AJ (*L'Armée juive*, the Jewish Army) soon after the Liberation (see chapter 6). He had attended a study circle in Toulouse run by convinced Zionists.[6] Claude Vigée has described how he felt the disintegration of

> the moral comfort of pre-war French Judaism. Hence what the event demanded of me was not merely a general revision of the values transmitted by my relatives, but rather a form of voluntary and direct commitment to the destiny of the Jewish people, to which, as contemporary history had proven so clearly to me,

my attachment extended back for thousands of years. Nor was
it proper for me to submit to it passively, receiving my participation from the outside, in the manner of an unjust condemnation decreed by our judges and assassins. The contact which
I had at that decisive moment with the young and not so young
people of our group in Toulouse, permitted me to make this difficult transition in my inner life and to accept, within a perspective which was simultaneously human, historical, and
political, that which had at first been in me merely a tempest of
emotions, an impotent reaction of indignation.[7]

He himself and several other participants in that circle later performed liaison and intelligence missions in 1941 and 1942 to organize the aid for foreign Jews without resources who were threatened with detention: "Then we
conceived plans for bolder action, where the necessity to oppose the mortal
dangers that posed an immediate threat to the Jewish people under
Hitlerian occupation was combined with that . . . of training ourselves, or
forming leadership units capable of taking regenerative action among the
abandoned Jewish youth, to orient it toward Zion and future life in Israel."[8]
These remarks indicate the itinerary followed by many young people whose
action within the Resistance began with attendance at study circles led by
the youth movements.[9]

For the youth movements the period extending until the mass arrests of
the summer of 1942 was a time of reorganization, adaption to the new geographical distribution of the Jewish population, the training of leadership,
and, finally, the creation of shelters and vocational training institutions:
children's houses and artisanal and rural centers. Each movement followed
its own respective calling in undertaking reorganization.

Les Éclaireurs Israélites de France

The first to regroup and go into action in the southern zone, the EIF provided a framework in which both native French Jews and immigrants had
experienced an integrated community since the 1930s. Involved in all forms
of Jewish activism during the war except political indoctrination—education, culture, publication, religion, mutual social assistance, professional
retraining, clandestine rescue, and armed combat—they were active in Paris
and throughout the southern zone.

The Intuitions of the Founder of the EIF

This movement's unequaled influence, as well as the suprising efficiency of its structure, was due largely to the personality of its national commissioner, Robert Gamzon. Professionally trained as an engineer and electroacoustician, he was passionately committed to education. In a letter written in 1943 he confessed his "need for love, to give, and for domination."[10] Moreover, a Jewish vocation, the demands of which could not be satisfied by the offerings of existing institutions, which lacked vitality, dynamism, and zest, led him to "invent" Jewish scouting in 1923 in Paris. Self-educated as a Jew, he expanded his Jewish knowledge under the influence of the poet Edmond Fleg and through the impetus of the rapid growth of his movement.[11] A man of action, he was also prone to contemplation, and he had created his own vision of Judaism, a utopian but coherent combination of faith in humanity, in progress, in the values of the Biblical message, in the historical eternity of the Jewish people, and in the universalism of its spirituality.[12] His insatiable passion for human beings had immunized him against controlling ideologies and dogmatism. Gamzon gave the EIF movement a pluralistic definition, corresponding to his desire and that of Fleg to welcome young people of every orientation. This definition was well served by his abilities as a negotiator and his capacity for compromise. In fact, the EIF was the only Jewish organization covering the entire country where native and immigrant Jews met without conflict even before the Second World War.[13]

Criticized for his "puerile" idea of scouting, Gamzon was nevertheless followed by numerous disciples. Guided by an often prescient intuition, in 1936 he had opened a self-administered community of young people in Paris, including cultural programs and workshops in expression and creativity, a true precursor of the youth and culture centers.[14] During the following three years he created workshops for artisanal training in Paris, an agricultural school in Saumur, and three shelters in the southwest intended to take in children sent from the capital to protect them from bombing.[15] These institutions, conceived to serve Jewish youth exposed to persecution and war, provided practical elements for a plan worked out by Gamzon immediately after the armistice of June 1940.

These accomplishments were not initially humanitarian or social in nature, though their role in this respect later proved to be of primary importance. They were educational. Their promoter employed the methods of scouting, enriched with Jewish content, with balanced component of both ritual practices and spiritual stimulation. This combination reflected

Gamzon's multifaceted but coherent and harmonious personality. Short, fragile-looking, but graceful and nervous, he possessed astonishing physical endurance. Because of the tenderness of his look, the caressing warmth of his voice, the sober clarity of his speech, adorned with lyrical accents free of all emphasis, he exerted a powerful affect on his listeners. Both ingratiating and demanding, he enjoyed holding intimate conversations with the young people and leaders of the EIF. A meeting with Gamzon was sufficient to give one a sense of being endowed with a richer potential than one had imagined, animated by desire to outdo oneself.

An attractive personality because of his personal charm alone, the founder of the EIF was also powerfully attractive because he embodied the self-rehabilitation of a pluralistic Jewish identity, leading to participation in a plan of action that anticipated the imperatives of the future. On July 19, 1940, in Clermont-Ferrand, still wearing his army uniform, Gamzon happened to meet the leader of the EIF of Strasbourg, Frédéric Hammel, who had been demobilized from his artillery unit the day before. The two men agreed in their analysis of the situation. They decided to exploit the movement's potential for creating and activating communities of young people.[16] The concrete plans made in Clermont were ratified on August 18, 1940 in Moissac by the national board, with the participation of all the chiefs "who were neither dead nor prisoners."[17]

Jewish Cultural and Spiritual Action

Declaring that as the "only movement that has remained organized," it took responsibility "for all the Jewish youth of France," [18] the board that had assembled in Moissac decided to expand the children's homes, in order to create scout groups in all the cities of the southern zone where there was an influx of Jewish refugees, as well as in North Africa, and to open rural and artisanal centers. These projects taken together obeyed a rule defined by Gamzon and Hammel: make the Jewish youth leave the city in order to give them an education that emphasized "the human and spiritual values of Judaism," and to orient them toward productive professions.[19]

Thus the movement intended to respond to "anti-Semitism in the form of the denigration of Judaism."[20] Gamzon wanted to "make all the young Jews of France into strong and courageous beings."[21] At this stage, no one yet expected that there would be either measures to eliminate the Jews from the national community or progressive repression leading as far as deportation. The Moissac program, which was carried out to the letter, took up and generalized initiatives that had already been attempted before the war and the armistice of June 1940. The difference appears in the means of application and in the priorities.

On August 18 the national board decided to appoint permanent, salaried commissioners, in view of the extent of the responsibilities accepted by the movement and in order to adapt the instrument to its declared ambitions.[22] Anyone who accepted appointment as commissioner was to give up all other professional activity. Considerable effort was made to recruit and train leaders. A preliminary training stage ("camp of chiefs") was organized in Viarose, near Moissac, in mid-September 1940. During the following year seven stages on various levels were held, with a total of more than 200 participants. After the promulgation of the Statue of the Jews in October 1940, the movement systematically recruited young teachers, officers, and other unemployed officials, and who, after a training period, enlarged the leadership of the EIF. The opening of a documentation center in Moissac, which contained a mobile library and offered mimeographed course syllabi, provided a permanent addition to the training program.

High priority was given to the deepening of Jewish knowledge, on the one hand, and to the creation of rural centers on the other. The first point was applied within the scout units and the assemblies of young people and children, as well as in the camps for chiefs. Its promotion was placed in the hands of Samy Klein and Léo Cohn. The former had been an activist in the traditional Yechouroun movement in Strasbourg and had chosen a rabbinical career. The latter, a German refugee, was a convinced Zionist and had received a deep and traditional Jewish education, enriched by musical talent and instruction, which were also placed in the service of his educational activity.[23] These two men made the various EIF communities into centers of Jewish fervor. The study of traditional texts, choral singing, and ritual celebrations drawing upon various sources were shaped by a language and an aesthetic that endowed it with an atmosphere and style attractive to young people. Creating an audacious and seductive synthesis of the austere and formal style of the consistorial synagogues and the impetuous style of the small Eastern European shuls, disdainful of all formalism, the liturgical life of these communities of young people, guided by the influence of Léo Cohn, took up a current of renovation that some called "Léo-Hasidism."[24]

The two chaplains provided models for identification for numerous members of the scouting hierarchy at its various levels. Their influence extended the impression made by the EIF beyond the movement, bearing the idea of a pluralistic but consolidated community to the Consistory, where Klein exercised responsibilities of the first order.[25] He established close cooperation with the Yechouroun youth movement, whose leaders composed several correspondence courses published and distributed by the Moissac center. Another member of the National Board, Simon Lévitte, the creator and administrator of the documentation center, cooperated actively with the Zionists. It was he who actually took the initiative of unifying the various Zionist groups scattered throughout the southern zone. Beginning with the creation of the *Mouvement de jeunesse sioniste* (MJS, the Zionist Youth Movement), Lévitte devoted himself entirely to leadership in the two zones, while at the same time fulfilling his responsibilities as a member of the National Board.

The programs of training courses or camps, including Jewish studies, pedagogy, scouting, calisthenics, and sports, as well as handicrafts, also enriched the life of scout units in the cities and their summer camps, as well as groups of children and young people. The most significant experiment was a training course where Gamzon gathered Jews whom the Statute of the Jews in October 1940 had condemned to idleness. Twenty-five teachers took a course from April 28 to May 14, 1941 near the House of the Vieux-Moulin in Beauvallon on the Estérel coast, the home of the president of the EIF, Edmond Fleg. For most of them this was the first initiation in Jewish life and studies. They devoted themselves diligently to the Hebrew language, Bible, history, sociology, philosophy, and religious customs and prescriptions. They held evening discussions and learned to sing with Léo Cohn. Many of the participants in the camp at Beauvallon experienced it as a major turning point in their lives. For the trainees it marked the transition from the Jewish condition lived passively to that of a newborn Jewish militancy, founded on humanistic and spiritual values. It revealed to the leaders the power of renewal and diffusion of the Jewish spiritual patrimony in the modern age. The various EIF groups in the southern zone gained new activists. The training received and the militant activity that followed it led many of them to total commitment to the movement's rescue network and then to armed combat.[26]

The idea of a documentation center conceived by Lévitte responded to two needs of different orders. Technically it was necessary to overcome the extreme geographical dispersal of the movement and the frequent shortage of experienced leaders. More substantially it was important to extend and supplement the action of the training courses by the circulation of written documentation. So that he could devote himself to the documentation center, Lévitte resigned as secretary general of the EIF and was replaced by Marc Haguenau. Beginning in November 1940, Lévitte operated three services: a small mobile library of a mere 300 titles that made hundreds of loans to readers dispersed in several dozen places in the southern zone and North

Africa, a file of Hebrew songs, and the publication and distribution of mimeographed correspondence courses and instruction leaflets. The courses were written mainly by Fleg, Klein, and Lévitte.[27] The mimeographed material was sent to leaders of scout units and study circles in sixty-four places (twenty-six in the southern zone, thirty in Algeria, four each in Tunisia and Morocco), including a total of more than 4,000 young activists, of whom approximately half were in North Africa.[28]

Within the perspective of the options taken by French Jewish youth in the twentieth century, the accent placed on the study of the Jewish cultural and spiritual patrimony as well as ritual celebrations represents a reversal in the tendency to leave Judaism. This phenomenon can be explained not only as a reaction to events in Vichy France, but also, in the case of the EIF, as a response to the plan of the movement's founder, Gamzon, and of his spiritual mentor, Fleg. Even before the war the movement benefitted from the double stimulation of those of its leaders who were Zionists, Denise Gamzon, Lévitte, and Léo Cohn, and by the leaders of Alsatian scouting, fervent traditionalists, who were represented on the national board by Hammel. The deep shocks born of the war and of the persecution of the Jews played a catalytic role in an evolution that had already begun and must be viewed in the more general framework of the history of the emancipation of the Jews of France.

The Development of the Rural Branch

At the closing of the Viarose training camp on September 18, 1940, Gamzon announced the opening there of the movement's first center of agricultural training, the Land Clearing Camp. The principle behind this initiative had been adopted by the national board meeting a month earlier in Moissac. Despite the improvised and preposterous character of the project, on fallow land with an uninhabitable ruin, without either instructors or budget, a collective of twenty-five men and women took over the camp. Among them were young demobilized soldiers who had been at the farm in Saumur and older members of the movement.[29] In mid-November the Land Clearing Camp moved to Lautrec (Tarn), occupying a group of farms that later became the main center of the EIF's network of rural camps. In 1942 the movement ran seven farms, one being a school, while the others were rural centers. Their size and membership is shown in table 5.1.

In the spring of 1942 the senior members of the movement, with the technical assistance of the young people from Taluyers, had created a new rural group in Saint-Germain (Ain) for which the Central Consistory

Table 5.1

SIZE AND MEMBERSHIP OF EIF's NETWORK OF RURAL TRAINING CAMPS, 1942

Name of property	area (ha)	numbers
Les Ormes and Les Étampes Properties in Lautrec Farm school	30	40[a]
Rural Group of La Grasse in Lautrec	27	8
Rural Group of La Roucarié in Lautrec	12	8
Rural Group of Taluyers (Rhône)	9	29
Rural Group in Saint-Péray (Ardèche)	30	7
Rural Group Le Pusocq in Baraste (Lot-et-Garonne)	60	8
Rural Group Charry in Moissac (Tarn-et-Garonne)[b]	58	24

[a]Trainees.
[b]EIF archives, report of June 30, 1942, not numbered. This document also includes the two *Hakhshara* farms (a Hebrew term meaning a farm-school preparing young people for life as pioneer farmers in Palestine) of the MJS in Blémont (Haute-Vienne Department) and Fretteserpes, near Grenade (Haute-Garonne Department), where thirty young people farmed eighty-eight hectares. The OSE had attached them administratively to the EIF to provide a better technical framework.

assumed financial responsibility. At that time the rural branch consisted of a total of forty trainees in Lautrec and about a hundred "land-clearers" spread among the rural groups. During the spring of 1942, it gathered about a hundred young adults removed from the detention camps of Gurs and Rivesaltes, some by the Social Service for Foreigners and others by the management of the refuge centers. Several dozen of these were included in the rural groups, while more than half of them were individually placed as day-laborers in the Auvillar region, which was transformed into a "Security Sector" by a man close to the EIF, Dr. Sigismond Hirsch.

The critical stage of this spectacular development had lasted more than a year, from the opening of the ephemeral camp at Viarose in September 1940. The establishments mentioned above had obtained surprising results by 1942, at least to the local peasants, who were skeptical about such experiments: the population was stable, the equipment was satisfactory both in tools and in livestock, and production was respectable from land that had to be cleared and was often of poor quality. Most of the young people had overcome the difficulties of a regime of rigorous physical labor that was like nothing they had previously experienced. But more remarkable than all that was the quality of collective life that had developed there. In relations with others and with the community, the rule of loyalty so dear to the scouts was universally adopted. Conflicts and crises were resolved by frank discussions, without the use of punishment. Literary, musical, and religious activity was of an intensity that reflected the fact that the promoters of these communities were neither farmers nor economists by profession, but rather men and women passionately committed to teaching or to art and avid for spiritual accomplishment. These promoters, notably Gamzon, Hammel, Pougatch, and Léo Cohn, were integral partners in the collective life with their spouses and children.[30]

The similarity between the "return to the soil," which was the slogan of the Vichy regime, and the enthusiasm of the EIF in promoting agricultural communities might suggest that the former inspired the latter. But chronology shows that the program for the return to the soil sponsored by the EIF drew upon other sources that had been manifest even before the war. Gamzon had introduced the idea of vocational training among the goals of the movement, which was an innovation with respect to other scouting federations. In 1934 he induced his colleagues on the national board to adopt a "motion on manual labor."[31] Among the initiatives intended to concretize the movement's interest in the area of vocational training was the opening in the spring of 1939 of an agricultural school in the Saumur region (Maine-et-Loire). Though it turned out to be very brief because of the outbreak of war a few months later, this experiment not only expressed the desire to translate the movement's declared mission into a concrete action, but was also an attempt to contribute to the reception of young German Jewish refugees. In 1939 the EIF magazine, Lumière, wrote that by encouraging the young refugees to turn to agriculture, "we are serving both France and Judaism," because "France, too, needs farmers and specialist laborers."[32]

The idea of serving Judaism by creating an agricultural school reveals the influence exercised rather diffusely by the Zionist youth movements connected with the pioneering organizations of Palestine. Imbued with socialist ideology, they proposed the kibbutz as an ideal model of a collective society. With the aim of preparing their youth for a future as productive farmers on a kibbutz in Palestine, they had created the institution of Hakhshara (Hebrew for "training") in several countries in Europe. These were agricultural training establishments managed collectively by their participants. As a movement the EIF was neither socialist nor Zionist. But the Zionist appeal for return to the soil by the youth certainly attracted it, to the extent that this program of vocational training responded to the ambition of transforming businessmen and intellectuals[33] into men and women who worked with their hands. Moreover, the structure of a community conceived according to collectivist principles was reminiscent in some sense of the manner in which the groups of senior scouts functioned, particularly during their summer camps.[34] Further, pedagogical considerations also led them to pre-

fer rural collectives to hierarchical organizations or to the individual place-
ment of young people in training courses. "The enormous experiment of
Palestine and the attempts made in Europe and France (in particular by the
EIF movement) prove that collective adaptation is feasible."[35]

With the establishment of the Vichy regime, the EIF adopted its vocabulary on this point. Their program of rural promotion was given the name of
"return to the soil." Let us add that the latter were in favor of scouting and
religious education, which were held to serve the system of values of
Marshal Pétain's national revolution. "Everything that concerns readapta-
tion to rural life is particularly dear to us," wrote Gamzon on September 14,
1940, to the Ministry of Family and Youth.[36] On the previous August 10, the
EIF had composed their "plan for a return to the soil," the preamble of which
stated: "Return to the soil, which has been desirable for many years, has now
become a necessity. A very large number of workers and intellectuals will no
longer have any other possibility of living. The problem is particularly acute
for the Jewish youth of France, following the elimination by the Germans of
the Jews from Alsace and the East."[37]

In May 1941, the Ministry of Agriculture provided the rural groups of
the EIF with equipment, clothing, and work boots, plus a daily allowance of
fifteen francs for those younger than twenty, "exclusively of French nationality," as well as a salary for three leaders in each center.[38] Diamant maintains
that the EIF had submitted to the will of the occupying authorities who
sought to "de-industrialize France and to make it into an agricultural
region."[39] Rabi, by contrast, places the EIF no less than the MJS and the AJ
(L'Armée juive, the Jewish Army) among the resisters. He explains that the
official aid was accepted by the rural centers for a reason "both factual and
psychological: pragmatism, the primacy of certain rescue actions, an initial
conception of defense rather than offensive combat, lack of political preparation, and possibly, too, for some, withdrawal into a spiritual ghetto which
constituted a permanent temptation."[40]

The same author refers to Gamzon's "legalism," for Gamzon, like his colleague in the northern zone, Fernand Musik, had taken part in the council
of the Vichy sponsored UGIF (Union générale des juifs de France, the General
Union of French Jews).[41] This also would explain, according to him, the
"delay" of the EIF in engaging in military action.[42] Nevertheless it does not
appear that the decisions made at any moment by the movement were subordinated to obligations undertaken toward the official authorities, nor
were they subordinated to the exercise of responsibilities within the UGIF.
Rather than actual legality it was the appearance of legality that was carefully
created and exploited without hesitation. "Within the UGIF we will be less

suspicious and freer to do illegal work," wrote Hammel.[43] Pougatch reports that at Vichy, Gamzon "gained the cooperation of men whom he could trust and who warned him in time about plans for mass arrests." He created "an information service, . . . thanks to which the lives of a number of young people (and adults, too) were saved."[44]

Need we mention again that when the Pétain regime was installed, Gamzon had resolved to go to London? He sent his wife and children to refuge in Portugal[45] so as to be free to continue fighting as a soldier of free France. A missed meeting had delayed his departure from France, giving him time to reconsider the priorities of the war, and he then chose to remain in place and fight in behalf of the abandoned Jews.[46] His relationship with the Vichy government did not derive from conviction that his duty as a patriot commanded disciplined submission, nor from the illusion that loyalty to Vichy would serve the interest of the Jews. For his loyalty was committed to Free France. Whether or not to obey Vichy was merely a problem of tactics, modifiable according to the circumstances. Official encouragement lavished upon scouting and the return to the soil permitted him to profit from legality, which the movement exploited. It did not make a religion out of legality, but rather an instrument, which was that much more effective because it could be used to camouflage illegal situations. Thus the senior girl counselors who worked in the Gurs camp as "voluntary detainees" appeared in the official documents as (non-Jewish) social service workers of the SSAE (Service social d'aide aux émigrants, Social Service for Assistance to Emigrants), to whom militant members of the CIMADE (*Commission intermouvements auprès des évacués*, Intermovement Commission for the Evacuees) in Lyons lent their name. Employing a stratagem to "authenticate" certain false identity documents, Gamzon disguised an escapee belonging to the GTE (*Groupements de travailleurs étrangers*, Foreign Laborers Groups) who had sought refuge in Lautrec in the autumn of 1941 as an escaped French prisoner of war.[47]

As soon as the national board of the EIF learned of the projected law to create the UGIF and to dissolve existing Jewish organizations, it met on November 11 and 13, 1941 and declared itself in favor of legality, on condition that it could preserve the action of the scout units, the children's houses, and the rural collectives. But at the same time the board developed an emergency plan for clandestine action if the movement were to be prohibited.[48] In January 1942 Gamzon wrote to the leaders of the EIF that the decisions had been made "to preserve as much as possible of our educational and social work."

Thus nothing in the behavior of the leaders of the EIF betrayed either the collusion with the regime or submission to the occupier that Diamant denounces. His explanations fail to take some of the sources into account and offer a tendentious interpretation of others. Certainly the tactic of playing the game of legality ran the risk of falling into the trap of an illusion of security. The fact that institutions of children and young people were known and listed by the authorities did make them easy prey. But today one cannot understand the mentality of those responsible for Jewish charities in the summer of 1942 and the decisions they made unless one remembers that physical danger was not visible. They did not have enough contact with the non-Jewish population, which was almost unanimous in the confidence it placed in Marshal Pétain and indifferent to the fate of the Jews. It was only after the mass arrests of the summer of 1942 that some of that population showed itself ready to help Jews hide. Elementary precautions were also planned for the foreign Jews, some of whom were threatened with detention in France itself.[49]

Nevertheless, Gamzon, together with Julien Weill of the OSE (*Oeuvre de secours aux enfants*, Children's Rescue Network) and Hirschler, director of the chaplaincy in the camps, developed a source of information from Vichy. Weill's natural pessimism endowed him with clairvoyance at that time, as he brooded darkly about future eventualities. Their source of information was the head of the SSE (Service social des étrangers, Social Service for Foreigners), officially responsible for the detainees as well as those conscripted in the GTE.[50] The system was to prove itself, for in 1942 it permitted the directors of the EIF to hide in their institutions the young people and children who appeared on the police lists of Jews to be arrested.

The period of organization and development was followed by one of major dangers. We shall see how the movement then continued its action in a camouflaged manner, in secrecy that was progressively extended over all its sectors, finally culminating in armed battle.

The Zionist Youth Movement (MJS)

Until May of 1942, no attempt was made to coordinate the various wings of Zionist youth. Geographical dispersion and the fragmentation of this youth into several movements limited the scope of the initiatives taken in Paris, Limoges, Toulouse, Montpellier, and Lyons on the local level. The bitterness of the ideological discord, which in some measure had stimulated the vitality of Zionist activities before the war, had become a paralyzing factor in occupied France and the southern zone. The tininess of each of the movements in addition to the consequence of the exodus had left them dismantled and cut off from all relations with their "mother home" in Palestine and made the difficulties of reconstruction insurmountable. From 1940 to 1942 a few of their leaders such as Emmanuel Lefschetz, the director of Maccabi in Paris, and Simon Lévitte in the southern zone worked within the EIF. Having no ideological affiliation, it was the latter who finally unified the dispersed elements of Zionist youth, who gathered for a congress in Montpellier in May 1942.

Before Unification

During the two years when Zionist activism seemed to be searching for its way and its leader, one can nevertheless take note of several local initiatives attesting to the presence of a will and a potential, needing only to be set in motion. We have described the emergence of the study circles. In Paris, Toulouse, Limoges, Périgueux, and Montpellier, the leaders were Zionist militants. In Toulouse during 1941 a group was formed that was preparing for armed battle, promoted by the Zionists and later called upon to deploy in several centers of the southern zone and in Paris under the flag of the AJ. At the same time, young people belonging to the pioneering movements, *Ha-Shomer Ha-Za'ir, Dror, Gordonia,* and *HeHalutz* opened two farms, one in Blémont, near Limoges, and the other at Grenade, in the Toulouse region. Palestinian fundraising organizations, *Keren Kayemeth Le-Israel* (KKL, the Jewish National Fund) and Keren Ha-Yessod (the Palestine Foundation Fund, associated with the World Zionist Organization), assumed financial and administrative responsibility for these farms, which belonged to the Zionist *Hakhshara* (training) program, preparing youth for life in rural collectives in Palestine.

The administrator and leader of these farms, Samuel-Moulik Szejner, gathered young people there, who, despite the war and the occupation, wished to receive agricultural training in conformity with their Zionist pioneering ideals. When the time came he became associated with the unification of Zionist youth. The farms also provided fighters with the AJ and candidates for emigration to Palestine via Spain. The local groups of the various pioneering Zionist movements ran educational activities in the southern zone. In Montpellier, a Jewish student refugee from Belgium, Otto Giniewski, assembled and guided a group of Zionist youth who met with local resisters and Spanish refugees and participated in the circulation of Gaullist leaflets. The most dynamic group during this phase seems to have been the one in Paris constituted in association with Rue Amelot around Henri Bulawko and his team.[51] Rather plump and round, with a jocular look, never without a joke, quick-witted and sometimes sharp-tongued, he was loyal to his friends and sentimental. Entirely devoted to his organization, no sort of work was beneath him.

The activity developed on four levels: education, assistance, rescue, and the fight against economic collaboration. The origin of this group was the assembly of young people seeking moral and spiritual support because official propaganda made pariahs of them both as Jews and as immigrants. They explored the Bible and Jewish history, aided by a Yiddish poet, Spire. There were lectures, all-night study sessions on the sabbath, and supervised activities for the youngest children, as well as outdoor excursions to the forest of Sénart or to La Varenne on Sundays. Singing was given a special place, mainly because the leader, Bulawko, wrote songs expressing at the same time the plight of the immigrant, the revolutionary fervor of the socialist, and the hope of Jewish national rebirth:

> Coming from every corner of the earth . . .
> We build a new world
> Above which our beautiful flag will float.[52]

This song crossed the demarcation line, thanks to young people who fled Paris and joined the groups of activists in the southern zone.

In 1941, the Parisian group began to suffer losses among its leaders, following the arrests and detentions of May 14 and August 20. Henceforth Zionist youth participated in the assistance action of Rue Amelot and took initiatives regarding rescues, enabling the most endangered Jews to flee to the southern zone. One path across the demarcation line benefited from the help of truck drivers who had belonged to the CGT (*Confédération générale du travail*, the General Labor Federation). Bulawko also learned how to obtain and produce false identity papers and ration coupons, necessary for successful escape from the detention camps.[53] Unlike *Solidarité* (see chapter 7), who had ordered its detained activists not to escape but to work for the political organization of the camp population,[54] the young Zionists encouraged escape, to the degree that they could supply the escapees and their families with false papers. Moreover, they were aided by the Jewish Communists of *Solidarité*.

Cooperation with the latter grew more intense after the formation of the *Comité d'action* (Action Committee) of the workers' parties on August 30, 1941, combining *Solidarité* and Rue Amelot. Zionist youth participated in the circulation of clandestine press published by the Jewish Communists, and they also interfered with the work of Jewish clothing manufacturers in order to slow down or sabotage production destined for the Wehrmacht.[55] Joint work with youth, organized in "committees," or cells containing five resisters, survived the failure of the Action Committee, which was disbanded in December 1941. During 1942, young Zionists joined the "committees" and prepared for armed combat, answering the call of *Solidarité*. "Several of my Zionist comrades," wrote Bulawko, "wished to form autonomous armed groups, but that was impossible, because, without the Communists, we had no arms. We finally accepted their offers."[56]

The shortage of equipment and people subordinated the organized Zionist youth of Paris to the action of the better structured organizations, *Rue Amelot* and *Solidarité*. It chose a path that distinguished it from the non-Communist Jewish organizations, who still gave absolute priority to rescue work in 1942. For the Zionist youth, this priority was obvious, in that they aided the escape of Jewish detainees and helped them cross over into the southern zone. But it was only a relative priority, once the militants began to take part in the actions of the *Solidarité* partisan groups in Paris in 1942. Many losses, and then the arrest of Bulawko on November 19, 1942, left this group leaderless. In fragments, Zionist youth resistance in Paris was reorganized by Lévitte, who secretly crossed the border in March 1943 to create a section of the MJF.

The Unification Congress

In May 1942 the scattered elements of Zionist youth in the southern zone found in Simon Lévitte the leader capable of regrouping them and promoting coordinated action. Born in Russia, he grew up in Metz, where his parents had settled after the 1917 revolution. A medical student in Strasbourg, then a student of agronomy, he was the local commissioner of the EIF in Metz but left for Palestine in 1936. After sharing the hard life of the pioneers in a kibbutz in the Jordan Valley, Lévitte became the Secretary General of the EIF in Paris. After the debacle, he reconstituted the administration of the movement in Moissac, where he created a documentation center designed to train the leadership.[57] A delicate man, with a long face and an elastic gait, he dressed conservatively but with an almost precious elegance, stood out with his air of an aesthete. Indefatigable, completely self-controlled, careful never to give offense, he inspired the people around him with the desire to serve. An excellent organizer, a devoted educator, and a convinced Zionist, he was preoccupied by the fragmentation of the youth, which was divided into small groups with differing political or ideological identities and reduced to ineffectiveness by paucity of members and means.

Similar divisions scattered the adult Zionist activists. But the prestige of the directors of the federative organizations, Marc Jarblum, the president of the FSJF (*Fédération des sociétés juives de France*, Federation of Jewish Associations of France), as well as Joseph Fischer and Nahum Hermann, who headed the pro-Palestinian groups, contributed to the relative cohesion of these Zionist circles. Lévitte took part in a Zionist conference that met at Lyons in December 1941. There he spoke with Fischer and with Dika Jefroykin, who was already in connection with the people who, a few weeks later, was to found the secret network of the Armée juive in Toulouse, and he decided to attempt the formation of a unified youth movement.

Lévitte immediately set to work organizing a congress. He decided to meet in Montpellier, where he knew a team of EIF leaders who were very favorable to Zionist ideas, and especially the local group of Zionist youth, organized on a strictly apolitical basis. On May 10, 1942, twenty-five young activists from the southern zone, including those responsible for the two *Hakhshara* farms, met at Montpellier. A bitter discussion ensued regarding the type of movement to be created: federative or unitary. A passionate speech denouncing the anachronism of parties and their ideologies in war time assured the victory of the unitary formula. Thus the congress of Montpellier founded the Unified Zionist Youth Movement (MJS), an unprecedented instance in the history of Zionism throughout Europe. It appointed an executive board, presided over by Jefroykin, and it appointed Lévitte as secretary general.[58]

The choice of the unitary formula was probably facilitated by the relative weakness of the parties as well as by the experience of the EIF, whose effectiveness no longer needed to be demonstrated. Nevertheless these factors would not have succeeded in shaking off the weight of the Zionist tradition, where party loyalty was almost a religion. The decisive impetus was given by the conviction of those dedicated to a unitary structure. The MJS was soon to know expansion and dynamism which its leaders attributed to the decision to free themselves from the control of the parties.

The congress also discussed the question of the legal façade of the MJS. At that time the UGIF was being established in the southern zone. The law demanded the dissolution of Jewish organizations, each of which was to become a division of the new Union. We shall see that in practice this was merely a formal change in name, which had a negligible effect on the freedom of action of each organization. Lévitte was inclined to endorse the solution adopted by the EIF, who continued their activities within the framework of the UGIF. This was also true of the leaders of the *Hakhshara* farms, which had recently been attached technically to the rural branch of the EIF. But the majority of the congress decided that the MJS would be clandestine.

Almost all the participants in the Montpellier congress were still unaware of the existence of the AJ, with the exception of Jefroykin, who was a member of its governing committee. No one alluded to armed resistance. The new MJS defined a program of activities in the educational and social area: courses and study circles in Jewish and Zionist education, physical training, vocational retraining within the framework of ORT, and finally social work in the service of local organizations and fund raising for the KKL.[59]

Lévitte, fortified by his own experience, immediately drafted plans for a training course or "leadership school." Maintaining contact by means of frequent trips and using the equipment of his documentation center in Moissac, in a few short months he created *gedudim* (Hebrew for brigades) or local MJS groups in thirty cities and towns of the southern zone. The Montpellier *gedud* was the best structured, punctually accomplishing all of the tasks listed in the plan and recruiting a large number of young people. The leadership school functioned for three weeks in August 1942 at Moissac. Zionist youth, "undisciplined and impatient,"[60] had finally found someone to assemble them in Lévitte, and they worked at double speed to make up for lost time.

However, *Jeunesse Mizrahi* (Mizrachi Youth), connected to the religious Zionist party and the youngest of the Zionist youth movements, had kept its distance from the reorganization effected by the MJS, with the exception of an active and influential group of young leaders, the Tseïré Mizrahi (Hebrew for "Young Mizrachi") who had gathered in Marseilles in March 1942. The chaplain, Kapel, had represented them at the unification congress in Montpellier and had been appointed to the executive of the MJS. Paul Roitman, one of the principal activists in the study circle of Toulouse, had not reconstituted the Mizrahi after the defeat. In July 1942, a summer camp he organized in Condom (Gers) assembled more than fifty veterans of the movement.[61] Strongly cohesive, at that time the Mizrachi had the potential for outnumbering any of the other small groups of Zionist youth. By joining the MJS, it could have nearly doubled its members. It did so only at a later stage, after the occupation of the southern zone by the Nazis. However, many of its activists were already at work in providing assistance to the detainment camps in the Toulouse region and in the GTE. Some of them had joined the first members of the AJ while it was being formed.

The end of the training course in Moissac coincided with the mass arrests of foreign Jews on August 26, 1942 in the southern zone. Just three months after its constitution, the MJS was called upon to accomplish missions not

envisaged by the Montpellier plan: to protect its own activists who were targeted for arrest and deportation, because they were foreigners who had
entered France after 1936, and to come to the aid of the population which
had hastily gone underground to avoid arrest.[62] Rescue activity was now to
take pride of place in the preoccupations of the MJS.

Publications and the Yechouroun Movement

The Jewish youth movements did not issue clandestine publications in
France before the summer of 1942. In Paris some Zionists in Bulawko's
group participated with comrades from the Communist UJJ (*Union de la
jeunesse juive*, Union of Jewish Youth) in distributing underground publications, pamphlets and periodicals published by *Solidarité* in Yiddish. Their
comrades in the southern zone were associated with the reproduction and
distribution of typed "information letters," published by the KKL in Lyons.
These sheets contained neither orders nor directives, nor commentaries or
analyses of the situation and events in France. Written with the assistance of
foreign Jewish press supplied by the KKL from Geneva, they provided information about Jewish life outside of Europe, particularly concerning
Palestine and Zionist activity.[63] In Toulouse, the engineer Moïse Finkelstein
of the AJ composed courses in Jewish history, the geography of Palestine,
Hebrew literature, and the ideology of the Zionist labor movement in
French and Yiddish and had them mimeographed.

The publications brought out by the youth movements themselves did
go beyond the legal framework of their activities: providing information
and instructions from the directors to the local leaders, and especially correspondence courses. Until the end of 1941, the only publication center was
that of the EIF in Moissac, headed by Lévitte. He put out a monthly communication bulletin, *Kishrei Avoda* (Working Connections, in Hebrew),[64]
containing from twenty to thirty typewritten pages. In addition to technical and administrative instructions concerning the functioning of the scout
units, one also found messages from the national board there, commenting
on one of the themes of scouting education or the next holiday of the
Jewish year, providing a brief description of the weekly Torah portions to be
read in synagogue on the coming sabbaths, the calendar, or a list of available titles in the traveling library, and the like. The documentation center
also published correspondence courses in Bible, Jewish history, literature,
trends in thought, Jewish life (ritual prescriptions), and Hebrew. In the
Lautrec rural center, Léo Cohn oversaw the creation of a wall newspaper,

Sois chic (Be Nice), which became the organ of the whole rural branch of the EIF in 1942.[65]

In January 1942 a similar center of correspondence courses, covering the same disciplines but intended for students at an advanced level, began publishing in Limoges. Created by the Yechouroun movement under the name of *Centre de formation religieuse des jeunes* (Center for the Religious Education of Young People), it was led by Jacques Cohn, a high school philosophy teacher and one of the founders of the movement in Strasbourg. Recruiting among the strictly religiously observant in Alsace and Paris, Yechouroun was attracted, on the one hand, by an intransigent isolationist tendency represented by the AIP (*Association des Israélites pratiquants*, the Association of Practicing Jews) and, on the other hand, by the desire to confront modernity. Its activists were sometimes limited in their commitments by the ambiguity of their position. Nevertheless, in Lyons, Marseilles, and Limoges, where they had sought refuge after the debacle, some of them were in step with the large Jewish organizations, particularly the EIF. Very diligent in attending study circles, they also took a notable part in bringing parcels to the poor detainees in the camps. Yechouroun operated and managed a kosher soup kitchen in Lyon.[66] Its correspondence courses were coordinated with those of Moissac.

In a more general way, coordination between the youth movements was desired by the Central Consistory. It had appointed Samy Klein, a veteran of the Yechouroun movement and the chaplain of the EIF, as chaplain for youth. In 1941, so as to enlarge the sphere of his activity and include, in addition to the youth movements, the children's houses, the rural and artisanal centers, and the religious education courses of the communities, Klein had created in Marseilles, under the aegis of Chief Rabbi Hirschler, the *Conseil directeur de la jeunesse juive* (CDJJ, the Leadership Council of Jewish Youth). This organization mainly saw to the rational coordination of the correspondence courses of the EIF, of Yechouroun, and, after the spring of 1942, also of the MJS, avoiding duplication and expanding circulation. At the rural center in Lautrec in August 1941 he organized a training course for leaders similar to the one in Beauvallon, with the participation of officials and teachers who had lost their jobs after the implementation of the Statue of the Jews.[67] In March 1942, Klein placed the CDJJ under the control of the Central Consistory in order to remove it from that of the UGIF.

The correspondence courses expanded considerably, mainly the elementary Hebrew course, sent out every week, for which the subscribers paid 80 francs for six months.[68] The center in Limoges created a course in the geography of Palestine ("palestinographie"), that it mimeographed in Moissac.

Beginning in the month of May 1942, Lévitte added courses in Zionism and the history of the pioneering movement in Palestine to his catalogue, meant for the newly created MJS. No one has studied the degree to which these publications were used by their subscribers. Seeing the poverty of the literary creation, studies, schooling, and religious life in the French Jewish community before the war, this rich blossoming in the precarious situation of the Vichy period could not have been predicted. It was stimulated by an undeniable demand. The subscribers to the Yechouroun courses in Limoges paid 4 francs per publication,[69] which was a considerable amount at the time. One month after its creation, the Center for the Religious Education of Young People served more than 200 subscribers, a number given in a report submitted to the *Police aux questions juives* (PQJ, Police for Jewish Questions) of Limoges, which intercepted all of Jacques Cohn's mail and telephone conversations. Two months later, the same police unit wrote to the Prefect of Limoges (April 1, 1942): "Seeing the constant growth of the addressees [of documents originating with the Center for Religious Education], I see it as my duty to bring to your attention the size that this movement seems to be assuming."[70]

Without the indiscretion and zeal of the inspectors of the PQJ, we would be far less well informed today regarding the printing of publications that helped initiate the young Jews under the Nazi jackboot in their cultural and spiritual heritage.

But of what were the writers of the Center of Religious Education for Young People suspected? The future Secretary General for Jewish Questions, Antignac, who was then only the chief of the PQJ in Limoges, admitted in his conclusions that, "the circulation of publications of strictly scientific character of relating to the Jewish religion is not prohibited by law" (report of February 15, 1942), and that "on first view," the intercepted documents "seemed to be purely a cultural and religious tie among Jewish correspondents" (report of April 1, 1941). But, he adds, "the activity of this movement could very well not be limited to purely cultural relations," and "one must fear that under the cover of these activities, the directors and chiefs might be delivering to these young people *propaganda definitely hostile to the gouvernment*."[71] Angered, the CGQJ (*Commissariat général aux Questions juives*, General Commission for Jewish Questions) had Jacques Cohn arrested and placed in detention on November 10, 1942, the day of the Allied landing at Algiers.[72] But the matter of the Center for the Religious Education of Young People continued to be the subject of reports addressed to the Prefect at least until June 28, 1943.

Some of those subscribing to the correspondence courses, counselors in children's houses and leaders in youth movements, used them in teaching.

Others consulted them to satisfy their thirst for knowledge of their people and for self-knowledge. The phenomenon is no different from that which led to the emergence of the study circles. Aside from the technical instructions transmitted by the youth movement hierarchy, the timeless themes developed in these publications reveal an apolitical tendency. The close cooperation between the EIF, the MJS, and Yechouroun, who produced and distributed material on the same subjects, shows an affinity for concerted action.

The formation of the MJS itself exemplifies the two currents expressed by a large part of Jewish youth: the blurring of ideological and political barriers and the desire for unity. This development was accompanied by a growing militant commitment, which was to become even stronger with the brutal deterioration of the situation in the summer of 1942.

6

⌒⤳⁂⤶

From Social, Political, and Cultural
Action to the Military Option

Looking back after the passage of so much time, when one considers the conduct of the Jewish leaders of France under the occupation, one might wonder why they were so hesitant in planning their response to persecution and why that response was so varied in its tactics and took so long to achieve unity.[1]

Close examination of the very diverse components of the Jewish population helps one to understand certain things. The president of a Jewish charity organization (the recipient of the highest civic and military honors, the scion of several generations of French patriots, and counting one or another of the heads of the Vichy regime among his intimate friends of long standing), would naturally interpret events in radically different ways than would the Russian (or Polish) born head of a Zionist movement, with ties to French socialist circles. Awareness of a common destiny was truly lacking at the start. It took no less than three years and increasingly cruel and brutal blows from the enemy to dissipate all the obstacles to the creation of a united front of Jewish resistance. The arrest and deportation of the heads of Rue Amelot and of the UGIF (*Union générale des juifs de France*, the General Union of French Jews) during the summer of 1943 did away with the last vestiges of misunderstanding among the Jewish organizations.

Anyone today who wonders why the response of Jewish resistance was relatively weak and late forgets that the personnel available to the Third Reich to accomplish its extermination plan were incomparably greater, far better organized and disciplined, and, furthermore, efficiently backed by the Vichy regime.[2]

The first blow could not be parried. The German order of September 27, 1940 for a census of the Jews in the northern zone[3] took those concerned and their leaders entirely by surprise. They had either to obey or to disappear into the underground. But nothing had been done to give that second option even a particle of feasibility. How, in a country that had become a police state, could one obtain a false identity from one day to the next? It required long apprenticeship in the resistance networks to be able to mass produce the full battery of official identification papers without which one could not survive in France between 1940 and 1944. One cannot improvise forgeries, either psychologically or technically. Thus almost all of the Jews went to the police stations in their neighborhoods and docilely complied with the census procedures.

Furthermore, while well aware that the census augured nothing good, people did not know what ills it boded. This leads one to mention another factor indicative of the inferior position of the Jews in their combat against the Nazis. While the latter were fully informed about the Jews, thanks to the census, they cleverly concealed their intentions and decisions so as to avoid any preventive resistance. In the first phase, during 1940 and 1941, their policies seemed to follow a plan to expel the Jews to the southern zone and then out of Europe.[4]

But people knew nothing definite. The measures of professional segregation, the despoilment, the detention of certain categories of foreign Jews, the prohibition against crossing the demarcation line, the coarse and damaging propaganda spread by the press and the radio, rumors of massive deportation of the Jews to Madagascar after the war,[5] and the expulsion to the southern zone of 3,000 Jews who had not fled Alsace and Moselle before the invasion—all of this did not constitute a coherent whole. No one had learned what was to be the Nazi solution to the Jewish problem. Hence no one could define a response or prepare for it. The Nazis kept secret their conference at Wannsee, on January 20, 1942, where it was decided to implement the Final Solution. They created a special vocabulary to disguise the truth: "forced labor," "convoys of laborers," "a Jewish population zone in southeast Poland," etc. The strategy succeeded completely. Wellers has published the testimony of Jewish escapees from the death camps, proving that no one knew the destination of the deportation trains or what was awaiting

them.[6] The London radio and the Jewish underground press began to publish the truth in November 1942.[7] Nevertheless, Jewish resisters as prescient
and lucid as Rapoport and Bulawko, deported from Drancy in the summer
of 1943, did not know what was being done at Auschwitz until the moment
they arrived.[8] Among both French and immigrant Jews, some believed that
the deportees from France would be treated with less barbarity than those
of eastern Europe.[9]

The principal cause of this state of mind was neither the effectiveness of
the cloak of secrecy spread by the Nazis and their accomplices nor lack of
information. The Jews did not know because they refused to believe the BBC
broadcasts and the underground pamphlets.[10] A psychological defense
mechanism gave them the idea that these bulletins were an invention of
anti-Nazi propaganda. News of the worst kind was mainly greeted with
skepticism. During the founding meeting of the Central Commission in
Marseilles on October 30, 1940, J. Weill stated that they must prepare themselves for a situation where Jews could no longer travel or meet. With his
goatee and thick eyebrows, his eyes sparkling with intelligence and sensitivity, with his soft gestures, his affectionate voice and confidential tone, his
somewhat precious courtesy, he was in imposing figure because of his
majestic self-assurance and the surprising breadth of his culture. But this
time, his warnings aroused protest among some listeners and hilarity
among others. During 1941 he informed the directors of Jewish charities
about the mass murders committed in Poland by the Einsatzkommandos.
This information came from Pflugfelder, a former police officer from
Strasbourg, who had emigrated to Switzerland and joined the British
Intelligence Service, for which he had carried out missions in Poland. But
Weill was unable to make a dent in his listeners' skepticism.[11]

Another reason for the imbalance of forces to the detriment of the Jews
derived from the military choices made by those who were in the same
camp in the battle against Hitler: the Allies. In their murderous obsession,
the Germans kept trains rolling to Auschwitz even when the general staff
was hampered by lack of transports to carry out its operations.
Correspondingly, the Allied command always gave military operations
absolute priority over humanitarian intervention. This rule was applied
on all levels of the hierarchy, in some cases even after the victory. In May
1945, American troops encountered a group of survivors of one of the
infernal death marches in Bavaria, consisting of wounded men and
women who were dying from lack of care. One of the surviving women
asked help from a Yiddish-speaking officer, who answered, "I understand.
But listen. The war is still going on. You understand? We are fighting here.

Right here. There is no one who can do anything now. . . . The war, you understand?"[12]

On the level of saving human lives, which was the major mission of Jewish resistance, no military support was forthcoming from abroad. "It is clear that Jewish resistance could not be part of the Allied strategy. They never thought of giving it a role. . . . No resistance movement was less favored,"[13] wrote Henri Michel.

The Unification of Aid Societies Imposed by the Government

From 1940 to 1942, the Jewish organizations had no doubt about their duty. Whether they were distributing help to the indigent, sending packages to detainees, dispatching teams of social workers to improve conditions in the detention camps, or running children's shelters, occupational training centers, youth movements, or study circles they were responding to needs resulting from the war and the occupation.

Immediately after the end of their torments, some of the survivors who had taken part in social work in the camps engaged in a retrospective self-evaluation, because they had discovered that the detention camps had served as an antechamber for deportation and death. By contributing to the organization and proper functioning of the camps, had they not promoted the enemy's plans? Should they not have acted to abolish them or at least undermine their activities, "employing all means to increase the number of escapes and to organize secret passage into Switzerland and Spain, . . . to provide false identity papers to a large number of the detainees. . . ? We tended to be too law-abiding, in the hope that that attitude would better serve the interests of the inmates."[14]

This dilemma emerged under the occupation everywhere in Europe, wherever the enemy dissolved the existing Jewish organizations and recombined them as a *Judenrat* (a Jewish council).[15] In doing so the Germans made cynical use of the Jewish tradition of community solidarity and the structures of their social and philanthropic bodies. During the first phase of the occupation, no matter what country one considers, the Germans gathered all the Jews and their institutions within the framework of a single and obligatory, solidly structured organization. Those holding responsible positions, preferably chosen from among people who enjoyed the confidence of the community, were made dependent upon the occupation authorities. In the particular case of France, the task of creating a Jewish council was delegated to the Vichy government, which, moreover, demanded that preroga-

tive. The *Commissariat général aux questions juives* (CGQJ, the General
Commission for Jewish Questions), a Vichy government agency, created the
Union générale des Israélites de France (UGIF, the General Union of French
Jews).[16] All the Jewish associations, charities, and organizations were dissolved and their assets transferred to the UGIF, with the exception of reli-
gious associations authorized by the Vichy government to retain their for-
mer private status, in keeping with the Law of the Separation of Church and
State of 1905. Unlike the Statute of the Jews in its successive versions,[17]
which was an autonomous initiative of the French authorities, the creation
of the UGIF responded to an explicit demand of the German command.
Moreover it functioned in the northern zone before the constitution of the
CGQJ, and it saw to the creation of the Coordination Committee of Jewish
Charities in January 1941. SS Lieutenant Dannecker had personally taken
charge of the creation and functioning of this committee. Less than a year
later, the UGIF replaced it in the northern zone, though it was formally and
administratively under the authority of the CGQJ at Vichy.

As noted, the constitution of a Jewish council, that is, the UGIF, belonged
to the first phase of the Nazi plan. It went together with the census of the
Jewish population,[18] the elimination of Jews from public functions, the
Aryanization of the economy and the liberal professions, as well as the
stamping of *juif* (Jew) on identity papers and ration cards (October 1940 in
the northern zone, December 1942 in the southern zone), and then, on June
7, 1942, in the northern zone, the obligation to wear a yellow star. Thus all
the Jews were placed on the margins of the national community, the first
step in the process of dehumanization. Replacing private Jewish charities by
a centralized public organization, administrated autonomously by Jews
appointed and supervised by the authorities, afforded the Germans several
additional advantages. The autonomous system of management allowed
them to economize on their own personnel while at the same time anes-
thetizing the distrust of the Jewish public and avoiding the possible risk of
seeing it take refuge in the underground. Because of the laws depriving the
Jews of work and thus of income, an increasing number of needy people
turned to the UGIF assistance offices, where they were received by Jewish
personnel, a circumstance creating a climate of confidence. Every appeal for
help—an allowance, a coupon for a soup-kitchen, treatment in a dispensary,
etc.—was accompanied by the creation of a family or individual file. The
Germans intended to use the files created in that manner for the waves of
arrests, either selective or massive.

Later, when the arrests took place, ostensibly for deportation to labor
camps in a mythical zone of Jewish population in the east, the Germans

obtained efficient help from the Jewish personnel who had been called upon to contribute to the smooth functioning of these operations by giving their members "certificates of legitimation," stipulating that they would be neither arrested nor deported. The bearer of such a certificate was expected to prove his zeal in executing orders, in order to avoid the risk of being deprived of it. This was also the case of the Jewish police established by the Germans in the ghettos of eastern Europe and in the camp in Drancy.

In general the system proved itself. It permitted the Nazis to carry out the Final Solution with the efficient, sometimes zealous, aid of Jewish auxiliaries. The latter usually believed they were serving a disinherited community, thinking that they were doing jobs that would otherwise have been given to Aryan officials recruited from among anti-Semitic milieus, or, more prosaically, they hoped to save their own lives. For the most part, they were deported and exterminated in their turn.[19]

Hence to belong to the system of the Jewish Council was the equivalent of being one of the delicate and invisible cogs that made the extermination machine turn.

But things never appeared in so simple and unequivocal a manner. Just as it would be incomplete and excessive to view every Jewish charity or cultural project as a resistance movement, so too it would be outrageous and unjust to see them as an instrument at the enemy's disposal from the moment they were absorbed, whether submissively or not, within the UGIF. The question calls for further analysis.

In the case of the Coordinating Committee in Paris and the northern zone, and then the UGIF in both zones, there were three options: to yield, to scuttle the Jewish assistance organizations, or else to go underground. The latter two choices presume a degree of clairvoyance almost entirely absent among the Jews, including the members of the responsible authorities.

The trauma born of the collapse of the French army and the occupation of French territory had given rise to a conquered mentality among most of the population. People thought that strict obedience to orders would guarantee their safety. The Jews were no exception.

Nevertheless one must distinguish between Jews of French nationality and immigrant Jews. The former had a vaguer awareness of the danger. Though they were also the targets of the first discriminatory measures—for example the exclusion from public functions and the Aryanization of the economy—they believed they would be protected by their long possession of French nationality and, above all, by their record of civil and military service, as well as by the official distinctions they bore. Some of them approved of governmental measures against foreigners, who were "in excessive numbers in the national economy," though they provided assistance to the victims of these measures as a strictly philanthropic measure and not out of community solidarity. From 1940 to 1942 the Central Consistory of the Jews of France, a religious organization under the authority of the Chief Rabbinate, reacted as the official spokesman for native French Jewry. In this capacity it separated itself from rescue and social assistance groups. Some of the latter were specifically meant to assist foreign Jews, such as CAR (*Comité d'assistance aux réfugiés*, the Committee for Assistance to Refugees) and HICEM (a Jewish emigration organization composed of the Hebrew Immigrant Aid and Sheltering Society, JCA, the Jewish Colonization Association, and EMIGDIRECT, a German Jewish emigration association). Others came from abroad, such as the AJDC (The American Joint Distribution Committee), or were created, directed, and administered by immigrant Jews, such as the OSE (*Oeuvre de secours aux enfants* the Children's Rescue Network), ORT (Organization for Reconstruction and Labor), the charities of the FSJF (*Fédération des sociétés juives de France*, the Federation of French Jewish Organizations) and the AIP (*Association des Israélites pratiquants*, the Association of Observant Jews).

Targeted by the plan to unify the Jews and called upon to establish leadership like the other organizations, the Consistory avoided this on the basis of its exclusively religious character and its legal status. Nevertheless, the leaders of the Consistory wished to serve as spokespeople for the authorities toward the French Jews and used their influence and authority on the personal level to "orient" the membership of the administrative council of the UGIF, which was under the jurisdiction of the General Commissioner for Jewish Questions, Xavier Vallat. The latter had asked the Jewish leadership to propose candidates to him. Deep disarray, the reluctance of some of the people chosen to accept such a post, and finally internal quarrels had caused long delays. Annoyed, Vallat made it seem that he was resolved to appoint men of his choice to the post. In the Consistory people were concerned to prevent the appointment of inexperienced administrators, unfamiliar with Jewish charities, and perhaps unscrupulous. Given Vallat's clear preference for appointing people agreed upon by the charities, if not delegated by them, the Consistory obtained leaders who were supposed to subordinate their agreement to two conditions: (1)The capacity of the UGIF would be limited to assistance, to social services, and to occupational retraining; (2) Its budget would be supplied by voluntary contributions, excluding any special tax, collective fines, or confiscations.[20]

Left out of the UGIF, the Consistory thus tried to exert its authority discreetly by placing its men at the organization's head. Despite disagreements with the president of the UGIF, Albert Lévy, and his secretary general, Raymond Raoul Lambert, permanent contact was maintained. The directors of the UGIF kept the Consistory informed and consulted it frequently.[21]

In contrast, no option was available to the organizations of immigrant Jews permitting them to exist openly outside of the framework imposed by the authorities. The political affiliation of Jewish communists organized in the MOI-Yiddish labor union made them marginal to all the Jewish community charities, both native and immigrant. Before the occupation they had been driven underground after the signature of the German-Soviet pact, when the French Communist Party was suppressed, and after the occupation they went through a period of even greater isolation. Their leaders immediately denounced the UGIF and the Jewish organizations that belonged to it as accomplices of the enemy. In May of 1941, their dispensary on de Turenne Street and their soup kitchen on Saintonge Street in Paris were forced to close when they were told that henceforth provisions would be administered by the Coordination Committee.[22] Their underground periodical, *Unzer Wort*, dated December 6, 1941, called the UGIF an "organization of subjection of the entire Jewish population."

But other Jewish relief organizations continued their action under the auspices of the Coordination Committee in the northern zone and later of the UGIF in both zones. The distress of the poor and the detainees weighed heavily upon the leaders chosen to constitute the board of directors of the Union. According to a report of the Central Commission submitted in October 1941 to the General Commissioner for Jewish Questions, the Jewish charities in the southern zone provided assistance to 22,500 people, not including the population of the detention camps.[23] In contrast to the other organizations, the FSJF (*Fédération des sociétés juives de France*, the Federation of French Jewish Organizations) and Rue Amelot avoided having their representatives appointed to the board of the UGIF. Despite a personal appeal, Jarblum refused.[24] He did not prevent the integration of the charities of the FSJF within the UGIF, but in the cities of the southern zone he created clandestine committees of his organization. On July 3, 1942, Lambert had him warned secretly of "the grave danger presented by these committees," if their meetings "should come to the attention of the authorities."[25] This tactic of playing a double game characterized Jarblum's policy, for he sought to promote cooperation between immigrant and native French Jewish leaders, but he was determined to avoid government control. Thus in 1941 he recommended the co-option of a representative of the FSJF by the Consistory. After this effort failed, on March 22, 1941, he wrote to Heilbronner, the president, "I thought that the Federation of French Jewish

Organizations could, in an advisory capacity, attend those meetings of the Central Consistory devoted to the defense of Judaism. . . . You have no right to divide the Jews as you are trying to do."[26]

Nevertheless the mutual assistance projects of the FSJF that were entitled "pro-Palestinian" were associated with the central commission. Once the UGIF had been created, the charities were formally integrated within it. This situation was reversed in June 1943. The projects of the FSJF within that part of the structure which had remained official were terminated,[27] and responsibility for mutual assistance was completely transferred to the clandestine organization. For its part, the Consistory co-opted one of Jarblum's colleagues, Joseph Fischer.

In the northern zone, Rue Amelot pursued a similar policy: attempting to promote unity between French and immigrant Jews, and removing the activity of Jewish organizations from government control. In September 1940, David Rapoport said to the Chief Rabbi of Paris, Julien Weill: "At this moment, we must unite!" At the official constitution of the Coordinating Committee in January 1941, Rue Amelot, present in the guise of the Mother and Child Project and the OSE, had the full agreement of its partner in the CBIP (*Comité de bienfaisance israélite de Paris*, the Jewish Welfare Committee of Paris), Marcel Sachs, to resist Nazi demands passively, and to administer a large part of the assistance through a secret fund. This tactic was rather quickly discovered by the SD (*Sicherheitsdienst*, the Nazi secret police), so in May 1941 Rue Amelot left the Coordination Committee, which then became an efficient organization after the departure of Sachs, and Baur and Stora were appointed to head it. These two were later appointed the heads of UGIF-north, and they tried in vain to bring in Rue Amelot. Nevertheless they agreed to continue to serve as a façade for Rue Amelot projects, giving up the idea of "centralizing them, as long as this is possible." They also agreed to hold "intimate meetings without minutes" of the medical-social commission of the UGIF, with the participation of Rapoport and Minkowski, representing Rue Amelot.[28] This double game, played with the complicity of the leaders of the UGIF, came to an end when Rapoport was arrested on June 1, 1943. At that point the projects of Rue Amelot at last became sections of the UGIF.

To summarize, opposition to the UGIF took various forms, each one expressing the temperament of a specific organization: the Central Consistory retained its independence through a legalistic argument which was accepted by Vichy; The Jewish communists were radically opposed to the UGIF and remained completely in the underground; The FSJF and Rue Amelot remained separate from the UGIF leadership and maintained their projects partially within it, including funds paid by the UGIF for aid, and partially underground.

In the northern zone, under pressure by the Nazi SD, which stood behind the control of the CGQJ, the UGIF became a centralized and efficient administration, responsible for aid and for supplying the camp at Drancy. In the southern zone, on the contrary, the UGIF had a federative structure, modeled on that of the Central Commission. The various organizations continued their prior activity under another name until August 1942, the date of the first deportations.

Emigration

The most obvious way to save the Jews would have been emigration. Embarrassed by the presence on its soil of those notorious "foreigners in excessive numbers in the national economy," France was officially in favor of emigration. In December 1940 the Prefecture of the Rhône Department, in an oral statement to the president of the FSJF, spoke of "the necessity of intensifying activity . . . aimed at the emigration of foreign Jews to countries overseas."[29] Vichy formally encouraged the HICEM. The government went so far as to authorize it to change money at the official conversion rate for the dollar in order to purchase ship tickets.[30] The HICEM was also permitted to open an emigration office in each of the detention camps.[31] The government allocated the camp of Milles, north of Marseilles, to detainees destined for emigration. An affidavit issued by HICEM was sufficient for the transfer of a family of detainees to this transit camp.[32] In February 1942, HICEM, having been officially dissolved, became the Sixth Directorate of the UGIF, but its activities remained the same.

Nevertheless, as we have seen, under the auspices of the HICEM there were only about 6,500 legal departures. The obstacles placed by conditions outside of France were doubtless many. But locally, the application of the declared policy of the government was often sabotaged by bureaucratic chaos and the bad will of the government. The offices of HICEM in Marseilles underwent several searches in 1940.[33]

Three doors stood slightly ajar for Jews who wished to leave France: the United States, Latin America, and Shanghai. Despite the limited number of visas obtained, many thousands of those who did receive them were unable to use them,[34] not only because the foreign visas had sometimes expired before (after long and harassing exertions), the Prefecture of Bouches-du-Rhône would finally grant an exit permit, but mainly because after July

1942, Pierre Laval prohibited the emigration of Jews who could be deported. Henceforth, for Vichy, the problem of surplus foreigners in the national economy was to be resolved exclusively by the Nazi plan for massive deportations. In the month of August 1942, the Milles camp and its branches in Marseilles, established for women and children, contained more than 1,500 Jews who possessed visas for foreign destinations, but were now forbidden to emigrate. The Sixth Directorate of the UGIF (HICEM) continued its efforts to have the foreign Jews who had arrived in France after 1936 deported overseas, and to have those of Greek, Romanian, or Hungarian nationality classified as not subject to deportation.[35] Later it furthered secret emigration.

The hope of emptying the camps by means of emigration, formulated in November 1940 by the HICEM leadership,[36] ultimately proved to be illusory. However, though feeding upon illusions, the HICEM leaders were able to mobilize moral resources that permitted them to develop within the Kafkaesque maze of the Vichy bureaucracy, through obstinacy and exhausting effort. The power of these illusions was contagious. It spread among the detainees, who were subject to moral collapse, apathy, and decline. "The hope that they could leave was the only moral resource that sustained them," stated W. Schah, the director of HICEM-France in the summer of 1941.[37] Having only a psychological effect, these illusions at least saved the detainees from despair.

Assistance in the Northern Zone

During the first two years of the German occupation, the survival of Jews deprived of means of subsistence and thus subject to internment depended on the ability of the Jewish organizations to provide help. On this level, they coped well. The disinherited, numbering in the tens of thousands, included refugees who had recently entered France without work permits, supporters of families who had lost their jobs to unemployment because of their flight to the southern zone, or because of the anti-Jewish laws,[38] families conscripted in the GTE (Groupements de travailleurs étrangers, Foreign Laborers Groups), as well as the sick and the infirm.

In the northern zone, Rue Amelot, the OSE, the CBIP, and the Solidarité organization created by the leaders of MOI-Yiddish provided for the must urgent needs. Public soup kitchens, medical and social dispensaries, and assistance offices resumed their activity. ORT opened professional retraining classes, and the OSE organized children's groups. The administration of these projects, with the exception of those of Solidarité, which foundered, passed under the control of the Coordination Committee in April 1941, which was replaced by the UGIF in January 1942.

Material assistance did not dissipate the moral disarray, common to both the poor and to those who were more fortunate. The many small synagogues dispersed throughout the IIIrd, IVth, IXth, XIth, and XXth arrondissements provided improvised centers for immigrant Jews in search of moral support. Informal meetings of the many *landsmanshaften*, well attended, were held in the soup kitchen premises, in synagogues, or in the homes of activists. The Jewish press had ceased to appear. The Coordination Committee, under orders from the Nazi SD, published a periodical, *Les Informations juives*, beginning in April 1941, a mediocre sheet of administrative announcements, received with contempt and sometimes hostility by the Jews. Following the publication of an announcement establishing obligatory dues, accompanied by an appeal to generosity in the name of community solidarity, the periodical received an avalanche of letters attesting to its unpopularity: "I request that you erase my name from the coordination list," or: "I would be grateful if you gave instructions that I no longer be importuned by an association which has nothing to do with me."[39] The terms used by the wives of detainees show that they viewed the Coordination Committee as a service belonging to the government and not to the Jewish community: "You had my husband detained on May 14, 1941 for no reason at all; I remain with three children without any resource. Despite that I have never asked you for help. I only ask you to return my husband." "If you wish to make contact with my husband, you should address the camp in Drancy. As for me, it's impossible for me to do so." "If you really need a big donation, write to my husband, who is in the Pithiviers camp, barrack number 6. He will send you a large donation, larger than large."[40]

Only one organization, *Solidarité*, aware of the importance of information, produced pamphlets and periodicals and secretly circulated them in order to bolster the morale of the Jewish population and to stimulate their commitment to militancy.

But no advice or orders reached the Jews when the authorities issued orders affecting individuals. The first German ordinance against the Jews, dated September 27, 1940, obligated all Jews to sign a special register at the police station nearest their homes.[41] On May 14, 1941, 5,200 adult male foreign Jews were called to the police stations individually, "on a matter that concerns you." No Jewish organization reacted. Was this a lack of clear-sightedness? Fear of removing the mask and exposing the Jews to reprisals? "Ignorance of the danger, inhibition, deafness, unpreparedness" confessed a *Solidarité* leader, A. Rayski.[42]

In the Seine Department, the census taken in October 1940 provided the authorities with a register of 148,000 Jews (65,000 households). On May 14, 1941, almost 80 percent of the Jews summoned, that is, somewhat fewer than 4,000, reported to the police stations and were interned the same day in two camps of the Loiret Department, Pithiviers and Beaune-la-Rolande. Was it a proportion of the same magnitude who obediently went through the formalities of the census? The data cannot be determined. The Jews, including the immigrants, no less than the entire French population, preferred to avoid conflict with the authorities. Taking into account this desire to "be in order," it is not unlikely that the proportion of those resisting the census was more modest than that of the foreign Jews who dared to avoid reporting to the police station on May 14, 1941. Be that as it may, there was no organized Jewish resistance to these two measures. Most of the 4,000 Jews who were detained never knew the taste of liberty, for they later died in the death camps.

Intervention in the Detention Camps of the Northern Zone

The massive and brutal emergence of the phenomenon of detention camps confronted the Jewish leaders with a new situation. Each organization acted in accordance with its temperament and in line with its previous choices. The CBIP, which the public no longer distinguished from the Coordination Committee, distributed aid to any family deprived of support who addressed it, and later it created a parcel service. *Solidarité* gave its action a clear political character: women's demonstrations at the camp gates and at the offices of the Coordination Committee, fund-raising in solidarity and the establishment of secret contacts with detained activists, in order to incite them to organize information and propaganda committees in the camps. Rue Amelot made ingenious efforts to help both the families and the detainees. Being the only Jewish organization that made great efforts toward the release of former military volunteers, the heads of large families, the sick and invalid, it directed its actions toward rescue.

Rapoport was at that very moment the most endangered of the leaders of Jewish charities in Paris. On May 13, 1941, the delegate of his dispensary, The Mother and Child, resigned from the Coordination Committee: "Our resources are definitely exhausted, so that from now on it will be impossible for us to maintain our role within the Coordination Committee."[43] This resignation followed a vain effort to persuade the CBIP and the OSE to withdraw as well, in order to extricate them from the machinery set up by the German SD. SS Lieutenant Dannecker then "summoned Rapoport and threatened to imprison him in a fortress if he did not cease his opposition, ordering him no longer to occupy himself with the charities."[44] Thus it became necessary to work in the shadows.

The local social workers of the Red Cross provided emergency care in the camps and sometimes transmitted messages to the families of the detainees. This circumstance gave Rapoport the idea of creating a channel of communication with the detainees. He asked the French Red Cross and the SSAE (*Service social d'aide aux émigrants*, Social Service for Assistance to Emigrants) to provide identification cards for social workers from Rue Amelot. The positive result of this action permitted the establishment of direct and constant contact with the detainees in the camps.[45]

Henceforth aid to the detainees expanded to include material assistance, cultural and political activity, and rescue. The similar but not concerted action of Rue Amelot and *Solidarité*, with the aid of the Red Cross and the SSAE, forced the administration to concede a few rights to the detainees: correspondence, parcels, visits, and furloughs, the free election of those who ran the canteens, and the opening of youth centers and cultural circles in the camps. The social workers from Rue Amelot coordinated the distribution of parcels and the allocation of special assistance to poor families and the sending of parcels to detainees without families.[46] The youth centers and cultural circles helped protect the detainees from moral collapse, stimulating a degree of cultural and political activism among clandestine groups, some Zionist, others communist. The young people from Rue Amelot sent books, office supplies, small sports equipment, and social games to Pithiviers and Beaune-la-Rolande. On January 4, 1942 a member of the youth club in Beaune-la-Rolande wrote:

> We are young people, around eighteen to twenty-one years old. . . . We have established courses in physics, chemistry, stenography, Yiddish. A calisthenics session is held every day. We give lectures on French literature, on scientific subjects, on history, geography. . . . We have created a drama circle and a chorus composed solely of young people. We have already put on a comic play which had great success in the camp, called "The Ideas of a Madman." This skit was improvised and acted by young people. . . . We have created a small journal. It's a little collection of our impressions and thoughts.[47]

The action also extended to the camps of Tourelles in Paris, Drancy (created in August 1941), and Compiègne, as well as Mérignac (near Bordeaux),

Tours, Poitiers, and Troyes. In the latter four camps, the occupation authorities had detained entire families living in the coastal regions of the English
Channel and the Atlantic. This caused considerable expansion of the
monthly expenses of Rue Amelot, increasing from 176,000 francs in
December 1940 to 421,000 francs in July 1941 and to 626,388 francs in July
1942. The rise occurred in the budget items of "Family Assistance" and "Aid
to Detainees," whereas the item "Soup Kitchens" decreased, because many of
the Jews arrested had frequented the soup kitchens, so that the demand for
them was reduced.[48]

Rescue operations were carried out on two levels, legal and underground: release and escapes. The social workers submitted applications for
the release of detainees to the police stations, trying without letup to support them, in case after case, by the recommendations and intervention of
prominent people willing to lend assistance. With the exception of the
release of about a hundred children less than fifteen years old from the camp
in Poitiers, we have been unable to determine the number of detainees saved
in this manner.[49] As for escape, this was relatively easy in the camps of the
northern zone, except for Drancy and Compiègne. Until July 1942, the
directors of the camps gave detainees furloughs and permitted the sick to be
treated in the city hospitals. Detained in the barracks of Tourelles, Oscar
Esseryk obtained permission on January 3, 1941, to go out and shop for a
parcel to be sent to his brother, a prisoner of war in Germany. He took
advantage of this circumstance to flee to the southern zone. By contrast,
another of his brothers, detained in Beaune-la-Rolande on May 14 1941,
received permission to leave the camp four times, in line with the general
rules of the camp. Having nowhere to flee, he returned to the camp each
time, and he died in deportation.[50] This was also the fate of most of the
other detainees. For, having escaped, a Jew and his family had to be capable
of eluding police pursuit. That is, they had to possess false identity papers
and another domicile, or else the means to flee to the southern zone.
Solidarité ordered its activists to remain in the camp. Rue Amelot was the
only Jewish organization that obtained false papers for escapees from the
camps in the northern zone. Rapoport, aided by Bulawko, who was in
charge of youth activities for Rue Amelot, personally oversaw this, in the
utmost secrecy, and with extreme prudence. Until July 1942, the possibilities
remained modest.[51] According to Adler, 300 Jews escaped from the camp in
Pithiviers.[52] A Red Cross report estimates that about a hundred people
escaped from the camp in Troyes.[53] On December 26, 1941, the Prefect of
the Vienne Department canceled the permission granted to young people
from the camp in Poitiers who were attending classes at the Lycée, "because
of the numerous escapes which have taken place recently."[54]

In June and July of 1942, almost 3,000 Jews from the camps of Pithiviers and Beaune-la-Rolande, and 20,000 from the camps of Compiègne and Drancy were deported to Auschwitz.[55] On July 16 and 17, Paris was the scene of the monstrous mass arrest known as the "Vélodrome d'hiver," after the bicycle racing stadium where those arrested were concentrated. Of a brutality and scope unprecedented in France, this disaster brought down upon the Jews confronted their organizations with a singular situation.

The Beginnings of the Underground in the Southern Zone

During the first two years of the Vichy regime, the Jewish population of the southern zone barely felt the blow of the continual deterioration of the Jews in the northern zone. They were not subject to German orders nor to the intervention and direct pressure of SS officers on the Jewish leaders. There were no mass arrests. The creation of the UGIF made no real change in the possibilities for action open to the Jewish charities. Until May 1942, the directors of the UGIF were occupied with setting up an administrative structure that had a more formal than operational character. The autonomy of the charities was preserved. The change in name had hardly any practical repercussions.

We have seen that one organization, the FSJF, was nevertheless not content with expressing reservations and apprehensions regarding the UGIF law and its enforcement. The president of the FSJF, Marc Jarblum, viewed it as one more step in the escalation of anti-Jewish repression, which was to be followed by other measures of increasing severity. Rather than place his faith in the promises of Vichy, he foresaw a situation in which the government would make the administrators of the UGIF into their docile puppets. Having avoided nomination in his capacity as a member of the Council of the Union, he occupied himself with the creation of clandestine FSJF committees in the southern zone. His goal was to create an apparatus that would be capable of assuming the responsibilities for assistance and rescue, in case the police seized control of the UGIF services. Each secret UGIF committee divided its members, approximately fifteen, into three sections responsible respectively for mutual assistance, documentation, and political intelligence.[56] The latter was run by Zionist militants, the leading elements of the committees. The documentation people maintained secret ties with the Fifth Directorate of the UGIF, charged with aid to immigrants, in order to gather information about those receiving assistance. The mutual aid section had to take care of indigent Jews who did not wish to report to the offices of the UGIF. Regarding funds for assistance, certain delicate problems could have arisen. But funding was largely provided by the AJDC as well as by donations and loans from individuals, passing through the Palestinian charities. The FSJF had enjoyed the confidence of these organizations for a long time. Moreover, Fischer, the secretary general of the KKL (the Jewish National Fund), Nahum Hermann, the president of Keren Ha-Yessod (The Palestine Foundation Fund), and Jefroykin, the administrator of the AJDC for France, sat with Jarblum at the head of the French Zionist Organization (OSF, *Organisation sioniste de France*). Thus there was no doubt that if responsibility for assistance had to be taken by the clandestine section of the FSJF, the financial means would be available.

Meanwhile, nothing changed in the legal status of the FSJF, aside from its new name: Second Section of the Fifth Directorate of the UGIF. This was the case with other charities, too. But none of them took precautions like those taken by Jarblum. The area of activity demanding the most energy was the detention camps. Thousands of food and clothing parcels were sent by the youth movements, the OSE, the Yechouroun Association of Lyons, the Association of Observant Jews (AIP, *Association des Isréalites pratiquants*) of Marseilles, and the FSJF.[57] Kapel developed a network of "adoptions," through which Jewish families of Toulouse and its region took on individual detainees. In March 1942, this action was taken over by Simone Hirschler, who extended it throughout the southern zone.[58]

The Nîmes Committee

The large Jewish aid organizations and many French and foreign charities employed their means and efforts in common. In response to the demand of the Ministry of the Interior, on November 20, 1940, they constituted the Coordination Committee for assistance in the camps, generally called the Nîmes Committee. Its president, A. Donald Lowrie, represented the American YMCA.[59] The main non-Jewish charities active within the Nîmes Committee, in addition to the YMCA, were the American Friends Service Committee (Quakers), the Unitarian Service, the *Secours suisse* (Swiss Rescue Organization), the *Secours national* (National Rescue organization), the French Red Cross, the *Service social d'aide aux émigrants* (Social Service for Aid to Emigrants), the *Commission intermouvements auprès des évacués* (CIMADE, Intermovement Commission for the Evacuees, headed by Pastor Boegner), and *Amitié chrétienne* (Christian Friendship).[60] The Central Commission of Jewish Assistance Organizations in Marseilles was represented here by its secretary general, Raymond-Raoul Lambert, and by a delegate from each of the affiliated organizations: OSE, ORT, HICEM, EIF (the Jewish scouting movement), FSJF, CAR, AJDC, and the camp chaplaincy.[61]

The Nîmes Committee managed to humanize the conditions for the detainees in the camps and the GTE in the southern zone. Its means of action included mobilizing the resources of the affiliated organizations, some of whom supplied food and clothing sent from Switzerland and the United States. The president, Lowrie, obtained important humanitarian concessions from Vichy, such as giving the detainees the right to send and receive mail and parcels, the establishment of a medical service, kindergartens, schools, and apprenticeships. Very well informed by solid, unembellished reports submitted by Dr. J. Weill to the Nîmes Committee, in his contacts with Vichy, Lowrie emphasized the disastrous impression for the reputation of France produced abroad by the barbarous conditions imposed upon those "sheltered" by the camps.[62] A report presented in September 1941 takes note of the death of 60 babies out of a total of 140 in two-and-a-half months in the Rivesaltes camp.[63] The Nîmes Committee obtained the free admission into the camps of Catholic, Protestant, and Jewish chaplains, the installation of resident social workers, male and female, in charge of distributing the assistance, and the replacement of personnel suspected of lying, of inhumane behavior, or of other abuses.

The humanitarian action performed by the charities connected with the Nîmes Committee represents a considerable investment in spiritual, psychological, social, and material resources.[64] The many teams that worked within this structure saved tens of thousands of human beings from decline, people whom the French government had placed behind barbed wire and watchtowers because they had been designated as "superfluous for the national economy." But they failed to save the majority of the camp population, from deportation to extermination, except for children and adolescents. On this topic, a study of Jewish resistance must take note of the part played by the Nîmes Committee in rescue, both legal and clandestine.

Created at the demand of the Vichy authorities, the Nîmes Committee functioned legally. The government felt the need to appeal to humanitarian charities in order to avoid some of the responsibility for administering the camps and to try to disarm some of the criticism voiced abroad concerning its policies regarding immigrants and refugees.[65] While it did not make the Nîmes Committee an instrument for applying its repressive measures, neither did it permit the committee to interfere with the "delivery" of convoys of deportees to the Germans.

The philanthropic action of the Nîmes Committee, the "tone of universal benevolence and pardon" that reigned in it, were the target of Nina

Gourfinkel's sarcasm: "The stultifying forbearance of confessional morality
. . . chiefly regards the poor victim as an opportunity for the benefactor's
self-perfection. . . . No one, not a well-meaning soul in that polite assistance
organization . . . shouted out: . . . existence in the camps is not what should
be improved—the existence of the camps must be fought, God damn it!"[66]

Having worked as the assistant to two resisters, Marc Jarblum, the president of the FSJF and of the Father Glasberg, a leader of *Amitié chrétienne*, she
identifies with the latter's demanding intensity.[67] As early as 1946, the
author of most of the reports submitted to the Nîmes Committee, Dr.
Joseph Weill, questioned himself regarding the very principle of the participation of Jewish charities in this organization:

> The moment one collaborates with an enterprise where human
> liberty and dignity are undermined, . . . one becomes somewhat
> of an accomplice. . . . Working to improve the camps . . . is little
> by little to come to . . . accept the camps as the condition of life
> for certain categories of people. . . . The detainees had to be
> helped to live; but they ought mainly to have been freed. If more
> vigilant attention had been paid to the manifest signs of the
> conqueror's policies, . . . the freedom of many people could have
> been saved."[68]

On the balance, the rescue action taken by the Nîmes Committee is not negative, even if it was disappointing, and properly so, for the most aware of its
participants. Three of the five commissions of the Committee worked for
the transfer of detainees to centers providing more humane living conditions and above all freed from the constant surveillance of the police: the
commission on hygiene and aid to children and the aged, the commission
on liberation, and the commission on foreign laborers.

Their action centered on the effort to release at least certain categories of
detainees: those who could emigrate,[69] those over sixty, young mothers, military volunteers and veterans, as well as, after 1942, the families of workers
enrolled in the GTE. The results were barely modest regarding potential emigrants and foreign workers and their families. But an appreciable number of
elderly and almost all the children were released from the camps. Regarding
the other categories, young mothers and military volunteers, they failed.
The actions undertaken by the Nîmes Committee did not save them from
deportation and death. In the spring of 1941, Vichy seemed disposed, under
certain conditions, to reduce the number of detainees, and it appointed the

Prefect André Jean-Faure as inspector general of the camps.[70] Their administration was transferred from the police to the Ministry of Labor. Jean-Faure confirmed that the criticism voiced by the foreign press was "dangerous because well founded."[71] The conditions of life were inhumane, they were overpopulated and underequipped, the food allocations were at starvation level, and the mortality rate was high because of physiological misery, dysentery, and typhoid. The inspector general acceded to some of Lowrie's demands. As a result the number of Jews in the camps and GTE in the southern zone decreased from 40,000 in the beginning of 1941[72] to 27,000 in July 1942, of whom 20,000 were in the GTE.[73] But this decrease did not result only from the liberation or "temporary" release of detainees, for almost 3,000 of them had succumbed to the dreadful conditions of the camp. In the Gurs camp alone more than 1,000 Jews died in 1941.[74]

Detainees who could prove they their monthly income was at least 1,200 francs could chose to live under police surveillance in a remote village.[75] The decision regarding the release of the aged, constantly postponed, was made only in 1943, after the death or deportation of a large number of them. Father Lagarde, the Catholic chaplain of the camps and an active member of the Nîmes Committee, sent 450 escapees to twenty-four safe houses dispersed throughout the southern zone.[76]

In 1941 the SSE (*Service social des étrangers*, Social Service for Foreigners) was charged with opening special centers to shelter families of those conscripted in the GTE. The women and children who benefited from this measure were not liberated, but they enjoyed living conditions less inhumane than those of the camps. The number of detainees in the camps was certainly decreased, but those living in the special centers were not secure from deportation.[77] Further, the same SSE sent male detainees between the ages of sixteen and twenty-five to rural and artisanal Jewish centers directed by ORT, Palestinian charities, and the EIF. Born of a clever administrative fiction resulting from trusting cooperation between Lesage, the head of the SSE, and the Jewish leaders, this measure permitted young people threatened by deportation to be spared temporarily.[78]

On December 3, 1941, a man invited to a session of the Nîmes Committee submitted a report on the activity of a newly created project, the *Direction des centres d'accueil* (DCA, Directorate of Reception Centers).[79] The author was a priest from Lyons, Father Alexandre Glasberg. Born in the Ukraine and of Jewish origin, Glasberg was one of the founders of *Amitié chrétienne* (AC, Christian Friendship) in Lyons, which assembled Catholic and Protestant organizations, including CIMADE. It provided aid to refugees and maintained contact with Jewish organizations and the

Central Consistory. AC acted under the moral auspices of Cardinal Gerlier, the primate of Gaules, and of the president of the Protestant Federation of France, Pastor Boegner. It was represented in the Nîmes Committee by Father Chaillet.[80]

Glasberg was one of the first to conceive of providing aid to the detainees as an act of rescue where the official cover of a charitable organization would mask illegal activity. In close cooperation with the FSJF and the OSE, and with their financial participation, he thought of creating centers to receive groups of fifty to sixty adult detainees, couples, unmarried, the elderly, Jews, and Christians. The teams of social workers voluntarily interned were made responsible for creating the groups so that the reception centers could be self-administered. It took Glasberg six months of exertions to overcome all of the chicanery of the prefectorial and municipal adminis- trations before the opening of the first DCA center. Glasberg was aware of the effect of Gerlier's name upon the zealous supporters of the regime, for he was known to be a fervent follower of Marshal Pétain. Thus Glasberg pre- sented the Cardinal's letter of support for his charity every time he encoun- tered the ill will of an official. He also obtained the participation of the SSAE, a private organization for aid to refugees to which Vichy had accorded a quasi-official status. The participation of Jewish groups in the DCA remained secret, with the exception of the report submitted to the Nîmes Committee. On November 25, 1941 the first center, opened in la Roche- d'Ajoux (Rhône Department), received a group of fifty-two detainees from Gurs, who were "on furlough, not to be released."

The DCA created four other centers in 1942, in the Departments of Gers, Hautes-Alpes, and Drôme. Called "Defense against Germany" by its advo- cates, the charitable organization produced proof that each detainee had a monthly income of at least 1,200 francs. The center constituted a supervised residence designated by the government for prisoners on furlough but not to be released. The DCA took responsibility for nearly 1,000 adult detainees, mainly Jews. When the threat of deportation emerged during the summer of 1942, Glasberg realized that the "furloughs" could be canceled and the Jews from the reception centers could be summoned back to the camps. Hence he had them transferred from one center to another, after "Aryanizing" them by providing them with false identity papers. To provide long-lasting protection to the occupants of all the reception centers, he had only to make the files of the furloughed detainees "disappear" from the offices. This task was given to the social workers in the resident teams.[81]

In 1941 and 1942, Father Glasberg was closely familiar with the teams of Jewish social workers in Lyons, as well as in the camps of Gurs and Rivesaltes.

His patched habit no longer surprised either the patrons of the kosher Jewish restaurant on Lanterne Street or the activists and beneficiaries who frequented the FSJF office on Sainte-Catherine Street, where he had a permanent spot. He spoke to people in a stentorian voice, and he also knew Yiddish.[82] Of middle height but with an imposing build, his nose was straddled by thick glasses for nearsightedness, and he had a brusque but contagious cordiality. He was capable of speaking harshly when he encountered an obstacle. He enjoyed good food but lived in simplicity. The role played by Glasberg in the rescue of Jews made him one of the promoters of Jewish resistance. His method, which consisted in transforming Jews into Aryans, using the guarantee provided by organizations officially recognized as non-Jewish charitable or social charities, was "invented" and applied in the northern zone by Rue Amelot at the same time. It served as the model for several Jewish rescue networks in the southern zone beginning in the summer of 1942, such as the FSJF and the OSE, who were involved in Glasberg's DCA from the beginning. As for him, the occupation of the southern zone in November 1942 was fatal to his activity. Pursued by the Gestapo, Glasberg had to hide under the false identity of a rural parish priest in the Diocese of Montauban.[83]

The Camp Chaplaincy

While the Central Commission was giving way to the UGIF in the spring of 1942, the Chief Rabbi of France, I. Schwartz, appointed René Hirschler as the general chaplain of the camps and the GTE in the southern zone. The chaplaincy service had hitherto been provided by Rabbis Kapel, Schilli, and Salzer. Liaison with the Jewish organizations responsible for administrative and financial matters then passed through the Central Commission, of which Rabbi Hirschler was the secretary general. But new problems had arisen. The detainees were dispersed among twenty camps, thirty GTE-assigned dwellings in remote villages, the reception centers of the DCA, and finally the special centers of the SSE. On more than one occasion the camp commanders refused to permit the chaplains access to the camps. The service was overextended and sometimes paralyzed. Furthermore, the Chief Rabbi of France insisted on preventing the administrative tasks that had until then been assumed by the Central Commission from passing to the control of the UGIF, so as to preserve the religious character of the chaplains under the sole responsibility of the Consistory.

The creation of the general chaplaincy permitted the reorganization of the service, the expansion of the scope of its action, and the preservation of its independence. Placing Hirschler at the head of the new organization allowed it to benefit from the executive experience he had acquired in administering the Central Commission and from his brilliant ability to adapt, supported by a very clear conception of his pastoral responsibilities as well as by uncommon skill in analyzing events. Predisposed to leadership, endowed with a great ability to work, a generous heart, and communicative vitality, Hirschler showed unfailing courage. Naturally tending toward efficiency and showing proof of imagination, he espoused a conception of the responsibilities of the rabbi that upset the French Consistorial tradition. His veteran colleagues were ministers, the spiritual guides of a community defined only by its religious dimension. Political expression was identified with affirmation of loyalty to the French homeland, and the exercise of charity was the sum of its social mission. Hirschler shattered this framework, which was more in harmony with the norms of Jacobin France than with the Jewish tradition, which speaks of man in all the dimensions of his personality. To his mind, the rabbi's spiritual mission must place him at the service of the Jewish people as a whole and not only of those loyal to the synagogue. In times of distress, the rabbi must also be a social worker.

Hirschler achieved official recognition of the general chaplaincy from the Vichy regime, enabling it to obtain orders granting the chaplains access to the camps and the GTE. He appointed six regional chaplains and local chaplains. His personal contacts with the detainees, thanks to frequent visits, gave him deeper awareness of their needs. He also appointed assistant chaplains chosen from among detainees with the appropriate qualifications. In 1942 they numbered eighty and were accredited by the camp authorities.

Following the example of Kapel and Schilli and stimulated by Hirschler, the rabbis of that generation (he was then thirty-six) and those younger than he devoted most of their time and effort to action among the detainees, despite criticism from the Consistory. Below we describe what was achieved in the religious and cultural realm. On the level of assistance and rescue, they provided an indispensable link between the population of the camps and the Jewish charities, taking note of the needs of the detainees, having the necessary arrangements made, and bringing aid. They located the most urgent cases of distress and supported the efforts of the resident teams to release the children. The chaplains were particularly effective in having detainees placed in supervised residences, a status that later permitted a number of them to escape deportation.[84]

The camps in the northern zone lacked any chaplaincy service. Rabbi Elie Bloch of Metz, who had taken refuge in Poitiers, was separated from his colleagues in the southern zone buttenaciously demanded the right to visit the detainees from the Prefecture of the Vienne Department and the local SD. Though denied permission, he nevertheless persisted in aiding them through the social workers of Rue Amelot, who had been transmuted into personnel of the Red Cross and of the SSAE. His action extended to all the camps in the northern zone, except those of the Parisian region. Bloch created a parcel service, brought in assistance, and successfully worked for the liberation of children and their placement.

It would be erroneous to regard the chaplains' action in isolation from that of the other social workers who came to the aid of the detainees. The release of detainees, for example, resulted from joint efforts, for only a multiplicity of efforts and initiatives could overcome the inertia and ill will of a bureaucracy mired in a labyrinth of official regulations swarming with contradictions. Success greeted the efforts of those who were most skillful in exploiting the incredible confusion of the rules. It was necessary to be imaginative, audacious, and capable of improvisation to obtain the release of a detainee as well as his escape. Kapel estimates the number of detainees released from the camp at Gurs between November 1940 and July 1942 at 2,000, while there were about 1,000 escapes.[85] The fate of the escapees is almost completely unknown, except for the few who risked the taxing and perilous crossing of the Pyrenees to Spain, a country that did not drive away the illegal arrivals from France.[86]

The Jewish Army

In Toulouse in August 1940 a handful of man were already dreaming of creating a Jewish combat organization. Two coalitions of Zionist militants of various political leanings, but who were determined to create an armed Jewish network, joined together in 1941 to create the *Forces armées juives* (AJ, the Jewish Armed Forces). One of these consisted of David and Ariane Knout and Abraham and Eugénie Polonski, who were committed to Jabotinsky's Revisionist Zionist doctrine. The other group, formed around Aron-Lucien Lublin, contained Zionist socialists. Contrary to all the other Jewish resistance movements, the AJ did not grow out of a previously existing organization, nor did its origin draw upon social work or cultural activity. It was a political credo that conceived and gave birth to the AJ.

Its founders were above all preoccupied by the situation of the Jews in the world and in history. The contingencies of the moment did not monopolize all of their attention. They viewed these in a universal context. Hardly more prescient than their coreligionists regarding the merciless war waged against the Jews by the Nazis, they analyzed the moral and psychological aspects of the Jewish tradition. A minority subject to discrimination, deprived of rights, and the plaything of arbitrary government whims, pitiful emigrants seeking a hospitable country, or citizens of liberal countries where their destiny led to assimilation and the loss of identity, the Jews of the Diaspora were humiliated and incapable of solving their problems and even deprived of all collective self-esteem. The Jewish condition in Palestine hardly seemed more satisfactory to them, for there, in the historical Land of Israel, they were subject to the British regime, which deprived the Jews of the rights of free immigration, the purchase of land, and self-defense against Arab terrorism. This appraisal of the situation led to the definition of a plan of action: to reorganize the Jews to constitute a military force, under orders from the Haganah, and thus to place the Jewish people in the position of an interlocutor in the concert of nations to affirm their demand for a state in Palestine.[87] This program of action unified the two factions under the combined leadership of Lublin and Polonski.

Each faction had been taking its own path for more than a year, while at the same time developing a common manifesto during many meetings.[88] This document illustrates the understanding reached between the two rival currents of the Zionist movement, the Revisionist minority and the socialist, liberal majority. Thus it constitutes the distinctive characteristic of Zionism in France during the war. As fragmented and dismembered as everywhere else, it formed a common front against the Nazi enemy. The salutary depoliticization that permitted the formation of the AJ prefigures the creation of the apolitical MJS (*Mouvement de la jeunesse sioniste*, Zionist Youth Movement) in May 1942.

"The Strong Hand"

During the 1930s a deep trench was dug, radically separating the majority of the Zionist movement from the Revisionists, who in 1935 took the path of dissidence and seceded from the Jewish Agency. At the Twenty-First Zionist Congress, convened in Geneva from August 16 to August 25, 1939, the central topic of debate was the White Paper, the name given by the government in London to the system of measures restricting Jewish immigration to Palestine. How should one react to the disappearance of the last hope of rescue for the Jewish victims of Nazism who were fleeing from Europe and found no country prepared to receive them? Some voices advocated the Revisionist option, formulated outside of the Congress: the call to arms in an attempt to abolish the White Paper. But the majority decided to place themselves on the Allied side in case of a supreme crisis. On August 29, the president of the Jewish Agency, Chaim Weizmann, wrote to Winston Churchill, "I wish to confirm in the most explicit manner, . . . that the Jews are with Great Britain and will fight at the side of the democracies. . . . The Jewish Agency has recently had its political differences with the mandatory authorities. Our desire is to set aside these differences before the higher and weightier needs of the hour."[89]

In France itself, a fervent adherent of Revisionist Zionism, Kadmi Cohen, a lawyer and publicist, passionately attacked the Zionist Congress, which, according to him, was guilty of collusion with the London government, under the influence of the very assimilated British Jewish communities. He regarded Hitler's anti-Semitism as an obstacle to assimilation, thus strengthening the Zionist movement. Cohen proposed to Vichy that it negotiate with the Germans to transfer the Jews of France to Palestine. For his efforts, he was arrested and deported in June 1943.[90]

The spirit of Kadmi Cohen's ideas is also found in one of those who inspired the AJ, David Knout. A Jewish poet of Russian origin, a soldier demobilized in Toulouse in July 1940, he wrote a small notebook entitled *Que faire?* (What Is To Be Done?). There he expressed the humiliation and frustration of the Jew, the target of every blow, and he denounced the Jews' lack of awareness, their inertia and passivity. Knout concluded with a passionate appeal for unity, for a surge of Jewish will and courage: "We are seventeen million. United, we are a force. Disunited, we are flesh to be massacred." He asserted "the necessity of creating a Jewish state in Palestine and to fight for the right to live as Jews outside of Palestine." In his confidential pamphlet Knout called for the immediate creation of a combat organization, demanding absolute obedience and silence of its members. Utter silence was the only means for the Jewish people to "centuple their force, fatally limited" by their numerical and material weakness.[91]

Encouraged by his wife, Ariane, Knout set about searching feverishly for followers among the flood of refugees swamping Toulouse in July 1940. It was in vain. The Zionist sympathizers or activists whom he discovered "mistrusted an autonomous force which would escape the control of the Zionist Organization."[92] "The idea seemed absurd and dangerous at the time."[93]

But Knout did attract the attention of a Revisionist, also of Russian origin, who had been living in Toulouse for fifteen years. Always taciturn in public, Abraham Polonski preferred to go unnoticed. He left activist responsibilities to his wife, Génia. She had taken part in meetings of the Revisionist party in Paris before the war. The meeting of this couple with David and

Ariane Knout led to the decision in August 1940 to create a secret organization, known as *Forteresse juive* (the Jewish fortress) or *Main forte* (MF, the Strong Hand). Its goal was to create a Jewish state in Palestine, endowed with power that would enable it to provide for the security of the Jews of the diaspora. Its law was absolute silence. Its slogans were: "present everywhere" and "confront." Its program was to create an armed force, with the participation of Zionists of all stripes.[94]

To underscore his own identification with the MF, Polonski used its initials for his underground name, Maurice Ferrer.[95]

Despite his intransigent loyalty to Revisionist Zionist doctrine, and aside from his true sensitivity to the exalted romanticism that had reigned at the inception of the MF, Polonski also had a practical spirit and was a virtuoso at organization. The leadership of the MF, composed of the two couples, Polonski and Knout, very rapidly fell apart. Génia, gravely ill, died in June 1941, and Knout took refuge in Switzerland in November 1942. But Polonski had found dependable followers in Toulouse, whom he charged with recruiting activists for the MF. He remained in shadow by personal inclination, for security reasons, and also because he had a precise notion of the power obtained by absolute secrecy. He was in direct contact with only a few followers, refusing to meet with more than one at a time.

In 1940 the recruitment was extremely modest. The Jews were not prepared for disobedience. "The idea of armed resistance was perceived as a sign of madness or as proof of total irresponsibility."[96]

The Revisionist fraction of the Zionist movement in France was a tiny group, without infrastructure or militant youth. But Polonski located an area where tactical necessities obliged him to seek joint action with other types of Zionists. MF remained hermetically sealed, held in reserve for the day when circumstances would permit it to confront the British. It never made an alliance with the other movements, organizations, or networks and did not reveal its existence. Thus it preserved intransigent ideological purity. Polonski's personal terminology distinguished between the secret domain, that of the MF, and the underground domain, that of the battle against the Nazis.

The Common Front of Socialist and Revisionist Zionists

At the same time, the idea of forming a clandestine organization had also taken root in the mind of another Jewish immigrant, Aron-Lucien Lublin. He had more than one thing in common with Polonski. Like him, he was an

electrical engineer and had opened a consulting office for rural electrifica-
tion in Toulouse. He had gone to Geneva with the Polonskis to attend the
debates of the Zionist Congress. But Lublin, a socialist Zionist, identified
with the majority at the congress. Polonski kept him in the dark about the
MF so as to remove political quarrels from their relations. Lublin and his
friends worked intensely to aid poor refugees and to feed the detainees in
the camps.

A study circle run jointly by Knout and Paul Roitman, a fervent religious
Zionist, expanded the influence of these two militant centers, which were
still strangers to one another.[97] Polonski invited Lublin to a meeting of
about ten people, where Knout read from his booklet, *Que faire?* The desire
to place the action to be undertaken under the sign of the battle for the creation of a Jewish state in Palestine and the decision to create a military organization received the unanimous approval of the small group. A manifesto
was drafted, containing several passages from Knout's text. On January 10,
1942, the *Mouvement national d'action juive Bné David* (Bnei David [sons of
David] National Movement of Jewish Action) was created. This name was
soon reduced to the initials AJ (*Action juive*) and fused with that of the
Armée juive (Jewish Army) chosen by Lublin and Polonski. The Comité central directeur (CCD, Central Administrative Committee) was formed and
two days later it supplemented the text of the manifesto that had been
adopted with a "plan of action."[98]

The manifesto states that "the extermination of the Jewish people is
already being carried out," and it denounces "the total failure of the ideology of assimilation." Its authors constituted "the national and revolutionary
movement of the young generation of Jews . . . [who must] prevent the
extermination and suicide of our people . . . [and prepare] a definitive solution of the Jewish question, which must be presented to the peace conference, in the sense of national independence judicially guaranteed. . . . A voluntary representative organization of the Jewish nation, . . . our goal is: a
Jewish state in Palestine and Palestine as the Jewish state."

The program of action composed by the CCD envisaged the formation of
a militia that would intervene "every time the conduct of a Jew can legiti-
mately be considered inadmissible." It organizes "aid to illegal immigrants"
and orders the formation of an information service and of a "group of volunteers prepared to fight . . . [who] will undergo military training," as well
as the institution of courses in Jewish history and Hebrew."[99]

The CCD of the AJ was directed by Lublin and Polonski. Mutual trust
reigned between the two men. For three years they took over the two-headed
command of the AJ. They were very different from each other physically.

Polonski was short, agile, very indifferent to elegance but careful in his dress, with a penetrating but impenetrable gaze, distant, and solitary, and he did not leave Toulouse. From the day that he took over responsibility for guerilla action, he arranged to be accompanied constantly by an armed bodyguard.

Lublin was tall and thin, well dressed, always smiling but with an enigmatic gaze, warm, and trusting. He did not surround himself with mystery, and his natural relaxation gave him an inoffensive air and added to his charm.

They were both indefatigable workers, obstinately combative, prudent and enterprising, austere and self-disciplined, excellent organizers, concerned both with details and with the whole picture. Polonski, who threw himself enthusiastically into ambitious and grandiose projects, nevertheless knew what was beyond the bounds of possibility. He had a feeling for command, aware of his competence and efficiency. He realized that Lublin was a convinced follower of the prevailing majority within the Zionist movement, that he was a socialist, and that he accepted ideological discipline. For that reason he had access to human resources—through the youth movements—and to finances that were largely unavailable to Polonski because of his Revisionist views, which aroused the suspicions of the other Zionist. The two men made up a reasonable, well balanced pair which was to prove its mettle.

The strict separation between dogma and action did not prevent those sworn to the MF from joining the ranks of the AJ. On the contrary, they produced some of its leaders. It soon became clear to Polonski that the type of action favored by Jews who were prepared to commit themselves was of a social or cultural order. The geographic proximity of the detention camps of Gurs, Rivesaltes, Noé, Récébédou, and Le Vernet imposed the duty upon the Jews of Toulouse to create mutual assistance teams. The chaplain, Rabbi Kapel, who accepted the ideas of the AJ, took charge of liaison with these groups with the goal of recruiting young fighters, while Knout searched among the adolescents and young adults who attended the study circles in Toulouse, seeking knowledge and militant commitment. Lublin saw to the recruitment of resisters by the AJ in other centers of the southern zone, notably in Montpellier, Nice, Grenoble, Lyons, and Limoges, for he was acquainted with the Zionist youth groups and social service teams. His friend Jefroykin, in charge of the French office of the AJDC, was appointed a member of the CCD and provided the AJ with funds necessary for its action.

The period leading to the great mass arrests of the summer of 1942 was one of preparation, the creation of structures, the choice of leaders, and of means of action. The phase of intensive recruitment and operations did not begin until later. In principle, every new member was required to go through an initiation ceremony during which he took an oath: "With my right hand on the blue and white flag, I swear loyalty to the Jewish army and obedience to its chiefs. May my people live again, may the Land of Israel be born again! Liberty or death."[100] The ritual took place in Polonski's presence, in an absolutely dark room, where a spotlight focussed on the new initiate allowed him to see only the symbols of the ceremony, a Hebrew Bible and the blue and white Zionist flag."[101] The AJ files contains 1,952 individual cards, the number admitted until August 1944.[102] The number of those who swore the oath is unknown, but Lublin estimates it at about 300. Actually the criteria for recruitment became less rigorous when, under the pressure of circumstances, attention was focussed exclusively on fighting the Nazis. Responding to the daily demands of the task of rescuing Jews, in its many guises, and in close cooperation with other networks, the leaders of the AJ forwent the requirement of the ritual oath or were satisfied with a short form of it to admit resisters who said they were non-Zionist.[103]

However, the hierarchical structure and the military orientation remained intact, as they had been defined by the manifesto of January 1942. "Jewish resistance preceded general resistance in France," wrote Knout in 1947.[104] Twenty years later, the historian Henri Michel, who for a long time had doubted the existence of Jewish resistance, concluded in his turn that the Jews "passed without transition, directly from oppression to partisan warfare; as to that partisan warfare, they were not the last to engage in it, following the example of others, and with their cooperation; rather, they were among the first, and all alone." This reflection was evoked by the Warsaw Ghetto uprising, which broke out in April 1943, "when there was not yet a single underground fighter in France,"[105], and it is perfectly applicable to the AJ, for in January 1942 it organized the recruitment of groups of volunteers in a military framework.

7

⸙

The Jewish Communist Organizations

When the war broke out, underground existence was already a familiar way of life for thousands of immigrants who were political or racial refugees. Since the economic crisis, the distribution of residence and work permits had been severely restricted. Whoever lacked these precious documents had to learn to avoid police scrutiny, which led to deportation or imprisonment.

Particularly in Paris, artisans doing piecework at home for small clothing or leather fabrication businesses were mainly operating illegally. Unable to obtain legal employment and a work permit, they were also defenseless against exploitation. Their employers paid them paltry salaries, not reported to the tax authorities, and provided no social benefits.

The most recent clandestine immigrants were former members of the International Brigades in the Spanish Civil War who had escaped from the detention camps. There were also militants of the PCF (*Parti communiste français*, the French Communist Party) who continued to publish and distribute its now-illegal publications after the party was outlawed in September 1939. The Parisian police had obtained "favorable" results in the repression of rebellious workers and those suspected of Communist "intrigues." At the same time, those living underground perfected their techniques.

Those who were both immigrants lacking residence and work permits and also Communist militants were very likely the most hardened. Numerically, the Jewish element was only weakly represented: three hundred members of the PC plus about 2,500 union members, mostly in the Yiddish section of MOI (*Main-d'oeuvre immigrée,* Immigrant Labor), which belonged to the CGT (*Confédération générale du travail,* General Labor Federation), under the tutelage of the PC.[1] These numbers do not include the mutual assistance societies, youth groups, sports clubs, and cultural associations created by left-wing immigrant Jews, some of which were practically speaking dependent upon MOI. The pieceworkers refrained from joining the union so as to be less exposed to repression by the immigration police, but some of them were Communists. Communist influence in the immigrant Jewish milieu extended beyond the members of the party and the labor union, notably by the circulation of the daily Yiddish newspaper, *Die Naye Presse.* Prohibited on October 10, 1939, it continued to appear irregularly as an underground paper under the name *Unzer Wort.* Also prohibited, MOI and its subsidiaries adapted to life underground, like the other parts of the PC.

This experience, which was later put to profitable use during the occupation, isolated the Jewish Communists from the rest of the Jewish population. Moreover, their reactions to events also distanced them from the other militants of the PC. Already confounded by the Hitler-Stalin pact, when the Nazis invaded Poland a few days later, with the USSR quickly following, they were disgusted and angry. Had the party not affirmed that the pact with Germany would prevent war? "May the name of Adolf Hitler disappear forever!" wrote Rayski in his editorial in *Die Naïe Presse* on September 4, 1939, the last issue to be published legally.

The Jewish Communist leaders got a grip on themselves. With the reflexes of disciplined militants, they attempted to "explain the inexplicable," though without going so far as to approve of the pact.[2] Disarray grew even greater with the defeat of the French army and the German occupation. The PC, which at that time took a "legalist line,"[3] broke with the immigrants. It was not until August 1940 that the party, under the direction of Jacques Duclos, renewed contact and charged Gronowski with reorganizing the immigrant milieus, placing him in charge of all the clandestine parts of MOI. In September he assembled the Jewish leaders on rue Custine at the home of one of them, Puterflam.[4] An anonymous MOI report written after the war claims that a special issue of *Unzer Wort* had been published much earlier, on June 25, 1940.[5] This unverifiable chronology is doubtless meant to support the official historiography of the PC, which "erased" the German-

Soviet pact and dated Communist resistance to the first hours of the German occupation. It is contradicted by reports, "official" or not, published after the war by Jewish Communist resisters.[6] All of these concur in dating the renewal of the political activity of clandestine MOI-yiddish to September 1940, following several weeks of confusion and hesitation.[7]

The PC line on the foreign policy of the USSR, which was linked to the Nazis by a pact, had left the Jewish militants of MOI inwardly torn and paralyzed in their action.

Solidarité and Secours populaire as Political Movements

The meeting called by Gronowski in September 1940 was felt by the participants to be the end of the isolation inflicted by the party. By that time, mutual assistance projects run by Zionists and Bundists under the hidden auspices of Rue Amelot had resumed their activity more than two months previously. It was decided at the rue Custine meeting to create a clandestine movement composed of neighborhood committees, which received the name of *Solidarité*. Two objectives were assigned to it: to raise the morale of the Jewish population and to distribute material assistance to the needy. *Unzer Wort* again began to appear, and a public soup kitchen on rue de Saintonge and a dispensary on rue Turenne reopened their doors.[8] Neighborhood committees multiplied, each consisting of five members, later reduced to three (according to the "triangle" formula used by the PC, so as to wall off the underground movement effectively). The *Solidarité* leadership appointed people responsible for sectors, an editorial team for writing *Unzer Wort*, and a technical team charged with printing and distributing it. In the spring of 1941 the leaders of the movement gave the activists the task of producing false identity documents.[9] The leaders left their families, homes, neighborhoods, and places of work. "It feels strange to look at your identity card, where the only thing that's you is the photograph. All the rest, name, first name, marital status, . . . has nothing to do with you, with your identity, which is certainly the right term here," wrote Rayski.[10] Committees of Jewish women and Jewish youth were also formed, on the same lines as those of *Solidarité*. Adler, following Ravine in this matter, writes that "while recognizing the importance of providing assistance, *Solidarité* saw this as only a secondary goal, the first being of a political nature: above all it was a question of waging a campaign both within and outside of the Jewish community that would alert everyone regarding the danger of anti-Semitism."[11] The primacy of politics in the action of

Solidarité is correctly emphasized by the author. This clarifies the specific nature of Communist resistance and constitutes the obstacle which for three years had thwarted efforts to create a united front of Jewish resistance. Non-Communist Jewish resistance networks constantly followed a line giving priority to rescue action.

It is not, however, certain that during the period between September 1940 and the beginning of hostilities against the USSR on June 22, 1941, that *Solidarité* did wage a campaign to sound the alert regarding the danger of anti-Semitism.[12] The underground publications of that period have disappeared. Their existence is known only by the reports of seizures by the police.[13] Adler's hypothesis does not take account of the policy of the PC at that time. *Humanité* as an underground paper denounced anti-Semitism selectively. In keeping with the imperatives of class conflict, it distinguished between "Jews without means," the victims of persecution, and "the Jewish capitalists," with whom the Nazis collaborated.[14] In a PC pamphlet mentioning the detention of the Jews on May 14, 1941, one reads: "Down with Aryan and Jewish capitalism." Rayski notes that "the name of Hitler, who had become a respectable statesman by virtue of the Ribbentrop-Molotov pact, was not mentioned in our press before May–June 1941."[15] The leaders of *Solidarité* had maintained the same passivity as the other Jewish leaders at the time of the German order of September 27, 1940, instituting the census of the Jews in the northern zone and, similarly, when 5,200 foreign Jews were summoned to the Paris police stations on May 14, 1941.[16]

At that juncture, the directorate of the movement was not free to issue instructions, because some of its members were busily traversing the southern zone to install committees along the Parisian model. Following a wave of departures among Parisian Jews who had reached the southern zone, the movement had lost its members in Paris. In June 1941, Ravine was charged with establishing an autonomous directorate of the southern zone in Lyons, in order to mobilize and regroup the Jewish militants of MOI. Called *Secours populaire* (Public Aid), the organization was active in five regions of the southern zone: Lyons, Grenoble, Nice, Marseilles, and Toulouse. Progress was slow because "the dominant organizations in the immigrant milieu"[17] were the FSJF (*Fédération des sociétés juives de France*, Federation of French Jewish Organizations) and the OSE (*Oeuvre de secours aux enfants*, the Children's Rescue Network), which provided support for thousands of families who were thus able to escape detention or assigned residence in a remote village.

Thus it seems that the major preoccupation of the *Solidarité* leadership at that time was the expansion of the movement. The detention of nearly

4,000 Parisian Jews in May 1941 was used as a springboard to give new impetus to the political action of *Solidarité*. On May 20 in a demonstration at the camp gates the wives and mothers of detainees demanded the right to visit their loved ones and to send them food packages. Detained militants received the order to remain in place and to create committees in the camps, charged with promoting cultural activity in the open so as to engage in clandestine political activity. Those who received furloughs returned to the camp in conformity with their leaders' instructions. For the latter, "detention did not seem to be the worst way to wait for better days."[18] In July *Solidarité* directed its action against the Coordinating Committee of Paris, denouncing it as being "the Jewish section of the Gestapo"[19] with ambiguity comparable to that of the PC. It ordered the closure of its public soup kitchen and dispensary because the authorities wanted to place their administration under the supervision of the Coordinating Committee.[20] From July 20 to 25, demonstrations by the wives of detainees at the Coordinating Committee headquarters on rue de la Bienfaisance took a violent turn.[21] Communist militants in the camps gained the confidence of many inmates. They published a handwritten bulletin and pamphlets. Following the execution by the Nazis of 95 hostages, including 53 Jews on December 15, 1941, the detainees held evenings of mourning. They took part in an appeal for funds launched in Paris by *Solidarité* for the widows of those who had been shot. The inmates of Beaune-la-Rolande raised 30,000 francs.[22]

This political action followed a party tradition of militant action among the masses. According to that imperative the presence of Communists among the thousands of detainees was thus necessary. Moreover, in 1941 it was "inconceivable to transfer thousands of people into the underground from one day to the next," since escapes could lead to reprisals against the Jewish population.[23] In May 1942, when *Solidarité* finally gave orders "to escape, to break down the gates of the camps and run away," it was too late.[24] All the Jews in the camps in Pithiviers, Beaune-la-Rolande, and Drancy were deported in June 1942.

Strikes and the Sabotage of War Production

The German surprise offensive against the Soviet Union and thus the entry of the USSR into the war on the Allied side brought deep relief to the Jewish Communists. The odious ambiguity of the sponsorship of a party supporting the German-Soviet pact was finally dissipated. Their disciplined submission to the orders of the PC had heightened their isolation from the other

Jewish organizations. Henceforth it was possible to attempt reconciliation, which became more of an imperative once the PC launched a campaign for a national resistance front, while anti-Jewish repression was becoming increasingly severe. In the spring of 1941 *Les Renseignements généraux*, the police security service, picked up the trail of the people distributing *Solidarité* publications and pamphlets and collecting funds. Eight arrests took place in April and seventeen in May. *Unzer Wort* was confiscated, as was a typewriter with Hebrew characters, forcing the leaders to order new precautions. On August 20, 1941 the police surrounded the XIth arrondissement and arrested 4,230 foreign adult Jews who were sent to Drancy.

The leaders of *Solidarité* and of Rue Amelot, with the exception of the Bundists, met on August 30 and formed a Committee of Union of the Workers' Parties which was to coordinate assistance and publish an underground bulletin. This publication, *Yiddische Stimme*, came out only once. But the young Zionists, guided by Henri Bulawko, joined the teams distributing the Communist underground press. *Solidarité* sought to convince Rue Amelot to close its public soup kitchens, but Rapoport refused: "Old men say that if we close the soup kitchens, they'll report to the Drancy camp."[25]

In this period of growing distress, the Jewish organizations in Paris were unable to protect the Jews. The coherence of the German intentions remained impenetrable. The Jewish leaders could only foster assistance projects and try to maintain public morale. The Committee of Union took part in a *Solidarité* initiative meant to send activists into resistance action against economic collaboration. The opening of the Russian front had considerably increased the German demand for warm clothing. The enemy placed orders with Parisian clothing manufacturers, where Jewish proprietors and labor were strongly represented. It provided the workers with certificates as *Wirtschaftlich wichtige Juden* (economically valuable Jews) which were supposed to protect their bearers from arrest and detention. The campaign of the Committee of Union developed in three phases: in October 1941 they called for a total boycott, which was not observed; in November and December, strikes in glove-makers and later in knitting factories severely impeded production; and starting in January 1942, the militants ordered the workers to produce goods with hidden flaws that would make the merchandise unusable, and to sabotage the machinery.[26] Conceived by *Solidarité*, this action was carried out with the participation of young Zionists from Rue Amelot.

But the Committee of Union dispersed at the end of 1941. The enemy had landed new blows and submitted the Jews to a regime of terror. In October bombs exploded in seven Parisian synagogues.[27] In December, 750

Jewish notables, mostly of French nationality, were arrested and interned in Compiègne. The previously mentioned execution of hostages took place on December 15. *Solidarité* decided to react vigorously. Encouraged by the strong public participation in a ceremony in honor of Jewish war dead in rue de la Roquette,[28] which the organization had directed skillfully on November 11, it launched the call to arms. The Committee of Union refused to join it and ceased to meet.[29] A misunderstanding had marred its formation. The representatives of Rue Amelot had placed themselves in the service of mutual assistance and rescue, whereas those of *Solidarité*, under the tutelage of the PC, were trying to extend their campaign of recruitment for armed action to all the immigrant Jews. Agreement could not yet be reached between those for whom Jewish resistance meant the battle for Jewish survival and those who identified that resistance with the war for the liberation of France, in conformity with the PC strategy.

The Call to Arms

On September 1, 1941, *Unzer Wort* published the text of an appeal in Yiddish originally broadcast by Radio Moscow. The Jewish poet David Bergelson said in it, "It is a question of the life or death of our people.... But our people will not die. It is the people of Maimonides, of Spinoza, of Heine, of Mendelssohn.... We shall not die, we shall live!" Composed in the name of Soviet Jewish men of letters and artists, the appeal called for Jews the world over to join the ranks of the combatants.[30] Several months passed before the *Solidarité* leadership transformed that appeal into a directive.

The PC leadership had organized recruitment for the armed combat groups of its *Organisation spéciale* (OS, Special Organization), ordering each unit to contribute a tenth of its members.[31] The Jews participated in the actions of the OS, which was constituted in the second half of 1941 and was then the only armed resistance unit in Paris. On April 25, 1942, Hersz Zimerman and Salek Bot, two *Solidarité* activists who were members of the OS, died when they were blown to bits by a bomb they were making, which exploded prematurely in an apartment on rue Geoffroy-Saint Hilaire.[32] At the same time, the directorate of MOI established the first unit of *Francs-Tireurs et Partisans* (FTP, the new name of the OS), consisting of Romanian and Hungarian speaking fighters from the MOI groups, almost all of whom were Jews.[33] At that time recruitment was still very difficult. If the PC had not disposed of immigrant volunteers, its OS and FTP groups would very likely not have gone into action until later.[34] The constitution of a specifically Jewish combat unit took place in August 1942, after the monstrous roundup of the Vélodrome d'hiver: the Second FTP-MOI Detachment, formed of Yiddish speaking volunteers.

The problem of the transition to armed struggle was not only the bone of contention between *Solidarité* and the other Jewish organizations. Among the *Solidarité* militants themselves it had aroused hesitation and reluctance. As long as anti-Jewish repression was limited to discriminatory legislation and the internment of men of working age (in the northern zone), the *Solidarité* leadership encountered opposition to armed resistance on every level of the movement. But the deportations to the east, beginning on March 27, 1942, and then the arrest of entire families on July 16 and 17 of that year brutally changed the mood of the activists. This explains the formation of the Second Detachment in August 1942.

Nevertheless, even then, the discomfort continued. The fighters had moral scruples about accomplishing their assigned missions, such as shooting isolated members of the Wehrmacht at close range. The military value of these actions seemed insignificant, and their price was excessive, for after each assassination by the Resistance, the enemy shot dozens of hostages.[35] The leaders of *Solidarité* undertook a campaign of explanation, claiming that the actions of the partisans was "of colossal importance." They sowed fear and demoralization among the Germans, removed divisions from the Eastern Front, interfered with military supplies, and were "incomparably more effective than the bombardments of the Allied air forces."[36] Rayski wrote a pamphlet in June 1942 in which he referred, like Bergelson, to Jewish history:

> Guerrilla warfare is not a new phenomenon in History. In going back to the distant past of the Jewish people, we discover this interminable guerrilla warfare, which was waged for many years by the Maccabees against the invader. . . . On the one hand, the exploits of the Maccabees demoralized the enemy troops, sometimes forcing them to withdraw from certain territories, and on the other hand, they drew a significant number of new fighters into resistance against the invader.

In response to the objection that the partisans' actions were of negligible military value, Rayski asserted its "political objective, that is, the influence that armed struggle could have on the morale of the population. . . . By far the most important factor is the political factor. The partisans must use it fully, bearing in mind that political victory remains their principal objective."[37] Should one interpret the Jewish reminiscences of this *Solidarité* leader as an opportunistic step taken in the service of PC orders, or as a sign of an emergent Jewish identity? It would not be out of order to suppose that the leaders of *Solidarité* sincerely felt themselves committed to the service of the Jewish people, whose very existence was threatened. They knew this feeling was shared by many activists. Total devotion to the party had not done away with awareness of the catastrophe that was befalling the Jewish people. According to Annie Kriegel, the Jewish Communists "took extraordinary comfort in the fact that at that time the salvation of the Jews and that of Communism were interdependent."[38] Jewish reflections such as Rayski's provide insight into what their authors were feeling when the joined the Resistance. They express one of the numerous aspects of their reactions, the ambivalence characteristic of a Jewish Communist. But it would be excessive to generalize. Some of them evoked Jewish memories, while for others they were without any deep significance. To these is applicable this observation of Léon Poliakov's: "The ideology of their resistance was as little 'Jewish' as that of the fighters active in the general French Resistance."[39]

The chronology of the call to arms promulgated by *Solidarité* and the formation of a MOI-yiddish detachment coincides with that of anti-Jewish repression rather than with the calendar of PC orders. The *Solidarité* leadership remained responsible for the equipment and political framework of the fighters enrolled in the Detachment. But the operational orders were issued by the general staff of MOI, hierarchically subordinate to that of the FTP of Paris and to the political directorate of the PC.[40] Authors and witnesses, in particular Charles Tillon, at the time a member of the PC directorate and a chief of the FTP, claim that MOI was not under PC control but was dependent upon Comintern.[41]

In any event, this dependency subjected the Jewish Communists to "a logic that has always given preference to the integration of minorities and socialist universalism without ethnic or religious distinction."[42] The ambivalence of their situation was expressed precisely in the fact that, though organized as a Jewish combat group and wishing to fight for the survival of their people, they were used and gave their lives only for "neutral" objectives chosen by commanders indifferent to the war against the deportation of the Jews. "I would have wished so much to have contributed to the saving of Jewish children rather than trying inconsequentially to kill a few more German soldiers," cried out Kriegel, who fought in the ranks of FTP-MOI.[43] Though the author of that reflection admits that it is "perfectly anachronistic," one could not find better confirmation of the choice made by other organizations of Jewish immigrants, which distinguished Jewish interests from those of the population at large.

Isolated from the rest of the people by an arsenal of laws and regulations that deprived them of their rights as citizens, marked out for detention and then for deportation, the Jews had above all to protect themselves. According to their organizations, absolute priority was to be given to rescue operations, a goal that did not coincide with those of the combat waged by the French patriots. Guerrilla action, of negligible military value, exposed the partisans to severe losses and provided a pretext for killing hostages. No one doubted that German defeat would lead instantaneously to the abolition of all threats to Jewish life. But the leaders of non-Communist Jewish organizations were convinced that the partisan units, as heroic and effective as their operations might be, did not have the power to hasten that defeat. Their strategy of Jewish resistance, devoted to protection and rescue, was thus based on the feeling that, were it not for their action, the restoration of freedom and rights for Jews would come only when there were no more Jews to liberate.

The distinctive features of Communist Jewish resistance did not derive only from their preference for the political factor and armed operations rather than rescue work. It was also different because it never had to confront the dilemma of legal action versus action that was partially or totally clandestine. Alone among the Jewish resistance networks, it maintained a constant tie with a large French political party. Though it had a potential for autonomy because of its remarkable cohesion, it nevertheless remained obedient to that party, despite the discomfort and ill-feelings that marked the period of the Soviet-German pact. The Jewish Communists developed political education more than any other kind, as well as the diffusion of information and orders by underground press and pamphlets. They deliberately avoided all Jewish cultural activity.

Nevertheless awareness of the true danger threatening the physical existence of the Jews came as slowly to the Communists as to the other sectors of the Jewish population. The turning point of the summer of 1942, in its tragic horror, was to oblige all the Jewish organizations, without distinction, to revise their analysis and action from top to bottom.

8

༄༅༄

The Consistory and Other
Religious Associations

The expression "psychological warfare" has become familiar in modern parlance, though it is as ancient as the human race: painting a hateful picture of one's adversary and portraying oneself in a favorable light. Hatred of the Jewish people has been taught for many centuries, accumulating an arsenal of psychological weapons of a power never equalled in history.

A dispersed nation, on the defensive, for generations the Jews had no choice but to adopt a policy of intercession, seeking to bribe the authorities in order to mitigate discriminatory decrees. At the same time they developed a perfectly autonomous spiritual and cultural heritage, providing the basis of their resistance in a hostile environment. Beginning with a common foundation of historical memory, or of religious traditions and literature, Jewish cultural creativity adapted to each generation and geographical location, forging an identity foreign to those around them but shared by Jews throughout the world, aside from certain local peculiarities. Extraordinarily rich, this heritage is the source from which they drew the power to survive. Until the dawn of modern times, Jewish religious and cultural identity was accompanied by certainty of a future national renaissance.

This situation ended in the democratic countries of Western Europe and America with the attainment of equal civil rights. In the case of France, in less than a century the emancipation of the Jews led them to assume an essentially French identity. The spiritual and cultural patrimony inherited from their fathers tended to be reduced to its religious dimension, remodeled in imitation of the forms and the aesthetic of the dominant religion. The creative genius of the French Jews, abandoning the language and culture left to them by their ancestors, flourished within general French culture. A century after the emancipatory revolution, France underwent an explosion of anti-Semitic passion and nationalist extremism illustrated by the Dreyfus Affair. Nevertheless the French Jews embraced French nationalism, which entailed the rejection if not the abolition of faith in Jewish national renaissance. François Furet has spoken of the phenomenon of the "internalization of the values of the adversary" and of "repudiated Judaism."[1]

Intercession with the Regime by the Consistory and the Rabbinate

The French Jews saw themselves as French patriots, an attitude taken by many immigrant Jews as well, starting in the second generation, and this self-image is reflected in the form of resistance to Vichy policies of discrimination and persecution adopted by the rabbinical and consistorial authorities. According to the classification established by Werner Rings, this was "symbolic resistance,"[2] expressed by courageous and vehement protests addressed to the chiefs of state and the government by the president of the General Consistory, the Chief Rabbi of France, and famous military veterans:[3]

> Neither a racial minority nor a political minority, but only a religious community, the Israelites protest against the defamatory accusations of internationalism and anarchical spirit raised against them, and they loudly proclaim their love of the Fatherland. (Protest of the Chief Rabbi of France, Isaïe Schwartz, to the Chief of State, against the Statute of the Jews, October 22, 1940.)

> I recognize no one's right or power to assess the love I have for my fatherland, love which is part of the patrimony of my heart, of my thought, sanctuaries which are inviolable by others.

(Protest of General André Boris, addressed to Marshal Pétain against the Statute of the Jews, November 10, 1940.)

We insist on declaring that, born French, we are French, and we shall always remain so. (Protest by several prominent Jews to Marshal Pétain, April 1941.)

The moment when rigorously exceptional measures deprive a minority of French citizens of their civil rights because of their confession, it is a duty of the representatives of their religious organizations to raise a solemn protest [against] acts which constitute the worst of injustices, founded on lies. . . . The law is not aimed at Israelites either as Frenchmen or foreigners, but in servile imitation of the occupying authority, it knows and acknowledges merely a Jewish herd where even *French* nationality is no more than an accessory without value or scope. . . . French Israelites . . . will nevertheless retain their faith in the destinies of eternal France to obtain just recompense for their rights, which are violated today. (Protest of the Central Consistory to Marshal Pétain against the law calling for a census of the Jews, July 1, 1941.)

I cannot believe . . . that you will not acknowledge with me that the day when reason reasserts its prerogative (and it will doubtless reassert them in the country of Descartes and Bergson), anti-Semitism, for its part, will lose its sanction. (Protest of Chief Rabbi Jacob Kaplan, addressed to the General Commissioner for Jewish Questions, Xavier Vallat, against the census of the Jews, July 31, 1941.)

Some authorized declarations, including yours, . . . have made the mass of French people believe . . . that those who have risked or shed their blood for France would be sheltered from the exceptional treatment which is striking the Israelites today and have made them second class Frenchmen. But this is not the case, and in addition to ingratitude contrary to the traditions of France, this is hypocrisy unworthy of her. . . . The fathers and descendants of our dead, our survivors, mutilated or wounded, declare with our voice that, far from rejecting France, despite everything they have undergone, they intend to add their silent sacrifice of today to those of the past. They thus hope doubly to merit, in a future more just and free, the title of Frenchmen which they will never abandon in their heart, even if it is torn out of them by force. (Protest read to Xavier Vallat by a delegation of Jewish war veterans, August 11, 1941.)

These appeals remained unknown to the population, both Jewish and non-Jewish. Jewish periodicals had ceased to appear. The bulletin of the Coordination Committee in Paris and later that of the UGIF (*Union générale des Juifs de France*, the General Union of French Jews) in the northern zone, created by order of SS Lieutenant Dannecker and subject to German censorship, contained only the laws and ordinances promulgated against the Jews and official notices of the Jewish charity organizations. The Rabbinate and the Consistory abstained from publishing written communications during the German occupation. Their protests to the authorities were unknown to the press and radio of the Allies or of the neutral countries. They faithfully expressed the sentiments of a large part of the French Jewish leadership, motivated by the "lucid desire to remain both an excellent Jew and an excellent Frenchman," as R. R. Lambert wrote in his private journal.[4] R. Cohen has noted that in 1940–41, native Jews suffered mainly from rejection by France. "Their discomfort was far more spiritual than material."[5] The familiarity of certain prominent Jews with several of the Vichy leaders, notably that of Jacques Helbronner, the president of the Central Consistory, with Marshal Pétain,[6] had placed them under the illusion that there was a desire and an ability to save the French Jews. For their part, a vigorous attitude reassured them in their own self-image as "excellent Jews and excellent Frenchmen." But ignorance of the real dangers and an erroneous assessment of the true quality and power of the heads of the Vichy regime made them persevere for two years in a discreet policy of intercession. The secrecy of their proceedings was meant to assure their efficacity. Had they been made public, even in the underground press, it would have placed these French Jewish leaders in grave danger and also jeopardized the very existence of the Consistory.

The assumptions of these Jewish leaders were not entirely without foundation. Vichy made some efforts to protect Jewish citizens and some foreign military veterans. The vigorous action of President Heibronner to prevent the creation of the UGIF was unsuccessful, but it did obtain an exception to the law ordering the dissolution of all Jewish organizations, permitting the Consistory to remain in existence and to act free of all official control, either French or German.[7]

Toward a More Active Response

This policy characterizes the reactions of only some leaders of the Rabbinate and the Consistory. To know more about the language used by rabbis from their pulpits one would have to possess the texts of their sermons or accounts of them, which are not extant. However, it is known that in Paris the synagogues were very well attended, sometimes "super-full."[8] Only a few of the sermons given in Vichy and Lyons by the Chief Rabbi, Jacob Kaplan, have been preserved.[9] Saying nothing of the actions of Schwartz and Helbronner in high places, they protested publicly against the Statute of the Jews: "We will not renounce our Jewishness to escape the rigors of a statute which, only in the eyes of the vulgar, might appear dishonorable" (Vichy synagogue, November 15, 1940). From the pulpit he read his personal letter to Xavier Vallat, protesting against the Jewish census law, and he distributed several copies of it, which were reproduced and circulated discretely.[10] Aside from this document, Kaplan refrained from publicly appealing to the French tradition and to patriotic sentiments. To raise the morale of the Jews assembled in the synagogue and to fortify their endurance and resistance, he appealed to Jewish values. On April 18, 1941, for example, he spoke indignantly of the spoliation, the Statute of the Jews, and the calumnies of the official radio station. Kaplan appealed to the history of the Jew, "always victorious," as an illustration of "every form of heroism: . . . Jewish history is the courage of courages . . . Do not let yourself be beaten down by your suffering."[11]

This language is closer to the feelings of those who had reacted to the French military defeat and to the anti-Semitic policies of the government with a surge of Jewish dignity and who had begun the study of the spiritual and cultural sources of their identity. Thus one may distinguish two tendencies within the leadership of French Jewry during the first two years of the Occupation. One remained attached to the model of Judaism that had emerged from the emancipation, believing that the symbiosis between religion and fatherland was unshakable, and managing their affairs during the crisis in prudent and discrete fashion. The other tendency viewed the Vichy anti-Jewish policy as weakening if not demolishing dreams of emancipation. Its reaction, more activist, encouraged the rebirth of Jewish traditions and assumed responsibility for the defense of the immigrant Jews. We shall see that, under the shock of the deportations of 1942, most of the leaders of consistorial Judaism rallied to the second tendency, passing from symbolic resistance to defensive resistance.

In the confusion that had followed upon the debacle of June 1940, in August of that year the members of the Central Consistory, who were dispersed in the southern zone, authorized Chief Rabbi Schwartz, then living in Vichy, to represent it before the authorities. On September 3–5, Schwartz convened the French Rabbinical Assembly in Lyons, and there they established the map of rabbinical regions in the southern zone, in response to the new geographical distribution of the Jewish population. One of the rabbis, René Kapel, requested and obtained appointment to the chaplaincy of the detention camps and GTE (*Groupes de travailleurs étrangers*, Foreign Laborers Groups) of the Toulouse and Central Pyrenees regions. On October 30 in Marseilles, Schwartz presided over the constitution of the Central Commission of Jewish Relief Organizations. At the same time several prominent Jews who had belonged to major government bodies united in Marseilles in early 1941 around General André Boris. They decided to create defense committees throughout France. It was then that Jacques Helbronner convened a plenary session of the Central Consistory in Lyons on March 16–17. He opened a permanent office on rue de Boissac and invited the "activists," who had met in Marseilles, to be associated with the Consistory as coopted members. Some of them accepted, notably the magistrate, Léon Meiss, who was called upon to play a major role at the head of the Consistory. Thus the division of French Jewish leadership, which Helbronner had feared, was avoided.[12] During 1941 other cooptations enlarged the Consistory to include a Parisian physician, André Bernheim, who directed the activity of the office on rue de Boissac, as well as several leaders of the EIF (*Éclaireurs israélites de France*, the Jewish scouting movement), Fleg, Gamzon, and Hammel.

A crisis broke out when the government created the UGIF and appointed Albert Lévy, a member of the Consistory, to head it. The latter accepted the appointment despite the categorical opposition of the President, Helbronner.[13] Relations remained tense between the leaders of the two organizations throughout 1942, to the point that they paralyzed the plan for joint action in Vichy in the month of August 1942 to try to spare from deportation the foreign Jews in the southern zone, whom Laval had delivered to the Germans in place of the French Jews in the northern zone.[14]

On August 25, the Consistory itself addressed a letter protesting the violation of the right of sanctuary and denouncing the lie of ethnic redistribution: "It is not for the purpose of using the deportees as laborers that the German government claims them, but with the clear intention of exterminating them pitilessly and methodically."[15] Unlike earlier protests, this one

was mimeographed and sent to several communities.[16] During the following months, in response to the increase in enemy strikes against the Jews,
Helbronner joined those of his colleagues who envisaged more active reactions and set aside his quarrel with the leaders of the UGIF.

Religious Services

The Consistory was determined to maintain religious ceremonies in synagogues as well as in improvised chapels in the cities and towns of the southern zone, which had seen an influx of Jewish refugees from Paris and the
Departments in the East annexed by the Reich, as well as from Belgium and
the Netherlands. Similarly it provided ritually slaughtered meat and unleavened bread for Passover, and it reprinted elementary manuals of religious
instruction.[17] Because of rationing of all food and industrial products, it
was necessary to overcome the obstacles raised by a nitpicking and hardly
helpful bureaucracy in order to obtain these results. The Consistory and its
rabbis showed tenacity in their efforts to maintain religious services. Any
other attitude would, according to them, have caused the loss of Judaism
and its adherents. Fascist action groups desecrated seven Parisian synagogues on the night of October 2–3, 1941, and that of Nice on June 12,
1942.[18] Despite these warnings and the evident danger, public prayers continued to be held. To close the synagogues would have been to capitulate to
the enemy. The heads of the Consistory were resolved to confront barbarism
and violence with openly displayed attachment to religious and spiritual
values. They believed that the maintenance of religious services was necessary to sustain the morale of the Jews who attended the synagogues.[19] The
latter responded not only to a religious appeal but also to the need to meet
with other Jews in hopes of gleaning some news.

Infinitely more difficult was the organization of religious services in the
infernal world of the detention camps. Considering the abysmal conditions
imposed on the population of these camps, for many detainees the practice
of religious rituals became the only possibility of fighting against dehumanization. "Filth, hunger, cold, despair are the common lot, yet some of
them fight against decline, while others let themselves be submerged in it,"
an OSE (*Oeuvre de secours aux enfants*, Children's Rescue Network) social
worker, a voluntary detainee in Rivesaltes wrote in her diary. One month
later, in December 1941, she wrote: "Everyone in the Jewish block celebrates
the first day of Hanukkah.[20] . . . With a trembling hand, one of the veteran
inmates lights the first small flame of the gigantic *Menorah* built by the

detainees. And the traditional song borne by hundreds of voices ascends in the night that falls on the camp. For a moment the suffering recedes, and I allow myself to be invaded by an immense hope."[21]

The rabbis serving as chaplains, following the example of Kapel, devoted themselves with zeal and ingenuity to developing religious activities in the camps. The provision of ritual objects used in daily life, the logistics of opening and managing kosher soup kitchens, as well as maintaining premises for public worship and religious education, depended entirely upon the chaplains' obstinacy and improvisational ability. The general poverty afflicting Vichy France and the refugee status of most of the Jews in the southern zone, whose aid was being solicited, greatly complicated their task. This was also true when it came time to organize High Holiday services for most of the Jewish detainees,[22] and the Passover Seder with unleavened bread and the other symbols of the holiday. The considerable efforts invested on these occasions provided a few hours of intense emotion, restoring a sense of human dignity to the population of the camps, who were subject to grievous decline. In a report addressed to the Chief Rabbi of France in January 1942, Kapel wrote regarding the religious ceremonies in the camp of Gurs: "There is more fervor and warmth than I have ever felt in our synagogues. . . . Hundreds of people are studying Hebrew and Jewish history, dozens forget their distress and devote themselves to Talmud study."[23]

In Gurs he had created a central assistance committee run by a detainee, Rabbi Léo Ansbacher, with assistants from each of the barracks in the camp. A similar arrangement was made in the other camps at the initiative of the rabbinical chaplains. Charged with promoting and administering social, religious, and cultural activities, the committee organized the distribution of charitable contributions of goods and clothing, and it worked to improve hygiene and prevent disease. With its encouragement, the detainees formed theater companies, dance troupes, choruses, and orchestras. The more learned inmates gave lectures and ran study circles in general culture, Bible, and Jewish history. During the literary and artistic programs, the prisoners "stopped thinking, at least for a few hours, about the hunger and anguish that tormented them. Without doubt these activities contributed to maintaining their morale and prevented them from declining into madness or seeking deliverance in death."[24] Painters and sculptors among the detainees exhibited their work. In the Milles camp, famous artists such as Max Ernst, Gus, and Hans Bellmer covered the walls of the Tuilerie with impressive frescoes, recently declared a national monument. The committee opened soup kitchens that served kosher meals and also provided the proper rituals for burials, marriages, and circumcisions. The chaplains obtained unleavened bread and kosher wine to celebrate Passover. Kapel had several thousand copies of the Passover Haggadah mimeographed, the text recounting the deliverance of the Hebrew slaves from Egypt which is read and chanted during the Passover Seder.

Study, Research, and Publications

In Lyons, the composer Léon Algazi created a center of Jewish studies for secondary and primary school teachers who had been discharged from the national education system because of the Statute of the Jews. With a budget allocated by the Consistory, Algazi proposed that each of them prepare a study on a theme of his choice in the area of Jewish culture. Several of them, who admitted they were completely removed from Judaism, set out to discover a heritage that had hitherto been unexplored by them.[25]

In Limoges Rabbi Abraham Deutsch created a Jewish high school with the material assistance of the Consistory. In the spirit of its founder, the institution sought to revive Judaism among Jewish pupils. The initiative had many points in common with those behind the opening of the Lycée Maimonide in Boulogne-sur-Seine in 1936. The war and the debacle had forced the latter institution to close: its principal had been taken as a prisoner of war in Germany, and its sponsors had been dispersed. Deutsch proposed a Jewish alternative to the secular school in order to teach the disciplines of the Jewish cultural heritage in addition to those of the national education system. Members of the consistorial circles, fervent adherents of the republican traditions, expressed certain reservations regarding this initiative, which they perceived as a Jewish version of a parochial school. Nonetheless they supported it, regarding it as a preparatory school for the French rabbinical seminary. The establishment received the official name of "petit séminaire israélite de Limoges" (Junior Jewish Seminary of Limoges). Because it was run under Consistory auspices, it managed to avoid control by the UGIF. The chaplain for youth, Klein, and those responsible for the Yechouroun youth movement recruited pupils from among very young community activists.[26] Although small in scale, due to the wartime circumstances, this school was a significant illustration of the trend among French Jews to react to events by promoting Jewish spiritual renewal. Deutsch and Klein, working within the Consistory, were resolved to work toward its radical transformation by "rejuvenating it and re-Judaizing it."[27] Rabbi Deutsch's private home in Limoges served as a center for Talmudic studies, as a classroom for the graduating class of his lycée, as a welfare office, as a center for the distribution of false identity papers, and as a rendezvous for Jewish resistance activists.[28] The Jewish Lycée of Limoges, within the complex reality of a community fighting for survival, sought to train Jewish leaders for after the war.

Aside from activities promoted by Zionist militants and the youth movements, we know of some other projects in which Jewish spiritual resistance was expressed. Although documentation is scarce, we do possess information about the *Ecole libre d'études juives* (ELEJ, the Free School of Jewish Studies) the *Amis de la tradition juive* (ATJ, Friends of the Jewish Tradition), and the *Association des israélites pratiquants* (AIP, the Association of Observant Jews).

Led by Rabbi Osi Wallach in Limoges, the ELEJ published correspondence courses based on adapted and annotated texts from Midrashic literature, revealing an author of uncommon erudition and originality.[29] On February 21, 1942 a police inspector from the Bureau of Jewish Questions wrote a report regarding the seizure from a Jew in Montpellier of a pamphlet about the religious significance of the Hanukkah holiday. The pamphlet, published by the ATJ, stated: "Other peoples found their existence upon material factors, sometimes on brute force, but Israel draws its vitality and duration from the spirit of sacrifice. . . . Israel treated as a pariah, ostracized by the human family, despite the most dreadful living conditions, has never lost consciousness of its dignity nor of its value."[30] A search of the head office of the ATJ in Marseilles was searched in September 1942, but no one was arrested or deported as a result.[31]

The AIP was founded in Paris in 1936 by a Hasidic rabbi who had emigrated from the USSR, Zalman Schneerson. Having withdrawn to Vichy and then to Marseille, the AIP had gathered a group of about sixty people and ran a synagogue, a welfare office, a seminary-yeshiva, a children's home, and a workshop for occupational retraining. Schneerson provided services to strictly observant Jews.[32] Situated on the margin of Jewish organizations, the AIP was the expression of a particular category of Jewish identity. Very popular before the war in Central and Eastern Europe as well as in Palestine, Hasidism possessed some fervent adherents within the immigrant Jewish community of Paris. Simultaneously rejecting emancipation, Zionism, and socialism, Schneerson conceived of Jewish existence as solely the scrupulous observance of rituals, and he raised an impenetrable barrier against the influence of the environment and modernity. His experience of secular persecutions had habituated him to react by creating a community with unbreachable cohesion, devoted to the study of sacred texts and to the observance of religious prescriptions in the enthusiastic atmosphere of the

Hasidic tradition. He and his followers felt secure in this framework, relying upon Providence. Schneerson did not perceive the unprecedented character of the Nazi menace, and the AIP was particularly vulnerable to deportations.

Nevertheless he was able to mobilize substantial resources among individuals and from the AJDC[33] to provide a major parcel delivery service to help kosher soup kitchens for the benefit of the detainees in the camps. Every package contained a personal letter from Schneerson, bringing moral comfort, to which the recipient often reacted with emotion:

> I also thank you with all my heart for the four candles. I lit them and prayed for my family and also for you, dear sir. . . . I was so astonished that after two years of detention there was a man like you, so charitable to me, who wanted to comfort my sad fate, and it is the good God who has inspired you to do good for me. I was very happy. . . . You give me courage by writing to me. (Rieucros Camp, September 5, 1941).

> I have received your parcel containing bread, fish, an onion, and some candles. You should know, sir, that I am truly grateful to you. From your candles I see that you want us to be able to celebrate our New Year, and I thank you for it sincerely. (Rivesaltes Camp, September 15, 1941).[34]

The spiritual effect conveyed by a letter doubtless helped humanize the fate of detainees deprived of all other sources of courage and hope. An identical example is provided by the parcel service operated in the northern zone by Rue Amelot. David Rapoport also enclosed personal letters in the parcels, producing the same effects:

> I assure you that detention is much easier to bear if one knows that there is someone outside who thinks of you and who you know won't forget you. In the nineteen months of detention which I now have behind me, I very rarely had the chance to sense active support which has such importance for one's morale. . . . Allow me to thank you again for being concerned for me so kindly without knowing me personally. (April 19, 1942).

> You do not neglect to add moral assistance to the physical assistance, and that double action makes your help effective.

There is also a glow around certain people, which sensitive souls instantly perceive. . . . You have done a lot more good for me, sir, than you doubtless think. Thanks to your understanding, a mother who bitterly follows her difficult path has been brightened for a few minutes, and that is enough so that she can find within herself new forces, courage, and energy. (November 21, 1942).[35]

The period of anti-Jewish persecutions that fell upon France had initially plunged its victims into a moral and spiritual crisis. Many were those who reacted by drawing upon the values of the Jewish tradition. This blocked the enemy's effort to dehumanize them by reducing them to the condition of pariahs before crushing them. The intense centers of Jewish spirituality that arose throughout France developed the forces that were to inspire the activists of Jewish resistance.

9

✧⁓✧

The Particular Case of Jewish Children

Shelters

When the Franco-German armistice was signed on June 22, 1940, approximately 2,000 Jewish children[1] were living in shelters in the southern zone. In February 1939 the Jewish Committee for Children from Germany and Central Europe had received the first convoy of Jewish refugee children from Germany and Austria in Montmorency in the Parisian region. Coordinating between the French immigration authorities[2] and the Jewish philanthropic organizations, this committee had the Ginzbourg and Rothschild families purchase properties in the Ile-de-France Department, then in the departments of Creuse and Haute-Vienne. The ose (*Oeuvre de secours aux enfants*, Children's Rescue Network) was charged with operating the shelters. After the outbreak of war, the French authorities recommended the removal of children from the major centers, which were threatened by aerial attack, and especially from the Paris region. They organized the transfer of the boarding schools of the *Éducation nationale* and of the *Assistance publique* as well as the children placed in their care by indigent French families. The eif (*Éclaireurs israélites de France*, the Jewish scouting movement) took the initiative for the similar evacuation of children overlooked by the official services, that is to say, those of recent immigrants without means.[3] Having obtained official authorization to shelter refugees in certain Prefectures, they opened four "evacuation centers" for children in the southwest, putting together improvised teams of female scout leaders, who administered the centers like permanent scout camps.

Separation from their parents as well as the geographical and sociocultural environment were particularly traumatic for these children, since they resulted from persecution of the Jews and from the war. These little refugees, thrown against their will into an adventure whose outcome was unpredictable, knew that their parents were exposed to the dangers from which it had been necessary to remove them. In Germany some of them had witnessed the deterioration of their parents, who until then had been a source of security, perceived as all-powerful, like almost all parents in the world. Moreover, they had been deprived of their homeland.[4] The situation was unprecedented for the pedagogical teams created by the sponsors of these shelters. The EIF applied scouting methods.[5] Lacking a professional staff, the OSE hired counselors from the young leadership of the youth movements. Its doctors installed equipment, and the daily regimen followed the rules of hygiene and preventive medicine.[6] A degree of cooperation between the two organizations helped keep living conditions in the various shelters at a relatively equal level.

No one then suspected that these Jewish children were destined for arrest, deportation, and dehumanization in the death and extermination camps. For more than a quarter of a century, the OSE had been perfecting its own method of reaction against persecutions in Eastern and Central Europe: gathering the children in shelters, which were to be islands of peace and security. The administrative and educational methods they developed had proved themselves, and in most cases they permitted the personalities and talents of the children to flourish. The system had been elevated to the level of a faith. The veteran leaders of the OSE were convinced that a Jewish child placed in a shelter was immunized against adversity. A consulting physician to the OSE from 1940 to 1943, Joseph Weill wrote in an autobiographical essay: "For the OSE, it had became a reflex, dating from the oppression of the czarist pogroms, to open reception centers after each calamity. . . . A large part of the OSE leaders, . . . intentionally kept at a distance from the major centers, withdrawn in the countryside, were led to withdraw into themselves . . . and they ultimately viewed the groups of children as an end in themselves. . . . The idea that these reservoirs of Jewish children . . . could prove to be death-traps barely grazed them."[7]

Newcomers to the field of protecting children, the EIF also discovered pedagogical responses to the problems posed by these groups of psychologically traumatized children. Aside from a certain lack of synchronization, there is a striking similarity in the development followed by these two organizations with respect to the rescue of children. The centers and shelters functioned entirely legally during the first two years of the Vichy regime. Their wards retain the memory of a happy group, well provided for on every level, in havens of security.[8] Lotte Schwartz, responsible for an OSE shelter that opened in November 1939 in Chaumont in the Department of Creuse, wrote: "It was not I who protected the children from the somber reality of the war, from Vichy, from the occupation. It was they, my kids, who formed a screen between me and despair."[9]

Historians of the genocide and Resistance try to determine the chronology of the operations and to explore the Jewish leaders' behavior toward the enemy during the time before a number of them committed themselves to the struggle. Not without irritation, Kieval states that the Jewish organizations in charge of children acted as though the enemy did not exist until July 1942 in the northern zone and August of the same year in the southern zone.[10] His observations do not shed light on their action any more than those of Szajkowski and Cohen, who emphasize that the EIF and the OSE were affiliated with the UGIF, a bureaucracy promoted and controlled by the occupier.[11]

Certainly, from the beginning of the Occupation several people had conceived of establishing a group for protection and defense, even for combat. A very small number went into action immediately. But concern for the protection of children even predated the outbreak of the war. Measures were taken on the level of social action, in broad daylight, with the agreement and, if possible, the assistance of the authorities. No one had a presentiment of the danger that children and adolescents would be incarcerated and deported. Nothing was predicted or undertaken to arm them against this danger. Kieval is correct. However, were fewer children saved than would have been the case because the OSE and EIF failed to take charge of them earlier than they did?[12]

To ask the question in this way is to run the risk of confusing the victims and the perpetrators in the process of the massacre of the innocents. Two contemporary perversions attempt to sow disorder among those who investigate the history of the genocide. One is the pure and simple denial of the facts,[13] the other is the abolition of the distinction between the executioners and their victims.[14] The "revisionist" falsifiers and their delirium of negation have been unmasked, notably by Georges Wellers, Nadine Fresco, and Pierre Vidal-Naquet.[15] The controversy regarding the dialectic of the relations between executioners and victims concerns more than the tragedy of the massacre of the innocents. The Nazi enterprise developed in three phases. First it turned the German people into a nation of potential assassins. It then extended this systematic dehumanization over the totality of the designated victims, cunningly reduced to ruin, notably by the establishment of an obligatory community, the *Judenrat*,[16] in order to force them to participate in their own extermination. The last phase was the implementation of the Final Solution in the death camps. Raul Hilberg and Hanna Arendt have concluded, wrongly in many cases, that the Jewish leaders placed at the head of the *Judenrat* were the effective tools of the Nazi bureaucracy, and that it would have been better had they refrained from exercising any responsibility. According to the former writer, the only admissible reaction was armed revolt. Arendt, for her part, writes that "resistance was impossible, but there was at least the possibility of *doing nothing*,"[17] instead of acting in the framework of the *Judenrat*. The severity and categorical nature of these judgments should invite serious reservations. Gershom Scholem admitted that discussion of this subject was both "legitimate and unavoidable." But aside from the fact that "certain aspects of Jewish history . . . pass our understanding," the same author notes that "our generation [is not] capable of passing historical judgment. . . . Who among us could say today what decisions the notables of the Jewish community ought to have made?"[18]

Contemporary historians, if they accept Scholem's remarks, must, above all, describe, with sensitivity, the circumstances in as much detail the available sources permit. It is of little importance whether historians have experienced the events personally, but they must be able to describe the ambiance and recount the reactions of the Jews before the enemy. If historians apply the rule formulated by Vidal-Naquet, "To understand historical reality, it is sometimes necessary *not to know the end*,"[19] they will be immunized against prejudices and tendentious speculations and will thefore have made a contribution to future debate. Perhaps later generations of historians will possess the instruments of investigation and the moral legitimacy to examine whether, for example, other actions and decisions would have permitted the Jewish leaders of France to save a larger number of children. As for us, let us try to describe what the protagonists underwent.

On the psychological level, the outbreak of the war in September 1939 caused the worsening in the condition of the refugee children in the Jewish shelters: the severing of all connections by mail or otherwise with their parents, who were unable to leave Germany or Austria, was accompanied by feelings of anguish about their fate with which it was difficult to cope, though they were sometimes repressed. The truth, still unsuspected, was that these children had been definitively deprived of their parental homes. When the French boarding schools of the Parisian region were evacuated for fear of aerial attacks, the prefectorial bureaucracy held off the delivery of the travel permits needed to transfer the residence of refugee children of foreign nationality. In the end, evacuation to shelters in the Creuse and Haute-Vienne departments took place, partially improvised and in haste, while German troops were already marching on Paris.[20]

After the armistice of June 22, 1940, Jewish institutions that could have sheltered children no longer existed in the northern zone. The facilities of Jewish boarding schools, vacation camps, orphanages, and dormitories remained temporarily unused. For nearly two years, the OSE, represented within Rue Amelot by Dr. Eugène Minkowski, restricted its activity to the administration of a medical-social dispensary on rue des Francs-Bourgeois. The Mother and Child organization, the headquarters of Rue Amelot, rehabilitated its orphanage in La Varenne in 1941, and there it sheltered a group of changing composition, including up to several dozen children.[21] During that year, the *École de travail* (Vocational School) on rue des Rosiers opened a small boarding facility, as well as apprenticeship courses, with the technical assistance of ORT. The situation changed radically in July 1942. Until then no one in the occupied northern zone had considered protecting children from possible arrest and detention. The psychological or other repercussions on children and adolescents of the census of the Jews ordered in September 1940 and then, beginning on June 7, 1942, of the obligation of every Jew over the age of five to wear the yellow star had not been perceived as requiring particular attention.[22]

The well established general impression, among the Jews, was that only men of working age were exposed to the risk of detention and deportation. The composition of the five convoys sent to the east before June 28, 1942 could have dispelled that impression, had the secrecy surrounding those deportations been broken earlier. The third convoy, leaving Drancy on June 22, 1942, transported 1,000 deportees, including sixty-six Jewish women who had been interned in the Tourelles camp. One of them had been arrested for planning marriage with an Aryan. The fifth convoy, leaving Beaune-la-Rolande on June 28, 1942, took 1,039 deportees, including thirty-four women who had been arrested in the Orleans region "to fill out the convoy."[23] The list of deportees in that convoy includes six adolescents from fifteen to seventeen years old.

However, the massive arrests and detentions of Jews by the thousands, on July 16 and 17, 1942, including infants and children of all ages, as well as the concentration in the camps of the Loiret Department of 4,000 children from ten to twelve years old, separated from their parents, caught the Jewish organizations entirely unprepared.[24] The rapid deportation of children completely undid all the efforts they had undertaken to rescue them.[25] In the autumn of that year, the Paris police arrested young adolescents suspected of violating the obligation to wear the yellow star and had them detained in Drancy.[26] The Jewish organizations of the northern zone then initiated the measures to protect children which will be described below. The situation was very different in the southern zone during the first two years of the Vichy regime. The population of the children's shelters in the Parisian region was transferred there. Moreover, the internment of foreigners applied by the French government affected entire families. The Nîmes Committee coordinated the efforts made to release children from detention.

The Release of Children from the Camps in the Southwest

The exceptions and concessions obtained in Vichy, permitting the liberation of one or another category of detainees, were subject to administrative conditions and impeded by the ponderousness and ill will of the bureaucracy, making their application random. A foreign or stateless child from a detention camp who wished to be admitted to a shelter was required to produce a certificate of domicile delivered by the prefect of the department where the shelter was situated. Most often requests for these certificates were rejected or postponed for prolonged periods.

The prefecture of the Hérault Department nevertheless proved to be understanding. Schilli, the rabbinical chaplain, as well as two directors of the OSE, Dr. J. Weill and Millner, maintained trusting relations with the prefect, Benedetti, and his secretary general, Ernst, who were active in the Resistance.[27] Ernst provided all the certificates of domicile requested by the OSE, which opened a transit shelter in the Department in Palavas-les-Flots, which received the children liberated from the camps. They stayed there while their administrative situation was regularized. Since the law imposed no other requirement for the movement in the southern zone of foreigners aged less than fifteen years, the children were then taken to the OSE shelters in the Indre, Creuse, Haute-Vienne, and other departments.[28]

The true drama took place in the camps, especially that of Rivesaltes, where the administration had concentrated most of the families with children in February 1941.[29] First it was necessary to overcome the administrative obstacles placed by the directors of the camps, motivated either by hostility or inertia, in the way of freeing the children. To overcome these obstacles required all the zeal and obstinacy the resident OSE teams possessed, along with the support of colleagues representing non-Jewish philanthropies. Too clever at "finding shortcuts through the thickets of procedures," the leader of the OSE team in Rivesaltes, Charles Lederman, was suspected by the camp directorate of encouraging escapes. After his removal in October 1941,[30] his replacement, Vivette Hermann, was soon "manipulating" the rules herself and became expert in "rejuvenating the adolescents over fifteen years old, who were therefore released."[31]

The cruelest moment was always that of separation. The traveling supervisor of the resident teams of the OSE, Andrée Salomon, was called upon to intervene in the most critical cases, in order to convince parents to entrust their children to a shelter, far from the sinister and inhuman reality of the camps. Her humane warmth and uncommon power of conviction made her a model with which the very young social workers constituting the resident teams could identify.[32] The latter were often overcome by the state of the environment: a windowless barracks, without beds or heating, muddy paths strewn with refuse, latrines without doors or walls, rare faucets providing water that was often polluted, undernourishment, the lack of sanitary equipment, vermin and rodents, the coarseness of the guards, the apathy of adults reduced to idleness, children left to themselves. In a journal entry dated January 25, 1942, Vivette Hermann wrote: "Behind the barbed wire, the detainees always lose their own personality. . . . Morality is weakened, filth and vermin invade their being."[33]

Despite this distress, the parents were hesitant to part with their children. Once the decision was made, however, they had to persuade their children to leave them. The departure for Palavas-les-Flots of convoys of liberated children gave rise to wrenching scenes, traumatizing the detainees who took part in them as well as the social workers in the resident teams.

Among the rescue attempts undertaken with the sponsorship of the Nîmes Committee, no action achieved the scale of that taken on behalf of the children. During the second session of the committee, on December 10, 1940, policy regarding the children was formulated. The initiatives taken to improve living conditions within the camps were incapable of protecting the youngest detainees from the psychological influence of an environment slipping down the slope into ruin.[34] The Nîmes Committee adopted the proposal of J. Weill to work to "establish children's colonies outside the camps." Nevertheless, during the month of January 1941, the Quaker representative in the committee declared himself in favor of using the financial resources to improve living conditions in the camps. He calculated that the return would be four times greater than that for action to liberate the children and take charge of them.[35] Today such a choice could appear cynical, but it more probably indicates candor and ignorance of the facts. The committee did not make that choice. The report submitted to it estimated that there were 5,000 detainees less than fifteen years of age. This figure combines Jews, Poles, Czechs, Gypsies, Spaniards, etc., and no available data allows one to establish their distribution precisely.

The total population of the OSE shelters in the southern zone did not exceed 1,300 wards. To make room for children from the camps, after 1941 some of those living in the shelters were placed, mainly in foster homes, though the statistics are lacking.[36] Three hundred places became available because that number of OSE wards emigrated overseas. A report dated June 5, 1942 states that 537 children had been placed.[37] In May 1942, two months before the first deportations from the southern zone to Drancy and Eastern Europe, 263 Jewish children out of a total of 843 children remained in the camps.[38] An OSE report of May 12, 1942 notes that "the problem of the children in the camps can be considered as virtually resolved."[39] At Rivesaltes there were fifty-five children, of whom thirty-four were about to be freed, as well as seven babies and twelve children from three to fourteen years old, "whose parents refuse to be separated from them." At Gurs there were fifty-six children, of whom thirty-five were close to liberation, and twenty-one had been retained by their parents. Some of those parents later followed the general example. On June 5, 1942, there were only seven Jewish children at Rivesaltes and thirteen at Gurs.[40]

OSE reports written after the war estimate that the organization freed more than a thousand children from detention and took charge of them prior to July 1942.[41] This figure does not include adolescents of fifteen years or older, illegally liberated, nor does it include Jewish children taken in charge by non-Jewish charities. The fragmentary information that has been gathered does not permit an estimate of the latter. One knows of the case of a group of forty-six little boys and girls placed by the Quakers in one of its boarding schools at Aspet, near Saint-Gaudens in the Haute-Garonne department on February 24, 1941, and one year later sent to the EIF center at Moissac.[42] Carl Landau, then twelve years old and the "dean" of this group, remembers that in that capacity he tried to protect his comrades. Relations were poor with the other pupils in the institution at Aspet, who called them "Boches" (Krauts). The director whipped incontinent children with nettles. He searched the rooms, where the Jewish children, haunted by poverty and hunger, hid food. On Saturdays, Carl refused to write at school, and he asked the teacher not to force the other Jews to write. Forced to stand in the back of the classroom because of this insolence, he became a Joan of

Arc figure in the eyes of his comrades. Carl also recalls sneaking rides on trains and stealing food to ease the hunger of his parents in Gurs, as well as various illicit transactions.

But these children dreamed of a peaceful, fraternal, free, and generous world. This dream was embodied at that time in the person of two Quaker social workers, who had accompanied the group from Gurs to Aspet, thus seen only during the short train trip. One of them, Ms. Rech, has kept a letter signed by each of the forty-six children, written six months after their liberation from Gurs: "Thank you for everything you did for us. Forty-six hearts beat for you, . . . to whom we owe so much." The letter is decorated with a drawing: a walled, almost fortified courtyard, presided over by a violent guard. The small artist, suffering from confinement and from the "muscular" pedagogy of the director of the boarding school, nevertheless retains hope: a graceful bird flies above the courtyard wall.[43] This combination of physical and moral suffering, of an adult maturity and sense of responsibility, of the rejection of a barbarous order, and of childish naivete, as well as the literary and pictorial expression of feelings and attitudes, is an eloquent illustration of the range of reactions of the martyred Jewish children.

Man was identified with the image of murderous bestiality. The animal was identified with the innocent victim, bearing the highest human aspirations. This shocking intuition is not an isolated case in the writ of accusation delivered in their own way by persecuted Jewish children. One finds an even more naked expression, bordering on the unbearable, collected by Gabriel Marcel from a young woman who had been a nurse at Drancy: "Feverish preparations for a deportation. One hears calls, cries, convulsive sobs. . . . A little four year old boy hides in a doghouse. 'But what are you doing, my little man?' 'I'm a dog. They don't deport dogs!' "[44]

In the beginning of 1943, the Quakers sent Jewish group of Aspet to Toulouse, where they were sent to several other shelters, including the EIF center at Moissac.

Jewish Children Emigrate to America

Before the first deportations from the southern zone in August 1942, the fate of the detainees in Gurs, Rivesaltes, and other places of detention, called *"centres d'hébergement"* (lodging centers) by the Vichy administration, seemed to be the worst that could happen to the Jews of France. Moreover, the high rate of mortality there, especially among the youngest children,[45] was more than sufficient to give the feeling that detention was a question of life or death.

Everyone classified by the administration in the undesirable category of "superfluous to the national economy" lost the right to stay freely in France. Unable to deport them because of the international situation, the regime turned to the expedient of detention, in a form unworthy of human dignity, and where the chances of surviving physically were close to zero. Before the intervention of humanitarian relief organizations, HICEM (the Jewish organization composed of the Hebrew Immigrant Aid and Sheltering Society, JCA, the Jewish Colonization Association, and EMIGDIRECT, a German Jewish emigration association) was authorized to list candidates for emigration from the camps. Was it not idle to devote oneself to an emigration plan, seeing that even before the war the borders of non-European countries were closed to refugees who tried to flee from Nazi persecution? Nevertheless, on October 6, 1940, the director of HICEM in Marseilles wrote to the European headquarters in Lisbon: "The result of my visit to the camp in Gurs is that enormous possibilities for emigration are conceivable within a rather short time."[46] Perhaps the French officials had informed him of the positive interest that the administration took in the execution of a large-scale emigration plan, for in his letter he expresses the certainty of obtaining every facility "in view of departure from France, from the authorities."

Regarding the emigration of children, steps were taken by HICEM beginning on September 11, 1940.[47] These affected children with family on the other side of the Atlantic who could obtain entrance visas for them and were willing to pay the costs of the trip. HICEM was called upon to arrange the formalities needed to obtain exit visas from France, transit visas for Spain and Portugal, as well as reservations on ships leaving Lisbon. At the same time, on March 5, 1941, OSE-France in Montpellier sent HICEM a list of 500 detained children as candidates for emigration. With the exception of certain individual cases, the obtaining of entrance visas for the children on this list depended on the results of the efforts made by American Jewish organizations, alerted by OSE-France, as well as by the American Joint Distribution Committee (AJDC) and HICEM delegations in Lisbon.

Only 311 entrance visas were ultimately delivered for children having no family in America before the mass arrests and massive deportations of children. The intervention of such prominent people as the Governor of New York State, Herbert H. Lehman, and Eleanor Roosevelt[48] with influential commissions on Capitol Hill and the immigration services was not fruitful until the second half of 1942, when it was too late.

It is almost superfluous to mention the shortage of places on maritime transport as well as the impediments to the emigration of children caused by a hesitant bureaucracy. Months went by until the French authorities, perhaps because of "lack of experience and disorder,"[49] delivered the exit visas, and the American consul completed the individual files of the children accepted for emigration. Once they received an entrance visa, these children were liberated from the camps, hence separated from their parents, but they sometimes had to wait in an OSE shelter for an entire year before leaving Marseilles. The 311 visas issued by the United States before July 1942 were all used. The complexity and ponderousness of the local procedures proba-bly made the emigration of a larger number of children a matter of chance, even supposing that American hospitality had been less grudging. But it is vain and superfluous to raise this question. For the flow of visas issued by wealthy America could be measured with an eye-dropper. Its spirit of initia-tive and administrative efficiency gave rise to the USCCEC (United States Committee for the Care of European Children), presided over by Eleanor Roosevelt.[50] But the quota conceded by the immigration authorities when it was still possible to bring children out of occupied Europe limited this com-mittee's scope of action to only 311 pupils. Everything—the myopia and rigidity of the political and administrative machinery in Washington and the archaism and ill will of the Vichy officials—seemed to be working in concert to keep undernourished Jewish children prisoner, subject to a regime that treated them like threatening evildoers, and doomed to certain death.

The first convoy of 111 children left the Marseilles railway station at the end of May 1941 and arrived in Lisbon via Spain after a trip of five nights and four days. Those whose parents were interned in Gurs were brought to the railroad station at Oloron, by police escort, in order to say a brief farewell. The children handed them the pieces of bread and lumps of sugar that had been given to them for breakfast on the train. One little girl of seven, liberated from the camp a year earlier, could not exchange a word with her parents: she could no longer express herself in German. Others were unable to identify their parents because of the physical decline caused by the privations they had endured in the camp. This meeting of several minutes in the Oloron railroad station was so trying that the OSE escorts rec-ommended avoiding it should there be further convoys.[51]

Even after the deportations from the southern zone had begun, people still hoped to have other convoys of children emigrate, for they did not know that President Laval had resolved not to let another Jewish child leave France, except in a deportation train.

Before the Mass Arrest of Children in the Northern Zone

Elsewhere we have analyzed the difference between the internment policy in the two zones. As a result, the situation of the Jewish children was in some respects less critical in the northern zone until June 1942. While the constant intervention and control of the German authorities interfered with any possibility of direct action by Jewish organizations, only a small number of Jewish children were interned there, less than 300 in all, in Troyes, Tours (the Monts camp), Poitiers (the Limoges road camp), and Mérignac, near Bordeaux. In most cases the population of the camp consisted of Spaniards, Gypsies, and foreign Jews whom the *Kommandantur* (office of the Commandant) had removed in complete family units from the Atlantic Coastal region. Only the Jews were confined to the camps, whereas the others were permitted to circulate freely.[52] In autumn 1941, the *Kommandantur* informed the Prefect of Poitiers that he was to free the French Jews, over whom it "did not recognize rights."[53] The French Jews in question were children and adolescents born in France of parents of foreign nationality and interned with them.

Until May 1941, the German authorities had mainly sent Jews to the southern zone.[54] Afterward came mass arrests, followed by detention, affecting foreign Jews belonging to the active male population. During the first two years of the Occupation, everything conspired to maintain the illusion that Jewish children were hardly threatened in the northern zone. The specific problems concerned children whose fathers were detained in Pithiviers, Beaune-la-Rolande, Compiègne, or Drancy, as well as those who were themselves detained with their parents in the camps in the Loire Valley.[55]

In the northern zone there was no equivalent to the organizations like OSE and the EIF, which were active in the south, promoting shelters and rural and artisanal centers staffed with Jewish educational teams. But the Amelot Committee took upon itself the care of children and adolescents whose fathers had been arrested and detained. It interceded to have children liberated from the Loire Valley camps. In some cases, limited in number, young people were transferred to the southern zone, after a clandestine border crossing, and sent to members of their family who lived there or to Jewish shelters.[56] Most often the Jewish charities placed their wards in foster families for a fee. The orphanage of La Varenne, administered by Rue Amelot, served as a transit shelter, with a shifting population of fifteen to fifty pupils.[57] In 1941 about a hundred children, wards of Rue Amelot, were placed "in the country."[58]

The extant documentary sources permit only a fragmentary account. The numerical data is partial, and it is unknown whether the placements made in 1941 sometimes used clandestine methods, such as "camouflaging" children by giving them a false Aryan identity. For example it is known that on November 24, 1941, twenty-one children from the camp in Poitiers were set free, followed by eighty others, under fifteen years of age, during the fol-

138   ORGANIZED JEWISH REACTIONS

lowing weeks.[59] It is also known that interned families were transferred from the Monts camp in Tours to the camp in Poitiers,[60] but we lack precise chronological and numerical data on this subject. However, 104 Jewish children under fourteen years of age had been listed in the Monts camp in February 1941, and ninety-three children of the same ages in the Poitiers camp on November 13, 1941. Could it be that children who had been interned in Tours in February were later sent to Poitiers when their families were transferred? The scanty nature of our sources do not provide and answer to this question.

Jacques Bielinky notes that about a hundred children were placed in the country in 1941 in an undated report on the action of Rue Amelot. Not having a precise chronology, it is not possible to establish whether these children were taken in after their fathers were arrested and interned in Paris, or whether the author refers to children released from the camp in Poitiers. Lists of names dating from September 1941 contain forty-nine detained children from one to thirteen years old, "placed in the country" by Rue Amelot.[61]

The establishment of contacts with Jews who were not detained seems to have been onerous for those interned in the camps on the Loire. Rabbi Elie Bloch, who had taken refuge from Metz in Poitiers, did not succeed in obtaining permission to enter the camps, in contrast to his colleagues in the southern zone. Young, firm in his resolution, efficient, sparing of gestures and words, with a generous heart, he had not hidden his sympathies for leftist parties before the war. Supported by a wife no less bold and active than himself, he managed to communicate with the detainees through the prefectorial and municipal services as well as through members of the gendarmerie who administered and guarded the camps. Aided by contributions in money and goods from the Jews who had withdrawn to the regions of Poitiers, Tours, Angoulême, and Châtellerault, Bloch succeeded in satisfying many demands of the detainees: for supplementary food, clothing, medicine, books, and ritual objects. Occasionally a sick detainee was hospitalized in Poitiers, giving Bloch or his wife an opportunity to establish direct but ephemeral contact. In mid-1941 he began corresponding with Rue Amelot, where people had already gained brief experience of action in behalf of detainees in the Loiret camps. David Rapoport arranged a monthly allocation of 10,000 francs to support Rabbi Bloch's action,[62] and he appointed a local social worker, Marcelle Valensi. In order to give her access to the camp, he obtained an appointment for her from the French Red Cross and from the SSAE (*Service social d'aide aux émigrants*, Social Service for Assistance to Emigrants), placing her in charge of "liaison between the camp social services and the Jewish organizations, as well as with the families of the detainees."[63]

At first Marcelle Valensi addressed the most immediate problems of the distress of the detainees in Mérignac, Tours, and Poitiers. Her letters[64] to Rapoport, very voluble, mention the wholesale purchase of unrationed articles and their distribution among the detainees. They provide information about life within the camps and the functioning of the social, cultural, and educational committees constituted by the detainees themselves. M. Valensi writes at astonished length about the Jewish traditions she was then discovering, in their own terms, and which were expressed in activities promoted by the detainees. One of her letters contains a detailed description of a children's celebration of Simhat Torah,[65] which she attended on October 14, 1941 in the Poitiers camp: "A moving, unforgettable day, that gives confidence in the fate of these persecuted people. . . . A new life has been organized. A marvelous adaptation to new conditions of life that defies all persecution."[66] Several times Marcelle Valensi expresses her admiration for Elie Bloch: "This rabbi is extraordinary in his assurance, his rapidity of thought, his intelligence. He constantly astonishes me.[67] I was astonished to meet, in this century so rotten with hypocrisy, a man so sincere with himself and with others, defying public opinion and all opinion, a man who has the courage of his ideas, his faith, and his feelings."[68]

But starting from November 1941, the activities of the social worker from Rue Amelot were concentrated on obtaining the release of children and adolescents. Having been delegated earlier to the camps of Loiret, Pithiviers, and Beaune-la-Rolande, she had devoted most of her efforts to trying to release the ill, military veterans, and those who were the sole supporters of their families.[69] Valensi and Bloch obtained permission from the Prefecture of the Vienne Department and from the local *Kommandantur* to take charge of children of less than fourteen years and to place them; later this was extended to fifteen-year-olds and to all those with French nationality, regardless of age. Before the end of 1941, the social worker reported the departure from the camp in Poitiers of 100 children aged from five months to fourteen years.[70] Several of them were placed with Jewish families in the region. One home in Migné-Auxonnes, not far from Poitiers, took in fifty children. But the hygienic conditions were so deplorable that some parents, when informed, demanded the return of their children to the camp. The prefect refused, and it was necessary to find other placements for these children with individual Jews.[71]

While pursuing her action in the camps, trying especially to secure the release of the sick, nursing mothers, and the elderly, Valensi also took an interest in the living conditions and scholastic progress of about a hundred children placed in Poitiers.[72] But in March 1942, she crossed the demarcation line, never to return. Later she resumed her activity in Marseilles.[73]

It cannot be established with certainty whether the children from Poitiers, released from detention at the end of 1941, were definitely saved. On February 11, 1941, the Gestapo arrested and then deported Bloch, his wife Georgette, and their baby Myriam. It then demanded the transfer of the Jewish children who had been placed in the Poitiers region to UGIF centers in Paris. Such transfers did take place,[74] but nothing permits us to establish with certainty that these were the children in question.

Nor do our sources tell us whether at that time the project of placing children in foster homes or in institutions was already being carried out in secret in order to remove the children entirely from the eye of the authorities. No one was yet aware of the perils lying in wait for these children. At that time, the Jewish organizations in the northern zone knew only the problem of children whose mothers could not take care of them because their fathers were detained in camps, as well as that of children suffering, or having suffered, from the sanitary and psychological conditions prevailing in the camps. Who could imagine the absolute horror of the Final Solution at a time when the *Kommandantur* ordered the prefect to release French Jews, over whom he did not recognize his rights? During the first two years of the occupation, Jewish schoolchildren, regardless of their nationality, suffered no discrimination in the schools.[75] Their parents had doubtless been deprived of their jobs, despoiled of their goods; thousands of fathers, mainly of foreign nationality, had been detained. But it did not yet seem as if the Jewish children themselves would be the direct target of the barbaric regime.

Everything changed brutally on June 7, 1942, when it became mandatory in the northern zone for every Jew, six years and over, to wear the yellow star. And especially on July 16 of that year, when thousands of Jewish children were arrested with their parents by armed policemen in their homes in Paris.

PART III

JEWISH CLANDESTINE ACTION
FROM AUGUST 1942
TO THE LIBERATION

10

⸙

The Establishment of
Underground Networks

On March 27, 1942, between five and six P.M., a long column of 550 Jews surrounded by armed German guards crossed the city of Compiègne, moving from the Royalieu camp to the railroad station. A train arrived from Bourget-Drancy containing an equal number of Jews, also mostly men between the ages of eighteen and fifty-five. The second contingent had been seized in Paris during the mass arrests of foreign Jews on August 20, 1941. Those of Compiègne were mainly French Jews who had been arrested in their homes in Paris on December 12, 1941. At 7:40 the train departed, with 1,112 Jews on board, arriving at Auschwitz on March 30.[1]

The previous June, four similar convoys had taken away 4,000 Jews detained in the camps of Drancy, Compiègne, Pithiviers, and Beaune-la-Rolande. In their documents the Nazis used the expression, "transport for forced labor," carried out as "reprisal against Jewry." Their instructions forbade use of the words "Deportation to the East."[2] At this initial, top secret, stage of the application of the Final Solution in Western Europe, the Nazis chose to disguise the deportation as the transport of hostages taken in reprisal for a series of attacks committed against German soldiers.[3]

The time of the first deportations coincided with a change in the personnel responsible for the Jewish question. On April 18, 1942, Pierre Laval

had returned to power as the head of the government after a period of dis-
grace lasting almost a year and half. In May he replaced Vallat with Darquier
de Pellepoix as the head of the CGQJ (*Commissariat général aux Questions
juives*, the General Commission for Jewish Questions). Laval appointed
René Bousquet to head of the national police, of which Jean Leguay became
the representative for the occupied zone. On the German side, a new police
chief in France, SS General Karl Oberg, established himself in Paris on June
1. In July, SS Officer Theodor Dannecker, now promoted to SS Captain, was
replaced by SS Lieutenant Heinz Röthke as responsible for the Jewish section of the RSHA (*Reichssicherheitshauptamt*, the Reich Central Security
Service) in France. His superior, Adolf Eichmann, had come to Paris on June
30 to give Dannecker the secret order to deport all the Jews of France,
regardless of their nationality.[4]

Simultaneously the Jewish population of the northern zone was being
ejected from society. The order to wear the yellow star was applied on June
8, 1942. One month later, the press announced that Jews could now shop
only between the hours of three and four P.M. They were allowed to use only
the last car in métro trains, and finally all public places were definitively forbidden to them.[5] In the southern zone, in July 1942 Vichy suppressed all exit
visas from France and canceled those already in the possession of candidates
for emigration.[6] Thus between April and July 1942, new French and German
officials were placed in charge of the anti-Jewish policies, while at the same
time measures demoralizing the Jewish population became widespread.

The Jewish organizations were almost entirely unaware of the preparations for the mass arrests and deportations that would affect 34,000 people
during the months of July, August, and September. Their information came
from French sources, which were also kept partially ignorant of German
intentions. This information concerned only the participation of the French
authorities in the arrest of the Jews and their delivery to the Nazis. Three factors determined the reaction of the Jewish organizations following the receipt
of the information: its quality; its interpretation; the chronology of events.

The northern zone should be treated separately from the southern zone,
since each developed differently during the tragic summer of 1942.

The Enemy Benefits from Surprise in the Northern Zone

The Mass Arrest of the Vel' d'hiv'

On July 7, 1942, a Franco-German technical committee began to plan an
operation, which the Nazis called "Spring Wind," for all of Western Europe.

The objective was to have the municipal police, with the help of the gendarmerie, mobile guards, and Doriotist militia members, arrest 22,000 foreign Jews of both sexes between the ages of sixteen and fifty in Greater Paris.
The lists provided by the Prefecture of Police to the teams in charge of the
arrests contained a total of 28,000 Jews, without regard to age. When the
police went into action on July 16, they were also ordered to take the children
living with the people to be arrested, as well as Jews over fifty years of age. In
two days, 12,884 Jews of all ages were captured, including 4,051 children.[7]

How did the other 15,000 Jews listed by the police escape arrest? Some of
them had illegally crossed over to the southern zone after October 1940, the
date of the census of the Jews of the northern zone, though their names still
figured in the files of the Prefecture of Police. Their number is impossible
to determine.

In early July a pamphlet in Yiddish published and distributed by
Solidarité warned of imminent massive detentions: "Do not wait passively
in your homes for the arrival of the bandits. . . . Hide, and above all, hide
your children, with the help of the non-Jewish population."[8] In the afternoon of July 15, the rumor of an operation the next day spread in all the
Parisian quarters where Jews lived.

In fact, in 1942 in the northern zone, there was no Jewish intelligence service for the purposes of rescue. The available testimony and documents are
silent on this subject. What they do teach us is that the authors of the pamphlet that was distributed in early July had apparently been informed by the
PC (Communist Party), which had sources in the Prefecture of Police and
had warned the leaders of Solidarité.[9] As for the rumor that was spread on
July 15, it originated with sympathetic officials in the Prefecture of Police,
who advised their Jewish acquaintances to hide.[10] Letters and reports arriving in America during the summer of 1942 stated: "During the arrests of
July 16 and 17, there had been a large number of indiscretions, notably on
the part of certain services of the Prefecture of Police. It may be said that
'everyone' had been warned."[11]

"On Wednesday night, a friend who had just left me was accosted in the
métro by someone unknown to him, who greeted him amicably and said
that he had known him in the workshop where he was employed. He pulled
him off the train at the next stop and whispered in his ear that he was a
police agent, and he implored him not to sleep at home. Then he went back
into the train."[12]

The information obtained through the PC lacked a vital detail: on what
date would the mass arrests be made? It was, however, correct regarding
another cardinal point: the order had been given to arrest entire families,
including children. The categories of Jews envisaged was not specified:

French and foreign without distinction? Would the wives and children of war prisoners be detained? What about war veterans and invalids? Ignorance regarding the date of the mass arrest was dissipated only on July 15, this time not with the help of a pamphlet put out by a clandestine Jewish network but thanks to leaks on the individual level. Some of the officials who had sorted the files of Jews to be arrested managed to reach a neighbor or acquaintance mentioned on the lists. One or more police superintendents warned certain Jews not to stay at home the following night.[13] The rumor rapidly spread.

The Jews interpreted this information in very diverse ways. This was the first time that the Jewish resistance movement circulated an order saying, "Hide!" Nothing like this had followed the orders to register with the police, the wearing of the yellow star, nor the order to report to the police stations on May 14, 1941, following which 3,733 Jews were detained in the camps of the Loiret Department. No leaks had preceded the mass arrests of August and December 1941 in Paris. Some Jews who knew of the *Solidarité* pamphlet calling upon them to hide to avoid an imminent mass arrest were incredulous. Others continued to believe, erroneously, that as before only men of working age were at risk. Most of the Jews believed that the families of prisoners of war were not in danger. Before July 15, no one knew how much time was available to go into hiding.

The chronology of the events was detrimental to the Jews. The information received via the PC at the end of June or in early July came from low-ranking elements in the Prefecture of Police who probably did not know the schedule for the Spring Wind operation. Those who had taken the orders of the Solidarité pamphlet seriously sought hiding places with neighbors or in the country, or else they obtained information regarding an escape route to the southern zone. Some of them were still seeking a path to safety on the night of July 15–16, when word of the impending mass arrest began to spread. In several instances only the adult males of the family had planned to flee.[14] The accounts of Rayski and Cukier, two leaders of Solidarité, the only Jewish resistance organization that had been informed and had given the alert before June 15, illustrate the fragmentary character of the information received. Neither man knew of the date of the operation. Not until the morning of the sixteenth did they notice that the French police forces had already begun their sinister task.[15]

Spring Wind was nevertheless a partial failure for the Nazis and the Vichy police, because, as Joseph Kessel notes, nearly 15,000 fewer Jews were arrested than had appeared on the official French police list.[16] Similarly, the operation was only a partial success for Jewish resistance, as nearly 13,000 Jews were indeed captured.

Today one can understand why the balance of rescue was not more favorable. Three factors were involved: the paucity of information; the illusions
of a large part of the Jewish population; and the insurmountable difficulties
of finding shelter.

Solidarité was a political organization whose leaders and activists placed
their confidence in the hierarchy of the clandestine PC. Mutual assistance
and rescue represented a relatively secondary area in its activity.
Information-gathering itself remained the preserve of the PC. By contrast,
Rue Amelot, originally a mutual assistance organization, had the primary
aim of rescue. But it was learning how to operate underground under conditions so precarious that the very idea of an intelligence service was lacking. Informed only on June 13 by the UGIF (*Union générale des Juifs de
France*, the General Union of French Jews), its leaders then warned those
receiving assistance in its soup kitchens and dispensaries.[17] When word
spread that the mass arrest would take place on the following night, it was
too late for the unprepared to find shelter. Among the Jews whom the police
found at home, many had chosen to remain there, either because they did
not take the rumor of the mass arrest seriously, or else because they had nur-
tured the illusion that their status—as military veterans, invalids, or women
and children—protected them from detention.

Thousands of Hunted Jews

Among the 13,000 Jews who were captured were some who had desperately
but vainly sought escape. To hide and escape the supervision and pursuit of
the police, it was necessary to "Aryanize" oneself, that is, to obtain a false
identity, falsify one's ration cards, find another house, or to take the risk of
illegally crossing the demarcation line into the southern zone. All of this
took time, as well as complicity within the government, or else that of neighbors or of people in the country. The Jewish organizations were not yet
capable of Aryanizing entire families. Until then they had only managed to
do so in a limited number of isolated cases.[18] On the level of individuals,
such an operation was not normally possible.

Under these conditions, one is astonished at the considerable number of
Jews who, on July 16 and 17, 1942, nevertheless succeeded in slipping
through the gigantic net. Rayski and Adler estimate reasonably that there
were 12,000. Precarious and temporary hiding places were found in an attic,
a basement, a back staircase, a hospitable concierge's lodge, a niche in a sympathetic neighbor's home—almost always a fortuitous solution, hardly
bearable for more than a few hours, in some cases, a day or two.[19] This

improvised rescue on such a large scale was the product of the combined effect of "the desire of the Jews not to let themselves be taken,"[20] on the one hand, and the courageous and helpful attitude of thousands of non-Jewish Parisians, on the other. Both were determined not to submit to the will of the occupier and his French accessories. The author of the previously cited letter of July 21, 1942 wrote: "I did not expect the moving sympathy shown by the non-Jewish population. Whole families were hidden, the keys to basements or vacant apartments were offered, and abandoned children were taken in on the spot."

Thus 12,000 people, entire families or not, went underground from one minute to the next, but they lacked shelter and the means to survive. In addition, an indeterminate number of Jews also fled their homes for fear of being arrested. Having ascertained later that the police had not looked for them, some returned home, while others remained underground to avoid the danger of future mass arrests. The previously cited report of August 25, 1942 described the tragedy:

> Several thousand people are currently hiding in Paris, in conditions that make one think of hunted animals. They cannot remain with the people who have given them refuge, not wishing to expose them to reprisals. They cannot return home, since their apartments have been sealed by the police. They no longer have a means of subsistence, and soon they won't even be able to obtain any food, for their sheet of ration tickets will have to be stamped. Among them are unfortunate mothers wandering with several children, not sleeping in the same place for two nights, and girls who don't know where to seek refuge, who will have no choice tomorrow other than to die of hunger or to fall into the hands of traffickers . . . suicide or prostitution.

The Jewish organizations were also decimated by the arrests and by the departure of pursued activists for the southern zone. Hence they could do nothing for the liberation or escape of detainees between July and September. The pace of deportations had become infernal: thirty-four convoys during these two-and-a-half months. Some Jews were deported the very day after their arrest.[21] In addition to those who were seized in Paris, the Nazis piled other foreign Jews into the cattle trains sent to Auschwitz, people captured in the entire northern zone, in Rennes, Nantes, Saint-Nazaire, Bordeaux, Tours, Poitiers, Angoulême, Niort, Angers, Le Mans, Laval,

Saumur, Troyes, Nancy, Châlons, and at various points along the demarcation line during failed attempts to cross. From August on, the detainees from camps in the southern zone were transferred to Drancy and then deported. This was then done to foreign Jews arrested by the Vichy police there. The implacable machinery set into action by the Nazis and their auxiliaries left no escape route for those who were transferred to Drancy.

The shock of the Spring Wind operation, despite its semi-failure, forced the Jewish organizations to change their actions completely. The safety of a large number of the 12,000 who had escaped from the mass arrest in Paris depended on assistance that could be provided by the Jewish charities to enable them to lead life underground: false identity papers and ration cards, false baptismal certificates, escape routes to the southern zone, lodging and monthly subsistence stipends, or the placement of children.[22]

Many neighborhood sections of *Solidarité* were dismantled, their members having been arrested or forced into hiding. The leadership was occupied with gathering information about what was happening at the *Vel' d'hiv'* (*Vélodrome d'hiver*, the Winter Bicycle Stadium, where the Jews were taken after the mass arrests) and in the camps. The goal was to publicize the atrocities in detail via the underground press:[23] in Yiddish, for the escaped Jews, to summon them to resistance; and in French, for the non-Jewish population, to gain its active assistance in behalf of the pursued families without shelter. This tendency to concentrate efforts on spreading information contrasts with the behavior of other Jewish resistance organizations, which scarcely used the underground press as an instrument in their fight. The Jewish Communists were the only ones who published bulletins for the non-Jewish population. This conduct illustrates the essentially political character of their action.

Urban Guerilla Warfare and the Underground Press

In response to the disaster caused by the monstrous mass arrests and deportations, *Solidarité* intensified its action on three levels: urban guerrilla, propaganda, and rescue. The emphasis was placed on the first two, since the Jewish Communist leaders were led by their training and experience to prefer political solutions.

The call to arms, launched in January 1942 following the execution of hostages on December 15, 1941, was followed by a rather long campaign of explanations intended to eliminate the qualms of hesitant activists about the timeliness and efficacy of this form of combat. But after the events of July 1942, Jewish adolescents began to demand arms. Solidarité then formed the Second Detachment, the only FTP (*Francs-tireurs et partisans*) unit using the Yiddish language, placed under the control of MOI (*Main-d'oeuvre immigrée*, Immigrant Manual Labor). At the end of 1942, the Jewish detachment numbered approximately eighty fighters as well as a reserve of very young elements.[24]

Regarding information, an exceptional effort was made to reach the non-Jewish French population. The official press and radio had not reported the mass arrests. The Jewish Communist leaders attached major importance to the publication of the atrocities committed on July 16 and 17 and to the inhumanity of the conditions prevailing in the detention centers. *Solidarité* militants made contact with nurses and social workers of the Red Cross, who testified about what was happening inside the Vel' d'hiv' and the camps of the Loiret Department.[25] The information was meant to advance two goals: to reinforce the spirit of resistance and to arouse the will to fight among men aware of "the relation that existed between the level of combativeness and the degree of information on Nazi plans and the process of their execution";[26] to encourage a humanitarian impulse to help the hunted Jews to hide and to take in their children.

In addition to *Notre parole* (Our Word), a bulletin written in French and addressed to Jews, *Solidarité* also produced anti-racist publications distributed among non-Jews: *J'accuse* (I Accuse), *Lumières* (Lights), meant for teachers and professionals, as well as *Combat médical* (Medical Combat), which circulated among physicians.[27] In June 1942, the *Mouvement national contre le racisme* (MNCR, The National Movement Against Racism)[28] formed around these three bulletins, recruiting from the membership of LICA (*Ligue internationale contre l'antisémitisme*, International League Against anti-Semitism) and among teachers. In early September, Solidarité circulated mimeographed pamphlets containing detailed accounts of the mass arrests, the hell of Vel' d'hiv', the delivery to the Germans of thousands of Jewish families captured in the southern zone and the deportations from Drancy.[29]

The MNCR also served as an auxiliary to Solidarité's children's commission by seeking foster families and non-Jewish institutions willing to accept Jewish children. For the latter it obtained false birth certificates thanks to complicity in the mayoral offices of the second and seventeenth arrondissements.[30]

The Organization of Rescue

However, assistance to the hunted Jews was mainly the task of Rue Amelot. Closed after July 16, its offices reopened on August 5. Rapoport and his colleagues, after long hesitations, provided their personnel with official UGIF identity cards. These were delivered between August and October. Of the leadership teams, "reduced to nothing" by the arrest and deportation of four of its members and the departure of several others for the southern zone, only Rapoport and Jacoubovitch remained. They reproached themselves for having delayed in providing their personnel with UGIF cards.[31] On the leadership level, the amiable understanding between the UGIF and Rue Amelot, defined on January 28, 1942, continued to govern relations between the two organizations. The UGIF provided a façade, without exercising control over the activities or accounts of Rue Amelot. Rapoport attended the "intimate" weekly meetings of the medical-social section of the UGIF, of which minutes were not kept.[32] They discussed coordination between the two organizations in the distribution of aid, dealings with the prefecture, taking charge of detainees, and the placement of children: "We provide the first assistance," explains an internal report of Rue Amelot of October 1942, "because the machinery of the UGIF is slower. . . . If the UGIF rejects a request, we keep the case in our charge. . . . Relations, both within this committee and in general, between the UGIF and ourselves are cordial."[33]

Rather than being reduced following the arrest of many of its clients, the monthly expenses of Rue Amelot for the distribution of aid rose from 321,936 francs in June 1942 to 512,198 francs in January 1943. The costs for placing children, which had been modest before the mass arrests, had to be multiplied by sixteen: rising from 18,201 francs in June, to 47,083 francs in October, and to 290,560 francs in January 1943.[34] Social workers were charged with the search for wet-nurses and the inspection of children who had been placed. A committee run by Henri Bulawko saw to the production of false identity papers and ration cards. Hunted Jews with no chance of safety other than camouflaging themselves as completely as possible turned to Rue Amelot.

People could only report to an office or dispensary of the UGIF, an official organization, under their true identity, with the yellow star solidly sewn to their garments. Any request gave rise to the creation of a file. Hence anyone who was or felt himself menaced in retaining his legal status and needed advice, help, an escape route to the southern zone, or a false identity sought discreet contact with Rue Amelot, where administrative formalities were suppressed. To go underground required leaving one's home, neighborhood, and job. Bulawko described the development of his false identity card service:

The first ones were given to us by a Communist official of a mayoral office in the Parisian suburbs (I think it was Pantin). . . . The

requests arrived in the Amelot Center . . . and David Rapoport
became more pressing. Some people living underground (they
had evaded the mass arrests) had to leave. And it was necessary
to provide them with credible papers.

Chance intervened. One day a girl reported to the dispensary. . . . On Sunday she was supposed to go to her godfather's
house, who was the mayor of a little borough in the large sub-
urban area, whom she served as a secretary. In answer to my
question, she stated that she produced the identity cards. That
was too beautiful—and it was true! She would bring me the
seals, teach me how to fill the card with a thumbprint, stamp it,
and cover the seal. At that time there was no national identity
card. The person requesting arrived with a blank identity card
(not uniform) that you could buy freely. I quickly bought up the
whole supply of the Uniprix [department stores]. I remember a
young salesgirl in the one on Faubourg Saint-Antoine who
asked me why I needed so many. I answered that it was for a
sports club."[35]

Later the methods were improved. The resisters fabricated seals with the
names of places "in the East (Alsace, if possible) destroyed by bombardments. That was where a number of Polish Jews would be reborn. That can
explain their accent when they speak French and make any verification
impossible."[36]

There are no extant sources for estimating the number of Jews who owe
their rescue to the illegal camouflage operations performed by the Jewish
resistance during the months following the mass arrests of the summer of
1942. These had been aimed at German, Austrian, Polish, Czech, Russian,
and stateless Jews. Those of other nationalities were not spared for long. On
September 24, 1942, 1,574 Romanian Jews were interned in Drancy, then,
on October 9 and 10, 1,965 Belgian, Dutch, Romanian, Bulgarian, and
Yugoslavian Jews who had been captured throughout the northern zone. On
November 5 came the turn of 1,060 Greek Jews. The mass arrests were prepared in the greatest of secrecy and with the shortest possible advance
notice, thus they remained entirely unknown to the Jews until their execution. Moreover, the action of zealous members of the Parisian police force
produced from twenty to thirty arrests daily from October to December.
After stopping in October, the deportations were resumed in November
with the departure of four convoys containing a total of 3,745 Jews.[37]

At the same time, the number of escapees from the mass arrests, seeking clandestine refuge in their turn, did not cease growing. Jews of French nationality doubtless felt less hunted than foreign Jews. But many of them had already tried to Aryanize themselves. Of a total of 41,951 deportees in 1942, about 6,500 were Jews of French nationality. The inmates of the Drancy camp on December 31, 1942 included 1,994 French Jews out of 3,031 detainees.[38]

Just like his colleagues among the personnel of Rue Amelot, Bulawko wore a yellow star and carried a UGIF card, which was supposed to afford protection from detention. Caught in a round-up in the métro station of Père-Lachaise on November 18, 1942, he was detained in Drancy and deported a few months later. His French nationality and UGIF card were ineffectual before a policeman's arbitrary decision: "I am accused of hiding my star with a book and a gabardine coat that I carry on my arm. I try to prove the absurdity of that accusation, but the cop knows only one logic: his. The round-up that he was in charge of has to be profitable. I am his only 'client' of the day, and he has no intention of letting me go."[39]

Bulawko's fate illustrates the extreme precariousness of the situation of the Jews whom official regulations exempted from deportation. It was also one of the most severe losses suffered by Rue Amelot. The false-identity service was cut off. While the medico-social teams devoted themselves almost entirely to the rescue of children, David Rapoport himself took over creation of false identities in response to the constant pressure of demand. But the police finally struck at the institution itself. On June 1, 1943, they arrested Rapoport and his liaison agent, David Oks, at Rue Amelot head-quarters. His helper, Jacoubovitch, had crossed over to the southern zone in May. Detained in the fort of Romainville and than in Drancy, from which he was deported, Rapoport died of exhaustion in Monowitz on July 2, 1944.[40]

After that arrest the soup kitchen and dispensaries of Rue Amelot were administered by the UGIF. But the children's rescue network continued to operate in total secret, under the direction of a veteran of the FSJF (*Féderation des sociétés juives de France*, the Federation of Jewish Associations of France), A. Alpérine.

The Zionist youth organized in the shadow of Rue Amelot found itself dismembered following the arrest of its leader, Bulawko. After the great mass arrests of the summer, cultural work had been interrupted. Many activists had left for the southern zone, others had joined the armed groups of FTP-MOI starting in October 1942.[41] Zionist youth did not regroup until March 1943, upon the initiative of Simon Lévitte, the founder of MJS (*Mouvement de jeunesse sioniste,* the Zionist Youth Movement) in Montpellier. In 1943 he made several trips between the southern zone and Paris, where he gave Emmanuel Lefschetz, already a leader of the EIF, responsibility for developing the MJS. Similarly, in the course of his visit to Paris in March 1943, Lévitte placed two other activists in charge of the rescue networks of these two youth movements, *Éducation physique* (Physical Education, associated with the MJS), and *Sixième* (Sixth, associated with the EIF).[42]

Jewish Resistance Thwarts the Deportation of Children from the Southern Zone

Vichy France was far less affected by the mass arrests of July 16 and 17 in the northern zone.Efficiently assisted by French and foreign humanitarian charities, the Jewish organizations managed to prevent the deportation of most of the children appearing on the lists of Jews to be transferred to Drancy and delivered to the Nazis. Even children already captured by the police and taken to assembly centers from which convoys for Drancy departed were mostly taken in hand by the rescue teams and placed in safe places. From August 7 to October 22, 1942, Vichy delivered 11,005 foreign Jews to Drancy, of whom 37 were children, divided as shown in table 10.1.

Table 10.1

FOREIGN JEWS FROM THE SOUTHERN ZONE TRANSFERRED
TO DRANCY, AUGUST 7-OCTOBER 22, 1942

Interned in Camps	3,936
Incorporated in the GTE (convoy of Aug. 25)	1,184
Mass arrest of August 26	
Number of names on the police lists	12,686
Number of Jews escaped from the arrests	5,393
Number of arrests on Aug. 26	6,701
Number of arrests, Aug. 27-Aug. 31	592
Total Arrests	7,293
Exempted (children and military veterans)	1,408
Victims of the mass arrests, transferred to Drancy (12 convoys from Aug. 29 to 22 Oct.)	5,885
Grand Total	11,005[a]

[a] Source: Klarsfeld, *Vichy-Auschwitz. 1943–1944,* pp. 158–159, 393.

All of the Jews from the southern zone delivered to the Nazis were deported to the East between August 10 and November 6, 1942.[43] But the German services had counted on 15,000 arrests, in addition to those in the camps in the South and the GTE (*Groupements de travailleurs étrangers*, Foreign Laborers Groups), on the basis of information supplied by Leguay, the representative in Paris of the Secretary General of the Police, Bousquet.[44]

The relative failure of the German plan to deport foreign Jews from the southern zone can be explained by a combination of circumstances:

- In late July several directors of Jewish organizations had obtained information in Vichy regarding the governmental decision to deliver 10,000 foreign Jews from the southern zone to the Nazis. They then obtained information regarding the date of the convoys, the categories of Jews concerned, and the exemptions to be granted.
- The precedent of the great mass arrests in the northern zone helped to alert the Jewish leaders in the southern zone, to dissipate some of the illusions that had remained, and to inspire clear-sighted and salutary decisions against the deportations.
- Several Jewish leaders importuned the authorities by lodging Jewish, ecclesiastical, and diplomatic protests with Pétain and Laval and by arousing a wave of indignation among the French population. The public expression of indignation by part of the bishopric supported the outcry of the rescuers and forced Laval to restrain his policy of "delivering" Jews to the Nazis.
- The organizations active in the camps had become familiar with the administrative and police machinery and knew its weak points. Trust and by now longstanding cooperation between the activists of various humanitarian associations grouped within the Nîmes Committee[45] facilitated the rapid formation of rescue networks.

Warning is Given

The dispersion of the Jews in the southern zone made the issuing of a warning among those targeted by the mass arrests more random than had been the case with a population concentrated within a few urban neighborhoods, as in Paris. Police reports show in fact that in the Departments of Bouches-du-Rhône, Rhône, and Haute-Vienne the Jews in the large centers were able to avoid arrest more widely than in small localities. Obviously one could not warn Jews whose place of residence was unknown, and the Jewish organizations often were unaware of the presence of Jews who had withdrawn to villages and hamlets. Nevertheless nearly 50 percent of the targeted Jews escaped capture; 20 percent of those arrested were saved from deportation and released because of legal or "abusive" exemptions issued by screening committees and humanitarian organizations.[46]

On July 17, 1942, Bousquet had his adjutant Fourcade telegraph to the prefects in the southern zone that the exit visas from France granted to foreign Jews had been canceled. HICEM (a Jewish overseas emigration association) alerted its Lisbon office, which sent its directors, Bernstein and Spanien, to France in order to negotiate the reestablishment of exit visas with Vichy. On July 18 Spanien was received at the *Sûreté nationale* (the National Security office), accompanied by the director of UGIF-south, Raymond Raoul Lambert. They learned from "horrified officials that Vichy had obtained the substitution of French Jews in the occupied zone by foreign Jews from the free zone."[47] They immediately alerted "representatives of French Judaism, American charities, and Christian circles for the purpose of official actions of humanitarian character."[48]

Lambert's first reaction was to seek the preventative intervention of the president of the Consistory and of the UGIF with Laval. But this plan was aborted when the president of the Consistory refused to take part. At first he did not believe the information received in Vichy by Lambert.[49] Tracy Strong, the secretary general of the YMCA and Donald Lowrie, the president of the Nîmes Committee, obtained detailed information in Vichy regarding the scope and date of the convoys leaving the detention camps for Drancy. On August 4 they informed the American ambassador to Vichy. On August 4–6 they met successively with several members of Pétain's cabinet, then with the Marshal himself. Laval also received the Quaker leaders, Noble and MacClelland. These actions only confirmed the information that had been received. The 1,000 foreign Jews possessing emigration visas were not granted exemptions.[50]

Moreover, the HICEM leaders, who understood that Vichy would keep its word to the Germans and deliver the agreed number of Jews, had no illusions about their efforts to restore the exit visas: "If our action should be crowned with success, our protégés [those possessing destination visas] will be replaced by other refugees who have no chance to emigrate."[51]

Bousquet's instructions authorized the SSE (*Service social des étrangers*, the Social Service for Foreigners) "to take charge of the interests of the Jews in each camp" with the collaboration of private charities, without "excluding *a priori* the Jewish charities," which, in any event, would be given "a limited place."[52] Lesage, the head of the sse, a militant philanthropist and a veteran member of the Society of Friends, maintained close ties with Robert Gamzon and Édouard Simon of the EIF, Rabbis René Hirschler and René Kapel, the chaplains of the camps, as well as with Joseph Weill of ose (*l'Oeuvre de secours aux enfants*, the Children's Rescue Network). He provided them with detailed information regarding the instructions secretly transmitted to the prefects of the southern zone by Bousquet on August 5 for the implementation of the mass arrests. Simon informed the commissioners of the EIF by a message.[53] On August 22, Vichy signaled the date fixed for the mass arrests by a secret telegram to the prefects: Wednesday, August 26, at dawn. Lesage immediately informed Weill, Hirschler, and Gamzon.[54] While the police were preparing to capture the Jews, the rescuers, secretly informed, sought to shelter the largest possible number of them.

The Circulation of Information Indispensable for the Rescuers

Today, in a society where information from the most diverse sources circulates freely, it is difficult to imagine the situation of a country receiving only limited information, screened by the authorities. The press and radio made brief mention of the fate inflicted on the Jews:

> Stateless Jews, convicted of illegal trade and speculation have been deported ... to a region where they can be forced to do useful work. .... The Jews continue to devote themselves to criminal actions, the damage of which is suffered by our compatriots, while these crimes are too often unknown. Police operations taking place currently have the aim of putting an end to it.[55]

Only those citizens who dared to flout the prohibition against listening to the BBC and the Swiss radio were better informed, as well as the witnesses of the arrests and those reached by the Jewish clandestine press. In the southern zone, most of the Jews had only fragmentary knowledge of the mass arrest of the Vel' d'hiv' and its aftermath. With censorship of the mails and fear of wiretapping, these private means of communication could not be used, either.

The best sources of intelligence, although it was slow and limited, were the Jews from the northern zone who managed to cross the demarcation

line after the monstrous mass arrests, as well as the bulletins of the underground Jewish press. The social milieus of the Jewish population withdrawn
into the southern zone were widely dispersed and very isolated. Reports of
the mass arrest of the Vel' d'hiv were not published by the clandestine Jewish
press until early September.

The leaders of the Jewish organizations were better informed. Their confidential sources were several officials in Vichy and above all Jews close to the
Consistory as well as Zionist leaders moving back and forth between the
southern zone and Paris. One of them, for example, a Gaullist resister, the
liaison man between the Consistory and *Amitié chrétienne* (Christian
Friendship), performed many missions in Paris and even in London.[56]

As of July 28, 1942 the Central Consistory addressed a solemn, well-doc-
umented, and vehement protest to the Vichy government against the acts of
barbarism, the massive arrests, and deportations of which the Jews of the
occupied zone were the victims:

> Considering that the primary duty of every civilized state is to
> safeguard the property, liberty, honor, and life of its citizens and
> to protect foreigners who have regularly received hospitality on
> its territory, [the Consistory adjures the French government] to
> try again by all the means of which it disposes to save the thou-
> sands of innocent victims to whom no other approach can be
> made other than their belonging to the Jewish religion.[57]

In addition to the revelations received in Vichy concerning the imminent
delivery of 10,000 foreign Jews from the southern zone to the occupiers,
there were others concerning the details of the arrests and deportations in
Paris, as well as fragmentary information, but of unprecedented horror, of
massacres of Jews in Eastern Europe. Some of the Jewish leaders understood
then that the Nazis were implementing a policy of the physical annihilation
of the Jews. On August 17, while the Chief Rabbi of France and the president
of the Consistory were absent from Lyons, Chief Rabbi Jacob Kaplan visited
Cardinal Gerlier, the Archbishop of Lyons and the Primate of the Gaules, to
ask him, in the name of the Chief Rabbi of France, to take action to rescue
the 10,000 foreign Jews who were about to be arrested and sent to Germany,
"not to work there but to be exterminated there." He tried to demonstrate
the falsity of the official version of "an ethnic regroupment in Poland."
Kaplan presented an eyewitness report of the passage of deportees arriving
from the camps of the southeast at the railroad station of Lyon-Perrache:

"There is no doubt that the majority of these unfortunates will not reach the end of their journey." He submitted several documents to the Cardinal, including a note on the massacre of 380,000 Jews in Romania.[58] In a message circulated in August 1942 among the leaders of the EIF, Simon reveals: "In Minsk, recently, 35,000 Jews were machine-gunned, and, since the German occupation, 700,000 Jews have been killed in Poland, women, old people, children, and men. Everyone passed through, either in gas chambers or in massacres."[59]

In a new protest of the Consistory to the government dated August 25, 1942, even more full of pathos than the earlier one, "indignation" and "revulsion" are expressed against the decision to deliver thousands of Jewish foreigners to the Germans. The emphasis is placed unequivocally upon the Nazi extermination plan:

> The Central Consistory can have no doubt about the ultimate fate awaiting the deportees, after they have suffered a dreadful martyrdom. Did not the Chancellor of the Reich declare in his message of February 24, 1942: "My prophecy, according to which in the course of this war it will not be Aryan humanity that is annihilated, but the Jews who will be exterminated, will be fulfilled. Whatever the battle brings us and whatever is its duration, this will be its final result." This extermination plan has been applied methodically in Germany and in the countries occupied by it, since it has been established by precise and consistent information that several hundred thousand Jews have been massacred in Eastern Europe, or have died there after atrocious sufferings, following the ill-treatment they received. Finally, the fact that people delivered by the French government have been assembled without any discrimination regarding their physical aptitudes, that among them are included the sick, the aged, pregnant women, and children, confirms that it is not with the aim of using the deportees as a labor force that the German government demands them, but with the unmistakable intention of exterminating them ruthlessly and methodically.[60]

The text also denounces, based on precise information, the inhuman treatment inflicted upon the deportees "from the moment of their embarkment in the unoccupied zone."

The leaders of the Jewish organizations were thus well informed, and several of them interpreted lucidly the real significance of the measures applied against the foreign Jews. Consequently they managed to arrange rescue measures. The rabbis of the chaplaincy, René Kapel sent to the camp in Gurs and Noé, and Henri Schilli to the one in Rivesaltes, tried to humanize the departure of the convoys of deportees (August 6, 8, and 11, 1942). With the help of social service teams and volunteer inmates, they managed to prevent the departure of almost all the children, distributed aid in cash, fruit, and other victuals. With the authorization of the police superintendent, Schilli accompanied the train as far as Montpellier, trying to reduce the moral and physical suffering of the deportees. The Quakers placed a batch of books in each railway car.[61] The children saved from departure were "sent to centers designated by the authorized regional delegate of the SSE." They were taken in hand by humanitarian charities, Jewish or not, having representatives in the camps, then they were secretly placed in safekeeping.[62] These, at least, were saved.

The Jewish organizations tried to do more and better in behalf of the foreign Jews who had entered France since 1933 and whom the police were preparing to arrest and transfer to the northern zone. Privy to the details of Bousquet's secret instructions, they decided to make use of the "screening committees" intended to designate possible beneficiaries of exemptions among the Jews who had fallen into the hands of the police. The SSE admitted representatives sent by OSE, the EIF, the chaplaincy, HICEM, UGIF, CIMADE, *Amitié chrétienne*, the Quakers and the YMCA to its commissions. On August 16, Hirschler assembled the chaplains in Marseilles to coordinate the warning system with them. He explained the types of exemption and gave instructions as to how to intervene in behalf of Jews covered by them. Between August 22 and 24, following information communicated by Lesage, his correspondents sent warnings to shelters, rural centers, and families that a vast police operation was to take place on the night of August 25–26 against Jews who had entered France after 1936.[63]

In several departments, the entirely improvised system of secretly warning Jews threatened by arrest, issued by people who until then had strictly observed legality, was very effective.[64] Many of those who acted held official positions in government, in the Jewish community, or in charity organizations. In the Department of Lot-et-Garonne, the police arrested only two out of two hundred Jews on the list. In Lyons, the 1941 census had counted 21,695 Jews, including 7,075 of foreign nationality. Delpech sets their number in 1942 at between 25,000 and 30,000, of whom 8,000–9,000 were foreign, taking into account those who avoided the census and the presence of refugees from the northern zone who had arrived in clandestine manner after the census. Four thousand of these were targeted by the arrests of August 26. But only 2,000 appeared on the lists prepared by the police, who captured 1,076 of them.[65] "Having made all of the screenings, only 545 individuals have left," the Regional Prefect, Angeli, reported to his minister.[66] In Montpellier there were no arrests at all, while in Béziers, in the same Department, the police action gave rise to "heart-rending scenes."[67] On September 15, 1942, a report of the French police submitted to the German authorities states that 10,522 Jews from the southern zone, of whom 3,920 came from the detention camps, had been delivered to Drancy.[68] About 5,400 of those subject to arrest remained impossible to find, while the screening committees effected the release of 1,048 people covered by the exemptions. The convoys from the southern zone arriving in Drancy between August 8 and September 15 contained 37 children,[69] while approximately 3,000 children whom Laval had decided to deliver to the Nazis either escaped the arrests or were released thanks to the screening committees. Although the promise made by Vichy to deliver 10,000 foreign Jews from the southern zone had been kept, Spanien, a HICEM official, termed the police operation of August 26 a fiasco, and not without cause.

Arousing Public Opinion

The attitude of the churches following the promulgation and application of the Statute of the Jews, the creation of the CGQJ and then the UGIF was disappointing on the political level. The vigorous stands against the racist hatred of Nazism taken by Pope Pius XI in 1937 and several French prelates, such as Cardinals Verdier and Gerlier as well as Monsignor Saliège in 1938, revealed some potential sympathy for the Jews within the Church. But the silence maintained in Rome and in French episcopal circles regarding the Vichy anti-Jewish policies had given the public the feeling that the Church was acquiescing in these policies. Before the summer of 1942, the only voice within the Catholic hierarchy that was raised against the anti-Jewish measures of Vichy had been that of Monsignor Saliège in a message of November 23, 1941.[70] The massive support of the clergy for Pétain and his regime confirmed this sentiment. This attitude contrasts with that of the Protestant Federation, whose president, Marc Boegner, denounced the injustice of the Statute of the Jews in March 1941 in letters addressed to the head of the government and to the Chief Rabbi of France.[71]

Things were not the same on the humanitarian level. Christian philanthropic associations, both French and foreign, took an active part, together with Jewish charities, in action in behalf of the detainees in the camps of the southwest. The Nîmes Committee, created to coordinate this action, was presided over and run by Pastor Donald Lowrie, the representative of the YMCA. Cardinal Gerlier and Pastor Boegner officially sponsored *Amitié chrétienne* and CIMADE, which came to the assistance of the foreign Jewish refugees and detainees. During the summer of 1941, Gerlier turned several times to Pétain and to the CGQJ in protest against the inhuman conditions reigning in the camp in Gurs.[72]

Further, the underground publication, *Témoignage chrétien* (Christian Witness), created in November 1941, analyzed anti-Semitism in its issues, attacking the racism of Vichy with vehemence.[73] When the mass arrests and deportations of the northern zone became known, as well as the Vichy plan to deliver the foreign Jews of the southern zone to the Nazis, the Jewish delegates to the Nîmes Committee and Chief Rabbi Kaplan increased their appeals to the clergy. Everything possible had to be attempted to bring to bear the influence of the Catholic Church on the Vichy regime and to make certain that those prelates whose humanitarian feelings for the Jews were known should act to exert pressure on the Vatican and on public opinion in order to change the anti-Jewish policy of the French government. Similarly it was hoped that the representatives of American Protestant charities on the Nîmes Committee would make the full weight of their influence felt. Through their contacts with the United States Embassy in Vichy and their frequent visits to Switzerland, they could transmit information that would arouse reactions in neutral countries by means of press campaigns and diplomatic pressure.

In fact, the wave of barbaric cruelty that broke on the Jews and the urgent appeals of Jewish leaders released a veritable storm of ecclesiastical and diplomatic protest lodged with Pétain and Laval, as well as criticism of the regime in public opinion. Following the overwhelming revelations received during his interview with Chief Rabbi Kaplan on August 17, Cardinal Gerlier wrote to Pétain on August 19 and had a pastoral letter read in the churches of his diocese on September 6. Pastor Boegner addressed a passionate appeal to the Marshal on August 20.[74] The Papal Nuncio, Monsignor Valério Valeri, was received by Laval on August 22.[75] The American chargé d'affaires delivered a note to the government on August 31, demanding that it place the 4,000 Jewish children captured in Paris in the care of Jewish associations.[76]

These actions and many others[77] had no immediate effect. But they did not leave the government indifferent. On August 25, two days after Monsignor Saliège had his admirable pastoral letter read in the churches, Laval made it known to the Vatican that he desired the retirement of the

Archbishop of Toulouse. He maintained that he was "very upset" regarding the consequences of this message, "not only in the strictly national context, where it will only sow discord within a population already so divided, but also in the international context."[78] Then, on September 2, the head of the government revealed to SS General Oberg the existence of "an unparalleled resistance within the Church. The chief of this opposition being, as it happens, Cardinal Gerlier." He asked to have no further demands made upon him regarding the Jewish question. In particular he did not want to have the number of Jews to be deported imposed upon him in advance. "The delivery of Jews isn't like that of merchandise in a department store."[79]

The chiefs of the SS and the sd in France, Oberg and Knochen, decided "in the higher interest of the Reich," which required a docile France, kept well in hand by its government, to forgo any reprisal measures that would create difficulties for Laval.[80] This was despite Röthke's obstinate insistence on obtaining the delivery of 15,000 Jews from the southern zone, in conformity with Leguay's estimates. Another consequence of the actions taken by the clergy was that Vichy refrained from passing a law rescinding naturalizations effected after 1933, a law that Laval had promised to Oberg.[81]

As a result, Jews in both zones were arrested at a slower pace. Eight convoys planned to depart from Drancy in September and thirty planned for October were canceled because of a shortfall of 38,000 Jews whom the Germans had expected the French police to capture.[82] The appeals of the Jewish leaders to the Catholic and Protestant authorities and to the American Embassy are only partially known. Nevertheless, the report submitted to the Consistory by Chief Rabbi Kaplan after his meeting with Cardinal Gerlier on August 17, 1942 has been published. The note of the American chargé d'affaires, H. Pinkney Tuck, of August 31 explicitly mentions the information presented by the AJDC in Marseilles, the UGIF in Paris, and the Chief Rabbi of France.

The Rescue Networks Go Underground

As in Paris, thousands of Jews who had escaped the mass arrests sought places of refuge and means of subsistence. It was necessary to avoid circulating, so as not to be exposed to an identity check, for the appearance of one's name on the lists drawn up for the mass arrests of August 26 could be fatal. The police captured 592 Jewish fugitives between August 27 and August 31.[83]

The distress of the hunted Jews led to the improvisiation of clandestine structures. On August 25, in Vichy, Gamzon met Henri Wahl, the district commissioner of the EIF, and two other leaders of the movement: "Mass arrests are imminent; you are all mobilized." The same day the leaders of the MJS left Moissac, following a training session directed by Simon Lévitte. These young people dispersed to Lapalisse, Limoges, Périgueux, Toulouse, or Montpellier and used the evening and night to warn targeted families of the mass arrest that was to begin a few hours later. The next day, a team from the MJS group of Montpellier organized to bring provisions to the escapees in their temporary hiding place. On August 27, the participants of the meeting at Vichy were present at the EIF offices in Moissac with other leaders of the movement. A month previously, these men had created the *Service social des jeunes* (SSJ, the Young People's Social Service), charged with the orientation of older adolescents, sponsored by the UGIF. In response to increased seriousness of the events, it was decided in Moissac to set aside three permanent workers, who would work for rescue throughout the southern zone: Henri Wahl; Ninon Weil-Hait, a voluntary detainee in Gurs until then; and Denise Lévy, who had just dispersed the girls of the Beaulieu center. Operating behind the facade of the SSJ, this team promptly organized the fabrication of false identity papers and sought stable shelters for hunted young Jews. The kernel of what was to become the *Sixième* had been constituted.

In Montpellier and Nice, Simon Lévitte formed similar teams during the following days, in the framework of the new MJS movement, also laying the groundwork for the underground rescue network of the Zionist youth, whose code name was "*Éducation physique*" (Physical Education).

At the same time a network specializing in the rescue of Jewish children whose safety could not be assured in the OSE shelters was secretly established by Georges Garel, a newcomer to Jewish charity work. The development and action of these three structures is described in the following chapter. Naturally their genesis was not preserved in the official minutes of meetings. Hence the historian must try to reconstitute it with the help of testimony and documentation, mainly reports written after the Liberation. The chronology of the beginnings of the *Sixième* was nevertheless made public by Roger Fichtenberg, one of the participants in the meetings in Vichy (August 25) and Moissac (August 27). An agent of the *Sixième* from the start, he has preserved his daybooks from the years 1942–1944.[84]

Idealists, mainly French patriots, scrupulously respectful of the law by education and reflex, the creators of these networks set about organizing the Jews threatened with deportation in totally illegal fashion. A passionate desire to thwart the murderous plans of the enemy by snatching away its prey stimulated their ingenuity and gave them the audacity to turn themselves into improvised forgers, exposed to major dangers. The structures they created operated in parallel with the youth movements and a medical-social service, drawing its leaders and agents from them. It was mainly after the occupation of the southern zone by the Wehrmacht as well as by Italian forces (who took over eight Alpine departments) that their operations gained in scope. The Garel Network, *Éducation physique*, and the *Sixième* separated their actions by region and perfected techniques of manufacturing false identity papers, helping Jews escape to Spain and Switzerland.

Another Jewish rescue network was born in Marseilles in the autumn of 1942 upon a personal initiative. Known as the *Service André*, its history is partially known thanks to the accounts of its founder and leader, Joseph Bass,[85] and of Denise Caraco-Sikierski, an agent of the network,[86] but above all by the pages written in 1946 by the historian Léon Poliakov, who was also an agent in that network.[87] A Jew of Russian origins, a specialist in patents and industrial property, Bass escaped from the Argelès camp and took refuge in Marseilles. In the spring of 1942 he gave a course in industrial drafting in the AIP (*Association des Israélites pratiquants*, the Association of Observant Jews) shelter. "Tall and broad, he seemed taller and broader than nature. He possessed the particular faculty for filling the place where he was with his presence. Impossible not to notice him . . . cordial and vociferous, he made an impression."[88]

In the autumn of 1942, finally in possession of a borrowed identity himself, Bass immediately threw himself into the rescue action. Initiated by two leaders of the *Sixième*, he gained the confidence of Maurice Brener, the co-director of the AJDC, who granted him a budget permitting him to form the Action Group Against Deportation, the forgotten name of Service André. Bass recruited agents, fabricated false papers, found places of refuge in institutions belonging to the Capuchins, the Dominicans, and Notre-Dame de Sion, as well as in the country, especially in Chambon-sur-Lignon. The network operated in Marseilles, Nice, Grenoble, Lyons, Saint-Étienne, and in the Haute-Loire Department, furnishing borrowed identities and hiding places to Jews of all ages.

Under the responsibility of the OSE, CAR (*Comité d'assistance aux réfugiés*, the Committee for Assistance to Refugees), FSJF, and OASI (*Oeuvre d'assistance sociale israélite*, the Jewish Social Assistance Mission), within the framework of the UGIF, the assistance work continued after August 1942, as in the past, to help Jews in need whom the mass arrests had spared. Providing aid to Jews who had gone underground was improvised and then organized by the OSE and above all by the FSJF. In addition to the Garel Network, Joseph Weill took the responsibility for constituting an underground team of the OSE, which acted in parallel to the administration and was led by Andrée Salomon.[89] It was patterned upon what had already put in place by Marc Jarblum, the head of the FSJF, after the official absorption of his organization by the UGIF. The workshops of the *Sixième* and of *Éducation physique* provided the false papers needed by those whom it was necessary to Aryanize. The sums demanded for this form of assistance were considerable. Weill and Jarblum quickly persuaded the AJDC delegate for France, Dika Jefroykin, who was also the president of the MJS and a member of the steering committee of the AJ (*Armée juive*, Jewish Army). The main provider of funds for the UGIF, Jefroykin's temperament and sensibility predisposed him to place the full weight of his influence behind clandestine forms of assistance, taking into account the new data regarding the rescue of the Jews. This also applied to the two leaders of the "Palestinian" charities, the KKL (*Keren Kayemeth Le-Israel*, the Jewish National Fund), and *Keren Ha-Yessod* (the Palestine Foundation Fund, associated with the World Zionist Organization), Joseph Fischer and Nahum Hermann, who depended on the AJDC for funds following the summer of 1942. These two Zionist activists were past masters in the art of signing for loans that the AJDC promised to repay after the war. Jefroykin made certain that the Jewish underground did not lack the means needed for its assistance and rescue work.

The Manufacture of False Papers

"A Frenchman normally carried, in the French State of Vichy, a half dozen identity cards and documents: an identity card, a military booklet, a certificate of demobilization, ration cards for food, textiles, and tobacco, to which a work certificate was added a little later."[90] Considerable documentation on papers forged by the Resistance, produced by a rather diverse selection of counterfeiting workshops, is conserved in archival institutes and by individuals.[91] A permanent exhibition in the Yad Vashem National Memorial in Jerusalem displays a rich variety of equipment and administrative documents from Jewish resistance groups in France.

The history of the manufacture of false papers comprises several phases, during which the methods and "products" constantly improved. Certain workshops began operating without possessing or fabricating rubber stamps. Identity and ration cards were "washed" with such widely available solvents as hydrogen peroxide or bleach, and then decidedly Aryan first and last names as well as other details would be written in. The work had to be done with care to avoid discoloring the paper or cardboard and erasing printed words, engraving, or the signature and seal of the authority that issued the document. If the seal overlapped something written by hand, the operation was impossible.[92] This primitive procedure was too precarious for several reasons, the most immediate one being the ration card. One could not receive monthly ration coupons except by presenting a card whose details corresponded with those appearing on a register in the municipal office in charge of issuing the coupons. The washing out of identity papers was abandoned when cards bearing the stamp *"juif"* (Jew) began to appear, according to the law of December 11, 1942.

Quite soon the false paper services learned to manufacture seals themselves. Some of them won the complicity of an engraver and thus obtained products entirely similar to the original. Others gained possession of original seals, either with the cooperation of an employee of the mayoral office or of the police station, or else by swiping a seal from an official's desk while his attention was turned elsewhere. Some of the older members of the MJS and the EIF were past masters in establishing good relations with mayoral employees in various localities, who gave them seals, knowing full well what they were doing.[93] Fichtenberg created an impressive collection of the most diverse rubber stamps for the *Sixième*, including those of military offices, used for the manufacture of demobilization certificates.[94]

It then became possible to fabricate new identity papers. A blank card widely available for sale in stores and the photograph of the person concerned were sufficient to complete the operation. The indispensable ration card posed a more delicate problem. Some Aryanized Jews retained their original cards, taking the risk of presenting them unaltered when ration coupons were delivered. Children placed in the countryside were given their original cards, which were first "washed" and rewritten with their borrowed civil status. The mayoral offices of small towns made no difficulty about registering the new little ration recipients on their rolls. Fortunately one official provided the false paper services with impressive quantities of blank ration cards, together with ration coupons, which were delivered collectively every time the documents were renewed.[95]

It became customary to call these precious documents *"bifs"* for some unknown reason. These *bifs* proved their worth in tens of thousands of cases, both for children placed away from home and for Jews who were not exposed to controls and verifications. Nevertheless, for people who traveled, and especially for active resistance operatives in a rescue network, the *bif* soon proved to be a dangerous document. A telephone check to the mayoral office or police headquarters by a slightly skeptical official could give away the forgery. Those who were caught in this fashion did not escape deportation.

A higher level of sophistication in producing false papers was achieved when resistance operatives learned to produce what they called *"synthés,"*

because they "synthesized" Aryanized Jews. A *synthé* was a properly registered document that could be presented in any identity check without danger. *Synthés* took the most diverse form. Most frequently they were the birth
certificate and identity card of someone deceased or a prisoner of war, delivered by a cooperative official. Sometimes non-Jewish Frenchmen, motivated by humanitarian compassion or the desire to help Jewish resistance,
permitted their own civil status to be copied by a Jew, who was thus
Aryanized, sometimes with the complicity of a municipal official who provided the necessary documents.[96]

In such cases, when one could not obtain the documents from the mayoral office, the workshops of the Jewish resistance did an excellent job of
creating the necessary documents by themselves. Parisian Jews who fled to
the southern zone thus assumed the identity of non-Jewish friends who had
remained in Paris and provided them with the details of their civil status.
Another method, discovered later on, consisted in using official affidavits. In
May 1944, an agent of the *Sixième*, who already bore a *synthé*, found himself
obliged to reduce his age by one year in order to avoid being taken to the STO
(*Service du travail obligatoire*, Compulsory Labor Service)[97].

Starting in February 1943 a massive effort was made to recruit young
Aryan males over the age of eighteen for work in Germany. He reported the
loss of his identity papers at a police station and then went to the justice of
the peace on rue Moncey, not far from Place du Pont, with two witnesses,
accommodating housewives whom he happened upon in the street. Based
on the declarations of these witnesses, the judge issued an official document
confirming the date of birth which they attested. The place of birth indicated was Fourmies, in the Department of Nord, a place whose mayoral
office and archives had been destroyed by a bombardment. The document,
immediately provided, permitted the young man to have duly registered
identity and ration cards issued legally. Since everything took place with
surprising ease, without the shadow of any administrative chicanery,the
enterprise clearly involved the tacit complicity of the justice of the peace and
the "witnesses," who were pleased to help someone evade the STO.[98] For after
the establishment of the STO the Vichy regime became ever more unpopu-
lar. One of the false document workshops had gathered very thorough documentation in order to produce demobilization certificates: a list of recruiting offices, mobilization centers, and military units belonging to various
places. The documentation covered sixty-seven departments.[99]

People who did not speak French or who spoke with a heavy accent
posed a delicate problem. Occasionally such a person had to make a long
train trip in order to reach a place of refuge. Now, the resistance had pro-

vided him with a French pseudo-identity, and he was taught to pretend to be a deaf-mute in order to avoid being unmasked. One false document service thought of combing the *Journal officiel* (the population register) of the 1920s and 1930s in order to select the names of non-Jewish naturalized citizens. They counterfeited these certificates of naturalization and identity cards to Aryanize Polish, Romanian, Russian, Bulgarian, and other Jews.[100] Another service managed to issue green cards for foreigners, provided with residence and work permits.

These accomplishments, as we have seen, were facilitated by countless acts of complicity, notably by municipal officials and policemen. Priests provided false baptism certificates.[101] Pastor Exbrayat of Limoges, an inventive and audacious man, taught the local leader of the *Sixième* how to use all of these techniques.[102] In Montauban and Nice, the bishopric sometimes sheltered a laboratory for the production of false papers belonging to the Jewish resistance, and the bishop himself occasionally helped the "counterfeiters."[103]

No one in French Jewish resistance circles had thought of disguising himself as a member of the Todt organization,[104] responsible for constructing the fortifications of the Atlantic wall and the Spanish border and requisitioning workers of various nationalities, including Jews. Now, the non-Jewish workers on leave or charged with a mission had access to the railroad cars reserved for the Wehrmacht, and on stopovers they received lodging and canteen coupons for the *Kommandantur*. Useless for Jews hidden in a given locality, membership in the Todt organization could, however, provide exceptional services to the resisters in rescue networks and to armed groups. This was ultimately discovered by the "Dutch group," which consisted of young Jews of German and Austrian origin who had taken refuge in the Netherlands before the war, where they had prepared themselves for a life as pioneers in Palestine in the rural Zionist groups of the HeHalutz movement. Following waves of arrests and deportations carried out in the Netherlands as in France starting in July 1942, these young people tried to pass over into Spain, whence they hoped to be able to reach Palestine. One group of them succeeded in crossing the borders to France in 1943 and made contact with the AJ, which was then organizing escape routes to Palestine via Spain.

One of these "Dutch" people, Joseph Linnewiel, had fought in a Netherlands resistance network and participated in the execution of a Gestapo agent, taking his papers, forms, and other precious documents. Linnewiel then assumed the identity of a Dutch worker for the Todt organization, a procedure that was also adopted by almost a hundred of his Jewish comrades from the Dutch group who had arrived in France and then by fighters of the AJ recruited in France. Disguised as workers in the open construction sites in the Pyrenees, they thus had easy access to the forbidden zone near the border, finally crossing over to Spain.[105] It took uncommon courage to dare to operate behind the façade of the swastika, not only risking discovery but also being the target of other resisters charged with striking down Nazis and other collaborators. The "Dutch" members of the AJ, whose German was native and who were completely unknown upon their arrival in France in the spring of 1943 were best suited to resort to this stupefying procedure. It was usable only for particular missions and finally became known to the Gestapo, which decimated the AJ in Paris in July 1944.

Several of the Jewish false paper services paid a very heavy tribute when the enemy captured agents carrying batches of cards and counterfeiting equipment, after which they would be subject to torture, deportation, or immediate execution. Jacob Weintrob, of the *Éducation physique* network, arrested at the end of September 1943 in Nice, was released after examination of his identity papers, which were, of course, false. But he was immediately seized again, upon which his capturers discovered the contents of his briefcase, which was full of counterfeit cards that he was planning to give to endangered Jews.[106] Marc Haguenau, the director of the *Sixième*, and his assistant, Édith Pulver, fell into a trap placed by Gestapo in Grenoble on February 18, 1944. Tortured atrociously, Haguenau met his death the next day after leaping out of the window of the Gestapo headquarters, while Édith Pulver was deported to Auschwitz, where she did not survive, suffering the same fate as Weintrob.[107] David Donoff, working for the *Service André*, the *Sixième*, and the OSE, was arrested in Lyons on June 27, 1944 while bearing false papers. He tried to flee and was shot down in the street.[108]

Some of the workshops attained an exceptional level of quality and productivity. In Lyons, that of Gilbert Leidervarger, an amateur engraver, provided seals for the *Sixième* and *Éducation physique* networks throughout France.[109] During 1943, the service run by T. Giniewski in Grenoble created thousands of *synthés* for the use of various groups of *Éducation physique* and the AJ. However, the workshop in Nice achieved the most astonishing performance. Pursued by the Gestapo from September 1943, it changed locations several times, slipping through the enemy's fingers at the last moment every time, despite the cumbersome equipment needed to issue large numbers of *bifs* and *synthés*. Under the direction of Maurice Cachoud-Loebenberg, this service supplied all of the Jewish resistance networks as well as the MLN (*Mouvement de libération nationale*, National Liberation Movement). Shockingly audacious, Cachoud was sent to Paris by the AJ, and there the MLN made him the head of its false papers service. Cachoud's case illustrates cooperation between various resistance networks and the exceptions sometimes made to the rule of isolation demanded by all clandestine activity.

Joseph Bass, shocked by the imprudence of these networks, preferred other sources for *synthés*. In Marseilles and Nice he used the services of a nurse of Corsican origins, Anne-Marie Quilici. For a fee, she obtained identity documents which she said had been validated by her friend, a police superintendent. Quilici also had contacts with the OSE and the *Sixième*. Arrested in Nice on September 28, 1943, Claude Gutman of the *Sixième* managed to send a message accusing Quilici of responsibility for his capture.[110] He was deported and died. Similarly two resistance operatives of the *Éducation physique* network who were captured in Nice by the Gestapo and interned in Drancy categorically accused the "nurse," in letters spirited out of the camp in October 1943.[111]

Of those who used false papers provided by the Jewish resistance, numbering several tens of thousands, almost all survived the war. As soon as it was possible, all of these survivors promptly resumed their own identities, with the most acute feeling of relief. Simply being Jewish or avoiding service with the STO—situations comparable only if one recalls that the risks were not the same—was a permanent violation of the law at that time. Anyone who was resolved not to offer himself passively as a target for the enemy immediately entered a clandestine and illegal existence, where the *bif* or *synthé* became an elementary and indispensable means of protection. Not only men and women capable of working but also thousands of old people and invalids, as well as tens of thousands of children would have had no chance of survival without these redemptive forgeries.

11

❦

The Rescue of Jewish Children

During the last six months of 1942, 1,032 Jewish children less than six years old and 2,557 between six and twelve, along with 2,464 adolescents from thirteen to seventeen, were deported from France.[1] None of them survived. Among the victims of the monstrous mass arrest of July 16 and 17 in Paris, not a single child could be saved by the Jewish organizations.[2] Despite an admittedly very limited number of precedents, no one had believed that women and children would be deported until then.

Children by the Thousands in the Deportation Trains

At first the Germans planned to place the children under sixteen of arrested Jews in charge of the UGIF (*Union générale des Juifs de France*, the General Union of French Jews).[3] Let us recall that they counted on the delivery of 22,000 Jews, but that nearly 10,000 of them, warned in time thanks to leaks from patriotic police officials or those who obeyed the dictates of their humanitarian conscience,[4] had fled their homes. Nevertheless, a number of women, children, and the families of prisoners of war did not believe themselves targeted and had taken no precaution, as we have already mentioned.[5]

At first the Germans had planned to create convoys of Jewish deportees of both sexes, aged from sixteen to fifty. As for the youngsters, Hitlerian racism, based on a biological doctrine, viewed the Jews as a danger, no matter what their age. Thus they had no intention of sparing the children. Their turn would come later. For the extermination program was to be applied in several stages. Especially in France, the Germans agreed at first to grant certain exemptions for French Jews and military veterans with exceptional service records, in response to the demand of the Vichy authorities. Their policy consisted in manipulating the French government in hope of gaining its active cooperation in the implementation of the extermination plan. The arrests, the guarding of the detention camps, and the escorting of the deportation trains to the border were all carried out by the French police and gendarmerie. This permitted the Germans to make considerable savings in manpower, which was in short supply. By organizing convoys of deportees without children under sixteen they sought to stave off the indignation and anger of public opinion and gave the Vichy government the impression that the children would benefit from exemptions.

However, the despicable and unexpected reaction of the head of the Vichy government, Pierre Laval, soon led the Germans to change the composition of the convoys of deportees and to include thousands of children of all ages. In preparing for the monstrous mass arrests, Laval agreed to make the French police responsible for them, but he demanded the exclusion of French Jews from the lists. In exchange he offered the delivery of 10,000 foreign Jews from the southern zone, explicitly stipulating that, for the latter, children under sixteen would be deported at the same time as their family. In a telex addressed to Berlin on July 6, Dannecker reported that "President Laval proposed that, during the evacuation of Jewish families from the unoccupied zone, children under sixteen should also be sent." On July 10, in the Council of Ministers in Vichy, Laval presented the following version: "With a humanitarian intention, the Head of the Government has obtained—contrary to the first German proposals—that children, including those under sixteen, will be authorized to accompany their parents."

For its part, the cGQJ (*Commissariat général aux Questions juives*, General Commission for Jewish Questions) took an inventory of places available for lodging children in the charity projects of the UGIF. There were only 300. The French officials in Paris needed no further invitation to demand that Laval's deportation policy for the southern zone should also apply to the Jewish children of the northern zone. Thus on July 8, 1942, when the Franco-German commission presided over by the head of the cGQJ, Darquier de Pellepoix, compiled the lists of people to be arrested, it included

28,000 Jews from the ages of two to sixty (fifty-five for women). The Nazi officers very promptly received the authorization they requested from Berlin to deport children under sixteen. Between August 14 and September 9, twelve convoys left Drancy, deporting approximately 5,000 Jewish children arrested in both zones and destined for the gas chambers.[6]

Marrus and Paxton correctly note that "far from attempting to save the children of the foreign Jews whom they delivered to the Germans, French authorities offered them, too, for deportation." If Vichy had merely accepted the initial Nazi plan, which postponed the deportation of children, in the southern zone, the Jewish rescue organizations, with the help of French and foreign humanitarian groups, would clearly have been able to assume all responsibility for looking after and rescuing the children whom the Germans had not yet demanded, and whom Vichy had the power and duty not to deliver to them.

Obviously it is more hazardous to imagine what would have happened in Paris if the lists of people to be arrested had been drawn up in conformity with the initial Nazi plan. Rather than being crammed into the Vel' d'hiv', more than 4,000 children would certainly have been left free and placed in the hands of the UGIF, despite the failure of the Jewish organizations of the northern zone to prepare for assuming a task of such size. The technical equipment, the financial means, and the human resources were lacking. This is true of the groups affiliated with the UGIF as well as those of Rue Amelot, which had protected its autonomy, and of Solidarité, the clandestine organization of the Jewish Communists. The improvised initiatives of Jewish charities and spontaneous humanitarian gestures of the Parisian population would certainly have contributed to addressing the most urgent needs of some of the children. Further, many dramatic and shattering experiences could not have been avoided. Nevertheless, nothing that might have happened to the children could have equaled the major sufferings endured following their concentration in the Vélodrome d'hiver, nor, even more so, the absolutely irreparable event of the deportation and massive massacre.

The delay originally planned by the Nazis in the sending of the Jewish children of France to Auschwitz opened up possibilities for rescue. The attitude of Laval and French officials led the Germans to abandon this delay. None of the children captured during the Spring Wind operation was saved by the Resistance.

What did happen to the children and adolescents who escaped arrest? For there were some.[7] They owed their escape to their own presence of mind or to that of their parents, or sometimes to sympathetic policemen, who responded to the parents' pleas, or to neighbors or concierges who spontaneously offered to look after the children. Occasionally children were fortu-itously absent from home when the police came to arrest them. We have no numerical data regarding the number of Jewish children who escaped arrest during the two dreadful days of Spring Wind and who never saw their par-ents again. Service Five (Children) of the UGIF distributed a circular among the staff of its activities on July 18, 1942: "We are creating a central file of all the Jewish children whose parents have been arrested in the past few days, . . . since some children have been lost."[8] There are no traces of such a file, if it ever existed. But the centers of the UGIF on Rue Lamarck, Rue Claude-Bernard, and Rue Guy-Patin took in about 400 children abandoned during the days following July 16 and 17.[9]

In fact, thousands did manage to escape arrest. Odette Melszpajz, who was then seven years old, lived in Paris on rue d'Angoulême with her mother. Her father was a prisoner of war in a *stalag* in Germany. The concierge of the building hid the little girl and her mother in his lodge before the arrival of the police on July 16, 1942. Having avoided arrest and after someone had removed the yellow star that was sewn to her dress, Odette was taken to a Parisian railroad station that very day, it is thought. Together with a group of four Jewish children, she was sent to the Vendée region, to Chavagnes-en-Paillers (near La Roche-sur-Yon) and placed in a foster family connected with the local Resistance. She was with the village blacksmith. Hardly had they arrived before the children were instructed by the mistress of the house how to make the sign of the cross and recite a short prayer. She categorically forbade them to tell anyone that they were Jewish and explained how they could pass for Catholic children from Paris.[10] To this day Odette does not know who organized the rescue. Perhaps it was one of the Jewish charities which, from the start of Operation Spring Wind, tried to come to the assistance of those who managed to avoid arrest.

The Clandestine Rescue of Children in the Northern Zone

Taken totally by surprise by the monstrous mass arrests in Paris, the Jewish organizations had hardly participated in the efforts made to warn the for-eign Jews targeted by the police. J. Adler claims that Solidarité was the only movement informed about the leaks from the Prefecture of Police during the first days of July 1942, thanks to the clandestine Communist Party. By July 9, knowing of certain preparations made by the CGQJ, the UGIF suppos-edly possessed "all the elements needed to predict the imminence of massive detention and deportation measures."[11] It should be recalled that until July

13 the UGIF did not inform the leadership of Rue Amelot or prepare medical teams or identity cards for children separated from their parents.
Solidarité militants did their best to sound the warning, without knowing
exactly who was targeted. They distributed a flier in Yiddish: "Do not wait
passively in your apartments. . . . If they come to arrest you, resist the police
by every means, . . . call for help, fight, do everything possible to escape."[12]

Summoned by Fernand Musnik, a member of the UGIF council and the
head of the underground EIF (*Éclaireurs israélites de France*, the Jewish
scouts) in the northern zone, teams of young scout leaders operated in
headquarters starting from July 15 in the centers in rue Claude-Bernard and
rue Lamarck. Intended to receive children arrested with their parents and
then released, these teams remained idle, since no child was released.[13] Not
until some wandering children were assembled, no one knows just how,
could the young EIF leaders, most of them high school students on vacation,
set to work.

Kidnapping and Camouflage

Jewish assistance and rescue organizations in the northern zone suddenly
found that the task of caring for children was now their major preoccupation. It was to remain so until the end of the occupation. By the hundreds,
children were separated from their deported parents or obliged to disguise
themselves under conditions that made separation a necessity. In the
administrative jargon of the time they were called "lost" or "abandoned children," and some of these unfortunates were labeled with terms borrowed
from customs officials: "blocked" children and "free" children.[14]

A child liberated from Drancy was a blocked child, recorded on a special
police register and at risk of being returned to Drancy at any time. In the
UGIF centers blocked and free children lived together. The latter were
entrusted by their parents, who had lost all possibility of looking after them.

After September 1942, Service Fourteen of the UGIF, in charge of liaison
with the occupation authorities, obtained the release of detainees in Drancy.
The pace of deportations was then relatively slow. While thirty-eight convoys had been sent to the East from June to September 1942, there were only
four during the period from October 1942 to January 1943.[15] The population of the camp grew because of the new arrests in Paris and the transfer of
Jews interned in the camps located in the provinces of both zones. Service
Fourteen augmented its activities and submitted 4,487 demands for release
between June and December 1942. It obtained 817, including 192 children

less than sixteen years old. The parents of some of these children were at liberty or in the southern zone, or one of them had been deported. Some of the children had been arrested for not wearing the yellow star.[16] The rules defining detainees as deportable were constantly revised, giving rise to dramatic and inescapable situations. Thus during the month of October 1942, parents with a child present in the camp were classified as "nondeportable." A UGIF note mentions that these parents did not want to "run the risk of being deported without their children. Now, once the children are released, the parents become deportable."[17]

In every instance, the children released from Drancy were placed with Service Five of the UGIF, directed by Juliette Stern, a member of the council, and submitted to the rules governing blocked children. Service Five also was responsible for a certain number of children "lost" during the monstrous mass arrests of July 16 and 17, 1942, as well as children given up by their harried parents, who were obliged to hide. These cases were not recorded in the special police register of blocked children. At the end of 1942 the number of wards of the UGIF reached 1,500. Stern had only 400 places among seven centers at her disposal, which she did not augment, preferring to place 1,080 children with non-Jewish families or institutions.[18] Contrary to Adler's conclusion, nothing indicates that the UGIF preferred to keep children in order to maintain them within a Jewish milieu and protect them from the risk of conversion when they were placed with a Christian institution or family.[19]

The members of the council of the UGIF responsible for the childhood and youth services were certainly known for their connections with the Consistory or for their activities in Zionist organizations. But they were no less active in the underground rescue networks, all of which placed their charges, whom they first took care to "Aryanize," with non-Jews. Juliette Stern ran the women's team of WIZO (Womens' International Zionist Organization), Professor Weill-Hallé was active in the ET (*Entraide temporaire*, Temporary Mutual Assistance) network, and Fernard Musnik cooperated closely with the Sixth Department (EIF) and with *Éducation physique* (of the MJS, *Mouvement de jeunesse sioniste*, the Zionist Youth Movement) until his arrest and deportation in September 1943. Their undeniable concern for preserving the Jewish identity of these children cannot be questioned. Moreover, they took care not to implicate the UGIF openly in illegal action, for fear of compromising it in the eyes of the CGQJ and the Nazi services. The blocked children were maintained in centers supervised by the police, with the exception of a certain number of those who were kidnapped by the Jewish resistance, supposedly acting unbeknownst to the UGIF.

Because of error or to a lack of prudence, free children also lived in these centers and were captured by the Gestapo on July 22, 1944.

Nevertheless, the leaders of the UGIF, as well as several of their co-workers, actively and efficaciously participated in the secret placement of children. They used members of the OSE (*Oeuvre de secours aux enfants*, Children's Rescue Network) personnel for this purpose, operating under the cover of their UGIF authorization card. A certain degree of cooperation was also established with the clandestine organizations, especially rue Amelot, the *Sixième*, and *Éducation physique* taking charge of the adolescents, and finally ET (*Entraide temporaire*, Temporary Mutual Assistance).

Analysis of the monthly financial reports of Rue Amelot shows that in July 1942 the committee spent a sum for the placement of children corresponding to the allowance for fifty-eight children. In January 1943, the committee paid 480 allowances.[20] A file containing 905 cards has been preserved, as well as another one, in miniature format, where the name and address of the foster family are replaced by a code number.[21] The latter is informative regarding the methods of underground operation, while the former contains the reports and observations of the inspectors, a true mine of information on the underground existence of these children in various circumstances. This is raw material for a study which remains to be carried out.

Everyone who worked to hide Jewish children was aware of the danger represented by lists, files, and correspondence regarding their work. They tried to disguise anything that could inform the enemy about the existence and location of these children. The most varied methods were improvised: the dispersion and isolation of the documents, the creation of coded files, the deposit of information allowing the decoding of the files with people passively linked to the Resistance and careful not to expose themselves to any risk. It was necessary to supply major necessities: to retain contact with the children so as to assure their welfare and to pay the monthly allowance to the foster parents, and to be capable, the day the occupation was over, of returning each child to its family and identity. If the enemy got its hand on these documents, the children and the families or institutions sheltering them would be exposed to immediate danger. In the best case, even if the enemy did not exploit the documents, their capture meant the risk of definitively losing track of some children. With the exception of one network which had succeeded in communicating a copy of its lists to the International Red Cross in Geneva, no network was protected against this risk. Fortunately the enemy was unable to put its hand upon any information regarding the camouflage of children. Most of the documents have nevertheless disappeared during the years since the war. The archives of Rue Amelot, today conserved by the YIVO Institute in New York, are the sole exception.

It is no longer possible to locate the lists, registers, and files of the OSE, WIZO, the *Sixième*, and *Éducation physique*. The 1,080 children and adolescents whom J. Stern placed with foster parents or institutions during the second half of 1942 were most likely taken in charge by these organizations, whose leaders retained contact with the UGIF. The part played by each of them can no longer be determined. J. Stern reported after the war that his family service for the placement of children was run by a team of WIZO women who hid their file with a private person. It had a monthly budget provided by the AJDC of 500,000 francs as well as donations and the "black fund" of the UGIF. It cooperated with secular and religious charities in Laon, Soissons, Amiens, Compiègne, Le Mans, and Auxerre. A list of eighty-six foster mothers living in the Seine-et-Oise Department has been preserved.[22]

As another humanitarian project, ET, devoted most of its efforts after the summer of 1942 to the rescue of Jewish children. A private initiative, entirely clandestine and involving people of different religions, ET was formed in 1941 in the shadow of a private charity operating openly, the SSAE (*Service social d'aide aux émigrants*, Social Service for Assistance to Emigrants). This organization was charged with providing assistance for the families of those conscripted in the Groups of Foreign Workers. Moved by the fate of victims of repression who did not fall into categories covered by its service, such as the families of men who had been shot to death and of Jews deprived of their work, its president, Mme. Lucie Chevalley, created the ET to come to their aid, unbeknownst to the authorities. She obtained the cooperation of Catholic, Protestant, and Jewish activist women. Some of these possessing great means agreed to provide very substantial subsidies and obtained considerable assistance from banks and large companies. An active member of the ET group, Denise Milhaud was taken into the service of the UGIF by Professor Weill-Hallé, a member of the council, as the chief of social services for the children's centers and dispensaries. Similarly her husband, Dr. Fred Milhaud, was included among the personnel of the UGIF as the physician for the children's centers. For two years beginning in July 1942, ET participated in the rescue of 500 children removed from the charge of the UGIF with the support of at least one of the members of its council, Weill-Hallé.[23]

The Jewish children's rescue networks benefitted from the secret support of publicly known charitable and social organizations, both secular and religious: the French Red Cross, *Secours national* (National Relief), Notre-Dame of Zion, the social services of *Habitations à bon marché* (HBM,

Inexpensive Housing), the Hospital of Créteil, the Hospital of Quinze-Vingts, the charity works of La Clairière of the Protestant church of the Oratoire du Louvre, the SSAE, public and private boarding schools, and many others which have been unjustly forgotten.[24] ET is unique in that it was created for the purpose of alleviating the suffering of Jewish immigrants and then that of saving Jewish children from deportation. It operated in shadow, without any legal cover, maintaining its budget with private donations, privy to dealings at the heart of the UGIF and working with its complicity.

Like the Jewish networks, the ET invented various artifices to camouflage its lists of children and of foster families and institutions. It used the 1921 account book of an inactive charity, *Sauvetage de l'enfance* (Rescue of Childhood), registering the contributions received, the vital statistics of the wards and their parents, and the names and addresses of the placements in the vacant pages. The dates of birth and of taking the children in charge were moved back by twenty years. The indication "in Biarritz" meant that the parents were in Drancy, "in Bayonne," that they were deported. Further, a file maintained in the Stella Hotel on rue Monsieur-le-Prince recorded the false identity of the children and the pseudonym of the person from the ET who was attending them. The latter file has disappeared.[25] The ET suffered no losses.

At the liberation, the Paris WIZO group had 1,250 children in its charge, placed with peasants, school teachers, truck drivers, and in religious boarding schools. In constant contact with J. Stern, this group had adopted the methods of supervision and surveillance of placements developed by Mme. Getting, the chief of social assistance in the Service Five of the UGIF. Her professional reputation won her the secret but effective support of several public social services. She was arrested by the Gestapo at the offices of the Service Five on rue de la Bienfaisance on July 30, 1943 at the same time as the personnel of the service. They were all deported, and not one survived. But nothing was seized in the offices, which were left to the discretion of the UGIF.

It is less easy to determine the role played by Solidarité in the rescue of children. A youth commission created after the mass arrest of the Vel' d'hiv. Solidarité distributed pamphlets in French calling upon "French wives and mothers" to take in "a persecuted Jewish child." It appealed to the non-Jewish activists of the *Mouvement national contre le racisme* (MNCR, the National Movement Against Racism), whose clandestine establishment it had promoted. It created a workshop to produce false documents, knows as "the Prefecture," for the children it placed in foster families. Part of this work was accomplished in cooperation with the young people of Rue Amelot.[26] Have records been preserved? If so, they are in the archives of the *Institut des études marxistes* (the Institute of Marxist Studies) in Paris, to which we were not granted access. Nevertheless, being a political organization, Solidarité was only marginally oriented toward assistance and rescue. During the summer of 1942 its leaders made the decision to intensify the armed struggle.[27]

It seems that the networks of the *Sixième* and *Éducation physique* in Paris mainly attempted to kidnap the blocked children, sheltered in UGIF centers. These operations were sometimes carried out with the discreet connivance of the woman responsible for the Service Five of the UGIF, Juliette Stern. The man who ran these networks in Paris, Albert Akerberg, met her with this aim once a week during the spring of 1944. "We operated in a simple way: during a visit to the dentist, for example, one or two children were taken away and sheltered in the country."[28]

In other cases wards were removed from the centers unbeknownst to the UGIF. The largest instance took place on Sunday, February 12, 1943. An employee of the center in rue Lamarck had given Solidarité a list of children about to be arrested. On February 12, forty women reported to rue Lamarck as volunteers to assist on the wards' weekly trip. Sixty-three children were taken to the headquarters of the Protestant charity, La Clairière, in rue Greneta, which was run by Pastor Vergara of the Protestant Church of the Oratoire du Louvre. After two or three days of improvised lodging, each of the children, duly "Aryanized," found shelter with a foster family or institution. Suzanne Spaak, alerted through the MNCR, was the soul of the entire operation. She sheltered several children in her home in Choisel while waiting for their final placement. She obtained the active participation of activists from the ET, which took charge of at least some of the children.[29]

The various networks seeking to rescue children all knew of each other. Each had secret relations with the UGIF, ranging from trust to reserve to antagonism. They avoided cooperating intimately, for reasons of security. Solidarité mistrusted Rue Amelot, which persisted in using the UGIF to screen its medical and social action. Nevertheless, D. Rapoport covered part of Solidarité's expenses for placing the children.[30] When Suzanne Spaak alerted the ET, D. Milhaud still knew nothing about the community of La Clairière: "I hesitated because I was not even sure it was Mme. Spaak."[31] Ties also were formed between the networks in the northern and southern zones.[32] The head of the *Sixième* in the southern zone, Marc Haguenau, chanced to meet Milhaud in Paris.[33] Caught entirely unprepared by the July mass arrest, the Jewish charities took in hundreds of lost children. The families of immigrant Jews, having escaped arrest, were hunted down. Unable to look after their children, they turned to the Jewish dispensaries and welfare offices. The first reception centers were improvised in the offices of charities or schools of the Jewish community on rue Lamarck, rue Guy-Patin, and rue Claude-Bernard. The clandestine EIF movement called upon its young male and female high school students, who were on vacation, to form teams of counselors and helpers. Two directors of the movement, Emmanuel Lefschetz and Georges Lewitz, immediately recruited other young men and women and trained them hastily so they could take the place of the EIF leaders after the start of the school year.[34]

The population of the centers kept changing because of the sound policy of placement practiced by the Jewish charities, concerned both by the shortage of room in their centers and by the desire to provide better security for their wards. After October 1942, the UGIF began to accept blocked children in their centers. No less than other children who had never been arrested or detained, they were psychologically shaken by their brutal separation from their parents and by uncertainty regarding their fate, and they were also ravaged by fear of being sent back to Drancy. The dreary look of the shelters, the absence of equipment to provide a minimum of hygiene and comfort, and the inexperience of the personnel deprived these children of any feeling of security, be it ever so ephemeral. In February 1943, arrests by the police were followed by an "abduction" by the Jewish Resistance.[35] In May of the same year, the UGIF took in other children released from detention in Drancy.[36] The dormitory and vocational school on rue des Rosiers were run by Georges and Ida Lewitz, veterans of Ha Shomer Ha Za'ir Zionist youth movement and clandestine EIF activists. Old-fashioned and poorly equipped, the institution consisted of occupational training facilities administered by ORT (a Jewish vocational training organization founded in Czarist Russia as *Obshchestvo Rasprostraneniya Truda*, Society for Manual Work). It took in a highly diverse group of adolescents. The behavior of some of the particularly deprived wards created an air of uncertainty within and around the establishment. The Lewitzes and several of their wards were deported in 1944.

In October 1942 when he was arrested in Angoulême with his parents, his two brothers, and his sister along with many other immigrant Jews, Robert Franck was fourteen years old. Born in France and possessing French nationality, he was the only one in his family to be released, along with ten other children in the same situation. A priest received the small group in a charity that he ran. Seeing that preparations for conversion to the church were being made, Robert wrote to Rabbi Elie Bloch in Poitiers, whose address had been given to him by his father. A few days later the ten children were placed with families not far from Poitiers. But six months afterward, following the arrest and deportation of Bloch,[37] they were all detained in the camp on the Limoges highway in Poitiers and then sent to Paris. Robert found himself in the center on rue Lamarck, and two weeks later he was placed in the vocational school on rue des Rosiers. The establishment included ten boys from thirteen to fifteen years of age and about fifty young people from sixteen to twenty-one years old. He remembers the efforts of the couple directing the institution to create an atmosphere of community, compromised by the cold, by the shortage of food, and mainly by the permanent specter of the threat of deportation. In April 1944, Robert received a mysterious letter, written in more or less these terms: "I am a friend of your parents. Please come on such and such a date, at such and such an hour, to this address in rue Alexandre-Dumas. Don't tell anyone about this letter." The young boy arrived promptly at the meeting and never returned to the vocational school. Metamorphosed into Robert François, he was placed in a non-Jewish milieu by the ET. He is the only survivor of his family.[38]

Rescue in the Southern Zone

Numerically, the dimensions of the tragedy were more limited in the southern zone. One reason for this is, paradoxically, the infinitely more cruel fate of the children there from 1940 to 1942, before the deportations, than in the northern zone at the same time. In the north, arrests and detention had spared women and children, while whole families had been crammed into the camps of the southern zone under atrocious conditions.

This circumstances particularly sensitized the Jewish assistance organizations and their associates in the Nîmes Committee to the plight of Jewish children. Teams of rescue workers living in the camps had legally obtained the release of almost all the children under sixteen, including an appreciable number of older adolescents, thanks to various tricks and deceptions.[39] Moreover, contacts with the government on every level of the hierarchy allowed them to identify and locate resisters or sympathetic and courageous officials in the bureaucratic machinery, constituting a true information network. Finally, the Jewish assistance organizations had developed a system of children's houses as well as rural and artisanal groups with logistic and educational experience. They were capable of receiving children and adolescents in satisfactory conditions.

The geography of the southern zone also offered possibilities for rescue unavailable in the northern zone. The common borders with two neutral countries, Switzerland and Spain, allowed the clandestine escape of children. However, the occupation of the southern zone on November 11, 1942, made these operations more dangerous, except in the sector of the Swiss border controlled by Italian troops until September 8, 1943.

The transfer of Jewish detainees to Drancy in preparation for deportation to the East began in the camps of Rivesaltes, Gurs, Agde, Noé, Récébédou, Le Vernet, and Les Milles on August 2, 1942. The French police made massive arrests of foreign Jews in the southern zone from August 26 to 31.

The Preventive Warning

We have seen that the secrecy surrounding the plan to arrest and deport foreign Jews in the southern zone was penetrated by the leaders of Jewish organizations earlier and more completely than it had been in Paris. However, these charity organizations were clearly incapable of paralyzing the impressive logistic preparations made by the police to seize 10,000 Jews and deliver them to the Nazis.

Nevertheless, all the reactions known to us show that the leaders of the organizations did not succumb to resignation or passivity. The appeals to high places and calls for assistance lodged with non-Jewish and foreign humanitarian groups as well as with the bishopric, and the warnings issued to threatened families and institutions, along with the actions of the chaplains in the camps, and Jewish rescuers serving as delegates in the screening commissions all express the spirit of resistance that prevailed before the danger. The attitude of Lambert, the head of UGIF-South, and of the affiliated bodies, in the summer of 1942 also dictated the defense of Jewish interests rather than submission to the power to which the organization was subject.[40]

The experience hitherto acquired in the field of saving children detained in the camps inspired hope that determined and well-coordinated action could preserve the children from the atrocious fate Laval had prepared for them. After succeeding in preventing the arrest of most of the wards of their affiliates, it remained to try to prevent the departure of those who were detained along with their captured parents. Their safety now depended upon the tenacious struggle waged against the police by the screening commissions.

Screening the Detainees of the Camps

The screening commissions were fighting an unequal battle but nevertheless managed to save many of the children. A dispatch of the Directorate of the Vichy police dated August 4 enumerated eleven categories of exemption, sparing "unaccompanied children less than eighteen years old" from deportation. It also stipulated that "parents with children younger than eighteen may remain in the free zone if they wish." But a telegram dated August 18 reduced the categories of exemption to six. Unaccompanied children became deportable. And the telegram stated: "Option of leaving children under eighteen in the free zone suppressed."[41] The contents of the dispatch dated August 4 was not brought to the attention of the various services in Vichy, including those of the SSE (*Service social des étrangers*, the Social Service for Foreigners), before that date. The Prefect of the Department of Tarn complained in his report on the "police operations of August 26 concerning foreign Jews" that "the circles concerned had, as everywhere, through a network of informers and through numerous indiscretions, gained knowledge of the arrangements and the very date of the measures prescribed by the Head of the Government even before official circles."[42]

The screening commissions had already used their information about the camps and tried, not without some success, to save people belonging to the exempted categories, especially children, from deportation. The main concern of the police officials was to deliver the required number of deportees. They composed lists without much regard to the details of the instructions they had received. Under the pretext of conforming to the instructions about the scheduled departure of the convoys, the police, who were annoyed themselves, sent away deportees even before the screening commission could accomplish its mission. And when an inspector of the commissioner responsible for the operation honored a request submitted by the screening commission, these men immediately designated other detainees to replace those exempted. This procedure transformed the rescuers into suppliers for the convoys: "The leaders of the Jewish organizations were placed in a moral dilemma, for they found themselves causing the deportation of one or another category of foreigners equal in number to the exemptions obtained by them for certain categories of refugees."[43] Following consultations it was decided to try above all to prevent the deportation of those possessing emigration visas and of children whose parents agreed to part with them.[44] That is, they concentrated on the only people whom they thought it was possible to have released from detention, and who could definitively be rescued from deportation. In effect this also applied to the children.

While there were almost no more children in the detention camps in July 1942 thanks to the work of the Jewish organizations, this was not the case regarding the camp in Les Milles and its annex, the Hotel Bompart in Marseilles, which was reserved for families who were scheduled for emigration. The cancellation of exit visas in effect transformed these into detention camps. Moreover, the police were ordered to arrest adolescents over sixteen living in shelters or artisanal and rural centers, so as to "regroup" them with their parents in the camps. Establishments of the MJS and the EIF managed to shelter all the adolescents and young adults targeted by the arrests. In early August, the directors of the center in Moissac sent all of its wards, almost 200 young people, on a camping trip near Bourganeuf, in the Department of Creuse. When the police arrived at the center, they found only the directors. The children returned on August 27, except for a group of fourteen adolescents whose names appeared on the police list. Under the cover of a mobile scout camp, they wandered in the Department of Corrèze for several weeks, until their leader, Léon Rosen, arranged a secret hiding place for every one of them, with the help of the bishopric of Tulle.[45] Similar precautions were taken by young people in Beaulieu, Lautrec, Fretteserpes, Le Pusocq, Charry, Blémont, and Taluyers.[46] This was not the case in certain shelters of the OSE in the Departments of Creuse and Haute-Vienne. In Rivesaltes and Gurs, the guards asked the parents for the address of their children placed in various institutions. The resident teams tried hard to persuade the detainees not to reveal the addresses. This was a difficult task for two reasons: they could not trust everyone; and, mainly, the authorities circulated the official explanation of a supposed reassembly of families in order to relocate them in a Jewish population zone in the East. For his part, Dr. Joseph Weill had informed Andrée Salomon, the head of the resident teams, about the massive massacres of deported Jews.[47] The gendarmes seized seventeen adolescents aged sixteen and over from the OSE shelters, though most of those who were sought managed to flee and find shelter, thanks to the presence of mind of the staff.[48] Moreover, the families of foreign workers located in SSE centers were gathered in Rivesaltes. Thus many children were once again detained in this camp, for the purpose of imminent deportation.

While extant statistics are fragmentary, it appears that most of the children were saved, although several dozen were indeed deported. A convoy that left Rivesaltes on August 20, 1942, contained eighty-two children from two to eighteen years old. The convoys of deportees from Drancy during September included children from Rivesaltes, Gurs, and Les Milles.[49] In the Rivesaltes camp, the deportable people were concentrated in Section K. Andrée Salomon, whose ardent determination and tranquil assurance impressed everyone, managed to have the children and young people lodged in a separate block, strictly guarded but well taken care of by volunteers from OSE, the Quakers, and the YMCA.

At this time the screening commission, electrified by Salomon's invincible energy and determination, harried the men responsible for the deportation lists: "She schooled almost all the officials of the Prefecture of Perpignan to become her accomplices."[50] Sometimes appealing to the rules in force before the deportations, sometimes to the categories of exemptions, the commission ultimately obtained the release of children under sixteen whose parents agreed to be separated from them. Before then the rescuers had used subterfuge and bribery to permit children to escape. One day, May Elms, sent by the Quakers, made several trips between Rivesaltes and Perpignan to escort about thirty children away from the camp. Twenty-five children were entrusted to a supposed delegate of the Swiss Red Cross.[51] Salomon had located "guards who knew they could make money by letting children escape."[52] Young girls over sixteen were disguised as nurses and provided with false exit passes. In the confusion that reigned, escape was relatively easy for young people (or adults) who knew French and were endowed with presence of mind.[53] Nevertheless, "each fugitive is immediately replaced, and the blackmail of the feeling of responsibility and solidarity prevents many men from fleeing."[54] Approximately six hundred children and adolescents were removed from the Rivesaltes camp in August and September 1942.

In the camp of Les Milles, Lambert, the general director of UGIF-South, and Spanien of HICEM (a Jewish overseas emigration association) took part in the screening commission:

> We work like galley-slaves, going through a thousand cards about individuals threatened with deportation. . . . We will save the children from two to fifteen. . . . A shattering spectacle. Buses taking seventy children away from parents who are going to leave this evening. . . . The fathers and mothers must be restrained when the buses leave the courtyard. What cries and what tears, what gestures of poor fathers who caress the face of a son or daughter before the final deportation, to retain the impression on the tips of their fingers! Mothers scream in despair, and no one can keep back his tears. . . . I cannot be present at each departure from the camp, and I hide to weep.[55]

But several days later, those exempted the day before were deported in their turn:

> The policemen are annoyed, and the quota is not reached. . . . Children are brought to the train without milk. Scenes of

despair multiply. I am ashamed of my powerlessness. . . . The people whom I saved from the first two departures are taken again this time without any examination.[56]

A social worker from the OSE saved a one year old child in her basket.[57] This incident took place on the night of September 1 and 2, after Vichy canceled the exemptions for children and while the camp at Les Milles served as the assembly point for the foreign Jews arrested on August 26 in Marseilles and the region. Brutal intervention by the police commissioner of the Bouches-du-Rhône Department, undid the work of the screening commission in violation of the regulations.

The Vénissieux Affair

Other departments were more fortunate. In Rhône, the approximately 1,200 unfortunates arrested on August 26 were gathered in an unused barracks in Vénissieux. Notable among the members of the screening committee were Joseph Weill and Charles Lederman of the OSE, Georges Garel, Lederman's brother-in-law and a newcomer to assistance work, Claude Gutman of the EIF, Father Glasberg of AC (*Amitié chrétienne*, Christian Friendship), Gilbert Lesage, the head of the SSE, a delegate of the SSAE, etc. After three days of determined effort, 108 children and adolescents and about 500 adults were exempted and released or permitted to escape. The determination of Lesage and Glasberg, veritable "hurricanes,"[58] overcame the authority of Police Superintendent Cussonac, who actually broke down and departed the second night.[59] Glasberg had the use of a black Citroën with yellow wheels, "a duplicate of the Prefect's car," which took Jews out of the barracks several times. Instead of inspecting the car, the sentinels saluted.[60] "We had to ask the parents who could not be saved to part with their children, promising not to baptize them. It was dreadful."[61] The rescuers placed baggage tags around the children's necks with their names and ages, dictated by their parents, not without falsifying the age of those over sixteen.[62]

On Saturday morning, August 29, under the supervision of Claude Gutman, buses brought 108 children to the EIF headquarters in La Croix-Rousse. Students and young Jewish scout leaders were hastily assembled and worked feverishly to put together what one would hesitate to call a reception. Less than forty-eight hours later, the children were all dispersed, some through OSE, others under through AC. The oldest boys, approximately twenty, left on a ten day camping trip in the Haute-Loire

Department, during which time a more stable placement was found for each of them.

But on Sunday, August 30, the Regional Prefect, Angeli, turned successively to OSE, AC, and finally to Cardinal Gerlier to demand the delivery of the children. The convoy containing the parents had been stopped at the demarcation line, and the police had received the order to include the children. Gerlier summoned Fathers Chaillet and Braun, Father Glasberg, and Jean-Marie Soutou, the leaders of AC, but he could not convince them to provide him with the addresses of the children's places of refuge. In the end, the Cardinal covered the action of the AC people. When the police arrived at the EIF center on the Mount of the Carmelites in Croix-Rousse, they found it empty and were scolded by the neighbors.[63]

Defeated, Angeli wrote to his ministry on September 3: "Jewish children were spirited away and placed in safety by *Amitié chrétienne*, thus, under the pretext of moral obligation, thwarting the will of the government." He announced that, by way of sanctions, he had placed Father Chaillet in a residence under police supervision. The number of deportees "only" reached 545, but, "if 100,000 had left, the noise around their departure could not have been greater."[64]

The Prefect of Lyons was not the only one overcome by indignation. For the opposite reason, other protagonists in the drama of Vénissieux retained a traumatic memory of it. This was notably the case of Garel.[65] While the buses were on their way toward La Croix-Rousse, on August 29, Joseph Weill took Garel to a hotel near the Perrache railway station. The two men had never met before Vénissieux. The physician and counselor of OSE begged his companion, an engineer in the private sector, a stranger to Jewish charities until that time, to promote a clandestine organization to receive Jewish children in non-Jewish institutions and private homes.[66]

During the following week, Lederman and Garel were received in Toulouse by the Archbishop, Msgr. Saliège, and they recounted the drama of Vénissieux to him. The prelate immediately sent them to his coadjutor, Msgr. Courrèges, and to Mlle. Thèbes, the director of the Sainte-Germaine charity. Within a few days, twenty-four wards of OSE, duly "Aryanized," were placed with families under the protection of that charity.[67] The Garel network was born.

Thus the Vénissieux affair was the origin of the first entirely clandestine network for the rescue of children in the southern zone. The men and women who had operated in Vénissieux held administrative posts, either in the community or privately, and were well known to the authorities. In response to the unprecedented situation, they had deliberately used their status to commit multiple infractions of the governmental rules in order to obey their humanitarian vocation. They were sometimes helped by incidents attributable to the disorder and torpor of the bureaucracy. Thus the instructions in the telegram from Vichy of August 18, revoking the exemptions in favor of children, were not communicated to Vénissieux until August 28. The police superintendent had already left. The message was intercepted—through good fortune or presence of mind?—by Glasberg, who stuffed it into the pocket of his cassock. The screening commission thus operated according to the terms of a circular written by the chief of service of the SSE, Lesage, who was also present in Vénissieux. This circular specifically demands conformity with governmental instructions, including the telegram no. 12,519 of August 18, 1942, and it states that "The Directorate of the Police of the Territory and of Foreigners, Ninth Bureau . . . has willingly given its accord."[68] Now a simple comparison between the texts of the government[69] and that of Lesage shows singular differences. The SSE circular, for example, exempts children under sixteen. The screening commissions used this text very effectively in Mâcon, Clermont-Ferrand, Limoges, and Montluçon, saving children and other exempted people.

An inquiry was opened by the judiciary police against Lesage and the SSE on August 24, because of leaks enabling Jews targeted by the mass arrests to disappear from their homes in time. Later the inquest was extended to include the complaints of police superintendents regarding the interference of SSE representatives while they were applying the "measures for assembling" foreign Jews. On October 5, 1942, Chief Commissioner Mortier made a deposition of fourteen pages, including numerous documents and appendixes. Through either indifference or complicity, this report, in which precise and irrefutable information abounds, neglects to compare the Lesage circular with the government instructions! In conclusion it affirms that the SSE was not "the main source of indiscretions, and it was not possible to establish which service was guilty of the leaks." Mortier notes an "absence of administrative maturity" in the service and blithely recommends advising his agents to "redouble their prudence." This policeman notes, not without some humor, the incompatibility between the human level, on the one hand, and the administrative level, on the other. He recommends maintaining the SSE, noting its "useful work on the social and humanitarian level."[70]

The case of the SSE is a striking example of the penetration of governmental administration by a man acting upon the explicit instigation of a Jewish resister, Robert Gamzon, in December 1940.[71] Afterward Lesage maintained permanent contact with Gamzon as well as with other resisters working in the area of rescue: E. Simon, R. Kapel, J. Weill, and R. Hirschler.

His information and administrative "trickery" enabled him to save a large number of foreign Jews from deportation, particularly children.

The Birth and Growth of a Camouflage Network

After the arrests and deportations of August and September 1942, the Jewish charities with children and young people in their charge maintained their official façade and continued to administer their shelters and centers. However, they removed all of their deportable wards. These, as well as children taken off the deportation convoys, were entrusted to their parallel and clandestine organizations.

Initially Weill planned to create a new body to provide assistance to children. By late August 1942 he was already determined to do everything possible to dissolve the OSE with its dispensaries and shelters. He conceived of a non-Jewish organization that would take charge of wards who had previously been "Aryanized." In entrusting that task to Garel, he chose someone unknown to the community of Jewish activists and to the authorities, making it easier to maintain the secrecy necessary for all underground activity.

Garel discussed this project with people in the archbishopric of Toulouse in early September 1942. He had turned to Msgr. Saliège upon the suggestion of Lederman, whom Saliège had assisted when, as a member of the resident OSE team in the Rivesaltes camp, he had arranged for detainees to escape. It had been hoped that the archbishopric of Toulouse would extend its patronage to the new project. However, it quickly became clear that the creation of a new body entailed serious practical difficulties and risked attracting the indiscrete attention precisely of those who ought to be in the dark. The idea of a central organization also contradicted the elementary rules of underground activity: dispersion and separation.

Hence the plan was abandoned. Instead, Garel decided to call upon existing lay and confessional institutions, encouraged by the advice of Msgr. Saliège and the spontaneous offer of the Sainte-Germaine charity to accept the immediate clandestine placement of a first group of twenty-four children.[72]

A letter of recommendation from the archbishopric opened the doors of a number of other institutions for Garel. A preliminary search revealed the potential for placing three hundred children in the Toulouse region. Garun extended his search to a large part of the southern zone. An impressive group of Catholic and Protestant religious bodies, as well as secular, public, and private organizations, cooperated or agreed to risk hiding Jewish children bearing false identities.[73] In most cases the aid consisted in giving a "cover" to the social workers of the network, some of whom were not Jewish—all the rest being provided with false papers—and in placing wards with families and institutions of reception.

In less than a year, the Garel network placed 1,600 children, more or less equally divided in four regional directions: Lyons (Center-East); Valence (Southeast); Toulouse (Southwest); and Limoges (Center). Everything was coordinated by the central directorate in Lyons, of which Garel was the head. Transfer of the children was entrusted to a group of female escorts, who had to make use of all of their audacity and presence of mind to protect the children from constant police inspections in the trains and buses, which were overcrowded and uncomfortable in any event. In each region, social workers periodically visited the wards who had been placed, watching over their material and moral well-being, arranging payment of the stipends as well as for possible contacts with families. Garel also coordinated a service for the manufacture and distribution of false identity papers and ration cards. He created a clothing distribution service with two secret depots in Limoges and Grenoble.

Severe measures were imposed to protect the secrecy of the placements, which entailed painful trials for the parents. The rule was not to divulge the address of the placement. The mail brought by the social workers was deposited with the ose dispensary. Some parents sought to rebel against this cruel discipline. This could be surprising only to someone who misunderstood the distress of these hunted Jews, anguished to the point of madness about the fate of their children, whose address had to be kept from them. Fortunately the rare but inevitable mishaps had no adverse consequences regarding safety. The system of separation functioned effectively. No social worker was ever confronted with a situation described by one who visited the northern zone in March 1944: "Certain parents have settled with the foster families. I insist on rapid departure. The chatter of the women, their accent, could attract notice and the tranquillity of the children could be compromised."[74]

Constantly preoccupied by the imperatives of security, Garel worked out procedures and orders for all contacts between his network and the outside. On the regional level, precise instructions guided the social workers in their dealings with municipalities and various local administrative services. Communications with the other resistance networks, Jewish or not, were subject to the authority of the regional leader. They made contingency plans for replacing operatives who might be arrested or denounced. The head of the network maintained what he called "deep connections," taking into account the possibility that the entire system might be discovered by the enemy. Coded lists of the children and deposits of money were placed with various people who were not exposed to danger. Copies of the lists were smuggled into Switzerland, where the OSE placed them with the International Committee of the Red Cross.[75]

A parallel network to Garel's, also devoted entirely to the rescue of Jewish children, arose in Nice in the days following Italy's surrender. Anti-Jewish repression, personally directed by the commander of the SS camp in Drancy, Aloïs Brunner, fell upon the city with unprecedented suddenness and ferocity on September 10, 1943. During the months of the Italian presence, the Jewish charity organizations had provided aid in broad daylight, lulled into a false sense of security by the protection of the occupation troops. No one dreamed of dividing families and placing the children in secure places. The wave of arrests begun on September 10 surprised thousands of Jews who, not having foreseen the disaster, were caught unprepared. Toward the end of the month, an arrest carried out at the local office of the OSE seized both the staff and the recipients of aid. Some resisters, members of the FSJF (Féderation des sociétés juives de France, the Federation of Jewish Associations of France), MJS, EIF, and AJ (Armée juive, Jewish Army), doggedly continuing to seek shelters and distribute aid and false papers, fell into the hands of the Gestapo.

Nevertheless, an unknown member of the Jewish community, Moussa Abadi, made himself a rescuer of children. Ostensibly appointed as the "inspector of independent education" by the Bishop of Nice, Msgr. Rémond, he sought out religious and lay charity organizations, as Garel had done. He recruited assistants and set about producing false identity papers and ration cards. Provided with financial means by Maurice Brener of the AJDC, the only Jewish activist whom he had previously known, he was placed in contact with Garel. The latter preferred not to annex the network that was being set up in the Alpes-Maritimes Department, though he did provide Abadi with abundant operational advice. He also sent him two proven OSE social workers. At the bishopric Abadi had the use of a room, which, with the personal approval of the bishop, became a workshop for the production of false papers. He took charge of nearly five hundred children and arranged their placement, without suffering any losses, although two of his helpers were deported.[76]

The Preventative Dismantling of Children's Shelters

The 1,600 wards of the Garel network all came from the OSE. They included those over whom the screening commissions had managed to gain custody and those whose parents had been deported. Several hundred other children had been placed in the hands of the OSE by families who were threatened with arrest and forced to hide.[77] But clandestine placement was not feasible for children strongly attached to Jewish ritual practices, nor to those suffering from certain disturbances, either temporary or long-term. Maintained in 1942 and 1943 despite Weill's pressure, the OSE shelters continued to provide a home for more than 1,000 children, including those whom it was impossible to place with non-Jewish foster families.

In early 1943 the directorate of the OSE still believed that it was unnecessary to begin the hasty dismantling of its shelters. It had not yet found a solution to the problem of children unsuitable for placement in a non-Jewish milieu. Moreover, the hasty closure of the shelters would have aroused the suspicions of the authorities and risked putting them on the trail of the underground network. Finally, the traumas of the mass arrests and deportations of 1942 had apparently not completely dispelled the sense of security provided by the haven of the shelters. It took more than a year for the directorate of the OSE to become convinced that the latter had become traps.

But as early as April 1943, in close cooperation with the underground networks of *Éducation physique* and the *Sixième*, the OSE began to smuggle its wards into Switzerland illegally. Gradually this rescue route made it possible to solve the problem of safeguarding children who strictly observed religious practices. The Swiss authorities proved hospitable to the children, while until September 9, 1943, the border in the Alps remained under the control of the Italian army, which was favorable to the rescue of Jews. During this period, several hundred wards of the OSE were taken to Switzerland. An interruption of three months followed when the Nazis replaced the Italians as occupiers, after which the clandestine passage points were reopened until June 1944.[78]

In 1943, the OSE opened two shelters in the Italian zone, where the occupying troops thwarted the pursuit of Jews by the Germans and the Vichy police, one in Saint-Paul, in the Haute-Savoie Department, and the other in Moutiers, in the Savoie Department. But the constant deterioration of the situation in the southern zone, occupied by Nazi troops since November 11, 1942, then the collapse of the Italian refuge following Badoglio's capitulation to the Allies on September 8, 1943, and, finally, the Nazi raid on the shelter in La Verdière on October 20, 1943, eliminated the last hesitations. At the end of October 1943, the directorate of the OSE created an evacuation service in Limoges which was charged with dispersing all the shelters. The closing of an establishment sheltering about one hundred wards could not go unnoticed. The evacuation service managed to persuade cooperative officials of the prefectorial administration to expropriate the buildings used by the shelters, which was gradually done.[79] This was tantamount to an official order to transfer the population. The Garel network took charge of a large proportion of these children. After January 1944, the reestablishment of escape routes to Switzerland permitted other children to cross the border.

While the operations of the escape service were in motion, the OSE continued to function openly. It then had in its direct, semi-clandestine care about 1,000 children who had been placed with families even before the creation of the Garel network, and around 1,500 children of families assisted by its medical-social centers. Moreover, it still had to dismantle several shelters, including the nursery and crèche of Limoges-Poulouzat and establishments mainly containing children suffering from behavioral problems or incontinence. On April 8, 1944 a Gestapo raid captured all the members of the directorate, who had withdrawn from Montpellier to Chambéry after the occupation of the southern zone, and they were deported. During his brief incarceration by the Gestapo in Grenoble, the director, Alain Mossé, managed to transmit a code message to the outside world, stating: "The babies of Poulouzat are in danger." The remainder of the shelters were hastily closed. The directorate of the medical center and school at Lourdes agreed to shelter thirty children suffering from incontinence. The institutions of the *Secours national* (National Rescue), situated in the departments of Seine-et-Oise and Loiret, received sixty other wards. This transfer to the northern zone was effectuated by a specialist in smuggling children into Switzerland, Georges Loinger.[80] OSE personnel who had escaped took what remained of the offices and dispensaries underground. They left social workers with the task of providing help for the children of families receiving assistance, operating on the model of the Garel network.[81]

A tragic loss took place while the institution was working entirely underground. In 1943 the OSE had entrusted about fifty wards to a private institution established in Izieu in the Ain Department. The site seemed to be "forgotten at the end of the world. . . . The camouflage that the Sub-Prefecture of Belley had given it and the hospitality of the local residents" seemed to protect the shelter. Nevertheless, an OSE social worker begged the director of the shelter to disperse the children in March 1944. The latter, Mme. Zlatin, left for Montpellier on April 3 to seek a place of refuge for her wards. During her absence, on the morning of April 6, men of the Gestapo Chief of Lyons, Klaus Barbie, seized forty-four children in Izieu as well as the staff of the shelter. They were all deported. One young woman, a member of the staff, was the sole survivor.[82]

The southern zone also knew a tragedy in which children placed with the UGIF by the German services were then taken back and deported. All the children in the shelter in La Verdière, in the suburbs of Marseilles, fell victim on October 20, 1943. The director, Alice Salomon, voluntarily joined the children.[83] Warned of the action the day before by the Gestapo itself, the UGIF directorate in Marseilles was divided. One member pressed for dispersing and camouflaging the children. But in the end they acceded in the face of the threat of massive reprisals against the Jews of Marseilles.[84] Other children in a similar situation, those who were called blocked children in the northern zone, were kidnapped by the Jewish resistance movement. A young women in the *Éducation physique* network, disguised as a nurse and provided with false German papers, abducted an eight-month-old infant in February 1944 and placed it in the shelter of La Tronche, in the Isère Department. The German police had decided to transfer it to Drancy, where its mother was detained.[85] In Lyons, in June 1944, resisters of the UJRE (*Union des Juifs pour la résistance et l'entraide*, Jewish Union for Resistance and Mutual Assistance) kidnapped six children who had been placed with the UGIF by the German SD (*Sicherheitsdienst*, Security Service) that had deported their parents.[86]

The Networks of the Youth Movements

The simultaneity of the EIF's descent into the underground and the formation of the Garel network is remarkable. Closely associated during the dramatic events of Vénissieux, the EIF and the OSE worked equally closely in taking charge of the 108 children who were saved at that time, camouflaging and placing them. They shared responsibility, entrusting the adolescents over the age of fourteen to the EIF.

But their method of action was less radically clandestine than that of the Garel network during the first months of their action. Gamzon and his colleagues had become accustomed to using the cover of the UGIF to all the activities of their organization and in large measure for its financing. The supervision of the Fourth Directorate, Youth had not interfered with its freedom of action. Nor, for that matter, had it hampered the MJS or Yechouroun, which were also placed under this administrative framework of the UGIF. Even better, sponsorship by the Vichy SSE of the shelters and artisanal and rural centers had made rescue operations possible, releasing and placing young detainees from Gurs and Rivesaltes. This sponsorship in fact was true complicity. In the name of the government, the SSE was responsible for the status of the resident teams in the detention camps, in particular that of the EIF led by Ninon Haït in Gurs. Moreover, on January 2, 1942, the SSE was officially charged with creating "Special centers for occupational training" to accommodate foreign Jews from fifteen to twenty-five years old.[87] Thus the SSE was given supervision over the centers of the "Jewish organizations: ORT, OSE, EI, CAR [Comité d'assistance aux réfugiés, the Committee for Assistance to Refugees], Keren Kayemeth le Israël [the Jewish National Fund],"[88] which thus became "special centers" of the SSE with regard to the government. Thanks to these two directives, dozens of adolescents and young adults who were detained in the camps were "incorporated" in the various establishments of the Jewish youth movements. For example, in 1942 the center in Beaulieu received forty girls from Rivesaltes, mainly aged over seventeen.[89] It is true that these young people were targeted by the arrests of August 1942. But, warned in time by Lesage, the directors of the centers removed those who were in danger before the intervention of the police, sending them to safe places of refuge.[90]

Taking note of these experiences, in the summer of 1942 the directorate of the EIF considered that an administrative structure modeled on the SSE combined the best means for preventing the deportation of young people. Thus, instead of taking the clandestine path, it created a replica of the SSE, the Service social des jeunes (SSJ, the Social Service for Youth), making it the sixth division of the Youth Directorate of the UGIF.[91] The SSJ personnel, led by Henri Wahl and Ninon Haït bore service cards of the UGIF, which paid their salaries. Its mission included: professional training, placements in the countryside, the distribution of aid, and "contacts with the concentration camps . . . to spare the young people dangerous overcrowding and to remove them from the camps and place them in children's homes."[92]

The clandestine activities of the SSJ, the manufacture and use of false identity papers and ration tickets, obliged it to take security precautions, but always under the official cover of the Sixth Division. The SSJ's field of action grew as its operations became diversified. The clandestine placement of children who had previously been "Aryanized" included approximately 350 wards. It became imprudent to concentrate the office, the false papers workshop, and the meetings of teams of workers in Moissac, the headquarters of the Fourth Division of the UGIF. For other reasons the leaders of the SSJ were obliged to operate with more discretion: the occupation of the southern zone by German troops, the increase of inspections in public transportation, arrests made by the Nazi police in addition to those made by the French, and finally the decision made on January 5, 1943 by the CGQJ to dissolve the Youth Department of the UGIF.[93] The combination of these circumstances pushed the SSJ completely underground.

In truth, the disappearance of the Youth Department changed nothing with respect to the administrative status of its Sixth Division, the ssj, for it was simply integrated within the Health Department of the UGIF. The personnel and budget went unchanged. Marc Haguenau, the official director of the ssj, maintained this fiction with audacity and cunning until his arrest in Grenoble on February 18, 1944. Instead of calling the service the ssj, its agents called it the "*Sixième*," which was merely an abbreviation for the Sixth Division! In early 1943 Wahl began to isolate his network, following the model of the structure created by Garel, dividing it into seven regions: Grenoble, Lyons, Clermont-Ferrand, Limoges, Toulouse, Marseilles, and Nice. He and his colleagues provided themselves with false identities. In April or May 1943, the network was also established in Paris, at the instigation of Simon Lévitte, who simultaneously created there a section of the *Éducation physique* network of the MJS. There was no difference between the two organizations with respect to the goal of their rescue operations. This double action was a response to the imperative of isolation. A single person, Jacques Pulver, replaced in February 1944 by Albert Akerberg, arranged contacts between the two networks as well as those between Paris and the southern zone.[94]

From then on the methods of work and the structures of the *Sixième* were modeled on those of the Garel network, though with less rigor regarding the security precautions. The heads of the *Sixième* permitted themselves more flexibility, because they counted on the spirit of discipline and the sense of responsibility of their assistants, almost all of whom were products of the scouting movement. This applied roughly to the *Éducation physique* network as well. Another distinction that had to be made concerns the strict specialization of the Garel network, which devoted itself exclusively to the placement of children, while the *Sixième* and *Éducation physique* also produced masses of false identity papers, rescued adults, and smuggled people across the borders

The invasion of the Italian zone by the Nazis on September 9, 1943 presented the resisters of the *Éducation physique* network with grave responsibilities. Established mainly in Grenoble and Nice, it had to reorganize the routes into Switzerland and to devise temporary solutions for children cast adrift following the brutal action of the Gestapo. The director in Nice, Jacob Weintrob, a dynamic and efficient man, was arrested on September 23, almost at the same time as his counterpart in the *Sixième*, Claude Guttmann.[95] Tortured, then deported, neither of them survived the inferno. This master stroke of the Gestapo nearly destroyed the two Jewish networks in Nice. This did not happen, though urgent precautions had become unavoidable. For example, the leaders of *Éducation physique* in Grenoble left the city and suspended all activity. The head of the network, Simon Lévitte, reshuffled the assignments and placed a very young resister, Georges Schneck, in charge of the local team. Schneck took over all the tasks connected with rescue.[96]

The *Sixième* also changed its personnel in the former Italian zone. It sent the head of the Agen region, Roger Fichtenberg, to Grenoble, with the mission of dispersing the children in the EIF shelter that had been established a few months earlier in La Grave, on the Lautaret road. Provided with a list of the nineteen adults and sixty-three wards from four to nineteen years old in the establishment, he gave each one a code name taken from the vocabulary of domestic equipment. When it became possible to send a convoy to Switzerland, or to find shelter for an adult, he would telephone La Grave and ask, "Send my blue shirt, my toothbrush, my pen, etc."[97]

Although Forbidden, Emigration Continues Clandestinely

Persistent efforts had been made for more than two years to have the children emigrate, yet it was not until April 1943 that the OSE began to smuggle them across the borders. In early November 1942, 500 children, gathered in Marseilles by the OSE with the help of the Quakers, were finally ready to leave for Lisbon on a special train. They were provided with American visas and reservations on an ocean liner from Lisbon to New York. But the exit visas promised by Laval to the American chargé d'affaires, H. Pinckney Tuck, were revoked by order of Réné Bousquet, the secretary general of the police in Vichy. Then, on November 8, the American landing in Algeria and the breaking of relations between Vichy and Washington definitively put an end to renewed efforts for emigration.

Earlier the American State Department had at last granted 1,000 visas on September 28, 1942, and then made public its decision to receive 5,000 Jewish children on October 15. This was the result of pressure, backed by precise information, exerted in the United States by the AJDC, the OSE HICEM, the Quakers, and the YMCA. In Vichy the same organizations had harassed Laval as well as Bousquet and Fourcade, the inspector general of the Interior Ministry. The latter pretended they were concerned with keeping families together and fulminated against the organizations that had taken over the children in Vénissieux, against the wishes of the government. "We will not let the children cross the Atlantic while their parents are left in Poland," exclaimed Bousquet. They finally authorized an experimental shipment of 500 children, after first demanding an American commitment not to permit publicity damaging to the good name of

France and Germany. But the French promise to release the children was not kept.[98]

Laval had chosen to deliver Jewish children to the Germans for deportation to the East rather than allowing them to leave for America. As long as hope had remained that it would be possible to send convoys of children overseas by legal means, no one had considered exposing them to the risks of secretly crossing the borders. The leaders believed, not without reason, that if such a convoy were intercepted by the French police, it would be sent to Drancy and delivered to the Nazis. Moreover, they did not know how the Swiss authorities might behave and preferred not to take the risk of rejection, which would have plunged the young wayfarers directly into the clutches of the French police. A change took place when in November 1942 the Savoy border with Switzerland passed under the control of Italian occupiers, who, it was gradually learned, effectively opposed the Jewish policy of Vichy and the Germans. Then, in April 1943, two leaders of Jewish resistance, Marc Jarblum and Joseph Weill, having taken refuge in Geneva to flee pursuit in France, negotiated with the Swiss authorities. They were successful, for the Berne government issued new instructions regarding illegal Jewish immigrants, sheltering convoys of children under sixteen from the risk of deportation from Swiss territory.[99]

This finally put an end to all the hesitations which had previously deterred resistance leaders from resorting to this rescue route. Passages, friendly and dependable addresses close to the border, and escorts were already known. The FSJF, the AJ, the EIF, and even the OSE had already used these resources for adults, notably to smuggle out activists for whom it had been learned that searches had begun. On September 15, for example, a dozen young adults, wearing scout uniforms with the insignia of the *Éclaireurs unionistes* (the French Protestant Scout Federation) arrived safe and sound in Switzerland, while their escort, who was arrested, was detained in Rivesaltes.[100] In October 1942 the Lyons police launched the search for "a certain Gutman, a Jewish scout official, absent from Lyons," who was suspected of organizing the passage of foreign Jews to Switzerland.[101]

The use of paid escorts who had proven themselves, along with the indispensable aid of non-Jewish resisters, including local elected officials, school teachers, pastors, and priests in the border area, permitted the passage of more than 1,500 wards of the Jewish charities between May 1943 and June 1944. While largely sucessful, some tragedy resulted. Three convoys were intercepted by the Germans: on October 22, 1943 and on June 1 and 5, 1944.[102] The Mayor of Annemasse, Jean Deffaugt, devoted unreservedly to Jewish resistance, managed to take charge of the children, on condition that they remain available to the German SD. With the aid of the Red Cross and the *Secours national,* he then had the children placed, and they were saved. But two of the escorts did not survive. Mila Racine, of the *Éducation physique* network, was deported to Ravensbrück, where she died in a bombardment. Marianne Cohn, of the *Sixième,* was savagely gunned down in Ville-la-Grand. Although *Éducation physique* had established a contact in Annemasse with each of them and prepared an escape plan, they refused to lend themselves to it so as to protect the children against possible reprisals.[103]

The organization of children's convoys toward the Swiss border entailed a quite large number of rather diversified operations: preparing the children; patiently practicing with each of them the way to behave in various eventualities; sewing a record of the real civil status of each child into his clothing; arranging rest stops and provisions; escorting, exploring, inventing new ways to cross the border; preparing measures for retreat and lodging in case of failure; administering the finances of this infinitely complex arrangement. All this was done under the greatest secrecy and where transportation and food supply were sporadic. Sometimes the Jewish resistance managed to send through convoys of from five to twenty children for several months in a row.

Violating the rule of segregation, the *Éducation physique,* OSE, and *Sixième* networks worked in intimate cooperation. An MJS team directed by Tony Gryn operated with incredible audacity. In October 1943, after two escorts of this team were arrested and Gryn was sent to Paris to direct the false identity paper service of *Éducation physique,* two men coordinated these operations, Emmanuel Racine, already active in the *Combat* network, and Georges Loinger. The latter took upon himself the sole responsibility for the final escort of dozens of convoys, containing a total of around six hundred children.

A physical education instructor, after his discharge from the army in 1940, Loinger had developed programs of physical exercise and sport in all the children's centers of the Jewish youth movements. Subjecting himself to strict discipline, sober, an extremely dedicated teacher, competent in his profession, he possessed exceptional endurance and was capable of surprising feats. He had created teams of counselors who applied his programs everywhere that he intervened. Without doubt he contributed to the development of a high level of physical and mental hygiene among Jewish youth and its leaders in the southern zone.

Loinger had been engaged in the action of the three organizations before they went underground, and he is a perfect example of the close cooperation of the Jewish resistance networks for illegal passage into Switzerland. With great effort, the rear bases of the networks prepared groups of children and then confided them to Loinger in Annecy, Aix-les-Bains, or Lyons. From there he took them along a very personal route, using the complicity of railway workers and his athletic experience. At the Annemasse railroad station, the workers marked a special exit for him, protected from police inspection, with the sign: "Exit for Vacation Camps." The group then reached the reception center of the SNCF (*Société nationale des chemins de fer*, the National Railroad Company), where the director, Balthazar, took over. The following stage was a sports field on the banks of the Arve, on the border. There Loigner organized games, and, at dusk, the children would disappear one by one across the Swiss border.

Other escorts invented an ingenious procedure for smuggling out children of a very young age. The Swiss police did not turn back couples with very small children. Using false papers specially prepared for the circumstance, pseudo-families were composed of unmarried couples and babies. The Jewish resisters took note of the points where the French customs officials and police had shown understanding and sometimes active complicity.

The spring and summer of 1943 were propitious for crossing the border, favored by the attitude of the Italian authorities, who were only present until September 8. An interruption of three months followed the interception of the convoy led by Mila Racine on October 22, 1943 by a German patrol. Taking stricter precautions, new routes were utilized in the spring of 1944. According to a report of the OSE-Switzerland addressed to the Commissioner of the Intergovernmental Committee on Refugees, 569 Jewish children entered Switzerland without their parents between January 1 and June 7, 1944.[104] The arrest of the group of thirty-two children led by Marianne Cohn on June 1 and then the Allied landing in Normandy on June 6 put an end to rescue operations across the Swiss border.

After the Allied landing in Normandy, a number of Jewish resisters joined the armed underground. But the demanding daily routine of saving children and making periodical visits to those placed with families and institutions was maintained by noncombatants, mainly women. They suffered further losses, but during this period the enemy did not succeed in seizing any of the children saved by the resisters.

How Many Jewish Children Survived the Nazi Occupation of France?

A prudent estimate sets the number of children saved by the Jewish organizations at between 8,000 and 10,000.[105] The statistical tables of S. Klarsfeld refer to a total of 75,721 Jews deported from France and include 10,147 children younger than eighteen.[106] One must note that the date of birth is missing for 4,851 of the people on Klarsfeld's memorial list. An indeterminate number of children is included in this number. The proportion of children among the total number of deportees whose age is known is 14.4 percent. Applying this, one arrives at a figure of approximately 700 children. In addition, the Jewish losses in France include another 5,550 victims: those who died in the French camps, those shot or summarily executed, and those who were deported from Belgium.[107]

According to the lists compiled by the Paris Prefecture of Police, based on the census of Jews in the Department of Seine, those under eighteen constituted 27 percent of the Jewish population.[108] The application of this rate to the total of 350,000 Jews present in France immediately after the armistice of 1940 places the overall number of people under eighteen at 94,500. But in 1944, those who had reached adulthood were only partially replaced by newborns, given the low Jewish birthrate during the war. Lacking accurate statistics, we estimate that the number of those below eighteen in 1944, before the deduction of losses, was 84,000. The number of children who escaped extermination is thus 84,000 minus 11,600, or 72,400.

According to the aforementioned statistics, the proportion of adult Jewish victims was 27 percent, whereas that of child victims was 13.8 percent. But if Laval's desires had not been thwarted by Jewish resistance, powerfully supported by part of the French population, the proportion of deported children would have been equal to that of the adults, or double what it actually was.

Let us further note that among the 72,400 children who escaped, approximately 62,000 remained with their parents[109] or were directly placed by them with non-Jewish institutions or families. The Jewish organizations, responsible for nearly 10,000 wards, also contributed to the safeguarding of children who remained with their parents, thanks to the distribution of various sorts of assistance and false identity papers. The available sources do not permit us to estimate the number of those who benefitted from this mode of rescue, but it is doubtless over 10,000, in addition to the wards of the organizations.

The rest owe their lives to the presence of mind of their parents, the help of neighbors or Resistance networks, or else to the good luck of not having been arrested, though they did nothing to hide.

The wards of Jewish organizations saved from extermination can be classified as shown in table 11.1.

Table 11.1

WARDS OF JEWISH ORGANIZATION SAVED FROM EXTINCTION

Children Under Eighteen	Estimate between	and
Emigrated Overseas	311	311
Having Crossed the Spanish Border[a]	88	132
Having Crossed the Swiss Border[b]	1500	2000
Placed with Non-Jews in the Northern Zone	1500	2000
Placed with Non-Jews in the Southern Zone	4500	5500
Total	7899	9943

a. Source: Avni, *Ha-Hatsala Derekh Sfarad u-Portugal*, p. 251.
b. Source: Keren-Patkin, "Hatsalat Ha-Yeladim Ha-Yehudiim Be-Tsarfat," p. 35 suggests an estimate of 1,000 children. It appears that she neither consulted all the archival sources nor used the work of Avni and Kieval.

Numbering the Losses

The losses suffered among the wards of Jewish organizations were felt keenly by those responsible for them and in some cases they sparked painful debates within communities after the war. They include around 450 children, of whom 350 were in the northern zone.

a.) The centers administered by the UGIF in and around Paris sheltered without distinction blocked children entrusted temporarily to the UGIF by the directors of the camp in Drancy and free children. The latter were social welfare cases and did not appear on the French or German police lists of Jews. The UGIF also cooperated in the placement of free children, under the camouflage of false Aryan identities. Because of the vagaries involved in taking charge of children and placing them, children belonging to both categories were always present in the UGIF centers. During the spring of 1944, the activists of the *Comité unifié de défense juif* (The United Committee for Jewish Defense, CUD) suggested to the UGIF that they simulate a massive kidnapping of all the children in the centers. This proposal was rejected.[110] The Jewish resistance decided to give priority to the blocked children, who were clearly exposed to a greater risk of being deported. The plan for massive escape having been abandoned, they turned to individual kidnappings, which were carried out from April to July, 1944, with the complicity, sometimes active, of the UGIF staff.[111]

However, from July 20 to 24, policemen under orders from Brunner, the commander of the Drancy camp, rounded up almost all the children still

sheltered in the centers. According to K. Schendel, the chief of the liaison service between the UGIF and the Germans, 500 children were transferred to
Drancy.[112] Of these around 270 were deported in convoy 77 on July 31,
1944.[113] The list of those on that convoy includes more than 300 children
under eighteen, of whom a third were deported with their parents and apparently did not come from the UGIF centers.[114] The other wards of the UGIF who
remained in Drancy after the departure of this convoy were not deported.

From 1945 to 1947 a panel formed by the CRIF (*Conseil représentatif des
Juifs de France*, Representative Council of French Jews) took testimony from
the directors of the UGIF. They admitted that they had rejected the demands
of the Jewish resistance for the closure of the centers and a mass escape of
the children. They claimed to have cooperated in the individual kidnappings, explaining that this operation had partially failed because the Gestapo
raid on the centers on July 20, 1944 had quickly seized the resisters charged
with dispersing the children. On January 14, 1945 the panel came to a decision regarding the controversy aroused by the action of Juliette Stern.
Though attributing part of the responsibility to her and also to Professor
Weill-Hallé for not separating the free children from the blocked ones, the
panel absolved them completely, alone among all their colleagues.[115]

Although the Jewish resistance incriminated the UGIF for having kept
Jewish children available to the enemy, in 1943 the authorities accused it of
"clandestine actions," among them "secret placement of Jewish children."
The distrust of the CGQJ had been aroused either by the perspicacity of an
inspector or by the involuntary or forced indiscretions of one of its officials.
The secretary general, Antignac, suspected that the UGIF in both zones was
using "the cover of its status as a public welfare organization [to mask] a sys-
tem of secret Jewish self-defense organizations." A report addressed to
Röthke of the SD mentions particularly Mme. Stern, Robert Gamzon, David
Rapoport, and other workers in the UGIF social services.[116]

Supervision of the financial management of the UGIF in the northern
zone never revealed irregularities in bookkeeping. Some of the funds allocated to the secret placement of children came from provisions of the UGIF
budget forwarded by the CGQJ under the cover of a clever system of false
receipts.[117] Antignac insistently demanded that Röthke conduct a "rigorously secret" police enquiry into Rue Amelot, "a false paper workshop" in
Mme. Stern's offices, on rue de la Bienfaisance, as well as in an OSE dispensary on rue des Francs-Bourgeois.[118] In the course of this enquiry, Röthke's
agents arrested David Rapoport in the Rue Amelot headquarters on June 1,
1943, and the employees who were present were arrested several days later.[119]
Stern's staff of rue de la Bienfaisance were rounded up on July 30, while she

was attending a funeral.[120]The Gestapo did not pursue her, and she had the lists and files which were left intact by the SD transferred to a safe place.

On September 4, it was the turn of two members of the UGIF council, Stora and Musnik. None of the victims of this series of arrests survived. The inquiry requested by Antignac never took place. But the action of placing the children continued, not without cooperation between the resisters of the *Sixième* and *Éducation physique*, on the one hand, and Stern, on the other.[121] That is why the arrests with their tragic consequences made by Brunner's agents on July 20, 1944 in the UGIF centers could be presented to the CRIF panel as a shared failure of the UGIF and of the Jewish resistance.

In addition to these 250 children, others were arrested in various UGIF centers in February 1943 and February 1944, and there were also the victims of the roundup at the vocational school on rue des Rosiers in May 1944—a total of about fifty children.

b.) Several dozen children secretly placed in private homes and institutions in the northern zone were lost. Instances of denunciation followed by the arrest of foster parents were very rare.[122] A UGIF inquest regarding thirty-one children detained in Drancy "whose parents are free" mentions ten cases of children who had been placed in foster homes, where they were arrested.[123] An observation noted by a Rue Amelot social worker visiting the children placed in the Nivernais region suggests that they are safer when their parents are unable to locate them.[124]

The total number of losses suffered by wards of the Jewish charities in the northern zone probably did not exceed 350. This estimate includes the children rounded up in the UGIF centers, approximately 300, and several dozen children arrested in their foster homes.

c.) Seventeen adolescents over sixteen were arrested in OSE shelters in the southern zone after August 1942, to be "relocated" with their parents with a view to deportation. Several of these were released due to the intervention of the screening committees. These losses can be estimated at around ten children.[125]

d.) The Nazis deported and gassed the entire population of three institutions: La Verdière (about twenty children), Izieu (forty-four children), and La Marcellière, a shelter in the Voiron region of the Isère Department, where the AIP (*Association des Israélites pratiquants*, Association of Observant Jews) had lodged seventeen children from its shelter at Saint-Étienne-de-Crossey[126]—in all around eighty.

e.) Among the children placed with non-Jews in the southern zone, around ten, according to a prudent estimate, fell into the hands of the police or the Gestapo and were deported.[127]

The losses in the southern zone thus came to around a hundred children, to which must be added the 350 wards of the Jewish charities in the northern zone. This conclusion combines the wards of the UGIF, an organization created by the Vichy regime and controlled by the occupier, and those of the Jewish charities, which, legally or not, acted to save their wards from the criminal actions of the government. This confusion in attributing the losses derives from the fluid nature of the divisions between the groups on the level of rescue operations. There were permanent contacts between the UGIF and the Jewish resistance. Far from limiting themselves to the expression of resentments and disagreements, these contacts often furthered the joint planning of assistance and rescue.[128]

Need it be emphasized that the major guilt regarding the losses mentioned here was that of the perpetrators of the massacre of the innocents, assisted by French auxiliaries, officials of the government, and Vichy police agents, and by informers. If the wards of the Jewish charities were not all saved, this is above all because of the unspeakable ferocity of the enemy in hunting them down. Moreover, some decisions taken on the Jewish side had unfortunate consequences. One example is furnished by the UGIF in Paris, which opposed the mass escape of the children in its centers in July 1944. There was also the refusal by Schneerson of the AIP to disperse the wards of the shelter in Saint-Étienne-de-Crossey one by one, under the cover of complete "Aryanization." After the Liberation, the community refrained from passing judgment on disobedience of orders from the heads of Jewish resistance. However, it did summon before its panel those responsible for the decision preventing the dispersal of the UGIF wards in Paris. After long debates, the panel concluded that the error of judgment committed by the leaders of the UGIF, which it called "an unfortunate and hasty decision," was not "a positive fault of the kind that would stain their honor."[129]

After October 1943 the clandestine FSJF and Zionist Federation demanded the dissolution of the UGIF in the southern zone,[130] as the UJRE had already done.[131] These organizations accused it of collaborating with Vichy and with the occupier, of turning children over for extermination, and of making the lists of recipients of aid available to the Gestapo, and also of being a trap for the UGIF staff and its clients. But after the Liberation, Jarblum reproached the UGIF in more balanced fashion. He wrote that this organization had served "the demands of the victors," who had neither the time nor the means to create a structure of German officials, and who wished to give the impression of freely consented collaboration. They also sought to "deflect the feelings of hatred and revolt created by their tyranny" against the heads of the Jewish community. Jarblum added that a resistance committee had formed in the Drancy camp, and that the UGIF served as the link between this committee and the CUD. Stora, a member of the UGIF council, was arrested and deported in September 1943. Brunner accused him of organizing secret contacts with the Drancy camp after the arrest of the staff of the service for detainees of rue de la Bienfaisance on July 30.[132]

In May 1944, the *Comité général de défense juive* (CGD, General Committee for Jewish Defense) brought before the CRIF a demand that the UGIF dissolve itself. UGIF of the southern zone supported the proposition,[133] but it made its application subject to the approval of the Union Council in the northern zone. On July 13, Edinger convened a secret meeting of the council, which voted not to dissolve. There were still 20,000 people wearing the yellow star in Paris, 10,000 families receiving assistance, and the UGIF was responsible for supplying the camp in Drancy. The council members considered that the distress of those receiving assistance and of the detainees would be aggravated if the UGIF disbanded. The president of the commission designated by the CRIF to study "the ways of closing the Union" concluded that it was necessary "to align the liquidation of the north with that of the south, and as long as the one was not possible, the other was not necessary." Lacking the agreement of the representatives of the CGD, the question was postponed until the general assembly of the CRIF. But the Liberation occurred before that assembly was held.[134]

Moreover, the lists of those receiving assistance and living under false identities, whose addresses were unknown to the police, never fell into enemy hands. Once Edinger gave Brunner an outdated list.[135] In Lyons, an AJ commando unit that had come from Nice on January 25, 1944 broke into the UGIF offices and destroyed the files and the lists, following the example of a similar operation effectuated in December 1943 in the UGIF offices in Marseilles by UJRE resisters.[136] Doubtless some of the resisters who had used the UGIF as a shield later realized their error.[137] Others, on the contrary, such as Serge Klarsfeld, believe today that the Nazis would have wrought even more destruction among the Jews had the UGIF been liquidated in 1943. Such a measure would have thrown tens of thousands of clients into the street, reducing them to starvation and thus making them easy prey for the SD.[138] Such a prospect authenticates the motivations invoked by the UGIF leaders, concerned with the safety of their clients. In the conclusion of his study of the UGIF, R. Cohen writes that "the monolithic image of the UGIF does not reflect the truth." He emphasizes the probity of its leaders and their perseverance in accomplishing their philanthropic goal.[139]

Outside Assistance to the Jewish Community

The rescue of Jewish children was a test of the attitude of the Vichy regime, its officials, the clergy, lay and religious organizations, and finally of the non-Jewish French population as a whole. Unlike most of the other directors of Jewish organizations who acted in secret, Marc Jarblum, who headed the FSJF and the OSF (*Organisation sioniste de France*, the French Zionist Organization), envisaged working without permanent coordination with non-Jewish associations and movements, even in the underground. The interests of their battle to liberate France from the occupier could not, in his view, coincide with those of the Jewish struggle for survival, especially regarding the immigrants.

In contrast, the Jewish Communist leaders were opposed to making their combat specific. They emphasized solidarity with the French resisters. Even for an operation as particular as the rescue of Jewish children, the only instance in France where aid to children demanded clandestine action, the Jewish Communists created structures without any Jewish identity: The *Mouvement national contre le racisme* (MNCR, National Movement Against Racism); and *Combat médical*.[140] The other Jewish resistance organizations had no ideological commitments except that of pragmatism. They used all available supports, including the official services of Vichy.

Thus one can discern three images of the French national collectivity. One evokes a people of collaborators, with the exception of a handful of resisters, whose attitude toward foreigners and Jews could, in any case, be indifferent or suspicious. Conversely, the Jewish Communists regarded most of France as being favorable to resistance, with the exception of traitors in the service of Vichy and the occupier. The others, finally, considered the first two images as abstractions, versus a situation that was more nuanced, complex, and subject to evolution. This is not vastly different from the lapidary phrase of Bernanos, claiming that France was totally committed to a "party of victory," first German victory, later the victory of the Allies.[141]

During the first two years of the occupation, the measures enacted and applied against the Jews aroused but little emotion in France with a modest number of signs of sympathy toward the victims. Teachers discharged because of the Statute of the Jews remember the silence and passivity of their non-Jewish colleagues when they were deprived of their employment.[142] One recalls the same absence of reaction on the part of the shop-keepers' associations when the Jews in the northern zone were required to place the sign, "Jewish Business," in their store windows, following the

German ordinance of September 27, 1940. A few rare shopkeepers protested discreetly by also placing the yellow sign in their windows for a few days.[143]

When the wearing of the yellow star was imposed in the northern zone on June 7, 1942, several dozen non-Jewish students, laborers, and office workers proudly wore yellow stars of paper in the street. A Jewish journalist linked to the activists of Rue Amelot, Jacques Bielinky, noted in his journal on June 11: "The first day, Sunday morning, two Jews were arrested on rue des Écouffes for going out without badges. The same day, on boulevard Saint-Michel, Catholic students were arrested for having put on the Magen David, not being required to." And on June 13: "It seems that about thirty Catholic students who were walking with Jewish badges were arrested and detained in Drancy. It is told that one of the arrested students, who was reproached for wearing the Jewish star, replied to the policeman: 'This isn't a Jewish badge!' 'How is that?' 'It's simple. These letters [*juif* = Jew] stand for: *Jeunesse universitaire internationaliste française* [French internationalist university youth].' "[144] Although spectacular, this gesture was modest in scope, indicating both the courage of the demonstrators[145] and the visible weakness of public protest. In September 1942, Cardinal Suhard, the Archbishop of Paris, punished two clergymen of his diocese for delivering false baptism certificates, presumably to Jews seeking to avoid arrest and deportation by disguising themselves as Aryans. In a circular distributed to all the priests in his diocese, Suhard presented his decision in a manner designed to discourage similar action.[146]

A report addressed by the HICEM office in Lisbon to New York in autumn 1942 describes with precision the mass arrests and deportations of July and August in both zones. The author sums up the popular reaction as follows: "Individually the French people disapproved of these measures, condemned them, and sometimes helped the 'hunted' to escape arrest, temporarily, but it did not feel capable of opposing them."[147]

The government and all the executive levels reached a low point with the French contribution to the deportation of 4,000 children from two to twelve years of age, arrested in Paris on July 16 and 17, 1942, parked in the Vel' d'hiv', then separated from the parents, and finally deported from Drancy between August 17 and 28.[148] Pastor Marc Boegner, the President of the Protestant Federation of France, approached Laval, who responded, "I am performing prophylaxis. . . . Not a single Jewish child must remain in France."[149]

But the French public mood, apathetic until then, had already begun to shift. The officials of the Ministry of the Interior who consulted the monthly reports of the prefects were perfectly well informed.[150] Generally absent from these reports until July 1942, the Jewish issue burst to the forefront during the summer. Even when the author of the report gave free rein to his anti-Semitic zeal,[151] he emphasized the emotion that had taken hold of the population of his region in response to the arrest of foreign Jews, including women and children, in July and August.[152]

These prefectorial reports reveal great diversity in the administrators' eagerness to serve the regime. In most cases the tone used is sober in describing the arrest and deportation of foreign Jews. They all emphasize the hostile reactions of public opinion.[153] In a small number of cases, the prefect is silent regarding the results of police action and dramatizes its effect on the public. Thus the regional prefect of Montpellier, Olivier de Sardan, wrote on September 3, 1942, that "men of the GMR [*Groupes mobiles de réserve*, Mobile Reserve Groups] took part in the operations of August 26 (Jewish affairs), where they were used to the maximum with impeccable conduct." Contrary to most of his colleagues, he made no final accounting of these operations. Did Vichy know that in Montpellier, even the foreign Jews appearing on the arrest lists had all been alerted and had left their homes before the arrival of the GMR?[154] The same report states that a "crisis of anguish and panic has spread among Jewish circles," and that "opinion is moved by repression which they claim is pitiless."[155] Jean Benedetti, the prefect of Hérault, reports on September 3, 1942, the "profound indignation" and "heartbreaking scenes" in Béziers. He wrote that "the operation had been announced some time earlier by the English radio, and in Jewish circles everyone was prepared for it." He concluded that "thus it could only succeed partially."[156]

The press of the French Resistance, in the main, waited until the end of the summer of 1942 before mentioning the persecutions against the Jews. Exceptions were *Cahiers du Témoignage chrétien* (*TC*), *Libération*, and *L'Humanité*. In March 1942 *TC* published a story called, "The Racists Portrayed by Themselves."[157] The eighth issue of *Libération*, dated March 1, 1942, reproduced a letter from Paul Claudel, the eminent Catholic poet and playwright, to the Chief Rabbi of France, written on December 24, 1941, where Claudel said, "the disgust, the horror, the indignation" that he felt "regarding the iniquity, the despoliation, the mistreatment of all sorts of which our Jewish compatriots are now the victims."[158]

L'Humanité mentioned the Jewish theme seventeen times between June 1940 and September 1942, then it kept absolute silence on the subject until the liberation.[159] *Franc-Tireur, Combat, Le Populaire, L'Insurgé, La Vérité*, as well as *Libération* and *TC* published the complete text of the pastoral epistle which the Archbishop of Toulouse, Msgr. Saliège, had read in the churches of his diocese on Sunday, August 23, 1942: "The Jews are men, the Jews are women. Foreigners are men. Foreigners are women. All is not permitted against them. . . . They are part of the human race. They are our brothers."[160]

The prefect of the Haute-Garonne Department and the regional prefect of Toulouse reported "considerable repercussions" of that letter. It was circulated by Catholic bookstores, sent to the cities of the southern zone, then "transformed into a political pamphlet by the adversaries of the regime and the Jews themselves, . . . copied, mimeographed, printed, circulated as a broadsheet."[161]

Saliège's example was followed by the bishops of Montauban, Marseilles, Nice, and Albi, as well as, in more reserved fashion, by Cardinal Gerlier in Lyons. The regional prefect of Marseilles emphasized in October 1942 "the profound and durable consequences" of the pastoral letter of Msgr. Delay, read in the churches on Sunday, September 6, noting that "the delivery of foreign Jews to the Germans is regarded by many as a national shame. . . . The Jews [have assumed] the figure of martyrs in the eyes of French opinion."[162] The bishopric of the northern zone was more discrete. It wrote a letter of "platonic and confidential"[163] protest to Vichy, signed by Cardinal Suhard, who decided not to read it in the churches.

This was the first time since the institution of the Vichy regime that a fraction of the bishopric was in disagreement with it. A growing part of public opinion had "the feeling that the Catholics are detaching themselves from the regime."[164] The unpopularity of the government grew incessantly when Vichy promulgated the Compulsory Labor Service law on September 4, 1942, and also with the German military reverses in North Africa and Stalingrad during the winter of 1942–43.

The reversal of French public opinion thus became perceptible in the reports of prefects from the moment they referred to condemnation of the atrocities committed against the Jews during the summer of 1942, as well as the repercussions produced by the reactions of several prelates. Before that time, prefects occasionally noted that "the population wishes the victory of the Allies," adding immediately that "the confidence enjoyed by Marshal Pétain remains complete."[165] But references to Pétain's popularity become increasingly rare in reports after September 1942. Is there any correlation between this shift in public opinion and the persecution of the Jews?[166] Although this question remains open, the shift in public opinion and the passage of Jewish rescue organizations from public to clandestine operations clearly do coincide.

The shift in public opinion was decisive in the success of the efforts of the Jewish resistance when it decided, almost from one day to the next, to camouflage thousands of Jewish children and remove them from the danger of governmental pursuit. This prodigious enterprise, unique in occupied Europe, would have been disastrous without the active complicity of thousands of non-Jewish Frenchmen, who were also willing to risk their own security to participate in the rescue of Jewish children. Doubtless the French resistance networks, oriented toward mainly political and military goals, took but a small part in this action. But countless individuals, prelates and clergymen, organizations and institutions, as well as some parts of officialdom, helped the Jewish resistance to save the lives of 10,000 Jewish children destined for the gas chambers.

The Children and Their Rescuers

This account of the activity of resisters working in the shadows and running major risks to rescue children allows us to imagine the fabric of their daily life and that of the children themselves in but a fragmentary manner. Their lives were complicated by the problems constituting the tedious routine of the occupation period: precarious public transportation, rationing and the shortage of innumerable foodstuffs and other items indispensable for daily life, curfews, the risks inherent in wearing the yellow star or being caught without it, police inspections, insecure domicile, the danger of denunciation. It was necessary to seek out unknown families and institutions throughout the countryside, to procure false papers and ration cards for the children, to teach them to forget their identity and to invent a new past, to provide them with a basic wardrobe, to transport them, to visit them regularly and pay for their upkeep, to keep up their material and moral well-being, and in some cases to maintain contact with family members without violating security precautions. This all had to be done by a very limited staff, sometimes decimated by mass arrests, without formal training, except in the case of youth movement social workers or teachers.

Most members of the Resistance, before the era of the maquis and the insurrection, developed in their normal environment. Without breaking with their families, neighborhood, work, or studies, they devoted a few hours daily or weekly to underground activity. All this was forbidden to the members of the Jewish networks for the rescue of children, harnessed to an arduous task and developing within perpetual clandestinity. Any error, forgetfulness, negligence, or fault on their part could compromise the well-being, security, and even the lives of several children and those who sheltered them. They were for the most part young people in their late teens and twenties. Their relationships were largely platonic, sometimes taking refuge in highly emotional letters. Too often relationships were shattered by the brutal separation of an arrest followed by deportation.

The periodic meetings with their wards were often trying, revealing cases of demoralization, disharmony with the surroundings, behavior problems, privation. Despite their own distress, they had to lavish kindness, to obtain indispensable clothing or shoes, to console, to raise morale, to find a new placement when the foster parent was clearly too hated or detestable, even dishonest or cruel.[167]

The wards of the clandestine networks certainly underwent physical and moral suffering during the wanderings of their underground existence. One is awestruck by the reserves of courage, presence of mind, and endurance that most of them were able to mobilize. For the vast majority of them, the supreme trial came at the end of the war, when they learned that their father, mother, brothers, and sisters would never return. Mainly they internalized their suffering. Those who have told the story of the war years did so with extreme sobriety. The Rue Amelot archives contain a large file of letters written by children placed in foster homes in 1943 and 1944. They all try to be reassuring.[168] When compared with the reports of the visiting social workers, they appear to reflect reality with regard to the satisfaction of their elementary needs. But it also happens that what children wrote was dictated by the moving concern not to worry their parents (they could not know their letters would never arrive), or else by fear of reprisals by the foster parents, who, they guessed, inspected their correspondence. In the Jewish orphanage of La Varenne in 1946, as well as in supplementary Jewish classes in rue Guy-Patin, in Paris, several dozen children from eight to sixteen years old wrote, "How I got through the German occupation." Many of them retain grateful memories of the time when they were placed in the country. Others mainly emphasize the Liberation, which meant the end of corporal punishments suffered in their foster homes.[169]

A look at the rare extant written testimony, letters dating from the years of the Occupation and impressions recorded a short time after the war, shows that the children's sensitivity and intuition distinguish between adults who reacted with cruelty and those guided by compassion. The contribution of the Jewish children to their own rescue is in having shown a sense of responsibility in not betraying their true identities. France did not know the nightmare and the dishonor of the caravans of children, all alone in the world, absolutely bereft, who wandered through Central Europe, abandoned to chaos. France is in debt to the rescue networks of the Jewish resistance, to their very numerous allies within humanitarian organizations and the Resistance, and finally to the thousands of peasants, workers, teachers, priests, men and women of all walks of life, who took in Jewish children and protected them.

For two years the resisters of the rescue networks waged this battle for the safety of approximately 10,000 children,[170] pitilessly hunted down by the most bestial perversion in history. The victory of these resisters is evident on several levels: they deprived the enemy of 10,000 of its prey, small and defenseless human beings; they defeated those who wielded force and power; and, finally, they gained a triumph for elementary human values that had been outlawed. Their epic struggle, carried on in darkness, but worthy of the most brilliant homage, made it possible to preserve the Jewish identity of most of the escapees who owe their lives to it.

12

❦

The Jewish Underground:
Solidarity and Vitality

A Jewish leader of the first rank noted in his private notebook on December 2, 1942: "The hours are passing and the news is good. The Russian offensives are developing. In North Africa there is progress. Is it already 1918, as people write in chalk on the walls? I believe so, as much as I hope so."[1]

On Sunday, November 8, the Americans landed in North Africa. On November 11, the Wehrmacht and the Italian troops occupied the entire southern zone. On November 27, the French sank their own fleet in the Gulf of Toulon rather than deliver the ships to the Germans. On the eastern front, the Wehrmacht suffered severe reversals at Stalingrad. Hope for the coming victory of the Allies was reborn.

The brutality and intensity of the elimination of the French Jews seemed to be declining. Notwithstanding, in Paris a special police unit created by Leguay on November 9 arrested and detained Jews in Drancy at the rate of twenty to thirty per day for three months.[2] But in the rest of France, a semblance of calm reigned with respect to anti-Jewish repression. Deportations had been interrupted since November 12. In the southern zone, the delivery of Jews to the Germans had stopped on October 23. Arrests following police inspections became rarer. The slowdown in police activity was accompanied by increasing ingenuity employed by the Jews in "Aryanizing" themselves.

At first the military occupation of the southern zone plunged the Jews into anguish. But it had no adverse consequences for them during the first weeks, except the definitive closure of the legal exits from France. We have seen that 500 wards of the OSE, about to emigrate to the United States and already gathered in Marseilles, had to be sent back to shelters in the center of France.[3]

The German troops exercised special vigilance along the Spanish border, where on December 30, 1942 a closed zone, fifteen kilometers deep, was established, swarming with customs officers and units of the Wehrmacht and Feldgendarmerie.[4] This measure made the illegal crossing of the border much more difficult. It was precisely on December 30 that a Feldgendarmerie patrol arrested Chaplain Kapel and the delegate of the UGIF in Carcassonne, David Geiger, on a bus on the Aulus-les-Bains line in the Ariège Department. They were both on their way to 375 Jewish refugees from Belgium who were assigned to residences in that area. Kapel had organized community life there, while the UGIF provided assistance to the poor. Alerted by Lambert, the Prefect of Toulouse demanded and obtained the transfer of the two leaders to the French police, who immediately released them. However the day before, one of Kapel's assistants, Paul Roitman, had been arrested in the same circumstances and detained in the Mérignac camp and then in the Fort of Hâ in the Gironde Department. An audacious but determined action by his younger brother Léon brought about his release as well.[5] These incidents, far from sowing panic, actually had a reassuring effect. Jewish leaders were comforted by the feeling that the action they had undertaken was bearing fruit: some were enabling wanted Jews to go underground, while others managed to have the enemy release newly captured prey.

A New Unleashing of Repression in January 1943

But the calm was soon to end. The feeling of relative security following the success of the children's rescue operations and the camouflage of foreign Jews, as well as by the impression that French Jews would not be delivered to the Germans, proved to be false. On December 9, the CGQJ ordered the UGIF to rid itself of all foreign personnel.[6] On December 11, a Vichy law required the stamping of *juif* (Jew) in identity cards and ration books.[7] On December 20, the Prefecture of the Alpes-Maritimes Department in the Italian zone decreed the transfer of the foreign Jews resident there to the Ardèche Department, which was occupied by the Germans.[8] On January 5, 1943, Darquier de Pellepoix ordered the UGIF to dissolve its Fourth

Directorate (youth) and to "assure the *effective and immediate* dissolution of the EIF."[9]

None of these directives were applied literally. Baur and Lambert, each on his own, negotiated with the CGQJ and succeeded in postponing the discharge of foreign personnel from the UGIF and in obtaining exceptions to the measure. The Italian authorities forbade the stamping of the identity papers of foreign Jews in their zone and prevented their transfer to Ardèche.[10] Regarding youth, the CGQJ never exercised the slightest control. The EIF continued their very thinly camouflaged activities.[11] Nevertheless, anguish once more spread among the Jews. The president of the UGIF, Albert Lévy, secretly emigrated to Switzerland toward the end of December. Discretely warned by a high prefectorial official, Chaplain Kapel crossed over into the Italian zone in Grenoble on January 31, 1943, to escape Gestapo searches in Toulouse. Having taken refuge in Isère, with the agreement of the Chief Rabbi of France, he resumed his social and cultural work with Jewish youth and with the Jewish communities of the region.[12]

The drama that was brewing burst out in Rouen and Marseilles. Between January 13 and 16, 1943, the French police arrested 222 Jews in Rouen, of whom 170 were of French nationality. They were all transferred to Drancy. Between January 22 and 27, along with thousands of arrests of "disturbing elements" by the French police during the evacuation of the Vieux-Port quarter of Marseilles, destined for destruction by German order, around eight hundred Jews were deported, including 585 of French nationality.[13]

No Jew had been warned in any way prior to the arrests. The deportation of whole families from Marseilles had taken place under inhuman conditions, without the knowledge of charitable organizations, Jewish and non-Jewish, and in their absence.[14] An exceptional concentration of police and gendarmerie forces in Marseilles during the days preceding January 22 was not sufficient to sound the alarm. The Jews of French nationality were not suspicious. According to rumors, in Marseilles there was to be a "purge" of people of irregular status and of anti-social elements. Lambert, General Chaplain Hirschler, and Chief Rabbi Salzer obstinately demanded the release of those captured, sending telegrams of protest to Pétain and Laval—in vain.[15]

Did these events signify that Vichy could no longer assure the safety of its Jewish nationals, or that it did not wish to? After placing its police at the disposal of the Nazis for the delivery of tens of thousands of foreign Jews, had the regime also decided to arrest and deport French Jews?

After an interruption that had begun in November, three convoys left Drancy between February 9 and 13, 1943, containing 3,000 Jews, of whom

1,000 were French. On February 9, the Gestapo captured the twenty staff members of the UGIF assistance office on rue Sainte-Catherine in Lyons. A trap laid in the same place caught sixty-six other victims, clients and resisters of the FSJF (*Fédération des sociétés juives de France*, the Federation of Jewish Associations of France) and of the *Sixième*.[16] On the night of February 10–11, the French police rounded up forty-eight children in the UGIF centers in Paris, as well as patients in hospitals, and old people in residences as well as people in their private homes: a total of 1,569 foreign Jews were detained, of whom 80 percent were over sixty or under twenty.[17]

This was further proof that the government wished to seize all the Jews, without distinction, persuading the resisters that any action, except the clandestine struggle for rescue, would be in vain. Children, old people, those not subject to deportation, those holding UGIF cards, military veterans, and Frenchmen—none was safe. Jewish officials demanded the application of still valid regulations, but these appeals were ineffective.

Official Judaism Moves Toward the Underground

There was nevertheless no radical and unanimous reaction on the part of either the Jewish population or of the leaders of the Jewish organizations. Reality was much more complex than is suggested by the accumulation of repressive operations of the months of January and February 1943 mentioned above. The attitude of the Vichy government was not yet one of pure and simple submission to the will of the Nazis. The precedents of Rouen and Marseilles, where the French police carried out the roundups, were not repeated in 1943. Until January 25, 1944, the French authorities refused to give the Germans the lists of French Jews.[18] The proposed law revoking the citizenship of Jews naturalized after 1927 was never passed.[19] Thus, despite the tragedies of January–February 1943, Vichy still seemed capable of limiting the Germans' freedom of action. Thus Lambert, at the head of UGIF-South, continued to assume his official responsibilities, acting with the support of the Central Consistory, which had set aside its reservations regarding the UGIF.[20] Lambert held bitter discussions with the CGQJ to protect his foreign staff. The Consistory became increasingly vehement in its appeals to Pétain and Laval, demanding, for example, that the French government react to "this serious blow to its sovereign rights, which cannot but move world opinion."[21]

The remaining official Jewish leaders, of the Consistory and the UGIF, were not entirely taken in by the game they continued to play. We have seen that in the two zones, the UGIF took an active part in the clandestine rescue of children. On February 5, 1943, Lambert had his council, meeting in Nice, nominate two "social inspectors," Dika Jefroykin and Maurice Brener.[22] Now these two men, co-directors of the AJDC, exercised responsibilities in the Jewish resistance movement. Jefroykin belonged to the directorship of the AJ (*Armée juive*, Jewish Army). Brener provided the *Service André* with means to act. Despite the nomination of two resisters to the top echelons of the UGIF, it is still difficult to determine precisely what role Lambert played in illegal activities. He makes no mention of them in his journal. But nothing stops us from supposing that he created the posts of social inspector, a fiction devoid of any defined task, so as to give Jefroykin and Brener a legal cover to facilitate their movement throughout France, under the protection of official UGIF identification cards.[23] In May 1943, these two men, along with Gamzon, went to Paris on a "special mission" for the UGIF:

> All three of us had obtained an *Ausweis* [laissez-passer] from the Germans, supposedly to arrange matters with the UGIF in Paris. We were thus received by the Gestapo chief in charge of Jewish affairs, Röthke. We conversed. Then we organized a network to transfer Jewish children from Paris to the south. We took care of the children from Rue Amelot, some children placed with families. We were helped by Dr. Minkowski and by David Rapoport.[24]

At about the same time, on April 29, Lambert was in Grenoble, taking part in the creation of the clandestine *Centre de documentation juif* (Jewish Documentation Center), which became the *Centre de documentation juive contemporaine* (CDJC, Center for Contemporary Jewish Documentation) after the war. This was an initiative of Isaac Schneersohn, with the support and presence of leaders from the Consistory and the FSJF.[25]

Behind its façade as an official religious organization, the Central Consistory established contacts between its charities and the rescue networks. In September 1942, it ordered the creation of improvised transit centers in synagogues for Jews who had escaped arrest but were pursued and without shelter.[26] In Lyons,

> the impossible was done to feed and lodge them. With the agreement of Cardinal Gerlier, the Primate of Gaules, and Pastor Eberhardt (who was later arrested from his pulpit by the

Germans and deported), the Captain of the Salvation Army, all these foreign Jews were lodged with private people, in convents, in branches of the Salvation Army, with *Amitiés africaines* (African Friendships), etc.

Many were terrified and did not dare leave the synagogue. They spent their day in the courtyard, where they did their laundry in the fountain and hung it to dry on the trellises against the wall. The synagogue entrance was an open grill, so passers-by could look in and see them. At night they lay on straw in the synagogue.

Every day there were 100 to 150 new people; we tried daily to pass on as many as possible to other shelters, so that from there we could manage to get them into Switzerland.[27]

In Toulouse, Nice, and Lyons the police raided the synagogues. During the night of October 20–21, 1942, three members of the Consistory tried to oppose the arrest of Jews who had taken refuge in the synagogue on Quai Tilsitt in Lyons. They too were arrested and found guilty of sheltering foreigners of irregular status. They were later released thanks to the intervention of President Helbronner with the police commissioner, who also had the refugees returned to the synagogue.[28] In 1943 and 1944, the seat of the Consistory, in Rue Boissac, in Lyons, served as a secret office for the distribution of false identity papers provided by the *Sixième*. The establishment of a permanent tie with the underground Jewish networks took place in autumn 1943, with the start of talks that led to the foundation of the *Conseil représentatif des Juifs de France* (The Representative Council of French Jews, CRIF) in January 1944.

During 1942–1944 the Jewish Communists had constantly demanded that the institutions of official Judaism dissolve themselves. They accused their directors of collaborating with the enemy and of giving the Jewish population a false illusion of the possibility of survival under the protection of the authorities. Synagogues and welfare offices were, in their view, merely traps facilitating the capture of Jews by the Nazis and their accomplices. The demand that the UGIF dissolve itself became general among the Jewish resistance networks in 1944, and commando units of the UJRE (*Union des Juifs pour la résistance et l'entraide*, Jewish Union for Resistance and Mutual Assistance) in Marseilles and of the AJ in Lyons destroyed the files of UGIF offices. One of the first debates on the agenda of the clandestine CRIF concerned the unanimous demand of the resistance organizations to close down the UGIF. But the Consistory kept synagogues and offices open, in "the conviction that the end of religious Judaism would signify the end of Judaism, and that it would be capitulation to the enemy to close the temples consecrated to the service of God."[29] Not until June 1944, following a Gestapo raid that led to the deportation of the staff of the Lyons synagogue and of some of the faithful present at the time, did the Chief Rabbi and the Consistory become resigned to closing their offices and plunging entirely into the underground.[30]

For their part the directors of the UGIF persisted until the end in keeping their administration going. Provisions for the camp in Drancy depended on it. In the summer of 1944, there were still 24,000 people wearing the yellow star in Paris, while the number of those assisted in the southern zone did not stop increasing during that year.[31] In determining the inventory of the work accomplished by the UGIF as well as its failures and the criticisms voiced against it, Klarsfeld writes: "without the subsidies distributed by the UGIF, how many needy families would not have been able to pay their rent, assure a minimum of subsistence for themselves, . . . how many would have fallen into the hands of the police, the gendarmes, the militia men, the Feldgendarmerie, or the Gestapo? . . . The UGIF helped incomparably more Jews to preserve their liberty and life than it contributed to maintaining Drancy."[32]

Regardless of the judgments regarding one or another of the leaders of official Judaism, their many acts of cooperation with the Resistance cannot be ignored. The enemy beleaguered these leaders. André Baur, the President of the UGIF, was arrested in Paris with his wife, and their four children on June 21, 1943, on the order of SS officer Aloïs Brunner, the commander of the camp in Drancy. One month later, on August 21, came the turn of the director for the southern zone, Raymond-Raoul Lambert, with his wife and their four children, on the order of Röthke, the chief of the Jewish section of the Gestapo. On September 4, Brunner seized two other members of the council of UGIF-North, Marcel Stora and Fernand Musnik. In Lyons, the President of the Central Consistory, Jacques Heibronner, was arrested with his wife on October 23, 1943. Then a detachment of the Gestapo captured the Chaplain General, René Hirschler, and his wife on December 23 in Marseilles. None of these people survived deportation.[33] Hunted by the police, the Chief Rabbi of France, Isaïe Schwartz, owed his safety to flight in December 1943 to a clandestine place of refuge in Ardèche. The rabbinical corps suffered the most severe losses: twenty rabbis were deported and died in the death camps, two rabbis, youth chaplains, were executed in France.[34] "The long list of employees and directors of the UGIF, like that of the rabbis and consistorial officials who were deported and, with their family, disappeared in Auschwitz, definitively prevents one from discussing these matters in terms of "resistance" or "collaboration," writes Annie Kriegel.[35]

The task accomplished by these two organizations, the Consistory and the UGIF, in 1943 and 1944 did not deviate formally from the role officially assigned to each of them: ritual and religious education on the one hand, and assistance on the other. Their leaders were imbued with the conviction that the survival of the Jews depended on their action.[36] Many of them led or encouraged parallel but clandestine activities within the framework of rescue work.

The action of the corps of chaplains led by René Hirschler is exemplary in this regard. In the southern zone they were officially accredited to the commanders of the camps and the GTE (*Groupes de travailleurs étrangers*, Foreign Laborers Groups), as were their priest and minister counterparts. They worked to establish religious and cultural centers, in assistance, and in rescue. After the deportations of August 1942, rescue had become the dominant preoccupation. It took forms that combined utilization of the labyrinth of the administrative rules with recourse to illegality. In the Gurs camp, in January 1941, Chaplain René Kapel created a central assistance committee led by Rabbi Léo Ansbacher, a German refugee detained in the camp. The camp administration accorded official sanction to his actions and gave him some privileges, for example relative freedom to circulate.[37] Counting on this precedent, Hirschler appointed more than 150 detainees in 1942 and 1943 as auxiliary chaplains in the camps and GTE. This status allowed most of them, with their families, to avoid deportation by using false identification papers, or else to cross illegally into Spain.[38] Ansbacher and his wife, warned in time by the OSE team of the camp that his deportation was imminent, escaped from Gurs on December 26, 1942. They managed to reach a place previously indicated to them and were taken in hand by a border-runner, who was paid with the proceeds of the sale of their stamp collection. After a border crossing full of dramatic adventures, they arrived in a Spanish locality, Ochagavia.[39]

Escape to Spain, like the action of the screening commissions, demanded the combined initiatives of numerous rescuers, activists in humanitarian organizations present in the camps, and chaplains. The escape routes could be hazardous and precarious. In December 1942, an officer in the Gurs camp, Sauvage, guided detainees to reliable border-runners.[40] But he was arrested, and it was necessary to find another escape route. Only enterprising people, endowed with good physical endurance, could risk crossing the Pyrenees, especially in winter. Among the hundreds of foreign Jews assigned to residences in Eaux-Bonnes in the Pyrénées-Atlantiques Department and in Aulus-les-Bains in the Ariège Department, visited regularly by the camp chaplains, the young and healthy men escaped to Spain before the January 20 transfer of all that population to Naillat in the Creuse Department.[41]

After the arrest of René Hirschler in December 1943, Rabbi Henri Schilli became the Chaplain General. He was unknown both to the Nazi authorities and to those of Vichy, with the exception of high French officials hostile to the Germans and to the collaboration policy. At this point in the war and the occupation, the official Jewish leaders had put an end to their appeals to the government. Those responsible for the appeals had all been arrested and deported or had disappeared into the underground.[42] Schilli directed the chaplaincy in the camps with courage and perseverance until the liberation. At work since the summer of 1940, he was experienced and efficient.

The Flow of Jews Toward the Italian Zone

The most massive obstacle to the application of the Vichy anti-Jewish policy arose after the occupation of the southern zone, where the Italian region extended from east of the Rhône over six whole departments (Haute-Savoie, Savoie, Hautes-Alpes, Basses-Alpes, Alpes Maritimes, and Var) as well as over the eastern parts of three other departments (Isère, Drôme, and Vaucluse). The Italian authority was in force until September 9, 1943, when the armistice concluded with the Allies by the Badoglio government was made public.[43]

On December 27, 1942 the Italian consul general in Nice refused to apply the Vichy law of December 11 requiring the stamping of the word *juif* on the Jews' identity cards and ration books. He also obstructed the French decision to transfer foreign Jews who had settled in the Alpes-Maritimes Department since January 1, 1938 to the Ardèche Department, which was occupied by the Germans. On December 31 the Italian military command notified all the prefects in its zone that it was forbidden to apply such measures, on the pretext that the Italian government "did not tolerate that people who might indulge in anti-German or anti-Italian acts should be removed from its surveillance."[44]

During the nine months of the Italian occupation, anti-Jewish repression was entirely suspended in that zone. Outraged at first by these blows to its prerogatives from a country that had not beaten France on the battlefield, the French government tried to reaffirm its sovereignty in the area of Jewish policy. Laval proposed the transfer to Italy of "foreign Jews who fall under the measures enacted by the French government." The Italian government refused this plan and the consul general in Nice explained that "his government intended to apply to the Jews residing in the Italian zone of occupation the same legislation that existed in Italy regarding the Jews, that is . . . a humane legislation."[45]

Irritated by this policy, the SS chiefs in France demanded intervention from Berlin. The German diplomats in Rome pressured the Italian government. Then Ribbentrop met Mussolini on February 20, 1943. After tacking and veering, the Italians pretended to concede by sending a high official, Guido Lospinoso, to Nice on March 20 to serve as Inspector General of Racial Policy.[46] Vichy ultimately bowed to the Italian policy of protecting the Jews, going so far as to invite the Consistory, discreetly but "urgently," to transfer itself, its members, and its staff to the Italian zone.[47]

Jewish circles in the southern zone occupied by the Nazis rapidly learned that the Italian army was opposed to interference by Vichy and the Germans in the territory under its control. The mass arrests carried out in Marseille during the last week of January 1943 set in motion a flood of migration of foreign Jews toward the Italian zone. The two Savoys, Grenoble, and above all the Côte d'Azur became hospitable places of refuge. On February 20, 1943, in response to a German demand regarding the deportation of 2,000 Jews in reprisal for the assassination of two Luftwaffe officers in Paris, the national police made mass arrests in the southern zone. The Italian command prevented the prefects in its zone from executing this order. In Annecy Italian troops surrounded the barracks of the gendarmerie and forced the release of Jews who had been arrested and imprisoned there.[48] The leaders of the MJS (*Mouvement de jeunesse sioniste*, the Zionist Youth Movement) moved to Grenoble, where they were joined by other leaders from Toulouse, Montauban, Périgueux, Lyons, etc.[49] Lévitte also transferred the documentation center which he had developed in Moissac to Grenoble.[50] A national congress of the MJS gathered in December 1942 near Grenoble, in La Grivolée, where the ideological charter of the movement was composed.[51] Along with educational activity, Lévitte recruited and trained agents for the *Éducation physique* rescue network. A workshop for the production of false identity papers, set up by Giniewski, provided *synthés* (false papers based on real ones) for the most exposed workers in the underground Jewish networks.

In view of the influx of foreign Jews in Nice, the MJS developed its group there, augmented by a section of *Éducation physique* with its own laboratory for producing *bifs* (less sophisticated forged papers) and *synthés*.[52] These two centers, Grenoble and Nice, specialized in escorting children to Switzerland. The clandestine border crossing was made relatively easy by the rather unwarlike conduct of the Italian patrols along the frontier. The coordination of social work between the *Éducation physique* and *Sixième* networks as well as convoying wards of the ose to Switzerland entailed the manufacture and diffusion of false identity cards and ration books, the placement of children, periodic visits to the latter and to camouflaged families to provide them with ration coupons, monetary assistance, and to relieve the distress of their isolation. In May or June 1943, the MJS and EIF movements strengthened their ties by the cooptation of Gamzon and Hammel into the executive committee of the MJS, the designation of a single directorate responsible for the rural groups and for the systematic coordination of educational and social activities. In August the MJS and EIF reached an agreement concerning the creation of a Zionist branch within the EIF, as well as joint training courses in scouting for the staffs of the two movements.[53] Since he came from the EIF and remained a member of their national team, Simon Lévitte was familiar with their effectiveness and organizational experience. Free of all partisan dogmatism, he shared the feeling with the two EIF leaders that their joining the MJS executive committee would be beneficial to both movements and to the rescue work in general. Let us recall that it was he who created, in March 1943, a section of *Éducation physique* and of the *Sixième* in Paris. Later their action was coordinated by Jacques Pulver, sent to Paris from the southern zone for that purpose in September.

The spring and summer of 1943 were particularly propitious for the growth of the MJS in Grenoble and Nice, where educational activities took place in an atmosphere of liberty born of the policy of the Italian occupiers. The Grenoble group had rented a chalet where the movement leaders met on weekends for training and relaxation. The participants in these training sessions would arrive at the chalet in a noisy group, by tram, without taking any security precautions. They sang Hebrew songs on the way.[54] Lévitte took charge of contacts with German-occupied France, orchestrated the transfer of children to Switzerland, and the Aryanization and camouflage of Jewish families. He also ran the documentation center. Correspondence courses in Jewish literature and the history of the Jewish people and of Zionism were composed, mimeographed, and distributed to MJS groups throughout France. Initially bearing the letterhead of the Fourth Directorate of the UGIF (Youth), the mimeographed courses were later issued under the fictional imprimatur of the Section of Historical and Religious Studies of the Law Faculty.[55]

Three children's shelters functioned in the Italian zone. One, opened in La Grave in the Hautes-Alpes Department by the EIF, was populated by children evacuated from Paris to the southern zone in June 1943 by the efforts of the *Sixième*. Another, in Sappey in the Isère Department, served as a rest home for children from Moissac whose health was precarious.[56] The third was the AIP (*Association des Israélites pratiquants*, the Association of Observant Jews, connected with Lubavitch), transferred in March 1943 from Demu in the Gers Department to the Chateau of Manoir in Saint-Étienne-de-Crossey in the Isère Department.[57]

The number of foreign Jews who fled to the Italian zone from the regions occupied by the Germans cannot be determined. The prefect of the Alpes-Maritimes Department estimated that in September 1943 there were 30,000 Jews in Nice and along the coast over a distance of thirty kilometers.[58]

The Dubouchage Committee

From the beginning of 1943, FSJF activists created a committee for aid to refugees in Nice. This body was known familiarly as the Dubouchage Committee, after the boulevard where the synagogue that lodged the assistance office is situated. It was headed by "a Russian Jew from Odessa, Yaakov Doubinski, a tall old man, over eighty, whose eyes were the same pure blue as the sky of Nice." He was endowed with an uncommon power of persuasion, thanks to which he raised significant sums.[59] The French police, searching for Jews whose papers were not in order, began to inspect the Dubouchage Committee offices. They were, however, removed by Italian soldiers, who then began to keep constant guard over the synagogue, not without canceling the arrests that had already been made and informing the superintendent of police in Nice that they had been ordered to arrest any policemen who molested Jews.[60]

The Italians applied the same policy of protecting Jews in their occupation zone in Croatia and Dalmatia. Anti-Semitism was not very popular in Italy. The racial laws of 1938 were never applied with vigor. In 1943 the Minister of Foreign Affairs showed great zeal in keeping Italy free of all complicity in the criminal actions against the Jews taken by its Nazi ally.[61]

The consul general in Nice, Alberto Calisse, was kept informed of the situation regarding the Jews by an Italian Jewish friend, Angelo Donati, a banker and former president of the Italian chamber of commerce in Paris. Donati studied the problems of Jewish security with Ignace Fink, the secretary general of the Dubouchage Committee, and with Michel Topiol, one of its members. Often, they would meet daily, especially during the changes that took place on March 20, 1943, with the installation of the Inspector General of Racial Policy, Lospinoso.

A note sent by the Italian high command to the Ministry of Foreign Affairs in Rome on April 3 exposes the Italian racial policy, taking note of the instructions received by Lospinoso from the government:

> The competent Italian authorities will take the necessary measures to repel . . . from our zone . . . the foreign or French Jews who try to pass from the German occupation zone to the Italian occupation zone. . . . The objective is to save the Jews living in the French territory occupied by our troops, regardless of their nationality, whether they be Italian, French, or foreign. . . . The police inspector Lospinoso . . . has informed the Command of the Fourth Army of the instructions he received personally from the Duce: To detain, by the end of March, all the Jews living on the French territory occupied by our troops, and to choose places situated about a hundred kilometers from the sea, for example, Haute-Savoie. . . . The army . . . will have to have hotels opened to serve as obligatory residences for the Jews.[62]

The measures, announced here in response to German pressure exerted upon the Duce, were, however, applied as a result of the cooperation among Lospinoso, Donati, and the Dubouchage Committee. The Jews who arrived in Nice from regions occupied by the Germans after March 26 were not turned away. The order remained a dead letter. Lospinoso enabled the Dubouchage Committee to offer Jews whose papers were not in order the option of having an assigned residence. The Italian army requisitioned hotels in the border Departments of Haute-Savoie (in Megève, Saint-Gervais, and Combloux), Basses-Alpes (in Moustiers-Sainte-Marie, Castellane, and Barcelonnette), and Alpes-Maritimes (in Vence and Saint-Martin-de-Vésubie). From March to July, 1943, 4,000 Jews were sent to these places at their own request. The Dubouchage Committee was responsible for accepting these requests, transportation by bus, and for the designation of the place of residence. It provided the people being resettled with the following form:

> Mr. and Mrs. _____ is/are authorized to take the bus to _____, on the date of _____. _____ seats.
> Assembly point in front of the boys' high school on Avenue Félix-Faure, at a quarter to six. Authorized baggage: one valise per person.

This form was stamped "Jewish Religious Association of the Ashkenazi Rite, Nice," in French and Hebrew, and it served as a temporary identity paper under the cover of the Italian authorities. The French police were forced to accede. The Dubouchage Committee submitted to Lospinoso lists of the names of those receiving tickets, classed according to their designated place of residence.[63]

Administered by Jewish assistance organizations, the FSJF, ORT, and the UGIF, these forced residences in the Italian zone were safe havens. But they lasted no longer than the Italian occupation, which collapsed in several hours on September 8, 1943, with the announcement of the armistice concluded between Rome and the Allies. During the five or six months of this interlude, the Jewish refugees created soup kitchens, schools, occupational training centers, chapels, and cultural circles in Saint-Gervais, Megève, and Saint-Martin-de-Vésubie, each of which contained approximately a thousand people. An elected committee administered the institutions in each locality. The UGIF of Nice covered the expenses for the food and lodging of those receiving assistance.[64]

Jews arrested in Nice for the crime of using false identity papers, numbering 162, were released upon the intervention of the Dubouchage Committee. Whenever a Jew was arrested and held in detention, the rule observed by Vichy was to send him to a camp upon the expiration of that detention. But the pressure of the Italian authorities, in support of demands of the Jewish committee, managed to suspend the application of this rule.[65] Moreover, in July the government replaced the regional prefect of Nice, Ribière, by Jean Chaigneau, who showed willingness to regularize the situation of all the illegal Jewish residents, making them immune to all sanctions. The new prefect explained to a delegation from the Dubouchage Committee, "I don't want to give the Italians the noble privilege of being the only defenders of the tradition of tolerance and humanity which is nevertheless that of France."[66]

Still, at that time worry seized the Jews of the Italian zone. The fall of Mussolini on July 25, 1943 and the ascent of the Badoglio government in Rome gave rise to fears of a German-Italian confrontation and the movement of Nazi troops into the Italian zone. The Saint-Martin-de-Vésubie committee gave a team of MJS leaders the mission of exploring an escape route to Italy.[67] An Italian note points out that "many foreign Jews have decided to cross the border illegally. . . . They prefer to undergo the rigors of Italian law rather than continue to run the risks to which they are exposed in France."[68] The same note suggested assigning several thousand Jews to residences in Liguria and Piedmont.

Informed of Badoglio's intention of making an armistice agreement, Donati went to Rome in early August. Completely aware of what would happen in France, he developed a plan to save 30,000 Jews from the Italian zone. He obtained the agreement of the government in Rome for the transit of Jews via Italy, and he negotiated with diplomatic representatives of Great Britain and the United States in the Vatican for the transport to North Africa on board allied ships.[69] At this time, Sammy Lattès wrote to Lambert on August 4 from Grenoble that people "in the charities [were preoccupied] with the problem of evacuation to Italy of the Jews of Megève and of Saint-Gervais, of foreign Jews in a general way, and also, if the case may be, of French Jews. . . . In fact the rumor is spreading that the Italians plan to evacuate the Jews of their zone to Italy and to regard them as civilian detainees. We will be definitively informed on this point, I hope, by Donati."[70]

At the end of August, Rome decided to withdraw its troops from France, with the exception of the County of Nice, where they were to gather all the Jews resident in their zone. The Italian government had thousands of passports printed especially for the Jews who were to be evacuated to Italy.[71]

On September 3 the armistice between Badoglio and the Allies was secretly signed. The Italian command planned to concentrate its troops and launch an offensive that would cause the collapse of the German forces and the liberation of Italy. At the same time, all the Jews under Italian authority would have been saved. Preparations for evacuation from the Alpine departments continued according to Donati's plan. But on September 8 the premature publication of the armistice with Italy by the Allied general staff transformed what was supposed to be the rout of the Germans into a debacle of the Italian troops. They were ready neither to take the offensive nor to retreat in good order. The Jews of the Italian zone were caught in a trap.

The Gestapo in Nice

Forward elements of the Wehrmacht arrived in the Alpine Departments on September 8. Two days later, the German occupation of Nice was complete, including the police. The Italian troops fled in disarray.

Eighty buses hired by the Dubouchage Committee made their way to Nice, transporting refugees from the assigned residences. The Italian command had a train leave from the Le Fayet railway station for the evacuation of old people, the sick, and children from Megève and Saint-Gervais. A ragtag convoy of a thousand Jews left Saint-Martin-de-Vésubie in panic, heading north and reaching Entraque in Italy after a march of more than two days. In the generalized, chaotic flight, Jews were received on special trains of the Italian army. A few dozen Jews from Nice had the good fortune of obtaining Italian laissez-passer and mixing in with the troops fleeing to Vintimille. Between September 5 and 11, from 1,000 to 1,500 Jews managed to cross the Italian border.[72]

The ferocious commander of the SS camp in Drancy, Aloïs Brunner, flanked by a special commando unit, arrived in Nice on September 10. His first action was to search the Italian consulate in Nice for files concerning the Jews. The staff claimed that these files had been taken to Rome, and Brunner arrested two diplomats. Donati's apartment was vacant. The Gestapo seized thousands of special passports that the Ministry of Interior in Rome had printed as part of the plan for Jewish emigration to North Africa via Italy.[73] A Waffen SS unit sent in pursuit of the refugees from Saint-Martin-de-Vésubie captured 410 Jews in the Piedmontese Alps on September 18. First interned in Borgo San Dalmazzo, they were all transferred to Drancy via Nice, between November 21 and 25, and later deported.[74]

The flushing out of Jews in Nice, executed with unprecedented ferocity, began on September 12. Along with Brunner's SS commando unit, members of the *Parti populaire français*, the French People's Party, led by Jacques Doriot, took part, along with a band of White Russian "physiognomists," bandits seeking to plunder rich Jews, and informers avid for the prize of 100 francs for every Jew delivered. Roundups in the 170 hotels and boarding houses and in apartment buildings, the accosting of Jews in the streets and railways stations, night and day, sowed terror. By the time of his departure from the Côte d'Azur on December 14, Brunner had captured around 1,400 Jews in the Haute-Savoie Department, in Grenoble, and above all in the Alpes-Maritimes Department, and to these must be added the 410 victims of the operation carried out in Piedmont. Compared to the 25,000 Jews whom the Gestapo expected to seize, this result was a failure.[75]

There were several reasons for the relative ineffectiveness of Brunner's manhunt, despite his formidable anti-Jewish fanaticism:

- His commando unit contained only about fifteen torturers, and it did not benefit from the cooperation of the French police. Chaigneau, the Prefect, destroyed the lists drawn up by his administration.[76]
- In general the population was helpful to the Jews. Seeing the result, one must supposed that informers were relatively rare,

despite the increases in the bounty offered from 100 francs to
1,000 francs and even 5,000 francs.[77]

• The rescuers belonging to the Jewish resistance movement,
although severely decimated by the Gestapo, opposed its devastating action effectively.

The teams of *Éducation physique*, the *Sixième*, and the *Service André*
obtained false identity papers, distributed help, and discovered temporary
shelters in the city and in distant places of refuge. Finally, to permit flight
from Nice, they discovered means of transportation other than the public
facilities which had become impractical because of the Gestapo inspections.

The Dubouchage Committee was immobilized during the first days of
the German occupation. Brunner had gathered a bundle of information
about the members of the committee. His men had put their hands on
Donati's secretary, Germaine Meyer. Tortured and then deported, she did
not survive.[78] Hunted and pursued, the leaders and activists of the FSJF who
had worked with the Dubouchage Committee left Nice themselves. Some
joined in the rescue action in Grenoble, Lyons, or Toulouse. Of the FSJF, only
Claude Kelman and four young social workers remained. In December
1943, the Gestapo raided his home, where it captured two of the social
workers, one of whom was deported. Kelman, too, had to flee from Nice. But
part of the underground assistance work of the FSJF continued under the
leadership of a non-Jewish Russian, Rogowski, the former Attorney General
of Petrograd under the Kerenski regime and a close friend of Marc Jarblum
and Yaakov Doubinski.[79]

The almost complete disappearance of the FSJF staff in Nice, leaving
thousands of Jewish refugees defenseless and without resources for their
basic subsistence, could have been a brilliant victory for the Gestapo. But
young people took up the battle. Elsewhere we have described the rescue of
children accomplished by Moussa Abadi, the creator of a network modelled
on the Garel Network. Léon Poliakov of the *Service André* has told how
Abadi took care of the "repatriation" to Saint-Étienne-de-Crossey of the
wards and personnel of the AIP who had fled to Nice in early September to
place themselves under the protection of Donati and the Italian troops. The
youngest ones were camouflaged as a vacation camp, the others were taken
in a series of convoys, hidden in a fruit truck on its way from Nice to Isère
with empty crates.[80] Exercising enormous precaution, the *Sixième* dispersed
the sixty children and staff from the shelter in La Grave, which had opened a
few months previously.

Aloïs Brunner Kept at Bay

In Chambéry, Annecy, Grenoble, Voiron, and Nice, the offices and dispensaries of the UGIF, the OSE, and the ORT had functioned without impediment during the Italian interlude. The teams of the *Sixième* and *Éducation physique* were filled out during this time, while they remained underground. The manufacture of *bifs* and *synthés* improved, the network of relations with resisters belonging to the government and to charitable institutions expanded. Young people combed the countryside in search of shelters for placing children as part of the Garel Circuit. Others escorted Jews of all ages to Switzerland and provided the cover of identity papers. All this was done to supply some of the needs of the regions under German occupation. In Grenoble and Nice in particular, the two clandestine rescue organizations of the MJS and the EIF remained intact during the Italian debacle. The Dubouchage Committee and the UGIF, including the OSE dispensary, had to close their doors during the general flight provoked by the reign of terror inflicted by Brunner's Gestapo, so the teams of Gutman (*Sixième*) and of Weintrob (*Éducation physique*) remained the only recourse for a large part of these hunted Jews.

How was contact made with the rescuers? There was no possibility of maintaining an office. Young people circulated among the hotels to unearth unfortunates. Very quickly identified by a growing number of hunted Jews, they were "assailed in the street, in squares, with supplications and appeals for aid. How many times did we arrive at hotels a few moments before or after the passage of the Gestapo."[81]

The two teams merged into a single group, later called the Maurice Cachoud group, consisting of twenty to twenty-five young men and women. Short of personnel but able to use the FSJF assistance funds, Kelman "wished to create only a single underground group, whereas we envisaged the existence of two organizations in case the Gestapo put one out of business. Unfortunately, that is what happened."

Within this group of young people "one team was charged with finding lodging, another with the fabrication of false papers, a third with the distribution of assistance, a fourth with relations with the authorities to seek out elements sympathetic to our cause."

During the first three months, the group distributed financial assistance, in the average amount of 250,000 francs, with funds provided by the FSJF and the UGIF and money raised by Raymond Heymann from individuals (more than 380,000 francs in three months). Later Maurice Brener provided the group with an allocation from the AJDC coming to an average of 220,000 francs per month until the Liberation.[82]

The Gestapo managed to decapitate the group in Nice in September, arresting Weintrob on the 25th and Guttmann on the 28th. Leadership was then assumed by a specialist in false identification papers, Maurice Cachoud-Loebenberg. After his departure for Paris in March 1944, where he was sent to the false paper service of the *Mouvement de libération nationale* (National Liberation Movement), Heymann became the group chief. The manhunt was unrelenting after Brunner's return to Drancy in December 1943. Systematic searches of hotels and apartment buildings, roundups in the streets and railroad stations with the help of a band of "physiognomists" were carried out in Nice and more sporadically in Grenoble, Chambéry, Aix-les-Bains, etc. Klarsfeld has demonstrated that Simone Jacob (Veil), aged sixteen, was one of the youngest escapees of France. She was deported from Drancy on April 13, 1944, having been arrested in Nice a few days earlier. The false paper workshops constantly had to move, whether because signs indicated that the Gestapo was on its trail, or because the landlord preferred to steer clear of something that was a mortal risk for him.[83] It became the supplier for the local resistance, which, in turn, facilitated contacts with the government, uncovering trustworthy officials willing to provide ration cards and the renewal of ration coupons on a vast scale, more than 2,000 per month. The German report on the arrest of Weintrob (September 25, 1943) shows that he had organized three convoys of twenty-five Jewish children, taking them to Switzerland. The *Sixième* and *Éducation physique* continued crossing the Swiss border with Jews, despite the threat of German patrols. The bishopric, pastors, the House of Jesuits, the *Compagnons de France*, the *Union chrétienne des jeunes gens* (Christian Union of Young People), and the Unionist scouts also contributed to the lodging of hunted Jews.[84]

Members of the local resistance made certain that an operation was undertaken against the gang of "physiognomists." Unwilling to delay any longer, the AJ dispatched its *franc* group in March 1944, and its methodical action got rid of these dangerous auxiliaries of the Gestapo.[85]

In addition to the 1,800 Jews captured from September to December 1943, the Gestapo had about 2,000 Jews deported from the former Italian zone in 1944.[86] The losses of the Jewish rescue networks in Nice, out of a total of forty-five, numbered nine dead, of whom eight were deported, while Maurice Cachoud, arrested in Paris on July 18, 1944, succumbed to torture. The action of these networks occupies a major place in the rescue of some 20,000 Jews in the former Italian zone. The personal losses of their main leaders during the first days of the German occupation did not weaken their determination. Among these young people, all of whom were under thirty, none pretended to have the strength to resist torture in cases of arrest. This theme arose frequently in their conversations. The specter of torture was ever more present because of the clandestine messages received from comrades who had fallen into the nets of the Gestapo and detained in Drancy.

These messages enumerated the information in Brunner's possession: "Actively searched for: Fischer, Kelman (very actively), Jefroykin, Topiol, Fink, etc. Brunner has declared that he absolutely wishes to put his hand on the Joint organization."[87]

The captured resisters did not let themselves become resigned, but rather organized an activist life among the detainees:

> We already have gathered a *gdoud* [Hebrew for regiment] and we hope to be able to do good work. . . . Every evening we meet and together we raise memories of the *gdoud*, accompanied with songs, in *Ivrith* [Hebrew], naturally. . . . There are possibilities for escape . . . (1) by the trucks that supply the camp; (2) by using a German uniform brought into the camp; (3) an act of force is possible, on condition that a car is available and a sufficiently numerous and trained maquis—a service for escape from Drancy ought to be set up.[88]

But there were no rescuers to aid the detainees to cross the barbed wire of the camp. Only these lines remain as testimony of an unconquerable will to survive.

No different from the other concentration camps, Drancy was never the target of operations mounted from the exterior. Were the installations of the bestial death industry impregnable fortresses? The Jewish resistance movement never attacked Drancy, above all populated by women, children, and old people, who were exposed to ferocious and pitiless reprisals. The general staffs of the Free French and the Resistance units regarded the war "solely from the point of view of military strategy"[89] and were indifferent to what was happening in the camps. But the resisters detained in Drancy were not defeated. The first chiefs of the *Sixième* and *Éducation physique* in Nice fell early in the battle, but the combat waged by the young men and women of their network did not cease. They won a splendid victory, saving the lives of almost ninety percent of the prey whom Brunner's Gestapo wished to seize.

13

⌒❀⌒

The Primacy of Tendencies Toward Unity
and the Dynamism of Spiritual Life

During the spring and summer of 1943, while Jewish refugees were converging on the Italian zone, the Jewish population of Paris was on the decline, not only because of the roundups but also because of constant migration to the countryside. Thus the popular base of Solidarité was constantly being thinned out. Local committees disappeared one after the other. The number of dues payers among manual laborers, including enterprises producing for the German army, diminished from day to day.[1] In March 1943 the police pulled off a masterful operation and seized 140 Solidarité and UJJ (*Union de la jeunesse juive*, Union of Jewish Youth) activists, including eighty in a single night.[2]

The directorate of Solidarité thus had to confront two realities. In the first place, the losses suffered indicated that the police had located the leaders of the organization but had refrained from arresting them, calculating that the leaders would lead them to other elements, and allow them to make more arrests. Furthermore, the Jewish Second Detachment in Paris had become too vulnerable, and the continuation of its operations became risky and precarious.[3]

In the second place, the supervision of the Jewish Second Detachment by the Communist Party and MOI (*Main-d'oeuvre immigrée*, Immigrant

Manual Labor) left the Jewish Communist leadership with little more than "the right to be kept informed to a very limited degree."[4]

The Redeployment of the Jewish Immigration Organizations in the Southern Zone

Everything argued in favor of a reconstruction focused on the southern zone. To remain in Paris meant exposure to the ever more probable danger of being eliminated. Moreover, there was "an anomaly with rather negative political consequences regarding the anonymity that accompanied the efforts and sacrifices of the fighters of the Second Detachment."[5] In other words, the Jewish Communists had lost the ability to defend Jewish interests in the capital. Henceforth their forces were exploited in service of the strategy and policy of the PC.[6] Rayski envisaged the transfer of men and political and military activities to the southern zone. The MOI leadership refused, calling the architects of this project "defeatists," because "the Communist cadres are not the sort of people to be placed in reserve."[7] Following another disastrous failure in June 1943, when eighty arrests definitely put the Second Detachment out of business, the transfer of the Jewish Communist center to Lyons was finally accepted by the directorship of the PC.[8]

The epoch of Solidarité and its affiliated organizations was over. Those who had conceived it in the Paris of the summer of 1940 found themselves in absolute isolation three years later. Not only had they lost contact with the population which they were supposed to protect and from which they could recruit activists, because of migrations to the south, but also relations with the other Jewish organizations as well as with the Communist resistance were more and more distant, if not conflicted. At this moment, however, the tendency within the resistance movement was favorable to redeployment. In its clandestine press the PC announced its desire to join the other resistance movements, calling upon them to form a "National Front." In May 1943 it participated in the founding of the *Conseil national de la résistance* (CNR, National Council of Resistance), placed under the control of the Free French in London and Algiers.[9] The organizations of Jewish immigrants in the southern zone, FSJF (*Féderation des sociétés juives de France*, the Federation of Jewish Associations of France), OSF (*Organisation sioniste de France*, French Zionist Organization), and the Bund (a Yiddish socialist labor organization, originating in Eastern Europe) had created a coordination committee. Between the two youth movements, MJS (*Mouvement de jeunesse sioniste*, Zionist Youth Movement) and the EIF, permanent cooperation had become the rule.[10]

Everywhere a certain dynamic of reorganization was modifying the structures active in the French underground. This phenomenon reflected not only the strategic options and tactics for battle, but also the gestation, already in progress, of postwar political institutions. The PC insisted on being part of a body such as the CNR, which it did not control, but which seemed to prefigure the form of government in liberated France. Following its example, the Jewish Communists were concerned with making sure they would participate in the community leadership that would survive the war.

The directorate of Solidarité, with the addition of Jacques Ravine, responsible for the organization in the southern zone (where it operated under the name of *Secours populaire*, Public Aid), held a meeting in an isolated building in the suburbs of Paris in the end of April 1943. It decided to reorganize all of the political entities—Solidarité, *Secours populaire*, the UFJ (*Union des femmes juives*, Jewish Women's Union), and the UJJ—forming the *Union des Juifs pour la résistance et l'entraide* (Union of Jews for Resistance and Mutual Assistance, UJRE). A declaration of principles stated that "the combat of the Jews must not remain anonymous."[10] This affirmation of identity entailed both a response to the centralizing tendency of the PC, which prevented it from addressing Jewish interests, and a step toward the non-Communist Jewish organizations.

Taking account of the decline of the Jewish Communist potential in Paris, the newly created UJRE developed its activities in the southern zone. Léo Glaeser, from the FSJF, suggested that it undertake a common program with the Coordinating Committee of Jewish Immigration Organizations. A meeting was held in the end of July 1943 in Grenoble, where the Italian regime was still in power. Agreement was reached to establish a *Comité général de défense juif* (General Committee for Jewish Defense, CGD), responsible for coordinating aid and rescue activities.[11] By its refusal to confine its activities to rescue, as its partners in the CGD demanded, the UJRE thus retained its freedom of decision regarding the armed struggle, an area kept apart from the responsibilities of the CGD.

The national directorate of the UJRE was established in Lyons during the summer of 1943, while two leaders, sent to Paris from the southern zone, tried to reconstitute a network there with the few survivors who were still present and whose eagerness for battle had remained undiminished. Not until January 1944 was a unity committee established in Paris similar to the CGD in the southern zone. It combined delegates from Rue Amelot, the OSE, the youth networks, and the UJRE. In this case, as in that of the creation of the *Sixième* and *Éducation physique* in Paris in March 1943, the unity committee owed its origins to the initiative of Simon Lévitte.[12] Charged with coordinating clandestine assistance and rescue, the committee also maintained liaison with the non-Jewish resistance regarding the armed struggle.

The CGD operated in Lyons, Grenoble, Nice, Marseilles, Toulouse, and Limoges. It appointed Léo Glaeser, the FSJF delegate, as secretary general. In more than one case, the coordination and cooperation between the rescuers of the various affiliated movements were beneficial. Thus in Nice, after the collapse of the Italians and the panicked flight of thousands of Jewish refugees, the resisters of the UJRE joined the rescue teams and also suffered losses.[13] In a report written in October 1943, Glaeser congratulates himself on "the loyal contact established with the new elements [UJRE]," in reference to the CGD action in Lyons, Grenoble, and Toulouse.[14] He arranged the distribution of the CGD relief funds until his arrest and death in Lyons in June 1944.[15] The UJRE delegate, Adam, replaced him.

In November 1943 the CGD published an underground leaflet in Yiddish, *Unzer Qempf* (Our Battle), where the pluralism of the committee is expressed and flourishes. This was a union of the two political trends into which the Jewish immigrants to France were divided. One trend entertained the dream of abolishing discrimination and persecution by promoting a socialist regime in France, and it included Communists and Bundists, who were deeply divided between themselves. The other trend proposed the Jewish nationalist dream, protecting the Jews and safeguarding their rights by establishing an independent Zionist state in Palestine.[16] The combination of political movements representing such radically divergent tendencies was possible only on the basis of limited aims. Each partner admitted that its own ideology was an option that did not exclude others.

The Bund had already chosen to work together with the Zionists from the beginning of the German occupation of Paris, in the framework of Rue Amelot, and also in the southern zone in Toulouse, Grenoble, and Lyons, with the FSJF. The geographical dispersion of its activists did not permit it to establish an autonomous organization, despite the establishment of contacts with an activist in Geneva who brought funds from the Bund in New York. Thanks to these contacts, the Bund resisters were able to publish their bulletin, *Unzer Shtimme* (Our Voice), sporadically in Paris and Grenoble. A group of young women led by Rachel Minc took an active part in the rescue of children in the Grenoble region.[17] Jacoubovitch, who headed Rue Amelot,[18] represented the Bund within the Jewish resistance organization in Paris, and Schrager, a member of the Coordination Committee of Jewish Immigrant Organizations and of the CGD, did so in the southern zone.

The political experience of the Bund people hardly encouraged them to seek common ground with the Communists.[19] On the contrary, they joined the unitary trend to avoid being left in isolation outside the CGD. However, the promotion of the latter, upon the initiative of the Zionists, expresses a substantial step taken by the UJRE in the direction of Jewish community. The Jewish Communists were undergoing a crisis of Jewish consciousness. They were torn between the orders of the PC and the struggle for Jewish survival, facing the immanent and imminent danger of the total extermination of the Jewish population. News of the Warsaw Ghetto Uprising, transmitted by the BBC during the very meeting held to establish the UJRE, aroused intense emotions among the Jewish Communist leaders. The desperate struggle of a few survivors out of a population of half a million souls elicited from Rayski, who was born in Poland, a lyrical effusion stemming from the depths of his Jewish past: "The specter of defeat rises before the hangmen. It appears to them through the faces of the millions of their victims, who emerge from their tombs, leave their crematoria and other factories of death. They advance, like an invincible army; behind them come the living, all of humanity, all the oppressed, united in the one idea of effacing the Nazi assassins from the face of the earth once and for all, so that no trace remains."[20] The immediate reaction was twofold. On the one hand, an exceptional effort was made to publish news of the tragedy in the Jewish Communist press (from which the above quotation is taken). On the other hand, they drew closer to the Jewish rescue organizations. The stirring example of the desperate heroism of the Warsaw insurgents was meant to stimulate the recruitment of new fighters. As for the desire to join the struggle to save those Jews who could still be saved, this expressed both a tactical choice and also a reassertion of Jewish identity: "We were only French. We have learned to become French Jews," wrote a UJJ bulletin the day after the liberation.[21]

The redeployment of the diverse political tendencies among which the Jewish immigrant organizations were divided, which took place in the summer of 1943, affected the coordination of mutual assistance, relief, and rescue work. The UJRE acceded to the refusal of its partners to entrust the CGD with military responsibilities. The FSJF admitted the necessity of organized Jewish participation in the armed struggle, but only at the moment of national insurrection. Its delegate declared that the moment had not yet come to call the Jews to enlist in the French resistance. According to him it was necessary to monopolize the forces in the service of rescue, given the absence of any aid on the part of the free governments. "The Jews have a score to settle with the democracies," reads a note of 1943.[22]

With the mandate of the cGD, Ruben Grinberg, the FSJF delegate, contacted the Central Consistory in October 1943. He wrote that the Consistory is "qualified to head a group of French and immigrant Jews."[23] On all sides people were already making plans for the delegation that would become responsible for representing Jewish interests before the authorities of a liberated France. Elsewhere we describe the discussions that took place between the cGD and the Consistory during the autumn of 1943, until the constitution of the *Conseil représentatif des Juifs de France* (Representative Council of French Jews, CRIF) in January 1944. Thus, under the aegis of the Resistance, the diverse elements of the Jewish population of France were united.

The Role of the Underground Press

The shortages reigning during the occupation affected not only foodstuffs, clothing, and other commodities, but also information. The press and the radio were subject to severe censorship. Listening to foreign broadcasts was forbidden and severely repressed. Fear of denunciation prevented some people from violating the regulations. Miniature transistor radios, permitting discreet listening had, of course, not yet been invented. A law of August 13, 1941 instituted the confiscation of all radio receivers owned by Jews in the northern zone.[24] Refugees, who constituted the majority of the Jews in the southern zone, thus had no radios to bring with them and were deprived of information.

Everywhere shortages produce a black market, and information is no exception to the rule. But unlike food and other products, information was free. The danger was getting caught. In Lyons:

> in June 1943, the curfew was at ten P.M., for there had been attacks against the Germans.
>
> As every evening, we were listening to the English radio (BBC) but very softly—because it was forbidden to listen—when someone rang the doorbell.... We hadn't thought that the ring at the door at ten o'clock could be the Gestapo. Usually it came at five or six in the morning....
>
> I opened the door. Two big and solid blokes: "German police!" entered....

Naturally we had turned off the radio and changed the station. . . . A few days ago, by lucky chance, I had removed all the copies of *Témoignage chrétien* [Christian Testimony, an underground publication], which the Germans were looking for, and which would surely have gotten us arrested.[25]

Word of mouth was an effective way to spread information. Scraps of information picked up while standing on line in food-stores and public transportation were passed on, interpreted, and distorted. The non-Communist Jewish organizations mainly published leaflets and bulletins devoted to enriching the readers' Jewish knowledge: correspondence courses produced by the EIF, MJS, and Yechouroun youth movements, *Igeret*, a newsletter issued by the KKL, edited by Joseph Fischer, giving information about the achievements and activities of the Zionists in Palestine and the free world, and the internal bulletin, *Sois chic* (Be Nice) of the rural EIF groups (nine issues appeared from November 1943 to May 1944).[26]

These organizations also sporadically reported news and commentary. The Bund published its newspaper, *Unzer Shtimme*, irregularly, first in Paris, then in Grenoble and later Lyons. The same applies to the organ of the left wing Zionist socialists, *Arbeiter Zeitung* (Workers' Newspaper). In 1942 the OSF circulated a vigorous condemnation of the Statute of the Jews, excellently written by the author Henri Hertz and entitled, *Le Silence complice du crime* (Silence, Accomplice in the Crime), with the epigraph, "Anti-Semitism Divides France (Anatole Leroy-Beaulieu)." Copies of this booklet were seized by the censors. Assuming that the "green document" (the booklet was printed on green paper) had been circulated among hundreds and thousands of readers, the Vichy propaganda services campaigned vigorously, on the airwaves and in the press, against this "insult to the laws of the Marshal" and its author, a mysterious and anonymous "senior jurist, a traitor to the regime."[27]

In the autumn of 1943, in Toulouse, the AJ launched an underground periodical, *Quand même* (Nevertheless). Begun by a professional journalist, Nahum Hermann, the publication attained a high level of excellence. It contained information about the persecution of Jews in France and the rest of Europe and about their resistance, political analyses, and news about Palestine. Created by a military network that had not grown out of any organization active before the war, unlike the other Jewish resistance movements, *Quand même* occupies a special place within the underground Jewish press. In order to conceal its location, the journal was datelined Geneva. The choice of the name had been difficult. After a fruitless discussion during which none of the names suggested was chosen, the resisters began discussing the situation, the bad news, the arrests, and Hermann concluded: "Nevertheless, we're going to get them!" One of the participants latched onto his word, and it was unanimously chosen as the name of the journal. After Hermann's arrest in Limoges in February 1944, and then the capture of two other members of his team and his printer in Toulouse, *Quand même* had to cease publication.[28]

By contrast, the Jewish Communists made a major effort to publish several periodicals and many leaflets and booklets on a regular basis in Yiddish and French.[29] This achievement cannot be appreciated without emphasizing the perils involved in these complex and risky enterprises: procuring paper and ink (commodities which were tightly restricted), their transport, the assembly and operation of printing houses, the door-to-door distribution of newspapers and leaflets. All of this was done totally underground. In addition to the teams of writers and printers, dozens of distributors unselfishly carried out missions for the underground press with insane obstinacy. The losses, thanks to relentless police pursuit, were dreadful in Paris, especially among the printers and distributors—the most exposed. Despite many setbacks, their publication and distribution were not interrupted.[30]

The role assigned to the underground Communist publications by their promoters was, in principle, the same as that played by party publications in ordinary times: to transmit the orders and political analyses of events prescribed by the leadership of the PC. This was done in order to maintain the leaders' control of the activists and to mobilize their bellicose spirit. This motivation, viewed as fundamental by every Communist leader, explains the dynamism and permanence of their press. To put out a newspaper had become a basic reflex and ritual, the movement's breath of life. It would have occurred to no one to view the publication of a newspaper as a voluntary option.

Thus, for four years, the Jewish Communist press called unceasingly for redoubled vigor in May Day action and on the anniversary of the Battle of Valmy (the French revolutionary victory over the invading Prussian army in 1792, an event commemorated by the Communists), urged the people to save the endangered fatherland. After June 22, 1941, it also celebrated the heroism of the Red Army and published special booklets to greet its anniversary. Commentary on Jewish events responded to the same preoccupations: the categorical denunciation of the UGIF as "a branch office of the Gestapo," and a more balanced criticism of enterprises working for the Germans,[31] where the Jewish workers, who paid a small percentage of their salaries as solidarity dues, were the movement's intended targets.[32] The Jewish Communists were the first and almost the only ones in France who circulated substantial information about the mass arrest at the Vélodrome d'hiver, the extermination camps in Poland, and the Warsaw Ghetto Uprising. Rayski reports that upon hearing, "for the first time, in October 1942, about the gassing of 11,000 deportees from France," the shocked leadership was left helpless and torn.

> To publish or not to publish? An atrocious dilemma, for whatever we did was bad. If we transmitted this information, were we not running the risk of arousing an action of fear, of panic, and plunging people into despair and resignation? But what a responsibility, not to divulge it! And what if it wasn't true, which was what we were hoping within ourselves?[33]

Unzer Wort and J'accuse published the information in November and December 1942. The other Jewish organizations, as we have seen, devoted relatively little attention to the publication of newspapers and leaflets. Was this a sin of omission? That is what the Communists reproached them with,[34] arguing that "there was never . . . an example in modern history when information was so essential for the defense of a people's life."[35] It is particularly risky to speculate on the influence of the underground press. To what degree did Unzer Wort reach Jews who read Yiddish? How many French-speaking Jews and non-Jews read Notre parole (Our Word), J'accuse, Fraternité, etc.? To what degree did those who read these publications place confidence in its information? "How can one believe in the unbelievable? Can reason understand unreason?"[36]

The historian Henri Michel has expressed skepticism, noting that the dynamism of the underground Jewish press "did not prevent its effectiveness from being without effect in preventing genocide."[37] During a round table discussion held in October 1983, French resisters, concerned by the fate of the Jews or actively associated with operations to rescue them, testified that they had known nothing of the Warsaw Ghetto Uprising.[38] Although its promoters might have overestimated the value and effectiveness of the underground Jewish press, respect should be paid to their complete sincerity and indomitable heroism. On the other hand, the dreadful price they had to pay does not authorize their survivors to denigrate the choice made by those who, like Rue Amelot, gave priority to rescue action, rather than publishing an underground organ.[39]

The Drancy Detainees Resist

After the French police operations in Marseilles and Rouen in January 1943, most of the arrests of 1943 were carried out by the Nazis themselves. While the Axis powers were suffering severe defeats on the Eastern Front and in Africa, Laval and Bousquet avoided the pressure of German security officer Heinz Röthke, who obtained neither passage of the law canceling the citizenship of Jews naturalized after 1927 nor the delivery of lists of Jews by the prefects.[40] In January 1944, after Bousquet was replaced by the chief of the Militia, Joseph Darnand, Vichy once again allowed its police to make massive arrests of French and foreign Jews, on order of the SD (Sicherheitsdienst, the SS security service).

Certainly an increasing number of Jews had learned to disguise themselves better. The combined action of anti-Nazi prefectures—and these became relatively frequent after 1943—and of the Jewish resistance had the power to cause the partial failure of any police operation, be it German or French. Brunner's fiasco in Nice has been described above. On September 9 in Toulouse the French police caught less than 10 percent of the foreign Jews whom they had the mission of arresting. An SEC (Section d'enquête et de contrôle, the police internal security department) denounces the leaks because of which the Jews were warned. It incriminates the police and the PTT (Poste, Télégraphe, Téléphone, the post office), which transferred the orders from Vichy:

The result was seen in the almost total failure of the roundups of September 9. Among theHere are the figures: 1,300 foreign Jews appearing on the lists used as the basis for the arrests in the Toulouse region, only 100 were rounded up. The latter are evidently those who were absent from their homes on September 9 and who returned too late to be warned. All the others, who did receive the warning,having been warned,either hid either (with Aryans, or else on farms), or else managed to join the railroad and communications guards along the tracks for one or several nights.[41]

In contrast, the arrests were formidably effective in those departments where the prefectorial services zealously executed the Nazi orders. On January 10, 1944, in the Gironde Department, a roundup directed by Maurice Papon, the Secretary General of the Prefecture, resulted in the deportation of 364 Jews. Of 473 French Jews who had been designated, the police caught 228.[42] In the Poitiers region, on January 28 they seized 484 Jews, while only 150 others who appeared on the list were impossible to find.

Despite the fierce determination of the Gestapo and the occupation of all of French territory, the number of deportations from January 1943 until

August 1944 (31,902) was lower than that of the period of March–November 1942 (41,951).[43] The relatively long intervals between the departures of convoys favored some resistance among the Jewish detainees. When deportation followed only a few days or sometimes a few hours upon their arrival in Drancy, the detainees were of course unable to organize themselves in the camp. No chaplain was ever authorized to enter Drancy or the other camps in the northern zone. The administration installed by the SS officer Brunner, who had all the French officials in Drancy eliminated on July 2, 1943, had two contradictory effects. The vexations, humiliations, and acts of bestial brutality committed against the detainees multiplied. On the other hand, the new Nazi administration selected detainees to be responsible for the functioning of the camp services. Those married to Aryans and specialists in various types of work, several hundred in number, were granted virtually official status in their jobs and were considered nondeportable.[44]

The MS (*Membres de Service d'Ordre*, members of the Jewish service for maintaining public order), the section chiefs, and their assistants, with a few exceptions, "created an atmosphere of fraternity."[45] During excavations in 1980 on the construction site of the Joliot-Curie gymnasium in Drancy, the workers brought to light a tunnel thirty-five meters long, dug at a depth of 1.50 meters. Leaving the basement of Stairway 22 of the camp, the tunnel ended less than two meters away from a trench shelter against aerial bombardments, situated outside the camp, not far from Jean-Jaurès Avenue.[46] These are the remains of the most ambitious plot hatched in Drancy. The underground tunnel was the work of a group of detainees who were planning a mass escape. Designed by an inmate, Major Georges Kohn, with the complicity of the Jewish commander of the camp, Colonel Robert Blum, the work of digging the tunnel began on September 15, 1943.

> It is difficult to describe in a few lines or to imagine the efforts that had to be deployed and the precautions that had to be taken: finding the equipment necessary to dig a gallery 1.30 meters high and .80 meters wide, lit by electricity and entirely timbered; to work at the end to cut through the earth, to remove it; to bear the heat, the lack of air. Every day or just about, someone had to climb up onto the roof to verify the direction or calculate the corrections to be made in the axis of the tunnel. It was also, alas, necessary to stop working for several days before and after the departure of convoys. As for the impatience of the workers, it caused us distress. It was difficult to get them to

accept that they didn't have the right to break through to the surface immediately after passing the barbed wire fence, that the chance for a few could not be obtained at the price of a collective repression upon all those remaining in the camp.[47]

The plan envisaged the escape of all the inmates of Drancy:

> The departure was to take place immediately after the evening roll call, on D-Day. The dispersion would take place until the curfew, then from the lifting of the curfew until the morning roll call. Monitors would take charge of the detainees, stairway after stairway, and lead them without a sound. The resistance in Drancy and the surrounding areas would be mobilized to expedite the opening of the tunnel at the height of the stairs in the shelter, to place trucks and hiding places at our disposition for the elderly, the infirm, women, and children.[48]
>
> There are three groups of workers, laboring night and day, a total of seventy men. The teams are protected by lookouts from the MS (the Jewish police of the camp) and by a warning system. . . . Stakes are sunk into the ground, behind which planks are slipped, to hold up the earth and prevent cave-ins. When the tunnel reaches fifteen meters in length, the work becomes painful, air is lacking. . . . A., the man who initiated this colossal job, is a pharmacist and will bring in sodium peroxide from the outside.[49]

Less than two months after the beginning of the work, when where was only 1.5 meters left to dig, the SS made a systematic search of all the cellars. Had there been a denunciation, or merely idle talk? At any rate, the tunnel was discovered, and a clue identified one of the excavators. Under torture, the SS identified fourteen of the seventy plotters. Deported on November 20, 1943, ten of them escaped from the train on the way to the east. In addition, sixty-five Jewish leaders of the camp, designated at random, and Colonel Blum, were deported by way of reprisal.[50]

A secret committee chosen by the Jewish staff and the MS tried to maintain the morale of the detainees by running a school, organizing study groups in many subjects, evenings of singing and even farewells before the departure of the convoys. The leaders of the youth movements gathered the young people, creating ephemeral educational groups and choruses. "In Drancy we saw acts of selfishness, cowardice, even crime, but they were swept away, cleansed, submerged in that marvelous human spirit which makes new souls emerge from the depths of misfortune."[51] The committee of detainees took over the camp administration when the SS fled, on Thursday, August 17, 1944. The following morning it freed the officers, non-commissioned officers, and veterans, who joined the uprising in Paris. With the support of resisters from the city hall of Drancy, the committee gave each of the 1,541 freed inmates a sum of money, an identity card, a ration card, and food for twenty-four hours.[52]

In their immense joy at recovering their freedom, these few survivors still harbored illusions regarding the fate of those whom they had seen deported. After the convoy of July 31, which deported 1,300 victims, of whom about 250 were children rounded up in the UGIF centers on July 22, Brunner fled from France, taking fifty-one hostages with him, including about thirty resisters belonging to the AJ.

The existence of the committee of inmates in Drancy and the tunnel team owes nothing to the Jewish organizations operating outside the camps. This differentiates them from the central assistance committee created by the inmates of Gurs with the aid of the camp chaplaincy. Similarly, the committees active in the camps of Pithiviers and Beaune-la-Rolande in 1941–1942 received support from Rue Amelot and Solidarité. Nevertheless, well structured and hierarchical, the secret organizations of Drancy worked in the areas of mutual assistance, of cultural activity, and of rescue. Their brief and tragic history fits into that of the Jewish resistance organizations.

The Spiritual Resistance of Hidden Jewish Families and Groups

On August 2, 1944, Darnand's services ordered the Prefect of Police in Paris to submit to the Gestapo a list of all the Jews in the Seine Department, including French citizens, which Röthke had been demanding since February 26. However, the Gestapo did not have time to organize a mass arrest before the insurrection broke out in Paris. The prefecture used delaying tactics against the Germans, who were forced to treat the French police with patience and tact, for it was indispensable for preserving order in the capital as well as in preventing attacks against German soldiers. For its part, the CGQJ (*Commissariat général aux Questions juives*, General Commission for Jewish Questions) was acting only sporadically by now. The fate of the

French Jews who had remained in their declared residences and wore the yellow star was relatively less severe in Paris than in several provincial departments.[53] Between October 1943 and May 1944 the Gestapo liquidated almost all the offices of the UGIF and arrested the staff and clients who were present. Exceptions were made of the offices in Paris and the Lyons region. In May 1944 the UGIF closed its offices in the southeast, which had been spared until then, while continuing its work by sending checks to clients or by sending social workers to visit them at home.[54]

By then, most of those receiving assistance in the provinces, mainly immigrant Jews, were camouflaged behind a false Aryan identity and a place of residence unknown to the official services. The *Éducation physique*, *Sixième*, and *Service André* networks sent out young people on social work missions. By the dozen, in the Lyons, Grenoble, Nice, Toulouse, and Limoges regions, they substituted for the UGIF personnel. Those with leadership experience and training in the youth movement excelled in establishing human contact with the families going far beyond the provision of support. During the monthly visits people rediscovered themselves as Jews. They brought reports of friends and acquaintances, various news items, ritual objects, and even unleavened bread for Passover of 1944.[55] The Jewish dimension of the meeting was the most comforting part, for, beyond the physical survival hoped for by these new Marranos,[56] it raised the glowing prospect for a world not only delivered from the Nazi monster but also open before every Jewish survivor whose identity could flourish in broad daylight.

The social workers traveled under the cover of false identities and orders for supposed missions provided by the non-Jewish charity organizations or the government agencies. When necessary, the Jewish resistance invented such charities or agencies. The chaos of the regulations was so great that it had become relatively easily to deceive authorities by presenting oneself under the colors of an organization that existed only on paper, by virtue of the imagination and audacity of the resisters. Two social workers moved about in May 1944 in the Haute-Savoie Department bearing orders delivered by a so-called "Office for the Placement of Children," which stipulated that they must travel "especially in the region of Cruseilles and La Roche-sur-Foron to study the possibility for the foster placement of children from the city of Lyons." To give more respectability to their document, they reported to the Prefecture of Haute-Savoie, where the words, "Examined in Annecy, May 22, 1944," were written on it, with the stamp and signature of the Secretary General of the Prefect.[57] The stationery of the "Office for the Placement of Children" was printed by the *Sixième*, in addition to that of the "Interprofessional Group for the Distribution of Products Indispensable to

Agriculture." In 1944 the person charged with the mission of this fictional group in Rhône Department was responsible for "research and supervision regarding the alimentary needs of cattle in the various regions of the department—examination of the hay supplies in the villages."[58]

However, the reader must not imagine that those bearing such orders were immune to all risks. While transporting false identity papers and ration cards for those being assisted, which was done frequently, some of them were searched, arrested, and deported.[59] The approaches to the Swiss border in the Haute-Savoie Department were patrolled by German troops, who were indifferent to orders of this kind. This is what cost the life of Marianne Cohn, who was arrested on May 31, 1944, while escorting a group of children to Switzerland.

The groups of older adolescents and young adults of the MJS and EIF movements in the southern zone passed through three successive phases while going underground: During the arrests of the summer of 1942, the rural worksites and centers in Moissac and Beaulieu sent young foreign nationals in the endangered categories to secure places; In November 1943, the directorate of the centers in Moissac and Beaulieu dispersed all the residents while the rural worksites began to evacuate families; in March and April 1944, all of the rural worksites closed their doors.

The leaders of the youth movements applied a specific method for bringing its groups underground. Instead of dispersing its members, they divided them into small communities. During the first stage, before the summer of 1942, the farm in Taluyers and the center in Beaulieu had taken charge of adolescents and young adults from the detention camps of Gurs and Rivesaltes.[60] To prevent them from being arrested, Hammel, the head of the rural group in Taluyers, had false identities created for them and placed them in a logging camp. This solution was transitory, followed by the opening of a new farm, Pierre-Blanche, in a very infertile region of the Vivarais mountains in the Ardèche Department. The cultivation of this rundown farm was very difficult, the food situation was critical, but Jewish life expanded with intensity.

In the autumn of 1942 escapees from the detention camps and the GTE (*Groupes de travailleurs étrangers*, Foreign Laborers Groups) and others who had illicitly crossed the line of demarcation, more than 100 young people in all, were delivered to the EIF.[61] The creation of small underground communities would have demanded means and staff beyond the abilities of the movement. It turned to the *Sixième*. More than eighty young people were then placed in farms around d'Auvillar, at the intersection of the Tarn-et-Garonne, Lot-et-Garonne, and Gers Departments. Sigismond Hirsch, a physician who had fled from Paris, was the mainstay of this operation by the *Sixième*. Well liked by the population, notably because he took care of indigent people without payment, he had also gained the confidence of the elected municipal officials, the gendarmes, and local notables engaged in the Resistance. He was able to manage connections with skill and delicacy between the young refugees, who had become farm workers and the farmers who employed them. The *Sixième* obtained the equipment necessary to lodge the young people on the farms and provided them with work clothes. The local gendarmerie did nothing to inspect their civil status. Called the "d'Auvillar security sector," the region also received Jewish children who were placed in the Ursuline Convent. This became a medical and pedagogical institute run by nuns who were refugees from Belgium. They assured the physical welfare of their wards and respected their religious identity. For example, they made Saturday a day of rest. The young people and children of the d'Auvillar security sector were never disturbed, but this impressive rescue operation cost the lives of Berthe Hirsch, the doctor's wife, and of one of their helpers. On October 18, 1943, the Gestapo raided a farm in Saint-Michel, where the Hirsch family lived, seven kilometers away from d'Auvillar. After a vain search lasting several hours and fraught with dramatic incidents—an escape attempt by Hirsch created a diversion that permitted the other occupants of the farm to destroy the lists of young people in hiding—they arrested the couple and two other resisters belonging to the *Sixième*. They were all deported.[62] The dispersion of the young refugees had to be undertaken hastily, but they could be located only with some difficulty, since the lists had been destroyed behind the backs of the Gestapo. But the operation on the Saint-Michel farm had no further repercussions, and calm was restored to the sector. The *Sixième* resumed its action of placing clandestine agricultural workers in the villages near d'Auvillar.[63]

After the arrest of Claude Gutman in Nice on September 23, 1943, the national team of the EIF ordered the dispersion of its children's shelters in Moissac, Beaulieu, and La Grave. The *Sixième* took over the wards and personnel of the latter, while the directors of Moissac, Édouard and Chatta Simon, themselves arranged the placement of all the occupants of the two shelters in the southwest. They did so in such a way that all the pupils could continue their studies. The members of the educational staff, familiar to the children, formed a team of social workers and maintained frequent contact with their pupils. In this case, too, despite the risks taken in the name of the education of these Jewish children, their security was preserved.[64]

At the same time, two new clandestine communities of young people were established. A member of the directorate of the center in Moissac,

Georges Lévitte, left for Istors, near Chambon-sur-Lignon in the Haute-Loire Department, with three staff members from the shelter. There they studied Jewish sources with two scholars, Professors Jacob Gordin and Georges Vajda, who had taken refuge in that hospitable Camisard (French Calvinist) retreat in the Cévennes. Lévitte wanted to train an intellectual elite capable of teaching Judaism to the survivors of the war. Known as the "school of the prophets," not without satirical intention, this small community remained closely knit until the day of the Normandy landing, when its members joined the FTP (*Francs-tireurs et partisans*) or the FFI (*Forces Françaises de l'Intérieur*, French Forces of the Interior).[65] Concurrently, in December 1943, a group of seven young farm workers from Lautrec, directed by Roger Cahen, a reserve officer, founded the first EIF community dedicated to military training. It was situated in an abandoned farm in the Sidobre mountain range in the Tarn Department.

During that winter the AJ established its first guerrilla training groups in the Montagne Noire in the Tarn Department. The members came from farms scattered in Blémont and Fretteserpes, with recruits from Grenoble, Lyons, Limoges, and Toulouse. Some of them had chosen to prepare for crossing the Pyrenees with the aim of reaching Palestine. A career officer, Jacques Lazarus, took responsibility for the military training.

The third and last phase in the liquidation of the centers was decided in early March 1944. The EIF national team, meeting in Lyons in the back room of a bistro known as Chez Jean, on quai Perrache, declared the closure, pure and simple, of all of the rural worksites, including the clandestine farm of Pierre-Blanche. It proposed smuggling all the women and children into Switzerland. Three options were offered to the men and unmarried adults of both sexes: armed combat in France through engagement in the EIF guerrilla unit or another resistance unit; social work in the ranks of the *Sixième*; crossing the Pyrenees with the aim of reaching Palestine. The same options were to be submitted to the staff and senior members of the EIF in the cities[66] were interpreted as a general mobilization order for the struggle.

A certain inertia delayed complete disbanding of the centers for several weeks. The rural groups wished to remain intact. But the various farms in Lautrec had already been partially dispersed. The young people from them split between the guerrillas of Sidobre and two small Jewish study communities hidden within a radius of twenty kilometers from Castres, constituting the "dispersed Lautrec sector." Itinerant spiritual leaders, Léo Cohn and Gilbert Bloch, taught in each of these communities, as well as in the guerrilla group, once a week. They planned an assembly of the entire dispersed Lautrec sector to celebrate the two Passover Seders together on April 7 and

8. But Gamzon was categorically opposed: "There is something blasphemous about tempting fate in that way." His comrades acquiesced, but not without criticizing him severely, mainly in the pages of the newsletter *Sois chic* in May 1944. He himself overheard young people commenting on his veto with much disrespectful sarcasm.[67] For the two Passover nights, Hammel brought together the two groups of Taluyers and Pierre-Blanche on the latter farm for one last time: "We decided not to post sentinels. On that night which must recall the one when God protected the People, nothing could happen to us."[68]

The complete dispersal was carried out during the following days. Sixteen young people from Taluyers were going to leave for Palestine via Spain. Toward the end of April, the buildings of all the Jewish rural centers were finally vacant, with the exception of the farm of Saint-Germain in the Ain Department. The team refused to disperse. It had taken security measures and maintained excellent relations with all the villagers. It was certain it would be warned in time in case of danger. However, on May 19, 1944, a German military unit captured all the Jews present on the farm. Five men, including the young rabbi, Aron Wolff, were shot on the spot, and another died in deportation.[69]

The zeal shown by an increasing number of young people for enriching their Jewish cultural and spiritual heritage is visible in some of the facts reported here. It sometimes led them to minimize risks, as is seen clearly in the planned Passover gathering in Lautrec. In Grenoble more than 150 young people of the MJS met in October 1943 in a hall provided by the Protestant congregation to celebrate Yom Kippur services.[70] From January 12 to 16, 1944, about thirty EIF leaders, some of them coming illicitly from Paris, led by the national team, held a Jewish study session in the chateau of Chamarges in Die, in the Drôme Department. Warned that a German train had arrived at the railway station, the participants spent the night and part of the next day on a plateau, a two hour walk from the chateau.[71] Whenever they noted a process of conversion to the Church among the wards placed in a Christian setting, the social workers overcame every difficulty and risk to transfer those wards.[72] In Paris, in the Claude-Bernard center of the UGIF, André Marcovici created an amateur Jewish theatrical group, *Les Compagnons de l'Arche* (The Companions of the Ark) in the spring of 1944. It surfaced with the liberation and developed its activity after the war.[73] In Saint-Étienne, the dispensary of *Aide aux mères* (Aid to Mothers), run by two fervent Catholics of exemplary courage, served as a resting place for convoys of children on their way to Switzerland and a meeting place for "Aryanized" Jews who assembled to hear classes and lectures by Edmond

Fleg, Léo Cohn, and Samy Klein.[74] In Nanteuil, in the Corrèze Department, the home of Albert Neher, surrounded by his numerous family, became an intense center of Jewish spiritual and artistic creativity, a scholarly center, and a house of prayer and study for the camouflaged Jews of the region. His sons, Richard and André, also wrote correspondence courses for the ELEJ (*Ecole libre d'études juives*, the Free School of Jewish Studies).[75]

The spontaneous reaction of young Jews scattered throughout France, their quest for spiritual depth, reveals that a change was taking place. Barely perceptible at the start of the war, it underwent prodigious expansion in the clandestine Jewish life of the years 1943–44. In the main, the participants in the study communities joined the combat units of the Resistance in the spring of 1944, especially after the Normandy landing. The rescuers and fighters who survived the war were to become the leaders in a Jewish renaissance in France and Palestine.

14

⌒⛬⌒

The Budgets of the Jewish Resistance

Tens of thousands of Jews owe their safety to the heroism and self-abnegation of Jewish resisters. The history of this epic also includes the budgets
that supported the assistance allowances, the placement of children, legal
and clandestine emigration, and the many other exploits of the rescuers and
fighters. The works of the Israeli historian Yehuda Bauer and our research
have brought to light interesting but general data. Considerable gaps
remain, and the results presented here are naturally approximate.

The exact distribution of expenses is impossible to determine, since we
lack the account books or financial reports of the various organizations. To
our knowledge, only those of Rue Amelot, ET (*Entraide temporaire*,
Temporary Mutual Assistance), and the Maurice Cachoud group were preserved. Thus one can at best attempt to estimate the total volume of the
expenses for which we have some data.

The monthly allowance paid to families and institutions sheltering children came to an average of 700 francs. A prudent calculation of the average
duration of the placements and of the number of children involved indicates an outlay of approximately 100 million francs, to which must be added
the cost of clothing, various equipment, medical and dental care. An analo-
gous method applied to the allocations paid to the families which were

"Aryanized" and deprived of employment produces an estimated cost of approximately 400 million francs. These two items constitute almost the entire expenses of ET and the Maurice Cachoud group. The constant railway journeys of the resisters belonging to the Garel, *Éducation physique*, and *Sixième* networks also ate up considerable sums which it would be hazardous to quantify.

The other items absorbed a relatively modest part of the budgets. Those resisters who had means, usually modest, worked as volunteers. Subsistence allowances, pared to the bone, were paid to the others. Although very onerous, the fees paid to the border runners were only a minor percentage of the total budget. By producing them on their own, by the tens of thousands, the Jewish networks economized in procuring false papers of every sort. They also paid very little for producing and distributing their publications, not including the copious underground press of the Jewish Communists. Sources that would permit an estimate of its cost are inaccessible.

Regarding military operations, the Jewish resistance movement took charge of the free groups of the AJ (*Armée juive*, Jewish Army) in the cities and of the escape of combatants to Palestine via Spain. The other units of Jewish partisans in the city and the countryside fought with the backing of the French resistance, which also covered most of the costs, especially regarding arms and equipment. These costs are not included in the following statistics.

The total expenses of Jewish resistance come to between 800 million and one billion 1944 francs, which, at an average rate of 100 francs per dollar, comes to the respectable sum of eight to ten million 1944 dollars. On Thursday January 11, 1945, the *New York Times* published a story by Dana Adams Schmidt datelined Paris with the headline: "Six Millions Lent Jews by French —J.D.C. Repaying Loans for Support and Hiding." The article states that the American Joint Distribution Committee was reimbursing approximately six million dollars lent by French people to aid and hide Jews during the German occupation. Since it was forbidden to send money from the United States to occupied France, the Jewish organizations depended on a committee authorized to borrow in the name of the AJDC. A certain number of Frenchmen, seeking a secure investment, did not demand interest and even offered to pay the Jews a premium to accept their money.[1]

With one correction, this information is confirmed in its broad outlines by a group of documents dating from 1940 to 1944. During that period, the AJDC spent $5,692,452 in France,[2] coming to approximately 600 million francs. The loans mentioned by the *Times* constituted a total of 240 million francs.[3]

The money spent by the Jewish resistance movement came from four unequal sources: Aid from the AJDC, from the Jewish Agency for Palestine, and from the World Jewish Congress (WJC); funds raised in France by the Jewish organizations; grants from the PC to Solidarité and the UJRE (*Union des Juifs pour la résistance et l'entraide*, Jewish Union for Resistance and Mutual Assistance);government subventions to the rural and artisanal worksites and to the social service for foreigners.

The American Joint Distribution Committee

Because the organization kept accurate accounts, the aid from the AJDC is the only source for which we possess exact information. To the sums figuring under the heading, "Operations in France," must be added some of the subventions paid by the AJDC to the Hebrew Immigrant Aid and Sheltering Society (HIAS) listed as expenses in the United States. operated in France through the HICEM office in Marseilles, about half of whose expenses were covered by the immigrants themselves or by their relatives overseas. The rest, coming to ten million francs, came from , which in turn was supplied by the AJDC in New York.[4]

The procedures of the AJDC had been worked out in the light of the experience of intervention in almost all the countries of Europe beginning in 1914. Everywhere it allocated budgets to local organizations, strictly respecting the law and without political discrimination. The sums distributed had to be used for monetary assistance or help in kind for the poor, loans to destitute artisans and merchants, and finally subventions for schools, cultural institutions, and professional training.

The vicissitudes of the period of hostilities had posed delicate problems in interpreting these principles. When the United States entered the war in 1917, American nationals working in the territories controlled by the central powers had to be repatriated. Responsibility for the philanthropic activity of the AJDC was then transferred to local Jewish committees, authorized to take out loans to be reimbursed after the cessation of hostilities.[5] The same method was applied during the Second World War.[6] Regarding France, the American personnel of the AJDC left Marseilles for Lisbon after the landing of Allied troops in North Africa on November 8, 1942. After the Marseilles office was closed, administration of AJDC aid was confided to the man who had been the French director since 1941, Jules Jefroykin. He was assisted by Maurice Brener, the personal secretary of the director of UGIF-south, Lambert. With the strong support of Joseph Fischer and Nahum

Hermann, the directors of the Zionist organizations (KKL, Jewish National Fund, and Keren Ha-Yessod), Jefroykin and Brener contracted loans, and the creditors agreed to be reimbursed after the hostilities. Thanks to this, although the AJDC was absent from France, it continued to supply the treasuries of the Jewish organizations.

Respect for laws and regulations imposed various constraints on the humanitarian action of the AJDC. The Treasury Department in Washington wanted to avoid having American money benefit its enemies. Hence the dispatch of funds to enemy countries or those occupied by the enemy was prohibited, unless licensed. The AJDC had to wait until the end of 1943 to receive the first license permitting it to contract loans in France up to a ceiling of $600,000.[7] Actually, until November 1942 this was not a problem regarding territory under the control of the Vichy government, which was regarded as a neutral country by American diplomacy. French legislation also had to be taken into account. This explains why payments by the AJDC were made through UGIF-south once it had been established.

In principle the British naval blockade forbade the sending of foodstuffs to the detainees in the camps of the southwest of France. Although London was disposed to agree to a possible exception in favor of a maritime transport under the flag of the Red Cross or the Quakers, the directorate of the AJDC in New York decided not to challenge the blockade.[8] In other cases the AJDC circumvented legal obstacles by having the Lisbon office make decisions without consulting New York.[9] Thus Joseph Schwartz, the European director, had funds sent to the northern zone from 1940 on, though this was enemy occupied territory. He made use of the good offices of the Quakers, whose Paris office paid Rue Amelot a monthly subvention of 100,000 francs.[10] Beginning in 1942, this subvention, gradually increased to 600,000 francs per month, was transferred in more clandestine ways, no trace of which has been preserved.[11] In November 1943 the AJDC representative in Switzerland, Saly Mayer, secretly sent fifteen million francs in cash to Dr. Eugène Minkowski, the director of the OSE (Oeuvre de secours aux enfants, Children's Rescue Network) in Paris, who administered funds for approximately 2,000 sheltered children and for family assistance.[12]

Generally speaking, Schwartz had given Jefroykin carte blanche in 1942, authorizing him to operate in France on his own responsibility on behalf of the AJDC. Did he know that his representative, a leader of Jewish resistance, at the head of the MJS (Mouvement de jeunesse sioniste, the Zionist Youth Movement) and the AJ, was financing the illegal activities of rescue, clandestine border crossings, and, finally, armed combat? Had the enemy discovered Jefroykin's activities, the matter might have damaged the status of the AJDC in Portugal and Switzerland. Moreover, Schwartz authorized recourse to the system of loans one year before the first license was granted by the American government. Had he informed the directorate in New York, he would have placed it in an embarrassing situation.

AJDC financing of operations such as illegal crossing of the Swiss and Spanish borders was also an infraction of the restrictions customarily imposed on the organization. Again, the directorate in Lisbon took responsibility for it, no later than May 1944. Its attitude was evidently influenced by information received about the unequalled barbarity of the war being waged against the Jews. The classical means of assistance, more necessary than ever, had nevertheless become trifling in a time and place where the Jews were hunted down.[13] Humanitarian action could no longer be kept within the framework of the law.

The situation changed on January 22, 1944, with the creation of the War Refugee Board (by the White House. The WRB was empowered to recommend measures to provide aid to the political and racial victims of the Nazi regime in occupied Europe. Thereafter it became relatively easy to obtain licenses from the American Treasury Department to transfer funds for humanitarian purposes.[14]

Washington authorized the Swiss office of the AJDC to spend $300,000 per month in the countries under the domination of the Third Reich.[15] Mayer then put an end to the system of loans, which was producing only about half of the sum obtained in Switzerland for the same amount of dollars.[16] He transferred allocations to France coming to a monthly budget of seventeen million francs, in addition to which there was a lump payment of forty million francs for passage to Spain. On July 14, 1944 in the Lisbon office, Mayer confirmed that he had provided the Jewish charities in France (OSE, FSJF [*Féderation des sociétés juives de France*, the Federation of Jewish Associations of France], and CAR [*Comité d'assistance aux réfugiés* , the Committee for Assistance to Refugees]) with their monthly budget until the coming November, a precaution regarded as necessary because of the Allied landing in Normandy.[17]

Remarkably, none of these underground financial manipulations gave rise to improprieties. Not a single case of misappropriation is known. The Jewish resisters committed every possible infraction with regard to French fiscal and monetary regulations as well as laws instituted against the Jews. They took part in illegal border crossings and operated an underground market. But nobody cheated, robbed, or extorted funds, nor did anyone commit a theft or armed robbery to obtain money or despoil the enemy. It was the solidarity of American Jews, channelled through the AJDC, that provided for the needs that local resources could not satisfy. It may be estimated that sixty percent of the total expenses of the latter were covered by the great Jewish philanthropic center of the United States. The beneficiaries were the recipients of aid, the ten thousand child wards of the Jewish resistance movement, the detainees in the camps, those who used the medical-social dispensaries and the soup kitchens, those who bore false identity papers, and, finally, the fighters in the free urban groups and in rural guerrillas.

The aid obtained from the international Jewish organizations, the WJC and the Jewish Agency for Palestine, was negotiated in Switzerland by Marc Jarblum. As a Zionist leader, he did not wish to seem totally dependent upon the apolitical AJDC. He had to dispose of funds allocated by the Zionist institutions. His instructions, transmitted to the AJ in France, stipulated that the sums from the Jewish Agency must be used for crossing the Spanish border and for armed combat. The extant documents covering Jarblum's activity in Switzerland give only fragmentary information regarding the amounts allocated by the Jewish Agency and the WJC. The means possessed by these organizations were in any event very modest. According to Bauer, the WJC disbursed six million francs. Three allocations of between 250,000 and one million francs are mentioned in Jarblum's letters addressed to the AJ from December 1943 to February 1944 regarding subventions from the Jewish Agency. The information is therefore too fragmentary to permit even an estimate.[18]

Local Fund-Raising

During the first months of the occupation, local fund-raising permitted the functioning of the soup kitchens and dispensaries administered by Rue Amelot, sustained in part by the Solidarité rescue fund and that of the Consistory charities.

Sketchy information exists regarding the funds raised by the Rue Amelot activists. From a monthly average of 100,000 francs in 1942,[19] they fell to 15,000 francs per month in 1944.[20] Meanwhile the arrests and migration to the provinces had reduced the Jewish population of Paris. All of those whom the racial laws had excluded from employment or professional activity were impoverished and no longer had the means to contribute.

Planned on a large scale during the second half of 1942, a fund-raising campaign presided over by the Chief Rabbi of France and administered by a member of the Central Consistory was undertaken in the southern zone.

The archives we consulted have preserved only the copious documentation detailing the goals and organization of the project as well as a letter describing a fund-raising meeting in Toulouse in July 1943.[21] No figures are known. The Maurice Cachoud group in Nice covered twenty-seven percent of its expenses by raising funds, on an average of 80,000 francs per month, from September 1943 to August 1944. We should note that news of the Normandy landing stimulated the generosity of donors, who contributed 156,000 francs in June 1944, in contrast to the 50,000 francs contributed in May and July.[22]

We have seen that the work of ET in rescuing Jewish children in Paris was financed by the contributions of wealthy individuals, businesses, and banks. Although an account book has been preserved, the gaps in it permit one only to estimate receipts of from three to five million francs.

We are poorly informed of the funds raised by Solidarité. Until the creation of the UJRE and its joining the CGD (*Comité général de défense juive*, General Committee for Jewish Defense) in August 1943, the Jewish Communists did not benefit from AJDC allocations. Indications of the volume of their assistance activities is entirely lacking. The activists collected donations and on payday in certain businesses they levied two percent of the salaries of their members and sympathizers.[23] The Institut Maurice Thorez does not open its archives, so we are unable to discover whether reports have been preserved that might provide some idea of the extent of the work accomplished on this level by Solidarité.

The Communist Party

Similarly we lack information regarding the sums allocated to Solidarité by the PC, which financed the underground press and the allotments paid to the permanent staff of the movement and to the fighters in the Second Detachment, FTP-MOI-yiddish. In 1942 each of the latter received 1,600 francs per month, with an additional 300 francs for every dependent child. At the end of 1943 the monthly allowance was raised to 2,300 francs. This sum had the purchasing power of only about 1,000 to 1,200 present-day francs, some four hundred dollars, an evaluation that does not take into account the shortage of food and the black market prices of 1943. Thus it comes as no surprise to read that the underground fighters "were always hungry."[24] From only this figure, the allowance paid to fighters, one must estimate the expenses of Solidarité financed by the PC at several million francs per year.

The Government

The Vichy administration gave the rural and artisanal worksites the status of professional training centers, entitling them to a monthly grant of 450 francs per pupil of French nationality and three salaries for the staff of each center, coming to a total of 4,200 francs. Thus the ten centers, containing 125 pupils who were entitled to the benefits, received an annual sum of 1,200,000 francs from the state.[25] The salary of some of the members of the resident teams of the OSE and the EIF in the camps of Gurs and Rivesaltes were paid by the SSAE (*Service social d'aide aux émigrants*, Social Service for Assistance to Emigrants) to straw men of the CIMADE (*Commission inter-mouvements auprès des évacués*, Intermovement Commission for the Evacuees, a Protestant organization) and of *Amitié chrétienne* (Christian Friendship), which also came from the state treasury. Since we have been unable to find the financial reports, we do not know how long these subventions were paid. Thus one cannot estimate the total amount used by the Jewish resistance movement.

The System of Loans

The anti-Jewish policy applied in France following the armistice in June 1940 included radical measures against Jewish property. The government regime confiscated real estate, blocked funds, the "Aryanized" commerce and industry, and the excluded Jews from most jobs and professions. Moreover, Jewish-owned apartments in the northern zone were the scene of extensive looting.[26]

Loopholes in the application of the labyrinthine legislation, which became increasingly complex as it became voluminous and elaborate, and the complicity, not always disinterested, of certain officials and employees, permitted Jews to withdraw from their accounts sums in excess of those "destined for personal maintenance," which had been set at 15,000 francs per month (about $2,500 in present-day dollars).[27]

Doubtless we shall never know precisely to what degree the economic measures taken against the Jews from 1940 to 1944 were flouted. Nevertheless it is obvious that some Jews had access to relatively large sums of money, and that they sought to keep it secure. Since assets placed in banks were exposed to confiscation and expropriation, these Jews preferred taking other courses, which they regarded as less risky, such as buying precious metals or depositing their money with trusted non-Jews. Some of them lent money to the AJDC.

That American Jewish organization already had experience with loans taken from individuals in countries at war in 1914–1918 to aid Jewish refugees. Its representatives accepted the obligation to reimburse the loans after the hostilities, without interest. The debt was expressed in dollars, according to the black market rate, making the system advantageous to both parties. In the beginning of 1943, for example, the Exchange Office paid thirty-five francs for one dollar, whereas on the black market the rate was eighty francs. In exchange for a loan of eighty francs, used on the spot to aid Jews, the creditor received the promise of reimbursement of one dollar after the hostilities. The system gave the contributions of the American Jews, collected by the AJDC, a return superior to that offered by the Exchange Office. The creditors received no guarantees, placing their confidence instead in the person who contracted for the loan in the name of the AJDC. After the closing of the office in Marseilles in November 1942, Jefroykin sent the accounts of loans to Lisbon via AJ convoys which crossed the Spanish border. He kept a copy, buried in the garden of a villa in Nîmes. The debts were honored in 1945 on the basis of those records. There were no disputes.[28]

A feverish rise in the black market doubled and even tripled the price of the dollar in 1944. The money allocated by the AJDC to Jewish resistance then took other routes. As we have seen, the creation of the WRB permitted transfers of funds via Switzerland. Authorized by Washington, dollars converted into French francs on the Swiss market were secretly introduced into France. After May 1944, every dollar thus produced 260 francs. The system of loans had done its part.[29]

Between February 1941 and October 1942, the AJDC borrowed 141,558,250 francs in France at rates ranging from 80 to 130 francs per dollar.[30] After November 1942, its representatives received 120 million francs in loans. These sums included 20,560,000 francs of donations raised by Zionist organizations and placed at the disposition of the assistance and rescue organizations in France through the channel of the AJDC, which transferred matching funds to Palestine.[31]

As long as the American agency acted openly in France, its contributions were directed to legal Jewish charities as well as to CIMADE, *Amitié chrétienne*, the DCA (*Direction des centres d'accueil*, Directorate of Reception Centers) of Father Glasberg, and the Quakers. With the establishment of the UGIF, most of the AJDC subventions passed through its treasury. But in February 1943, Jefroykin secretly convened a "consulting committee" in Nice. It consisted in leaders of the KKL, the UGIF, the Central Consistory, and the OSE. Not without difficulty, Jefroykin persuaded the committee to approve the clandestine use of AJDC funds in a proportion to be left to his discretion, but which gradually became preponderant.[32]

The problem of secretly manipulating these considerable sums was solved thanks to non-Jewish institutions that agreed to replace banks to permit the circulation of the Jewish resistance movement's funds without danger. Thus the Faculty of Catholic Theology in Lyons safeguarded the deposits made by Fischer.[33] The AJ, however, which was the first stop for funds smuggled in from Switzerland, created a cache in the basement of a newspaper distributor which served as a cover for its irregular corps of Lyons.[34]

Across the Swiss Border

Links between the Jewish resistance movement and the outside world beginning in 1943 passed through Geneva, where information was exchanged and the financial aid provided by the AJDC, the Jewish Agency, and the WJC was funneled into France. Hunted down by the SD (*Sicherheitsdienst*, the SS security service), Marc Jarblum and Joseph Weill had taken refuge in Switzerland in March and May 1943, respectively. They became zealous spokesmen before the international Jewish organizations in Switzerland for the movements to rescue Jews which were active in France, and each of them established a line of communications across the border. They sent tens of millions of francs across the border with their instructions, and in return they received information about the persecutions and about the resistance movement, which they transmitted to the local Jewish leaders and to the Allied representatives in Switzerland.[35]

Weill used:

> a team of resisters working in Chênes-Bourg (a suburb of Geneva) and Annemasse. As folksy as possible, it was directed by a pharmacist from Geneva, an ingenuous bon vivant, a passionate anti-Nazi and a pure Gaullist sympathizer. A good, discreet, pure curate with one leg, who was able to derive unsuspected profit from his wooden leg, a few customs inspectors, actually Swiss, the owner of a steamroller in Ambilly, and Gabriel, . . . a house-painter, who lived near Annemasse.[36]

That line of communications, secure and well drilled, extended to Maurice Brener. Jarblum's line used the services of a professional bicycle racer[37] and a garage owner in Bossey in the Haute-Savoie Department, who was in contact with the irregular AJ corps in Lyons. These border runners took a commission of 1.5 percent of the sums smuggled through. As noted, the AJ had opened a newspaper distribution shop in Lyons, at 149, Grande-Rue de la Guillotière. This was a meeting place, an arms cache, and the last link in the chain by which Jarblum sent contraband and money. The shop sold daily and weekly collaborationist newspapers to a clientele that had no idea that the woman managing it was a Resistance fighter. Tens of millions of francs passed through that store without arousing the suspicions of either the French or German police.[38]

During the last six months of the occupation, the allocations of the AJDC reached all the Jewish assistance and rescue organizations through the channel of the UGIF to a small degree, and through the clandestine OSE and the CGD. But the sums allocated to the AJ both for its network for crossing the Pyrenees and for its armed action, came without any intermediary, thus escaping supervision by the other leaders of the Jewish resistance movement.[39] Since they were incorporated in the FFI (*Forces Françaises de l'Intérieur*), the Jewish guerrillas were armed and equipped by the *Comité français de la libération nationale* (CFLN).

The major role of the American Jewish contributions in the budgets of Jewish resistance is worthy of study. The arrival of the AJDC in France in 1933 took place within the framework of a strictly circumscribed event: the influx of Jewish refugees from the East, driven out by persecution. Expressing the solidarity of American Jews, this humanitarian agency increased the volume of its expenses in France in proportion to the growing distress of the Jews. (See table 14.1.)

Table 14.1

AJDC EXPENSES IN FRANCE, 1933–1944[48]

Year	Amount($)	Annual Average
1933–38	826,658	138,000
1939	698,761	698,761
1940–42	2,286,729	762,000
1943–1944	3,405,523	1,702,000

After the liberation, the AJDC continued its work of helping the Jewish refugees, but it mainly contributed to the restoration of Jewish social, educational, and cultural institutions in France, as well as the reconstruction of synagogues. In 1945 it allocated nearly two million dollars to these projects.[40]

Certainly the first intervention of the AJDC was inseparable from the circumstance created by the influx of refugees. It coincides with the arrival in France of other international Jewish humanitarian organizations: ORT in 1920, HICEM in 1927, and OSE in 1935. Before the war French Jews saw these charities as institutions preoccupied by the interests and needs of the Jewish immigrants. Eminent members of the Consistory supported these charities and sat on their administrative boards, whereas most French Jews did not feel concerned. The same applied to the international organizations of a political bent, the Jewish Agency for Palestine and the World Zionist Organization, most of whose leaders and activists were recruited among the immigrants.

The change that took place during the years of the occupation, when the internal splits within the Jewish population of France diminished, is partly the consequence of the intervention of the AJDC. By its size and evolution, it demonstrated that the manifestation of Jewish solidarity without boundaries is of irreplaceable value in the Jewish struggle for survival. The moral influence exerted by American Jewish aid on the forces preparing to work for the renewal of Jewish life in France cannot be overlooked.

15

⟡

The Groundwork of the
Postwar Community

The spokesman for the Jewish population of France at present is the *Conseil représentatif des institutions juives de France* (CRIF, The Representative Council of French Jewish Institutions). This organization, born in the underground in January 1944 in Lyons, brings together all of the Jewish institutions of the country, covering the most varied areas: religion, education, culture, mutual social assistance, and community activism.

The CRIF has no precedent in the history of the Jews in France, whereas in Great Britain, for example, an organization representing all the Jews, the Board of Deputies, has existed since the beginning of the nineteenth century.[1] Certainly one must mention the *Comité de coordination* formed in Strasbourg in 1936, which, though local in scope, was the first organization to do away with the distinction between native born and immigrants as well as between the religious, cultural, political, and social dimensions of Jewish life.

Sooner or later the diverse elements into which the Jews were split would probably have constituted a coherent ensemble, but it would have been cut off from those whom the process of assimilation had distanced from all participation in Jewish life, until they reached the final phase of the loss of identity. Persecution and resistance set profound forces in motion, favoring the

unity of the Jews and the renewal of Judaism among those who had already
taken the route of assimilation.

A Common Front for Rescue

The reorganization of the Jewish community took place in 1940, dictated by
the interests of the fight for survival. The present study has described the
chronology of this reorganization. It began with the alliance between the
Zionists and the Bundists within the framework of Rue Amelot. Then followed the foundation of the AJ (*Armée juive*, the Jewish Army), which united
two opposing factions of the Zionist movement under the same flag. The
MJS (*Mouvement de jeunesse sioniste*, the Zionist Youth Movement) brought
together people subscribing to the rival ideologies that had previously
divided militant Zionist youth, uniting them in a common spirit. The MJS
and the EIF (*Éclaireurs israélites de France*, the Jewish scout movement) each
coopted members of the other's leadership teams to give more vigor to their
ties, which were already numerous. Finally we noted the foundation of the
CGD (*Comité général de défense juive*, General Committee for Jewish
Defense), that marks in its fashion the return of the Communists of the
UJRE (*Union des Juifs pour la résistance et l'entraide*, Jewish Union for
Resistance and Mutual Assistance) to the bosom of Judaism, but above all it
accomplished the union of all the Jewish immigrants.

The foregoing summary describes operational alliances which were valid
in the very circumscribed context of the war. Their goal was to make a common front against the enemy in order to perform rescue work more effectively. The partners in this alliance conceded that their ideological character
had to give way temporarily before the imperatives of Jewish survival. The
Bundists, for example, did not have to adjust or modify their anti-Zionist
and anti-Communist credo, but they postponed all political contention to
better days. To ally themselves with political rivals or with those subscribing
to another doctrine, it was enough to overcome reflexes that had become
anachronistic and to understand that what was at stake in the war against
the Nazis transcended the ideologies dividing the Jewish people.

Among the immigrants, the union was favored by their cultural affiliation and by the consciousness of belonging to the same community of
fate. Could it have been brought to include French Jews without the obstinacy of a handful of apostles? Marc Jarblum, Nahum Hermann, Joseph
Fischer, Ruben Grinberg, Lucien Lublin, and Robert Gamzon were at the
origin of more than one alliance. The attention and authority achieved by

these men demonstrate the popularity of the idea of union among the Jewish activists.

After the formation of the CGD in August 1943, the operational reordering of the underground Jewish organizations was complete. It proved its mettle in Nice a month later, during the Italian debacle. But the agreement realized in this fashion did not include the military domain. Moreover, the men of the CGD hoped to achieve agreement with the official representative of French Jewry, the General Consistory.

The Failure of the Youth Unification Committee

During the negotiations in Grenoble in July 1943 for the formation of the CGD, the UJRE had demanded the participation of all the partners in recruiting fighters, the unification of the armed detachments, and a permanent financial allocation for these detachments. But the FSJF (*Féderation des sociétés juives de France*, the Federation of Jewish Associations of France) was not prepared to approve joint action on that level. Its leaders remained convinced that it was necessary to dedicate all forces to rescue. "We must spare Jewish lives. They have already shed enough blood," states a leaflet entitled, *The Jews and the War*, published secretly in Toulouse.[2] Jewish army units, placed under the orders of the Gaullist or Communist resistance movements, were not to be sent to battle, in their opinion, except at the hour of national insurrection. This disagreement did not prevent the creation of the CGD. Its promoters decided that the coordination of the armed groups would be achieved by a future Youth Unification Committee.[3]

The formation of that committee was arduous. The Jewish Communist press published in Grenoble launched appeals to unity to "young Zionists and scouts."[4] Then it denounced "the inexplicable decision" of the "Zionist cartel" which declared that "Zionist youth is not yet ripe for unity."[5] To the pamphlet, *The Jews and the War*, the UJRE replied with a declaration entitled, *Jews in the War Against Fascism*, pleading for the recruitment of fighters.[6] But in a report addressed to the PC in December 1943, the leadership of the UJRE acknowledged the responsibility of its youth organization, "which was unable to carry out an intelligent and persistent policy of unity."[7] The coordination of the combat groups was in fact difficult to conceive. Those of the UJJ (*Union de la jeunesse juive*, Union of Jewish Youth) were integrated into detachments of the FTP (*Francs-tireurs et partisans*) in Lyons, Grenoble, Marseilles, and Toulouse. Those of the AJ, by contrast, in the same cities, operated uniquely in the service of the Jewish rescue networks.

The *Comité d'action et de défense de la jeunesse juive* (CADJJ, Action and Defense Committee of Jewish Youth) was nevertheless created in Grenoble in February 1944. Defining itself as a youth section of the CGD, the CADJJ combined the MJS, the Bundist Youth, the UJJ, and the EIF. Its charter[8] stated that it was charged with "the coordination of combat and defense groups as well as of guerrilla units belonging to the CADJJ."

However, deprived of a budget, this committee had only a theoretical existence. Since the thinning out of the Second Detachment and the dispersion of what was left of it in Paris in October 1943, no autonomous military unit had been formed by the Jewish Communists. They certainly constituted the majority of the members of the Carmagnole Battalion in Lyons and of the Marcel Langer Brigade in Toulouse. Viewed on the personal level, the engagement of a number of these Jewish fighters belongs under the rubric of Jewish resistance. But the epic of the partisan units of which they constituted the main element belongs to the history of Communist resistance and not to that of Jewish resistance. While the experience of battle in the ranks of the MJS and the EIF tended to deepen the identification of youth with the sources of the Jewish heritage, that of the UJJ, according to the personal testimony of Annie Kriegel, sought to submit them to "an apprenticeship . . . which would purge them of their impurities, and notably of Jewish impurity: . . . in 1944, when weary and broken, but triumphant, we left the inferno, in appearance we were no longer anything but Communists, in the strict sense of the term."[9]

That is why the creation of the CADJJ was merely a formality, accomplished under the pressure of the promoters of the CGD. The generation of immigrants owed the possibility of agreement in the common battle, despite the ideological splits, to its cultural homogeneity. The children of the immigrants, in contrast, had taken paths too divergent to manage to meet in action. The men of the CADJJ signed a charter that in fact remained a dead letter, simple homage granted to their parents as a sign of respect. Between the young people who served a Communist apprenticeship and eliminated Jewishness from their lives and those who studied Hebrew in order to participate in Jewish religious and national life, there was no common ground. Effective coordination within the Jewish resistance movement was thus achieved not on the level of military operations but rather on that of rescue action.

Thinking of the Future Under the Shadow of Death

The ultimate stage in restructuring Jewish organizations remained to be reached: the definition of a joint platform that would express the interests of the Jewish population of France beyond partisan ideologies and in the perspective of the day that would follow the torture.

For some of the leaders were thinking about the postwar community. The emergence of the representative political institutions of free France is not irrelevant to this. The *Conseil national de la Résistance* (CNR, the National Council of the Resistance), a sign that "all the movements and parties of the resistance" were rallying politically to de Gaulle, held its first meeting on May 27, 1943 in Paris, while the "Gaullist State" was founded the following June 3 in Algiers, with the formation of the *Comité français de libération nationale* (CFLN, French Committee of National Liberation).[10] During the summer of that year, Joseph Fischer composed a draft text defining the Jewish representation before the CFLN and the future government of the republic. Approved by the Coordinating Committee of Immigrant Jews, the draft was submitted to the Consistory, which appointed a committee to study it.[11] At the same time, the UJRE proclaimed "the necessity of a true representation of French Judaism. . . . Within that representation, the organizations of immigrant Jews would sit beside those of the French Jews."[12]

While some thought about the structure of the institutions, others were preoccupied with promoting Jewish renewal. It was they who assembled study groups for the training of tomorrow's community leaders. For both, the aim was to "change the miserable image of our Judaism."[13] As Rayski said, "it demanded superhuman will to think of the future under the crushing shadow of death."[14]

The Charter of the Representative Council of French Jews

Talks between the leaders of the Consistory and the immigrant Jews extended over six months. The Gestapo kept tightening its vice, especially seeking out leaders of "official" Judaism. Let us recall that following the arrest in Paris of André Baur, the Vice President of the UGIF (*Union générale des Juifs de France*, General Union of French Jews) on July 22, 1943, three official Jewish leaders were arrested in the southern zone: Baur's southern counterpart, Raymond-Raoul Lambert, on August 21 in Marseilles; the President of the Central Consistory, Jacques Heilbronner, on October 23 in Lyons; and the Chaplain General, René Hirschler, on December 23, in Marseilles. On Friday night, December 10, three grenades thrown into the synagogue in Lyons wounded ten of the faithful assembled for prayer.[15] Under such conditions, it took unparalleled coolness and audacity to insist on planning the Jewish institutions of the future. After Heilbronner's arrest,

Léon Meiss took it upon himself to continue the talks in the name of the Consistory. Tall and well-built, his face filled with reassurance and gentleness, with a very mobile but never fleeting glance, he harbored a smile that was both witty and enigmatic. Economical and sometimes solemn in his gestures, he knew how to listen and made sober use of his voice with its soft but occasionally nasal intonations. The partners met in cafés, "never the same ones, between Vaulx-en-Velin and Lyons."[16]

After September 1943 the cGD, acting as the spokesman for the immigrant Jews, entered talks with the Consistory. At that point a completely unprecedented situation emerged. The men placed in command of the UJRE felt no sympathy toward the religious representatives of the French Jewish bourgeoisie, who were traditionally close to political power, nor did they know them. Similarly, Meiss had never met a "Jewish extremist," as he put it.[17] A long history of disagreements, misunderstanding, and mutual distrust created a psychological distance between the two parties that was difficult to cross.

However, by the very fact that they could envisage a united Jewish representation in France, the heads of the Consistory showed that they had revised their old conception of Judaism reduced to its religious dimension. The Consistory in its historical definition thus renounced its monopoly over Jewish representation. This task was now to be shared with the Jewish immigrants, grouped in organizations displaying a political or national Jewish identity.

As for the cGD, none of its partners conceived of a Jewish representation without the participation of the delegates of French Jews. It even declared that it recognized the Consistory's moral authority to lead the restructuring of the French and immigrant Jews.

Such attitudes had swept away the psychological obstacles that might have prevented bringing talks to fruition. The Jews' precarious living conditions constituted the only difficulty in pursuing the conversations. Hunted down without cease, the negotiators had to camouflage themselves and resorted to a multitude of ruses to protect the secret of their meetings.

The cGD demanded that the charter of the future representative council declare its support for the resistance and issue a radical condemnation of the UGIF, from which the Consistory had distinguished itself from the beginning. The Zionists wanted the charter to proclaim the right of the Jews to a national home in Palestine. The Consistory wanted these points to be passed over in silence, for some of them were mere formalities, and it put forward one precondition: each partner must produce guarantees against any use of the representative council to benefit a political party.[18]

The first clearing of the brush was the work of Fischer. He proposed distinguishing between the role assigned by Vichy to the UGIF on the one hand and the intentions and activity of its leaders on the other. Having obtained agreement on this point, he arranged a first meeting between Meiss and Rayski. From the start the head of the venerable religious organization and the "Jewish extremist" found the proper tone for a frank and trusting exchange.[19] A commission charged with drafting the charter was then constituted.

Adopted unanimously in January 1944,[20] the CRIF charter calls for the abolition of all discriminatory laws and for the restitution of all Jewish rights and property. It defines the council as the only body qualified to represent the Jews of France before the French government, "as soon as circumstances permit," as well as before foreign Jewish organizations and international bodies. It states that the president of the CRIF shall be the president of the Consistory or his delegate.

It was agreed not to have the charter proclaim the support given by the CRIF to the resistance, so as to maintain what remained of the legal status of the Consistory as responsible for synagogues where people continued to hold religious services. Similarly it was decided to remain silent regarding the UGIF, since in itself the creation of the CRIF constituted a rejection of the Vichy institution.

The thorny problem of support for the Zionist movement was resolved in a spirit of compromise. Those drafting the charter accepted both an amendment proposed by the UJRE stating that the council would encourage "the most complete understanding between the Jewish and Arab populations of Palestine, in the greatest democratic spirit," and also an amendment proposed by the Consistory stating that "the national status of the Jews of Palestine will in no way affect that of the Jews of other countries and the ties that bind them to their fatherland."[21] These two clauses were joined with the text of the charter demanding the abolition of the British White Paper of 1939, the freedom of Jewish immigration to Palestine, and the establishment of a national Jewish home there.

We have seen that in July 1944 the CRIF appointed a committee headed by Meiss which debated, as demanded by the CGD, the immediate closure of the UGIF. The voluminous protocols of the work of this committee show that the decision to dissociate the leaders of the UGIF from the role assigned by Vichy to that organization was scrupulously applied.[22]

The unanimous choice of Léon Meiss, valued for his tact and open mind, had permitted the Consistory to retain leadership in the body representing the Jews of France. But the Consistory had changed. It no longer embodied the values of the era of emancipation. Its status as the institution responsible for religious services doubtless remained unchanged. But the cruel experience of genocide, the dizzying magnitude of the losses suffered, and the intolerable outrages inflicted by a French government had contributed to changing its perception of Judaism, or rather the perception of its leaders. They now recognized the legitimate presence in the community of all those who conceived of Jewish identity in a dimension other than the religious one. Thus it was necessary to share the mission of representing the Jews with Zionist organizations or those linked to a political party. The development of the Consistory provides a rather good illustration of the inner development of the Jews of France. On the decline before the war, it underwent a dynamic awakening in resistance to the Nazis and revealed forces capable of producing renewal.

The restructuring effected in the night of the occupation in order to present a united front to the enemy did not survive the war. But two organizations born in the torment have remained active to this day: the CDJC (*Centre de documentation juive contemporaine*, Center for Contemporary Jewish Documentation) and the CRIF. In both cases their promoters had envisaged the community of tomorrow. Having taken perfect measure of the unprecedented character of the tragedy undergone by the Jews, the founders of the documentation center conceived of a specific institution charged with studying and preserving as authentic a memory as possible.

The ambition of the CRIF was to contribute to the reconstruction of the postwar community. An organization with the vocation of representing the Jewish institutions of the country is certainly not qualified to take up the work of community activism nor of promoting a renewal of Jewish life. But it symbolizes the idea of union and consolidates the process of diminishing the splits and discord that had fragmented the pre-war Jewish population and had been overcome during the Resistance. Thus it creates conditions encouraging the establishment of ties of another sort between the various elements of that population. Overthrowing tendencies that had predominated before the war, the resisters who founded the CRIF left it with a coherent institutional framework capable of defining Jewish interests in the name of all the organizations.

16

❧

The Armed Struggle

The Jewish resistance movement took part in guerrilla action against the Germans not only because it identified with the strategic thinking of the Allies, including the French Resistance, who held that the only way to halt the war crimes committed by the Nazis against civilian populations was to crush Germany by force of arms. In addition, the Jewish movement wished, of course, to save Jews from extermination, so that bearing arms against German troops was but one aspect of the struggle. Its military role is therefore inseparable from its determination to contribute to the defeat of the Nazis.

The imperatives of salvation and taking up arms were not always in accord. Indeed, we have already mentioned this problem. However, the two goals ultimately coincided at the end of the road, with the launching of the assault against Hitler's forces and their French auxiliaries.

The case of the AJ (*Armée juive*, Jewish Army) is a perfect illustration of the Jews' desire to take up arms in the name of their feeling of solidarity with all the Jews, and of their national Jewish consciousness. A military network from its genesis, the AJ first used its fighters against agents of the Gestapo or of the Militia who were hunting down Jews. But at the time of the final assault, all its men fought at the side of the French resistance.

Solidarité-UJRE (*Union des Juifs pour la résistance et l'entraide*, Jewish Union for Resistance and Mutual Assistance), while in the vanguard of those who undertook guerrilla operations against the Nazis, did not wait until the end of the hostilities to engage in rescue work as well. Other resistance networks, EIF (*Éclaireurs israélites de France*, the Jewish scouts) and *Service André*, became militarized only in the final phase of the war in France.

Jews in the National Resistance: A Military Response

Nevertheless it appears that the numerous Jews who took an active part in the Resistance viewed their role primarily in military terms rather than as a rescue mission. "In the Resistance, the Jews acted no differently than other Frenchmen," writes a specialist on the history of the Resistance, Henri Michel. He maintains that "the participation of Jews in the Resistance was the highest, proportional to the population of Jewish religion or origin, of all the components of the Resistance, considered in their religious or ethnic aspect."[1] Though admitting that it is impossible to cite numbers, or even percentages, the eminent historian states:

> one finds [Jews] in all the manifestations, in all the regions, and at every moment where the Resistance asserted itself: in the entourage of General de Gaulle in London, as among the non-Gaullist emigrés in England or the United States; in the resistance movements in the occupied zone, and those of the so-called free zone; among the first groups of the 'special organization' of the Communist Party and among the adherents of the Socialist Party; in the underground press, in all the stages of its production; in the rural fighting groups—notably in Vercors; among the FFI [*Forces Françaises de l'Intérieur*] and finally in the liberation committees. Often Frenchmen of Jewish religion or origin were the creators or leaders, the organizers of parachute missions and maritime operations, heads of networks, emissaries of Free France in occupied France, commanders of rural fighting groups. One resounding action was the Putsch in Algiers on November 8, 1942, accomplished by several hundred volunteers who were, in the majority, Algerian Jews.[2]

Can this action be called Jewish resistance? The answer given to this question by resisters giving subjective testimony is not uniform. "Owing my survival and that of my family to the aid of resisters, pure and simple, I owed it to myself to fight at their side," explains one of them, claiming that he belonged to the Jewish resistance movement in that he fought with a rural fighting group of the national resistance.[3] This is not an isolated case. But another witness affirms: "My resistance was not specifically Jewish."[4] Was his behavior identical to that of other Frenchmen in the Resistance, as Henri Michel states? Not at all, because he had "suffered personal injury by the fact of the German regulations and the anti-Semitic legislation of the Vichy regime," states Léo Hamon, who places himself among the Jews who reacted "for their dignity as citizens and Frenchmen." Continuing this train of thought he concluded:

> Perhaps, too, there were quite a number of us who had, according to an expression that has become classic, 'a certain idea of France,' the fatherland of the Revolution and of the rights of man, in which the Republic had taken the place which, in the Bible, was that of the People of the Covenant. . . . Some of us, seeing ourselves as mobilized in the service of that France, even came to regret being enclosed and confined in the quality of Jewishness, which moved in the direction of the enemy's manipulations. . . . I was not part of the Jewish resistance, I was part of the French Resistance.[5]

The historian must respect testimony in which everyone interprets the meaning of the combat he himself waged. It would be inappropriate to cut off the open debate on this theme. But regardless of the idea that every resister had of his own identity, no differences appear with respect to the goal of this combat: to save defeated France from Nazi domination. The framework of the present study concerns the organizations and networks that strove to save Jews from the genocide perpetrated by the Nazis. This framework does not coincide with an account of Jewish action in the Resistance. The distorted character of the latter sort of inventory is suggested by those who, like Marc Bloch and Léo Hamon, insisted on the French identity of their resistance, foreign "to any pretended racial solidarity."[6] Two historians articulate this view: Béatrice Philippe writes, "It is difficult and tiresome, even shocking, to make an exhaustive accounting of the number of Jews who participated in the Resistance";[7] and Lucien Steinberg states, "It would be absurd to separate the various combatants of the Resistance, in other words, to create a ghetto there."[8]

Armed resistance does not, therefore, belong to the framework of this study except where it coincides with humanitarian resistance. This is the case

regarding military operations aimed at striking down enemy agents implicated in the deportation of Jews or at destroying the instruments of that
deportation. This is also the case with participation in the guerrilla warfare
waged in the final phase of the occupation to liberate a certain part of the territory, and with popular insurrection designed to precipitate German defeat.

Seen from this angle, the armed resistance of Jewish organizations was a
defensive battle waged by victims of aggression who were threatened with
physical annihilation. This definition takes note of the motivations that animated the partisans engaged in the irregular Jewish corps and rural fighting
units. On the level of the leaders, however, political choices inspired the initiatives that were taken, and this is the case with two organizations:
Solidarité-UJRE, which identified with the options and imperatives of the
PC, despite certain disagreements; the AJ, created by militant Zionists to
serve the program of Jewish national rebirth.

Their political character explains the early date at which these organizations began to operate on the military level. They were the first to respond
to the pressure of dynamic elements within Jewish youth, impatient to take
armed vengeance for the deportation of their relatives.[9]

Urban Guerrilla Warfare

The Irregular AJ Corps

The abovementioned organizations were also the only ones that operated
militarily against the agents of the deportation of Jews. The irregular corps
formed by the AJ in 1943 in Toulouse, Nice, Grenoble, and Lyons gathered
intelligence at first. They created files containing information about the personnel and activities of the CGQJ (*Commissariat général aux Questions juives*,
General Commission for Jewish Questions) and of activists of Darnand's
Militia.[10] After the Italian debacle on September 8, 1943, Jews were hunted
down in the streets, hotels, public places, and transportation facilities in
Nice, then in Grenoble, Lyons, Limoges, and Toulouse. The Gestapo
directed these operations, mainly using men of the Militia, of the PPF (*Parti
populaire français*, French People's Party, a fascist organization) and also of
more or less experienced informers. In Nice, as has been noted, a team of
"physiognomists" operated. It was composed of White Russians and Italian
Fascists, some of whom owned nightclubs and stores selling luxury items.
From January to March 1944, 660 Jews were captured in Nice, transferred to
Drancy, and deported.[11]

The irregular AJ corps in Lyons was the first to procure arms, purchased earler from Italian soldiers.[12] The other irregular corps, in Nice, were handicapped by their failure to have yet procured arms in the autumn of 1943. In the beginning of 1944 the Nice group succeeded in tracking down some of the most redoubtable of the "physiognomists" responsible for the capture of hundreds of Jews every month. The irregular corps turned to the local resistance but obtained from it neither arms nor direct intervention against these dangerous informers. In March it went into action itself, after obtaining several revolvers and ammunition, to the detriment of an arms dealer in Marseilles. In May the local resistance finally procured explosives. From April to June the young men and women of the irregular AJ corps in Nice, after patient surveillance, assassinated two Russian auxiliaries of the Gestapo, a Militia member from Saint-Martin-de-Vésubie, and some informers. In June it was incorporated within the local FFI with the name of the irregular *Éclair* (lightning) corps, and it planted bombs in a nightclub named *L'Écrin* and an antique shop, both of which were headquarters of anti-Jewish activities.[13] The band of "physiognomists" disappeared from the streets of Nice in April 1944, and the number of Jews arrested diminished by 80 percent from April to July.[14]

Less is known about similar actions by the irregular AJ corps of Lyons and Paris, formed in April 1944 by fighters coming from the southern zone. The extant reports are scanty.[15] The men, arms, and munitions used in Paris came from the southern zone, transported by intrepid female liaison agents. There, too, the AJ operated with the FFI within the framework of the irregular corps *Alerte*. AJ units took part in the battles of the Liberation in the ranks of the FFI in Paris, Lyons, Grenoble, Nice, and Toulouse.[16] The chief of the irregular corps of Lyons, Ernest Lambert, was arrested in the Perrache railway station on June 29, 1944. He was murdered, after torture, on July 8. Infiltrated by the Gestapo, the irregular AJ corps in Paris was captured on July 18 and 19 in the course of an operation described below.[17]

The Second FTP-MOI-Yiddish Detachment

While a number of its activists had participated in the guerrilla warfare fought in Paris by the *Organisation spéciale* (OS) of the PC as early as November 1941, not without suffering severe losses, in August 1942 Solidarité formed the Second FTP (*Francs-tireurs et partisans*)-MOI (*Main-d'oeuvre immigrée*, Immigrant Manual Labor)-Yiddish Detachment. Incredibly courageous, its men and women obtained arms and explosives by their own means, attacking German soldiers and police agents, and robbing rock quarries (for the explosives) in the suburbs. Operating under the orders of the FTP command, they carried out a great many armed attacks against isolated elements of the Wehrmacht, restaurants, hotels, and cinemas frequented by German troops, and also against military vehicles and garages.[18] The directors of Solidarité made patient efforts to convince their fighters that this form of guerrilla action was necessary to hasten the defeat of the Nazis, so as to put an end to the persecution of the Jews. They also had to explain that the massive reprisals made by the enemy against hundreds of hostages, mostly Jews, had a beneficial effect on the French population, in that it aroused hatred against the Germans. This was the doctrine of the PC.[19]

The special brigades of the prefecture of police struck hard against the Second Detachment. After engaging in extensive surveillance, they twice succeeded in planting a "turned" resister in the unit.[20] In March 1943 they seized approximately 140 militants, the main body of the Second Detachment and its reserves. Eighty more arrests were made in June 1943, putting the group out of existence. At that point the PC, after having refused to do so in May, because "the Communist cadres are not the sort of people to be placed in reserve," agreed to transfer the directorate of Solidarité, which had meanwhile become the UJRE, to Lyons. But instead of stationing the survivors of the Second Detachment in towns harboring considerable Jewish population in the southern zone, the PC incorporated them within two other FTP-MOI units in Paris. Most of them (150 fighters of every nationality) were trapped, in November 1943, by the special brigades and turned over to the Gestapo. Twenty-three of them, including eleven Jews, were condemned in a court martial in February 1944. This was the show trial of the so-called Manouchian Group, produced by the Nazis with the intention of discrediting the Resistance by showing that it did not emanate from French patriots, but from revolting foreign terrorists. Throughout all of France, walls were covered with thousands of "red posters" with the headline: "Liberation by the Army of Crime." They reproduced the photographs of ten of those condemned, including seven Jews, with their unpronounceable names.[21]

The liquidation of the FTP-MOI units in Paris led to painful debates. Some people have gone so far as to accuse the PC of deliberately sacrificing these fighters because they were immigrants and Jews. Rayski, followed by the historian Stéphane Courtois, nevertheless observes that this accusation "is not the kind that clarifies factual reality or makes it explicit in its political and historical context." Both a witness and participant in these events, he maintains that in its determination to build its political prestige on the basis of the stunning actions of FTP-MOI, the PC committed the error of waging a guerrilla struggle as if it were ordinary warfare: "Whereas in war, the essential point is not to lose ground, to cling to it whatever the cost, for guerrilla struggle, what is essential is to know how to let go, not to linger on the field, and to limit losses, the supreme concern of all partisan combat."[22]

There was no Jewish military unit similar to the Second Detachment in the southern zone, although the large FTP-MOI formations of Lyons and Grenoble (the Carmagnole-Liberté Battalion), of Toulouse (the Marcel Langer Brigade) and of Marseilles (the Maurice Korsec Battalion) contained a very large proportion of Jewish fighters. The UJRE formed Jewish groups of "patriotic militias," whose action is little known, for lack of accessible sources. The assumption of direct responsibility for Jewish interests is evident only regarding two operations carried out in Lyons in July 1944: the armed abduction of seven Jewish children placed in the l'Antiquaille hospital, under the control of the Gestapo, which had deported their parents, as well as the assassination of Marc Carrel, the regional head of the CGQJ and a leader of the PPF.[23] These UJRE combat groups took part in the battles of the Liberation in several cities in the southern zone.

The Limits of Battle Against Deportation

We know of no attempted armed intervention to liberate the inmates of any of the places of detention, or of deportees being transported in railway cars. First, the military capacity of the Jewish resistance movement was insufficient to carry out an operation of that scope. Second, the fear of provoking reprisals that would harm more victims than would have been saved by the Resistance had a paralyzing effect. The leaders could not imagine that the detainees and deportees were inevitably condemned to extermination.

It was impossible for a sane person to credit the existence of the death factories. No one wanted to shoulder the responsibility of causing the death of some of the occupants of a train on its way to Auschwitz.Such an operation had, in fact, once been attempted by the Jewish resistance in Belgium. On April 19, 1943, an armed commando unit attacked a deportation train, resulting in 231 escapees, but also in the deaths of twenty-six other deportees. The attackeers, too, suffered losses in sufficient number to have prevented the commando unit from taking charge of the escapees from the train, so that many were recaptured by the Nazis.[24] Those responsible for the operation experienced it as a failure and attempted no further operations of this sort.

It was only after the war, when the truth was revealed, that the survivors took a different view. The psychological process explaining the decisions made by the resisters has been described by Raymond Aron: "On the level of

clear consciousness, my perception was more or less the following: the concentration camps were cruel, . . . the death rate was very high there, but gas
chambers, the industrial assassination of human beings, no, I admit, I had
not imagined them, and, because I could not imagine them, I did not know
about them." That testimony complements that of Georges Wellers: "Only
the perverse, the mad, men without faith or law, are capable of inventing
monstrous slaughter-houses for humans, or even to imagine the possibility
or believe in their existence."[25]

Hence urban guerrilla action offered a very narrow field of action to the
Jewish resistance movement. Before the popular insurrection broke out, the
irregular AJ corps were the only ones who waged this warfare. The overwhelming advantage of the enemy was partially psychological. It was
absolutely impossible for the Jewish resisters to conceive that the true stake
in its war was the physical extermination of all the Jews.

Let us add that the irregular urban corps struggling against deportation
developed in total isolation. Not only were they aiming at a target that the
other partisans ignored, because it did not fit into their military objectives,
but also they were deprived of two instruments, radio and aviation, which
were, in contrast, accessible to the other underground fighters, the rural partisan groups. Henri Michel, the historian, points out that "radio removed
the rural partisan from his blindness and intellectual isolation," whereas aviation provides him with arms, equipment, provisions, and leaders parachuted in.[26] Suffering from the limitations of its means, in March 1944 the
AJ sought to establish contact with London by radio and air. It fell into the
an ambush laid by the Nazi secret services, which seized fourteen of its men
in July 1944.

The Dismantling of the Irregular AJ Corps in Paris

The affair was set in motion when the chief of the irregular corps in Nice,
Henri Pohorylès, confided in the FSJF's trusted agent, Rogowski, that the
severe shortage of arms was paralyzing AJ plans. The former Attorney
General of Petrograd remembered that one of his acquaintances, a young
Russian Jewish woman, had revealed to him that her lover was an agent of the
Intelligence Service (IS). Charged with the mission by the heads of the AJ, in
May Pohorylès met in Marseilles with Charles Porel, supposedly an IS agent.
He was, however, really Karl Rehbein, a decorated and experienced agent of
the Abwehr. The contacts continued in Montauban and then in Paris, where
"Pohorylès" had been sent to reconstitute the irregular corps that had been
dismantled following the capture of five members of the Dutch group. The

Gestapo had raided their hotel room in Versigny on April 27, also seizing their equipment for the fabrication of false identity papers and German travel documents.[27] It was agreed that all the officers of the AJ underground would be introduced to the IS agents after the reception of a coded message on the BBC, confirming the arrival of its two emissaries in London.

These two, René Kapel and Jacques Lazarus, left on July 17. Within less than two hours they found themselves at Gestapo headquarters, on rue de la Pompe. The next day the Nazi police captured six men of the AJ, who had gathered to listen to the BBC. Among them was Maurice Cachoud-Lobenberg, the head of the MLN (*Mouvement de libération nationale,* National Liberation Movement) false document service.[28] He was tortured and executed, but he never talked. Traps were laid in the apartments where the members of the irregular AJ corps met, leading to further arrests, which brought the total to fourteen, twelve men and two women.[29]

Despite torture, they kept silence about the AJ's irregular corps and rural partisans. Transferred to Fresnes, then to Drancy, on August 17 they were placed on a train carrying what would prove to be the last deportation of Jews by Brunner, the SS chief of the camp, who took them with him in his flight from France. Almost all of them succeeded in a daring escape, leaping from the moving train in the Saint-Quentin region. They testified in the trial of the torturers of rue de la Pompe in December 1952 in Paris. Rehbein, tried in absentia, was also implicated in the massacre at the waterfall in the Bois de Boulogne of thirty-four young resisters, whom he had gathered by making them believe he was going to distribute arms.[30]

Completely dismantled by the "downfalls" of April 27 and July 17–19, the irregular corps of Paris nevertheless managed to reconstitute as a combat unit that distinguished itself at the side of the FFI irregular group, Alerte, in combats for the liberation of Paris. Their lack of political experience and unfamiliarity with secret warfare were partly responsible for the defeat inflicted by the Abwehr against the heroes of the AJ. But imprudent actions committed through an excess of credulity are not sufficient to explain the unfortunate course of events, which was a result of the exceptional professional competence of the German secret services, which also wrought devastating damage to the large networks of the Resistance.

Jewish Rural Partisans

Part of the story of the Jewish rural partisans in France is generously documented. The Israeli historian Haim Avni has thoroughly researched the illegal passage of AJ fighters to Spain. The testimony he gathered from 1960 to 1963 as well as his penetrating study fill in the gaps in the work of Émilienne Eychenne, a specialist in the history of escapes from France to Spain. Fragments of the log of an AJ partisan unit, where men preparing to cross the Spanish border received military training, have been preserved by individuals.[31] The sources concerning a unit of the AJ-*Service André* of the Vivarais-Lignon Plateau and the AJ squad incorporated in the *Corps franc de la Montagne Noire* (CFMN, Irregular Corps of the Black Mountain) come from reports addressed to the directorate of the AJ (partially preserved) and from the log of the CFMN kept by its chief, Major Roger Mompezat.[32]

Abundant documentation recounts the daily chronicle of the EIF-AJ partisan unit of Vabre (the Mountains of Lacaune), the Marc Haguenau Company.[33]

The Escape of Fighters to Spain

When the AJ formed a partisan unit in Bic, near Alban in the Tarn Department in November 1943, its aim was to establish a base for escorting men who intended to cross the Spanish border.

The first attempted escape to Spain of young people connected to the Jewish resistance movement who wished to reach North Africa or Great Britain to join the French forces was an initiative of the *Sixième*, which had no follow-up. Wahl had made contact with men who ran the border in the Basses-Pyrénées Department. A convoy of ten Jewish escapees, leaders and senior members of the EIF, was taken in hand by a border-runner in Bedons on December 22, 1942 and arrived in Spain after a ten day march. But a German patrol had intercepted two other members of this convoy in the railroad station of Bedons, and they were deported to their death.[34]

In addition to the risk of arrest in the border zone, crossing the Pyrenees was extremely difficult because of the dangerous topography of the mountains and its unpredictable climate (impenetrable fogs, snowfall, and avalanches) and the unscrupulousness of some of the border-runners. From late autumn of 1942, the AJ planned to form convoys of young people who were supposed to pass through Spain on their way to Palestine, where they were to join the Allied forces.[35] This idea conformed more than any other to the program defined by the AJ: to mobilize Jewish youth to combat the Nazi enemy and to work in favor of Jewish national rebirth in Palestine. The appearance of the first elements of the Dutch group in France at the same time was a stimulant of the first order.

As in France, mass arrests and deportations of Jews had taken place in the Low Countries in July 1942. It was then that young Zionists active in the pioneering movements, mostly refugees from Germany and Austria, began to seek escape routes to Switzerland or Spain, in an effort to reach Palestine. The idea of Switzerland was soon abandoned, since that country was "a large prison until the end of the war." After the passage between the Netherlands and France was tested with the help of the Dutch resistance, the first arrivals reached the southern zone from Holland in November 1943. After putting out feelers for a long time, they made contact in Lyons then in Nice with underground Zionists in France, active members of the MJS (*Mouvement de jeunesse sioniste*, Zionist Youth Movement) and also the AJ. The AJ had not yet attempted passage to Spain. In April 1943, thirteen young Jews from the Low Countries on their way to France were arrested in Antwerp. They managed to pass themselves off as workers for the labor camps of the Todt Organization in France who had taken an illegal leave in the Netherlands. The Wehrmacht sent them to a labor camp on the English Channel and a submarine base in La Rochelle. There they familiarized themselves with German bureaucratic procedures, and during an air raid at the base in La Rochelle they snatched various official forms. Thus equipped, they set about counterfeiting identity papers and travel documents that permitted them first of all to bring comrades from Holland into France, and then to equip the members of convoys escaping to Spain, including those of the AJ.[36]

The heads of the AJ in Toulouse had gathered some information about the fate in store for illegal border crossers at the hands of the Spanish regime. They knew that those who claimed to be French or who were regarded as French generally ran the risk of being sent back or even handed over to the French authorities. But they did not know that this practice was progressively abandoned after the Allied landing in North Africa in November 1942, when Spain obtained various American supplies.[37] Those escapees who claimed to be stateless or Canadian, for example, were condemned to internment of variable duration and then released. The aid of a consulate or of a humanitarian organization such as the Quakers or the Red Cross could avoid or curtail internment in some cases. The AJ decided to smuggle two delegates across the border to Spain. Their mission was, through the AJDC office in Madrid, to organize some arrangement to receive the escapees and send them on to Palestine. They crossed the mountains by a route passing through Saint-Girons and Mont Vallier in the Ariège Department in May 1943. Other small convoys followed by the same itinerary. From May to October the AJ smuggled forty-two men to Spain. Thirty of them came from the Dutch group. The price paid to the border-runners ranged from 10,000 to 30,000 francs per person.[38]

The two delegates who arrived in Madrid encountered the suspicion and skepticism of the local AJDC. Their mission was a failure.[39] But in Toulouse, the AJ chiefs created the *Service d'évacuation et de regroupement* (SER, Evacuation and Relocation Service) in October 1943. It was given operational autonomy and placed under the direction of Jacques Roitman.

Henceforth escape to Spain went from the improvisational phase to that of organization. Under Roitman's leadership, candidates for border crossing were gathered in a partisan unit, that of Bic, which had been created to serve as a base for escape convoys. There they underwent a course including both Zionism and physical, pre-military training. A career noncommissioned officer, Jacques Lazarus, took responsibility for this partisan unit. He had been enlisted by the AJ in March 1943 and had instructed individuals and irregular corps in Lyons, Grenoble, and Nice. The shortage of arms was a source of worry for the leaders, who were forced to develop plans for escape and camouflage in case of an alert. Lacking telecommunications equipment, lookouts mounted guard equipped with whistles. During the winter they received some pistols brought by a woman liaison agent sent from Toulouse. The local resistance, to which the base in Bic was linked, gave the order for withdrawal in March 1944 after the arrest of an officer in Albi. The AJ partisan unit first moved about fifty kilometers to the south, in the mountains of Lacaune, then, in April, they moved on to Espinassier in the Montagne Noire.[40]

Roitman established the standard equipment for each escapee. He surveyed the border zone from the Mediterranean to the Haute-Garonne Department, where he inspected various alternative escape routes. A woman liaison agent was charged with discreetly escorting each group of escapees. At the moment the border-runner took charge of the group, she would hand him the submachine gun she had been carrying unassembled in her baggage. Then she would return to Toulouse to make her report. The first convoy of twenty-eight escapees set out on December 6, 1943 but turned back because the border-runner thought the mountain was impassable because of snowstorms. The members of the group withdrew to the base in Bic and made a second attempt in mid-January. This time they were provided with travel documents from the Todt Organization, counterfeited by the Dutch group. But the border-runner did not show up. He had been arrested. It was not until February 28, 1944 that the first SER convoy, comprising thirty men, finally left for Spain, where it arrived on March 5 after a harrowing journey.[41]

Four more convoys ran the border between March and April. The system of contacts of the Dutch network was dismantled during that time by a series of arrests near the Belgian and Swiss borders and then in Paris. The capture of the leader of the Dutch resistance, Jop Westerwiel,[42] in March 1944 deprived the Jews of indispensable contacts that had permitted escape from Holland. The Gestapo raid on the Hotel Versigny in Paris on April 27 put an end to the use of false German papers by the AJ.

A departure route from Oloron-Sainte-Marie, where the secretary of the municipality came to the assistance of the escapees, helped four SER convoys. The border-runners demanded 5,000 francs per escapee. In early April 1944 a border-runner was arrested, then released. The SER then gave up the use of that route.[43]

Let us recall that the EIF and the MJS had begun the definitive dispersal of their rural worksites in April 1944. Several dozen young farm workers from them opted for departure to Palestine via Spain. Thus the SER was charged with an unprecedented number of candidates for escape. Until then AJ recruitment for departure to Palestine had been relatively modest, since young men of fighting age sometimes preferred to enroll in local French partisan groups.[44]

Subject to pressing the entreaties of hunted Jews who wanted to take refuge in Spain, the head of the SER agreed to have the combat groups joined by a very limited number of escapees for the purpose of rescue. The progress of convoys through the mountains during the spring of 1944 was impeded more than once by the slow pace of escapees over forty, who had not undergone prior physical training. But Roitman did not allow himself to be dissuaded by his AJ comrades, who reproached him with compromising his Zionist work by occupying himself with "emigration of philanthropic character."[45]

On May 3, 1944, a convoy of fifty-nine people, including sixteen young men from the rural worksites of the EIF in Taluyers and Pierre-Blanche, eight people from Holland, and a dozen older people not affiliated with the AJ, began on a route that passed by Mont Vallier. In order to renew the failed mission of the two delegates who had left for Madrid a year earlier, the AJ chiefs designated Jefroykin, who was the head of the convoy, as the liaison. The casual attitude of the border-runner, the physical incapacity of several of the "civilian" escapees, bad weather, the fatal fall over a precipice of one of the Dutch resisters, and the lack of provisions after three days of wandering turned the convoy into a seven day nightmare. One of the older members of the party died of exhaustion and cold in the mountains, and a young AJ member arrived in Spain seriously injured.[46]

The next convoy, similar in composition, took place on May 17 on board a train in the Saint-Cyprien railroad station in Toulouse. But before the departure, the Gestapo arrested the chief of the SER, Jacques Roitman, on the station platform. Five passengers for Spain were also arrested, including Léo Cohn, the chaplain of the EIF rural worksites. The forty remaining escapees arrived in Saint-Girons, where they learned that their border-runner had been assassinated, which left them no recourse but to return to their base.[47]

Taken in hand again by Léon, the young brother of its chief, the SER continued its activity despite this succession of difficult setbacks. During the summer months, six convoys of escapees, each comprising from twenty-five to forty-five people, arrived safe and sound in Spain. Most of them took a route that passed through the principality of Andorra.[48]

Meanwhile, in Madrid, Jefroykin succeeded in having the AJDC take charge of the escapees who arrived unscathed. Even better, on July 18 in Barcelona he met Eliahu Dobkin, a member of the executive committee of the WZO who had arrived from Jerusalem, who provided the AJ fighters who had escaped to Spain with immigration certificates for Palestine. Placing itself under the authority of the WZO, the AJ was accredited to be represented in Palestine by an emissary having authority to recommend the assignment of fighters from its organization.[49] One of the major objectives of the unfortunate affair, in which the AJ had believed that its emissaries were going to be flown to London by the IS, was thus achieved at the very moment when they were facing Gestapo torture without breaking.

Meanwhile, in Toulouse the chiefs of the AJ had complemented the SER in March by creating the *Service d'évacuation et de regroupement des enfants* (SERE, Evacuation and Relocation Service for Children), which assumed the task of evacuating children across the Pyrenees to Spain, intending to send them on to Palestine. Andrée Salomon of the OSE (*Oeuvre de secours aux enfants*, Children's Rescue Network) had in fact turned to the AJ with this in mind, because of the growing riskiness of the crossing into Switzerland. The leaders of the OSE, hesitant about sending children on such a hazardous journey, decided that only very sturdy children with relatives in Palestine would be evacuated to Spain.

Directed by Gisèle Roman, the SERE team, with its humanitarian aims, had nothing in common with that of the SER, which was military in character. The two agencies were not aware of each other's existence until June 1944. The SERE took charge of small groups, never larger than twelve children, in Toulouse. The children had been brought there under the responsibility of Andrée Salomon. The route to Spain passed via Andorra. After a night on the march, the little escapees were lodged in a hotel, where a bus took them to Spain. From April 6, the date of the first SERE convoy, until August 1944, eighty-eight children thus arrived in safety. Four of the convoys in the month of July were combined SERE-SER operations, when the latter began to use the Andorra route.[50] No untoward incident occurred.

Despite the abundant documentation and testimony that has been gathered, there still remain lacunae that make the overall picture of escape to Spain imprecise on a number of points. taking account only of data that has been established with certainty, we obtain the figures shown in table 16.1.[51]

Table 16.1

THE ACTIVITY OF SER AND SERE, 1943–1944

1. Escaped to Spain		
1943	10 AJ men	
	32 men from the Dutch group	42
1944	124 adults from France	
	59 men from the Dutch group	
	88 children	271
Total		313
2. Left for Palestine		
February 1944, on the *Nyassa* (adults)	18	
October 1944, on the *Guinée*		
(175 adults, 79 children)	254	
Total		272
3. Losses:	2 lost in the mountains	
	6 deported, of whom two survived	

Jewish Guerrillas and Partisans

The military history of Jewish resistance is the best known part. Communist Jewish historiography is not the only one that accorded a privileged place to armed combat.[52] Authors who belonged to the AJ have also focused attention on the military aspects of that resistance.[53] Similarly Rabi uses terminology in which "Resistance" designates armed struggle, "which has become of supreme value, . . . considered as superior to non-Resistance." Asking whether "it was progress or regression?" he concludes that not only for those who took arms, but also for those "who died at the hands of the executioner without waging an armed combat, we must also pronounce the ritual *kaddish*."[54]

Eventually rescue operations were no longer classified as "nonresistance," but this change occurred late in the war.[55] The place that rescue deserves was only timidly suggested during a colloquium organized in Paris in October 1984 by the Association for Contemporary Jewish Historical Research,[56] where the heroes of rescue work were promoted, not without some condescension, to the status of "the stretcher-bearers of the resistance."[57]

As a matter of fact, almost all of the chiefs of the Jewish partisan units belonged to the leadership of the rescue networks. Among their members, partisans and liaison agents, many were veterans of these networks.[58] To them, salvage and military operations were one and the same battle. This is confirmed by the name given in June 1944 to all of the EIF partisans of the Tarn Department: the Marc Haguenau Company. Haguenau had been the Secretary General of the EIF and became one of the chiefs of the *Sixième*. He died in Grenoble while in Gestapo detention. "I thought that he would have liked to be with us, and he is, at least in name," wrote Gamzon.[59]

Jewish partisans operated in two regions, on the Vivarais-Lignon Plateau and in the Tarn Department. Le Chambon-sur-Lignon, as we have seen, with its Calvinist Protestant majority, admirably encouraged by Pastor André Trocmé and his colleagues, was the most hospitable site in France for hunted Jews. Entire families from Saint-Étienne, Lyons, and Nice took refuge on the plateau, which also served as the point of departure for an escape route across the Swiss border. The concentration of numerous disguised Jews and the support of a population that took risks to save the victims of anti-Jewish persecution favored the formation of a Jewish partisan unit in the region.[60] Being a country where the Catharist tradition remained vital among the Protestant communities, the Tarn Department also offered favorable conditions for Jewish partisans, though it was less homogeneous in its population than the Vivarais-Lignon Plateau. Its geographical proximity to the Pyrenees border also made it suitable for the establishment of a base for the departure of organized escapes to Spain. But above all, after 1940 the Castres region had harbored the largest assembly of EIF worksites, that of Lautrec. Its men had become familiar with the topography of the area. They knew the political proclivities of the local elected officials, functionaries, merchants, clergymen, etc.

In every case the Jewish partisans submitted to the authority of the chiefs of the local armed resistance and operated under the responsibility of its military hierarchy. Though they remained autonomous on the level of their staff, training, provisions, and the daily life of the units, they took no operational initiative other than the actual training of partisans. One sole case of disobedience is known. The EIF partisan group of La Malquière, in the Mountains of Lacaune, obtained arms in February 1944 by appropriating a Resistance cache containing a recent parachute drop.[61] The local partisans were handicapped because the members divided their time between work on their family farms and military activity: "The partisans have no barracks; the officers dispose of no means of constraint. The soldiers know that they are free, and no punishment can be inflicted on them."[62] By contrast, the Jewish units, constituted of men with no attachments in the region, were more stable. "Their group forms a coherent, disciplined ensemble, that makes a better impression," wrote the commander of the CFMN.[63] Because of these qualities, the Marc Haguenau Company was designed by the FFI general staff in Vabre to receive the numerous parachute drops made on the "Virgule" grounds from June 25 to August 8, 1944.[64]

The Partisans of Le Chambon-sur-Ligon

Documentation of the Jewish partisans of the Vivarais-Lignon Plateau is very fragmentary. Formed toward the end of the winter of 1944 by the head of the *Service André*,[65] the initiative was taken up by the AJ, which sent an instructor to Toulouse, Léon Avraham, who had served in the Foreign Legion. In addition to local recruitment, fighters came from Lyons. The only extant fragment of a log refers to the days from July 12 to August 4, 1944, a period of intense military training, including riflery, the occupation of terrain, anti-tank defense, and a course in first aid. Under the orders of the local FFI, the unit took part in skirmishes harassing the retreating German troops. Between August 25 and 30 it went to Lyons, where it joined the forces engaged in the popular insurrection.[66] Relatively speaking the Chambon region was spared repressive house to house searches by the enemy. During their advance toward the north, "the lateral elements of the army of De Lattre did not enter into combat against the Germans, because the FFI had preceded them, and the [Haute-Loire] Department had already been liberated."[67] The AJ partisans of the Vivarais-Lignon Plateau suffered no losses during these operations.

The Blue-White Squad of the CFMN

After having moved toward the south of the Tarn Department, under orders from the FFI in Albi, in April 1944 the AJ squad, now commanded by a reserve noncommissioned officer, Pierre Loeb, established itself in

Espinassier, an abandoned hamlet in the Montagne Noire. It was incorporated into the CFMN, which was in the process of formation. Created by Major Roger Mompezat, the irregular corps made use of a radio link with London, maintained by Major Richardson, a British officer parachuted into France in October 1943, and of light arms dropped in the Tarn Department by Allied aviation during the first months of 1944, enough to equip 500 men. Mompezat concentrated several partisan units in the region of the Pic de la Nore sector to the southeast of Mazamet. Henceforth the AJ squad carried out a double mission, acting as a base for the SER and as an operational unit integrated within the CFMN. Its permanent membership of thirty-five men sometimes rose as high as fifty, including the candidates for escape sent by the SER for a military training course.[68]

On May 31, among the messages broadcast by the radio from London, the chiefs of the CFMN heard: "As usual, a flying fortress with four motors." This was the announcement that the Normandy landing was imminent. On June 5 they received two more messages: "We have something to refresh ourselves with in the garden," and "Whoever likes rare meat has good taste." This was the order to begin guerrilla warfare. During the following days, the men of the region assembled on the Pic de la Nore. The officers set up squads and platoons, appointed leaders, and distributed navy blue uniforms, booty from a raid by Mompezat's men on a depot of the secretariat of the Youth Commission in Toulouse.[69]

The AJ resisters placed a blue and white ribbon on the epaulets of their new tunics. The unit then became the "Blue-White Squad."[70] The daily life of the Blue-White Squad is recounted laconically in the weekly reports sent by Loeb to the AJ chiefs in Toulouse: morning ceremony of saluting the Tricolor and blue-white flags, military instruction and exercises, courses in the history of Zionism, late night sessions and singing, operations to harass German convoys, the reception of parachute drops.[71] Its participation in the evening sessions of the CFMN made it quite popular: "The evening, long in this season, is devoted to games. . . . The leaders of these evening festivities are . . . especially the members of the Jewish squad, which contains some excellent singers."[72] On July 14, the CFMN marched to Revel, then to Dourgne. After a "copious" dinner served in the camp, "at eighteen hundred hours, the Jewish squad presents a performance that it had been preparing for several days: a few whimsical acts, choruses, and finally a review whose characters are evidently the officers of the irregular corps."[73] Well integrated, appreciated by the command for its discipline, the AJ unit intrigued one of the officers, who often had arguments with Loeb. One day he told him: "I'm sick and tired of your Jewish problem. Change your name, marry Christians, and in one generation there won't be a Jewish problem anymore."[74]

At that time the CFMN included more than eight hundred men. The troop movement on July 14 was a convoy of twenty trucks flanked by several light vehicles. The leaders had decided to make the force of the partisans known, increasing the ambushes and the harassing of enemy convoys and carrying out the spectacular demonstration of July 14. In contrast, the Vabre partisan leaders preferred the tactic of small, dispersed, and autonomous units. The debate between the proponents of these two conceptions, "the large, mobilizing partisan group," on the one hand, and small, highly mobile units on the other, has not yet died down. Using the examples of the massacres that had annihilated the large partisan group of the Plateau of Glières in the Haute-Savoie Department, of Vercors in the Isère Department, and of Mont Mouchet in the Haute-Loire Department, Henri Michel argues that the doctrine of large partisan groups "has shown itself to be tragically erroneous." Mompezat believes, on the contrary, that "it was to a great extent thanks to the spectacular demonstrations and incessant actions of the irregular corps [of the Montagne Noire] and the fear it inspired within the enemy that the German garrisons of Mazamet and Castres surrendered later, without fighting."[75] London gave Ravanel the mission of unifying all of the fighting forces within the framework of the FFI for the Toulouse region. In June 1944 he placed Major Pierre Dunoyer de Segonzac at the head of the FFI of Zone A in the south of the Tarn Department. The latter revealed in 1947 that "the Montagne Noire ... constantly escaped my jurisdiction," while Ravanel confirms that "the CFMN was in fact the only formation that refused to be integrated within the FFI."[76]

On July 20, 1944, the Wehrmacht launched a large-scale offensive against the CFMN camps, deploying aircraft, armored vehicles, and infantry. After a twelve-hour combat, in which the CFMN held off the enemy, inflicting severe losses on it and losing four men, its chief gave the order for a general disengagement. The Germans abandoned the field without pursuing the resisters, and Mompezat assembled the CFMN almost intact, and made preparations for a new enemy assault. Nevertheless, because the notables of the neighboring villages had asked him to avoid reprisals against the civilian population, he ordered those men who had nothing to fear from the Gestapo to return to their homes, instructing the others to disperse in small, mobile units. A liaison antenna known only to the officers of these units was maintained in the Montagne Noire, while Mompezat returned to Toulouse to place himself under Ravanel's orders at last. On August 12, having returned to the Tarn Department, he issued the order to assemble the CFMN on

August 17 and 18 in Agoudet, in the Hérault Department, sixty kilometers east of the Pic de la Nore.[77]

The Blue-White Squad, unharmed in the combats of July 20, led a life of wandering, changing camp almost every night for four weeks. Its chief, Pierre Loeb, has reconstructed the log of that period in minute detail.[78] He maintained contact with the CFMN liaison antenna as well as with the leadership of the AJ in Toulouse, and he himself took over the problems of supplies. On August 1 he received the order to reduce his men to the minimum and to camouflage the arms while they waited. Loeb sent away twenty of his men. Dispersed in Toulouse, Limoges, and Lyons, they took part there in the combats of the liberation, where two of them were wounded. Two other resisters belonging to the Blue-White Squad were arrested in Toulouse and kept in detention until the liberation. They had been recognized by German prisoners of the CFMN who had escaped after the July 20 attack. Also in Toulouse the Militia executed two members of the irregular corps of the AJ in an apartment they used. They wounded a fighter from the Blue-White Squad who managed to escape, and they caught another, who died in deportation.[79]

Present in Agoudet on August 18, when the CFMN reconstituted itself, Loeb and those who remained in the Blue-White Squad engaged in very difficult skirmishes, the most demanding experienced by the irregular corps, while harassing the retreat routes of the German troops in Saint-Pons and Murat.[80]

In the joy of the recovery of liberty, mingled with mourning for comrades and relatives who had been killed and anxiety for the fate of the deported, the SER and SERE networks emerged from the underground. The former became the *Service européen des recherches* (European Search Service) and occupied itself with the unification of families and the orientation of former camp inmates from the southwest of France. The latter became the *Oeuvre de protection des enfants juifs* (OPEJ, the Organization for the Protection of Jewish Children), which took charge of children who had been placed with non-Jewish families and institutions, and whose entire families had been deported.[81] The AJ reappeared in liberated France as the *Organisation juive de combat* (OJC, Jewish Combat Organization). It was recognized as part of the FFI network under that name. The lists of men submitted to the government do not contain the names of the AJ leaders. After the Liberation they decided to hold themselves in reserve for the organization and mobilization of Zionist emigration to Palestine. They realized they would have to avoid the attention of the British services charged with interfering with that emigration.

Of all the losses suffered by the AJ, none is attributable to a breakdown, to an inside informer, or to the betrayal of any of the resisters in that network. The norms of secrecy and discipline and the oath of fidelity imposed by the leaders proved themselves.

The greatest part of the expenses of the AJ were absorbed by the SER and later by the SERE. Those responsible for these services regularly received the sums necessary to finance the escapes from the chiefs of the AJ.[82] In May 1944, after Jefroykin's departure for Spain, the two chiefs of the AJ had to separate. Polonski remained in Toulouse, while Lublin established himself in Lyons, the financial base of Jewish resistance at that time. Fischer, too, was there. He remained the only one in France responsible for the transfer of AJDC funds. Similarly it was the irregular corps in Lyons which received the sums sent by Jarblum from Geneva. In that way, Lublin was able to supervise personally the transfer of the funds necessary for the AJ to Toulouse, Nice, and Paris until the Liberation. He also took it upon himself to cover the financial needs of the military branch of the EIF, according to an agreement signed on June 1, 1944 by Gamzon and Lublin in the name of their organizations. The two men worked for a long time in drafting this agreement, which accorded with an aim that AJ had set for itself from the beginning. It arranged in detail the military coordination between the units that had been established, and it contained the seed of the possible fusion of the armed forces that had been constituted under the aegis of the Zionist ideal on the one hand, and of a pluralistic conception of Judaism on the other.[83]

The Marc Haguenau Company

The EIF took up the military option in two phases. On December 16, 1943, a group of eight leaders and young farm workers from the worksite in Lautrec, which was to be dispersed for reasons of security, created an undercover camp in a small group of dilapidated buildings, La Malquière, an isolated corner in the Mountains of Lacaune to the east of Vabre. On April 29, 1944, a similar group, also from Lautrec, whose site was closed at that time, created a second hideout in the ruins of a farm, Lacado, seven kilometers from La Malquière.[84]

In early March 1944, the national team of the EIF had decided to "mobilize" the young people of the worksites as well as the leaders and senior members of the movement.[85] Young women leaders, "*cheftaines*," combed the southern zone during April and May, visiting three hundred people to whom the national team's decision was addressed. The "mobilized" youth divided themselves between teams of the *Sixième*, escape to Palestine, enlistment in the partisans of the national resistance, and finally joining the EIF partisan units of the Tarn Department.

For a young man living at some distance from the Tarn Department, it was less risky at that time to join a group operating close to his place of residence. One resister belonging to the *Sixième* in Lyons, who was nevertheless determined to join the EIF partisan group, left the city on June 4 and arrived in Limoges without difficulty the same night. But the following night he was held up at the railroad station of Brives, because the German troops had declared a state of siege. It was June 6, the day of the Normandy landing, and in Tulle the Resistance had just carried out a spectacular operation, which was savagely repressed. After a week of very risky efforts, he obtained an authentic German *Ausweis* (pass) issued by the *Kommandantur*. He then quit Brives by road and arrived in Vabre on June 15.[86] Other resisters also reached the sector, each one having lived through an adventure along the route. At the end of June the military units formed by the EIF in the mountains of Lacaune contained 120 partisans.

The groups of La Malquière and Lacado set the style of the EIF partisans. The team from La Malquière, resisters aged from eighteen to twenty-eight, included two men who had been officers in 1940, one of whom was a graduate of the prestigious École Polytechnique, a noncommissioned officer who was an agronomic engineer by profession, an orthopedic assistant, a tailor, a furrier, and two high school students. The Lacado group was not very different. The FFI commander of the Vabre sector gave the following description of the Jewish partisan unit:

> The most unusual group was that of the Jews. They were not from the area but had come from all over the place to Sidobre, which had originally been a place of refuge for them. Several of them had only recently been naturalized. They were all strongly attached to their religion and dreamed of settling in the Promised Land. These were, by the way, Robert Gamzon's faithful. . . . He was a man with a great heart whom I had often met and appreciated. The group contained a significant portion of students from the universities and *grandes écoles* [advanced technical colleges].[87]

The experience of scouting and of life in a rural community inspired their daily existence in these partisan camps, described in detail in their logs. In the morning, some prayed while others read a literary text appropriate for spiritual meditation. Most of the days were taken up with physical and military exercises. But rather frequently these partisan units supplied personnel, quite experienced and competent, to the local peasants. This created a climate of trust between the Jewish partisans and the population, and also provided abundant supplies of farm products. The Friday night Sabbath services were celebrated exactly as before in the rural worksites, and on Saturday morning the program included a reading from the Bible with commentaries. Frequent evening song sessions alternated with night exercise. On May 22, the chief of Lacado read a long document about the atrocities committed in Poland and about the Warsaw Ghetto uprising. La Malquière possessed a good radio set that received evening concerts. On June 3, the pastor of the village of Lacaze attended a Bible reading. On many occasions his rectory was a stopping point for Jewish partisans who were on the move.[88] A text by Gamzon describes a visit to the Lacado partisan camp:

> It is noon. Around large wooden tables placed on the bare earth in front of the farm, the boys are sitting and waiting for their soup. The soup is served. No one begins. Bread is distributed, and the head of the section cuts it into small pieces, sprinkles it with salt, and, with scull-caps on their heads, the whole section chants the *Berakha* (the blessing on bread).
>
> Here they are, the "bandits," the outlaws, "the criminal dregs of the common law," of which the Vichy press speaks!
>
> They come from everywhere on earth. They're all Jews; they were all in the EIF agricultural centers and were directed to the underground by these centers. They try to maintain their style of life, their correct behavior, their dignity, their honor.
>
> It is curious, by the way, how all these boys, who have sometimes lived like hunted beasts, many of whom escaped from the Vichy government concentration camps, the ignoble camps of Gurs and Rivesaltes, are thirsty for dignity, for a consensual discipline. I have no difficulty in obtaining from them those "external signs of respect" so dear to the French military regulations, and which I wanted to apply rigorously, precisely because here we begin a military life. This does not prevent comradeship and friendliness, but "rules are rules," and two hours lateness in returning from a leave mean two days in the brig![89]

We have seen how, in February 1944, the partisans of La Malquière obtained their first arms. Those who executed the raid came away with thirteen submachine guns, twelve revolvers, ammunition, and twenty grenades.[90] But the local FFI leaders agreed to wipe the slate clear of the incident. Relations developed with the heads of the resistance in Vabre. La Malquière became a military training school for refractory recruits of the region.[91] Near this hideout, a rounded hill called "la Blando" (salamander) in the local patois, was chosen as the grounds for parachute drops under the code name of "Virgule" (comma).[92]

In May new men began to arrive. La Malquière became crowded. On June 7, the day after the Normandy landing, the camp was transferred to Larroque-La-Farasse, to the southeast of Lacado. The hospitable village of Lacaze, huddled at the bottom of the gorge of Gijou, was halfway between the two camps.[93] On June 11, with a complement of sixty men, the EIF partisan group became the Marc Haguenau Company, consisting of three platoons, under the effective command of Gamzon, known as Lieutenant Lagnès. He placed himself under the orders of Dunoyer de Segonzac, recently appointed commander of the FFI in the Vabre Sector. Training became more intensive. On June 25 the company received its first parachute drop at the Virgule grounds.[94]

That evening the radio monitor of the two camps had received the following message over the BBC: "From the screech-owl to the white blackbird: the loader only has twenty bullets." This was the code announcing that during the night an airplane would fly over the Virgule, dropping fifteen 200 kilo containers, for a total of three tons. This message was repeated frequently during the following evenings, with several variants: "the loader only has three times twenty bullets" announced three airplanes; "two friends will see this evening whether the loader only has twenty bullets" warned of the arrival of two parachutists.

The men and equipment dropped on Virgule were destined for the whole FFI sector of Vabre. Its commander had designated the Jewish company to receive parachute drops because it was well staffed, disciplined, and had a constant membership. The physical endurance of the men of Lacado and Larroque was put to a rude test. More than once they had to spend the night on the Virgule grounds in vain: "August 4, parachute drop of arms and sabotage equipment; the fifth, despite the message, a vain wait: the airplanes didn't come; the sixth, an American commando unit with fifteen men and a jeep, arms, and baggage fall from the sky."[95] From June 25 to August 8 seven parachute drops took place at Virgule.

Like most of the partisan units throughout France, the Lacado platoon included three SS deserters, admitted by request of the SS leaders of Vabre. One of them, Hans, made himself indispensable as an automobile mechanic, another was a virtuoso in grenade throwing and instructed the Jewish partisans. Three weeks later, an FFI officer of Vabre took Hans as a chauffeur. One day four officers were in a van driven by Hans. They stopped on the road to examine the map and were surprised by a motorized German patrol that opened fire. The partisans managed to get out, but Hans disappeared.[96]

In June the FFI of Vabre robbed a depot of the *Compagnons de France*, a paramilitary organization of the Vichy government, in Labruguière, and they obtained khaki cloth from industrialists in Mazamet. Thus they equipped the three hundred partisans with solid boots and uniforms, which were sewn by the hidden Jewish tailors in the region.[97] Segonzac tried to give a certain coherence to the heterogenous ensemble of his group:

> What is there in common between the Marc Haguenau group, sustaining its solitude with Talmudic lessons and dreams of Palestine, and the Paul group, where naive little guys, but talking down to earth like in the true Gallic manner, are coddled by a fugitive gendarme, as indulgent as a grandma? . . . The partisans of the Tarn Department have a particular form that appeals to my taste for unity and combination. Jews, Catholics, and Protestants in equal numbers.[98]

On July 14 he had his partisans parade together, not in a town, as the CFMN had done a little to the south in Revel, but more discreetly, on the road, a reasonable distance from Vabre:

> The "Partisan Police," in navy blue shirts, had put up barricades. From Vabre the public had come up in trucks and busses, in its Sunday best for the classic July 14th parades: firemen, gendarmes, working men and women, bourgeois, peasants, children.
>
> All the civilian and religious authorities of the country were there: mayors, "superintendents of the resistance," school teachers, priests, and ministers.[99]

The creator and director of the leadership school of Uriage from 1940 to 1942,[100] Segonzac had been joined in the Tarn Department by part of his team, notably Hubert Beuve-Méry, Gilbert Gadoffre, Jean-Marie Domenach, etc. From July 21 to 24, two platoons of the Marc Haguenau Company took a military and civic training course:

During an entire day, a FFL (*Forces françaises libres*, Free French
Forces) parachute officer explained to us how one prepares and
executes a surprise attack, how one liquidates an enemy sen-
tinel, how one gets the most out of rudimentary armaments.
The sturdiest of us had to give way to his demonstration of close
combat. . . . One afternoon, covered in his vast loden cape,
Beuve-Méry came to talk about the past with us: a tragic evoca-
tion of errors and betrayals by someone who saw them from up
close. [Gadoffre], for his part, spoke about the future, and especially about university reform.[101]

Until July the FFI of Vabre had more or less avoided contact with the enemy:

We had only defended ourselves, without too much difficulty,
by the way, because of our fluid encampments outside of inhab-
ited centers. . . . The German garrisons of Mazamet and Castres
and of the Vintrou Dam seldom ventured into a rough and
wooded terrain. At the most from time to time they made some
motorized armored raids which bothered us so much the less,
because their passage was signaled to us by telephone.[102]

When they passed to the offensive, ambushing enemy convoys and the elimination of the garrison of Vintrou, Segonzac rarely put the Jewish platoons
on the line, though they made an ample contribution in receiving the parachute drops:

I felt scruples, too, about risking the lives of lads who had
undergone so many trials with their families. Among the Jews
above all, some of whom had lost everyone. That decision . . . is
not one I made easily, and, still today, I don't know if it was well
founded. Classically warfare doesn't make allowances for sentiments. . . . Can one, on the battlefield, be both an effective leader
and at the same time a humanist?[103]

Nevertheless, during the night of August 7–8, a German armored column
raided the Virgule grounds. Radio London had announced: "Four friends
will see tonight whether the loader has only twenty bullets." The Marc
Haguenau Company, which "had received all the parachute drops until

then, is rather tired. It is decided to let about twenty men rest and to call for reinforcements from the Germain platoon [belonging to another company of partisans in Vabre]."[104]

Gamzon directed the operation. Upon landing, the four parachutists, two officers and two radio operators, were immediately placed in light vehicles by Segonzac. Then there was a burst of machine-gun fire. German armored vehicles attacked the grounds. Acting coolly, Gamzon led the disengagement of the partisans, under heavy fire, without suffering any losses, with the exception of four containers abandoned on the spot. During the following hours the enemy arrived directly at the Larroque camp, then at the Lacado camp, annihilating them. Fighting in the Larroque sector left seven dead, included Lieutenant Gilbert Bloch,[105] and two wounded among the partisans.[106]

"The Germans had been alerted, and we still don't know by whom," Segonzac wrote later.[107] The Wehrmacht armed column had advanced through the sector as though completely familiar with its terrain. The Larroque and Lacado camps, well hidden by the terrain and vegetation, were accessible only to someone who knew them. Thus it was evident that the enemy had been led by a guide who was remarkably used to all the recesses of the country.

Several days after the attack, Gamzon was summoned to Vabre with eight armed men. Hans had just reappeared:

> I meet Captain Campagne who greets me with these words: "I have a present for you!"..."What present?" "Hans!" "Should we shoot him?" "I won't tell you that. You'll do what you think right. One thing is certain, that he lied to us, and so you can suppose anything."...
>
> It would be so simple to put a bullet in the back of his head. I take out my revolver.... No, this is idiotic. We aren't killers, *not us*! If he's to be condemned to death, it has to be done correctly. ...I command *men* who fight for an ideal of justice and truth against Nazism, and it would be losing our own battle to think like Nazis.

During seven days of inquests and verifications, no proof against Hans emerges, while his own statements are confirmed. Gamzon had him brought to Vabre.[108]

One of the partisans in charge of the inquest came forward with an explanation that swept away the hypothesis of treason:

"I spoke to some peasants from Lacaze and Viane. Everywhere the krauts were led by kids from the countryside whom they picked up along the way and who guided them, under threat of death. We talked to the kids, who admitted it completely."[109]

Repeated use of the Virgule grounds for such a long time leads one to wonder about the somewhat irresponsible lack of foresight on the part of the FFI command.

We spoke in vain to the higher echelons, but they knew as well as we did that the grounds were known, and the phrase, "The loader only has twenty bullets," is known throughout the countryside, and that the local kids are present at all the parachute drops, picking up chocolate and grenades themselves, but unperturbed, they continue making parachute drops on the same grounds. . . . Sooner or later there will be a catastrophe, we're convinced of it, but at the same time there's that incredible sense of security that's always given by a habit.[110]

Forty years later, a teacher in the Catholic seminary of Pratlong, near Vabre, tried to reconstruct the events of the eighth of August in detail, interrogating dozens of residents and former partisans. He collected all of their testimony in a fascinating booklet produced in homage to "those seven young men who were cut down so that we might live in freedom." He confirms that

Since there had been six parachute drops rather close to each other, the code name had spread: try to keep something secret that's being announced to you! People talked about it, and more and more people came, mostly young people; people came especially from Viane, but also from Lacaze, from Camalières, Esperausses, and the surrounding farms. People didn't enter the grounds, of course—There were even a few "swipers." On the night of August 7–8 there were actually a lot of people: "it was like a festival," "a formidable amount of loose talk."

Looking for the Virgule grounds that night, the Germans picked up young men on bicycles who were on their way home. Once they held hostages, it was no problem to be guided directly to their objectives.[111]

From then on the Marc Haguenau Company led a nomadic life in the woods, from bivouac to bivouac. The comrades who had been killed were buried in Lacaze: "We went down . . . to Viane, where people lent us civilian clothing. . . . The whole population of the countryside was there."[112]

For more than half of the men, the attack of August 8 was their baptism by fire. After the losses suffered, there was the feeling of having sustained a painful defeat and, another consequence of the German raid, the partisans were forced to wander aimlessly. "The wind of demoralization began to blow."[113] One morning, before the assembled company, Gamzon opened his Bible and read:

> Before you join battle, the priest shall come forward and address the troops. He shall say to them, "Hear, O Israel! You are about to join battle with your enemy. Let not your courage falter. Do not be in fear, or in panic, or in dread of them. For it is the Lord your God who marches with you to do battle for you against your enemy, to bring you victory."
>
> Then the officials shall address the troops as follows: "Is there anyone who has built a new house but has not dedicated it? Let him go back to his home, lest he die in battle and another dedicate it. Is there anyone who has planted a vineyard but has never harvested it? Let him go back to his home, lest he die in battle and another harvest it. Is there anyone who has paid the bride-price for a wife, but who has not yet married her? Let him go back to his home, lest he die in battle and another marry her."
>
> The officials shall go on addressing the troops and say, "Is there anyone afraid and disheartened? Let him go back to his home, lest the courage of his comrades flag like his."[114]

Galvanized by their chief's spiritual energy, the Jewish partisans renewed their courage. On August 15, in the evening, gathered in a clearing, they heard a lecture by Gadoffre on Great Britain and the Commonwealth. The same day, the army of General de Lattre landed on the coasts of Provence. On August 17, Segonzac assembled all of the partisans of his sector near the factories of Mazamet with the aim of taking offense action against the German garrison of the city. He himself held meetings with the local resisters. Then, having noted signs of an eventual enemy retreat, he decided to postpone the attack and withdrew his troops.[115]

On the nineteenth, the German soldiers in fact loaded their automatic canons and large quantities of equipment on a train fifty cars long. Segonzac chose a place about two kilometers east of Labruguière on the Mazamet-

Castres line, where the curved tracks were enclosed between two embank-
ments at a height of three meters. He deployed the Marc Haguenau
Company on the south of the line, and, facing it, on the northern embank-
ment, a small unit, the Antonin platoon. Antonin was a "squadron commander of the active army who had recently come to offer his services with
praiseworthy but tardy enthusiasm."[116] While the partisans were digging
their firing positions, and the American commandos were blowing up the
railroad at various points between Mazamet and the site of the ambush,
Segonzac, accompanied by a noncommissioned officer from the EIF partisans who served as an interpreter, went to tell the German commander of
Mazamet: "Your train will not get through, give yourselves up!" But the
enemy officer refused to capitulate without fighting, and he set his convoy
in motion at seven P.M. A patrol walking in front of the locomotive was
charged with detecting mines and breaks in the track. The train, slowed by
repairs to the previous sabotage, took three and a half hours to cross the
eight kilometers that separated it from the ambush.

It was a dark night. The fingers of the partisans clutched the triggers of
their weapons. The locomotive crossed a broken section of track and
stopped at the end. A Jewish partisan officer pressed the detonator of an
eighteen kilo plastic explosive charge. There was a deafening explosion, and
the battle began. "It was clamorous, because my troops fired like rookies, I
mean wildly, and the Germans responded with ardor, mainly with automatic 37 mm. anti-aircraft canons, with explosive tracer shells, piercing the
darkness with ravishing flashes."[117]

In less than an hour all the partisans' machine-guns were jammed. The
chief gave the order to withdraw to a nearby position. During the rest of the
night, he sent out patrols at brief intervals to throw grenades so that the
Germans would be unable to repair the track. The Germans fired flares as a
call for help, but a powerful garrison in nearby Castres, with some 4,000 men,
only about ten kilometers away, did not respond. The dissuasive effect of
guerrilla warfare, "operating like an influence, an impalpable idea, expanding
like a gas,"[118] had at last paralyzed the enemy. When dawn rose, Segonzac put
into action the only mortar he possessed. A Jewish partisan patrol then saw
German soldiers, wrapped in white cloth, unarmed, walking toward them:

> Sixty krauts, their hands in the air, haggard, stunned, bloody,
> stood in a line. Our boys . . . walked in front of the krauts, who
> were stunned and trembling, and said to them, "*Ich bin Jude!*"
> (I'm a Jew!).
>
> The Germans' only reaction was to turn green and tremble
> harder. They don't look so proud, those glorious conquerors of

Europe. They're convinced we're going to shoot them all and treat them the way they treated our pals a few days ago, but without doubt we're too beastly dumb or too human, and not one of my boys even made a threatening gesture toward them.[119]

The outcome of that victory: one gendarme killed, three Jewish partisans wounded; on the enemy side, five killed, many wounded, and sixty prisoners, and considerable spoils. During the day of August 20, while looking for a place to keep the prisoners, Gamzon was involved in a road accident. He was immobilized for several months with a fractured vertebra.[120]

Meanwhile, in Castres, Segonzac obtained the capitulation of the entire garrison without a battle. On Monday morning, August 21, on board methane-powered trucks, the Marc Haguenau Company was wildly cheered in the streets of the city. Reoccupied by German troops coming from the south, Mazamet was liberated on August 22, after a brief and violent assault launched by the Larroque platoon.[121]

The Tarn Department was liberated. The Marc Haguenau Company became the Second Commando of the Bayard Irregular Corps, which was then established by Segonzac, boarded a train in the Castres railroad station on September 6, determined to continue fighting until the total crushing of the Nazis. In Lapalisse it continued its progress northward on methane-powered trucks and participated in the fighting to liberate Nevers. Then it joined with the First Army of De Lattre in Autun.

The incorporation of the Jewish partisans in the regular army was attended by an unpleasant surprise. The soldiers of foreign nationality, nearly a quarter of the men, found they were offered enlistment in the Foreign Legion. The Jews again felt the winds of xenophobia that had inspired the racial discrimination of the Vichy regime. Revolted, but also full of frustration, they exchanged their uniform for civilian dress.[122]

All the French members of the troop who had matriculation certificates were insistently offered six months of training at the school for officers in Cherchel, Algeria. This was the case of the majority of the remaining members of the Marc Haguenau Company. All of them refused, however, impatient to leap upon Germany and to be those who liberated the Jews held in concentration camps.[123] They fought a hard war in the Vosges, in Alsace, and across the Rhine, losing two more members on the battlefield.

It was the vocation of rescue that had mobilized them for this combat. The military phase was merely a transition. But they did not yet know what had happened in the Nazi camps.

~❧~

Conclusion

The collective memory of the French views Jewish resistance only as a sub-category of the history of the Resistance. It recalls that the partisans and guerrillas of the Jewish units took part in combat for the liberation of France, and that they pursued the invader until his capitulation. Why then set them apart? Were they not included with the rest of the resisters when the restored Republic confirmed their participation in the fight against the Nazis?

It seems that the Jews, too, on the whole, have taken part in the celebration of the Resistance as the collective memory perpetuates it, obeying the officially defined French criteria for the distribution of rights and honors. The fighters have received the share of glory that they deserved. The rescuers, Jewish or not, have returned to anonymity and sunk into oblivion. Heroic resisters, hunted down and sent to their death for smuggling children into Switzerland, have not benefitted from the posthumous homage that would have been accorded them, if, instead of children, they had taken responsibility for leaflets or arms.[1]

Thus we must state that the concept of Resistance has not embraced Jewish resistance. To take account of the latter, one must oppose received ideas. If one is not resigned to the amnesia, which has already lasted fifty years, one must finally admit that Jewish resistance was different from the

French national resistance. The latter did not take charge of the protection of Jews, who had all become excluded from society, whether French, immigrants, or foreigners. It was against this "civil society," as Annie Kriegel has pointed out so well, that Hitler waged *his* war within *the* military war.[2]

Thus if the balance sheet of the national resistance is essentially military, that of Jewish resistance is above all civilian. The Jewish networks certainly did play a part in the military exploits of the Resistance, massive in the urban guerrilla warfare in Paris, relatively modest in the insurrections in the other large cities, larger in the escape of fighters via Spain, and major in the liberation of Castres. But, self-evidently, no territorial objective was linked to the military operations of the Jewish resistance movement, which were carried out under the hierarchy of the Resistance.

In this civilian accounting, the preponderant element is rescue. Three out of four of the Jews present in France in 1940 survived the war. Tens of thousands of these owe their lives to the Jewish resistance organizations, which provided them with subsistence grants, false identity papers and ration cards, and lodging secure from police searches. They also extricated them from concentration camps and helped them to flee from France to Switzerland and Spain. The circumstances under which this help was dispensed defy all enumeration. It is likely that more than half of the survivors lived through the war because they were able to develop what Kriegel calls "strategies of survival," on the individual or family level. These strategies "were adapted to the demands of dispersion and decentralization, and of mobility, increasing the chances of escaping from the heavy bureaucracies of persecution."[3]

Excluded from power and condemned to physical annihilation, the Jews were scattered in a society which, after the autumn of 1942, reacted in a way that could sometimes thwart the homicidal will of the government. This applies to Western Europe as a whole. As much as it favored Jewish rescue and resistance operations, it was also favorable to the survival of a large number of escapees who adapted to underground life individually and on their own initiative with the help of friends or neighbors.

But the number of children who were wards of the Jewish resistance movement can be evaluated with more accuracy. Almost ten thousand children, as we have seen,[4] entirely taken in charge by the Jewish networks, were saved. Statistics indicate that 27 percent of the adults and 13.8 percent of the children among the Jews in France were murdered by the Nazis. In other words, the losses suffered by the children were relatively half as heavy as those suffered by the adults. This is not because the homicidal barbarism was less fierce against children, nor that the latter were less vulnerable. On the contrary: no deported child survived; whereas approximately 3 percent of the deported adults returned. Hence the Jewish resistance movement saved 10,000 children from the hands of the assassins. It sometimes snatched the children away from danger under dramatic circumstances, despite all risks.

As determined as they were, the rescuers of children could not have succeeded without a number of brilliant intuitions. Without them, it would be impossible to conceive the implacable decisions, contrary to logic and even to conscience, that permitted the safeguarding of so many children. Before removing them from the hands of the executioners, they had to be removed from their parents. "Your maternal instinct must instruct you to separate yourself from your children and not, as usual, to hold them close to you," says a leaflet addressed to Jewish mothers.[5] "Indescribable scenes were played the moment one separated them from their parents," recall the rescuers who were on duty during the drama of Vénissieux.[6] In the detention camps, every child abducted from a convoy being formed was replaced by the police with another detainee, placing the rescuers in a moral dilemma: "We will save the children from two to fifteen years old. Is that human?" asked a rescuer in his *Notebook*.[7]

Also impressive was the trying task of creating a system of foster families and institutions and the metamorphosis of the children into little "Aryans."

The most surprising thing could be that these rescuers, including many young men and women coming out of the youth movements, were so determined to maintain awareness of their Jewishness among the children whom they placed. How did they do it?

This aspect of their mission defies description, because it is dependent upon the quality of relations created between each rescuer and his or her wards. The tie was maintained by the monthly visit, necessary to pay the monthly allowance and inquire into the child's welfare. At that time a discrete conversation gave the child a chance to resume his true face for a moment, remembering his family and his Jewish experience. One thus imagines a world shared only by the child and his visitor, sending an invisible bridge over the clandestine present to the past and to the dream of rebirth. For the most part, these children overcame the indescribable psychological confusion arising from the inhuman uncertainties of their physical welfare.

"Wanting to save . . . not only children, but Jewish children, destined to remain so," as Vidal-Naquet put it,[8] is a faithful definition of the work accomplished by the rescuers of the Jewish resistance movement. Some of their leaders had received the final wishes pronounced by the parents during the heartbreaking scenes of separation:

They entrusted their little ones to our faithful guardianship. . . .
Many blessed them with the Biblical formula in use for millen-
nia among the Jews, placing their hands on their foreheads, without shedding a tear; concentrating all of their paternal love in the
few verses murmured out loud with fervor, offering their destiny
and lives to the safety of their little ones. But they told them to be
brave, to be worthy of their Jewishness, not to forget, and, with
an abrupt gesture, they turned away to hide their emotions.[9]

The rescuers overcame multiple obstacles that opposed their action, and
they scrupulously obeyed the wishes of the deported Jews. In doing so, they
went against the current of sloughing off Judaism that characterized the
1930s in France. The rapid decline of community institutions, extreme fragmentation, internecine quarrels, the general absence of activism, and the
signal poverty of Jewish studies and creativity had been the most visible
characteristics of French Judaism. But, under the occupation, the circles
engaged in the Jewish resistance movement had undertaken the systematic
task of returning to the sources. One would search in vain for a rational
explanation of this, even though the demanding and cautious historian,
Vidal-Naquet, stated that "when a community—even a partially imaginary
one—is threatened in its very substance, is it not natural for it, under the circumstances, to try to revitalize itself in a tradition that has, when all is said
and done, its own noble lineage, and which, even were it to have none, is *its*
tradition?"[10]

The revival of a moribund Judaism is thus, along with rescue work, the
other major element of Jewish resistance. Many of the enduring institutions
of the postwar community derive from initiatives taken by the Jewish resistance movement from 1940 to 1944. The colloquia of French-speaking
Jewish intellectuals were made known thanks to the poet Edmond Fleg and
the composer Léon Algazi. From 1941 to 1943, these two men held Jewish
study sessions in the southern zone for instructors driven from the univer-
sities and high schools by the laws of the Statute of the Jews. Their annual
meetings are a factor in the renewal of Jewish authors and scholars in
France, while the volumes of collected papers from these colloquia made it
possible to disseminate the sources of Jewish culture expressed in contemporary language. They acted as a creative stimulus and contributed to the
growth of publication in the Jewish area.

Out of the mass of underground study groups that grew up in 1943–1944,
meant to train the leaders of the future community, the EIF opened a leader-

ship school in 1947. The students attended for a year, living in a community and devoting themselves to Jewish study before attending university.

The idea of a Jewish day school as an alternative to secular schooling was attempted only once in the period just before the war, but after the Liberation it began to develop. By 1948 there were two primary schools and five high schools. The responsibilities undertaken in the creation, direction, and staffing of these schools by a handful of young teachers, former students of the Jewish high school founded in Limoges in 1942 and former resisters with the Jewish partisans, illustrate the spiritual and cultural influence of Jewish resistance on the renewal of French Judaism.

In founding the CRIF (*Conseil représentatif des Juifs de France*, Representative Council of French Jews) the Jewish resistance movement unveiled a potential for deep change in the mentalities of the Jews in France. Let us recall that before 1940, the leadership and official representation of the Jews belonged to the Consistory. The strictly religious definition of the latter dictated its conception of Jewish interests, ignoring acute problems of anti-Semitism, the influx of refugees, and Zionism. Its conservative attitude, nourished by the ideology of the emancipation, left it unprotected before the splits that fragmented the community and in confronting the increasing loss of Jewish identity.

In conclusion let us say that the experience of Jewish resistance introduced into France a durable, pluralistic definition of Jewish identity. It contributed to effacing the split between natives and immigrants. The tendency to slide down the slope into the loss of Judaism has not disappeared, but it is relatively counterbalanced by the inverse process of the return to the sources accomplished by men and women "who have returned to a Judaism which is both strict and learned."[11] Similarly, the slide away from Judaism is opposed by a strong current of Zionist activism, unprecedented in France in that form.[12] For the Jewish resisters, to participate in the foundation of a Jewish state, in the reception of Jewish refugees from Europe and the Islamic countries, and in combat against the aggression of the Arab armies was the continuation and expansion of the battle for survival they had begun in France. Following the example of some of their leaders, even among those who were not politicized, a rather large number of rescuers and fighters in the Jewish resistance movement joined pioneering collectives in Israel.

The seeds of some of these changes can be found in the charter of the CRIF, which was drafted and adopted by the resisters. These men turned their back on the ideology of emancipation and opened the way to the political, cultural, and national affirmation of Jewish identity in addition to its religious aspect. Regardless of the burdens of the past, particularly in the persistence of several of the former splits, what had been a disparate ensemble, breathing its last and barely conscious of its decline, rediscovered durable dynamism and creative power in the upsurge of resistance.

But since the Liberation French Judaism has made its way without taking sufficient care to preserve the memory of the heroic work accomplished by its rescuers, of whom such a large number sacrificed their lives. Filling in the gaps and rebuilding the ruins certainly mobilized the community's available forces. Nevertheless, this forgetfulness remains inexplicable to this day. The time has come to restore that obscured and mutilated memory to its full splendor.

Notes

Chapter 1. France from 1938 to June 1940 and the Problem of Foreign Nationals

1. Serge Klarsfeld, *Memorial to the Jews Deported from France, 1942–1944; Documentation of the Deportation of the Victims of the Final Solution in France* (New York: Beate Klarsfeld Foundation, 1983).

2. According to Léon Poliakov, *Histoire de l'Antisémitisme*, vol. 4, *L'Europe suicidaire, 1870–1933* (Paris: Calmann-Lévy, 1977), p. 317.

3. Michael R. Marrus and Robert O. Paxton, *Vichy France and the Jews* (New York: Basic Books, 1982), pp. 31–32.

4. François Goguel, *La Politique des partis sous la Troisième République* (Paris: Editions du Seuil, 1946).

5. Marrus and Paxton, *Vichy France*, pp. 41, 46.

6. Goguel, *Politique*, p. 339.

7. Marrus and Paxton, *Vichy France*, p. 33.

8. A Russian-born Jew, Stavisky was implicated in a colossal scandal involving fraud and political corruption, exposed in December 1933.

9. Marrus and Paxton, *Vichy France*, p. 33.

10. Ibid., pp. 45, 46.

11. Goguel, *Politique*, p. 339.

12. The Communist Party was not associated with the Union of the Left, but it diverted its votes to the Union candidate in the second round of elections.

13. The left won a majority in 1924, 1932, and 1936. In all three cases, it barely managed to remain in power for two years, coming to six years in all. During the twenty years

between the two world wars, the right governed for fourteen years in France, although the country voted more often for the left. See Goguel, *Politique*, pp. 543 ff.

14. *Journal officiel*, May 3, 1938, reproduced in the French edition of Marrus and Paxton, *Vichy et les Juifs* (Paris: Calmann-Lévy, 1981), pp. 388–391.

15. Marrus and Paxton, *Vichy France*, p. 57.

16. *Journal officiel*, November 13, 1938, reproduced in the French edition of Marrus and Paxton, *Vichy et les Juifs*, pp. 394–398; Vicki Caron, "Prelude to Vichy: France and the Jewish Refugees in the Era of Appeasement," *Journal of Contemporary History*, 20 (1988):. 157–176.

17. Quoted by Marrus and Paxton, *Vichy France*, p. 58.

18. Yehuda Bauer, *My Brother's Keeper: A History of the American Joint Distribution Committee* (Philadelphia: Jewish Publication Society of America, 1974), pp. 138, 237–239; S. Schwarzfuchs, *Les Juifs de France* (Paris: Albin Michel, 1975) claims that between 1933 and 1939 half a million Jewish refugees stayed in France for periods ranging from several weeks to several years, see p. 286.

19. According to Moshe Catane, *Encyclopaedia Hebraica* (Jerusalem: Encyclopaedia Publishing Company, 1976), 28: 961.

20. Including the 400,000 refugees from Spain after the collapse of the Republicans in January 1939. The majority of these returned to Spain after a few months.

21. For a detailed analysis of the contradictory versions of this affair, see Marrus and Paxton, *Vichy France*, pp. 59–63.

22. Marrus and Paxton, *Vichy France*, p. 67.

23. Schwarzfuchs, *Les Juifs de France*, p. 297.

24. With the exception of those who were in captivity in Germany.

25. The expression is taken from the report appended to the decree of May 2, 1938, cited by Marrus and Paxton, *Vichy et les Juifs*, p. 388; see also Hanna Schramm and Barbara Vormeir, *Vivre à Gurs* (Paris: François Maspero, 1979), pp. 199–244.

Chapter 2. The Jews in France in 1938–1939

1. Doris Bensimon and Sergio Della Pergola, *La Population juive de France* (Jerusalem, 1984), pp. 32–35. The authors do not take account of the fact that the Jewish detainees were not included in the census. Moreover, they state that the 24,000 Jews of French nationality (according to Klarsfeld's *Memorial*) represent 27 percent of the native Jewish community, which according to the data from Vichy comprised 90,000 people in 1941. This figure evidently refers to Frenchmen by descent, and one must add to it the prisoners of war in the same category. However, the 24,000 Jewish deportees of French nationality include both Frenchmen by birth and by naturalization, of whom there were 180,000 in 1939. Thus a total of 13.3 percent of French Jews were deported. One must also correct the data given by Bensimon and Della Pergola regarding the number of foreign Jews (120,000 in 1939, 170,000 in 1940), of whom 32 percent were deported or died in French camps. See Bensimon and Della Pergola, *La Population juive de France*, p. 347.

2. The estimates of Serge Klarsfeld, *Vichy-Auschwitz. 1943–1944* (Paris: Fayard, 1985), pp. 179–180, correspond with our own. He estimates "at 330,000 the number of Jews living in France at the end of 1940," not including those detained in the camps in the southwest.

3. Pierre Vidal-Naquet, *Les Juifs, la mémoire et le présent* (Paris: François Maspero, 1981), pp. 96–97.

4. Léon Poliakov, *Histoire de l'Antisémitisme*, 4:281–284; Lilly Scherr, "Les Juifs de France à veille de la Seconde Guerre mondiale," *Yod* 15–16 (1982): 12–18. Simon Schwarzfuchs, *Les Juifs de France*, p. 287; Béatrice Philippe, *Etre juif dans la société française* (Paris: Montalba-Pluriel, 1979), pp. 209–210.

5. Vidal-Naquet, *Les Juifs*, p. 104.

6. Schwarzfuchs, *Les Juifs de France*, p. 284.

7. Michel Roblin, *Les Juifs de Paris* (Paris: A. & J. Picard, 1952); David H. Weinberg, *A Community on Trial: The Jews of Paris in the 1930s* (Chicago: University of Chicago Press, 1977); Paula Hyman, *From Dreyfus to Vichy. The Remaking of French Jewry, 1906–1939* (New York: Columbia University Press, 1979).

8. Weinberg, *A Community on Trial*, pp. 36–47. The author told me that he was unable to find the archives from the *shuln*. In several cases their existence was precarious and ephemeral, and it is doubtful they can be recovered now. The daily frequenting of one of these *shuln* in Metz from November 1938 to July 1939 has left me the memory of a warm community center without hierarchy or decorum, with a quality of direct and intense fervor. An expression of a culture perceived as exotic by Western Jews, the *shuln* appeared to be nourished by a vigorous essence, in contrast with the static atmosphere in the consistorial temples.

9. Most of these organizations were close either to the Zionist parties or to the Communist Party.

10. Hyman, *From Dreyfus to Vichy*, pp. 307–308.

11. Ibid., p. 20.

12. Ibid., passim.

13. See mainly Lloyd Gartner, *The Jewish Immigrant in England, 1870–1914* (Detroit, 1960); Milton Gordon, *Assimilation in American Life* (New York: Oxford University Press, 1964); Hanokh Bartov, "Conformisme et sionisme du judaïsme anglais," *Dispersion et Unité* 10 (1970): 138–148; Marshall Sklare, "Le judaïsme américain et la célébration du bicentenaire," *Dispersion et Unité* 16 (1976): 188–197; Steven Aschheim, *Brothers and Strangers: The Eastern European Jew in Germany and German Jewish Consciousness, 1800–1923* (Madison, 1983).

14. Bartov, "Conformisme," p. 145.

15. Charlotte Roland, *Du ghetto à l'occident* (Paris: Editions de Minuit, 1962).

16. Hyman, *From Dreyfus to Vichy*, pp. 206–233. The author notes that by 1928 the children of immigrants constituted the majority of students in the rabbinical seminary.

17. Ibid., p. 123; Weinberg, *A Community on Trial*, pp. 9, 47–48.

18. Ibid., pp. 48–49; Hyman, *From Dreyfus to Vichy*, pp. 124–125, 323.

19. Ibid.

20. Ibid., p. 135.

21. Ibid., p. 136; Arnold Mandel, *Les Temps incertains* (Paris: Albin Michel, 1950), passim.

22. Hyman, *From Dreyfus to Vichy*, pp. 52, 135; Weinberg, *A Community on Trial*, pp. 38, 66.

23. Hyman, *From Dreyfus to Vichy*, pp. 273–277.

24. Ibid., pp. 277–286.

25. Ibid., p. 307; Weinberg, *A Community on Trial* pp. 104, 130.

26. Henri Bulawko, "Témoignage sur la résistance juive en France occupée," Paris, November 30, 1982, unpublished, in the author's possession, p. 3.

27. Alain Michel, *Les Éclaireurs israélites de France pendant la Seconde Guerre mondiale* (Paris: Editions des E.I.F., 1984), pp. 20–22.

28. Hyman, *From Dreyfus to Vichy*, pp. 286–297; Lucien Lazare, "L'empreinte fonda-trice des Éclaireurs israélites de France," in *Tribune juive*, no. 863 (March 22, 1985).

29. Ibid.

30. For more details on the occupations they held, see Weinberg, *A Community on Trial*, pp. 25–36, Hyman, *From Dreyfus to Vichy*, pp. 74–79 and 133–119.

31. Weinberg, *A Community on Trial*, p. 36.

32. Following the divisions among the political parties in Palestine.

33. Weinberg, *A Community on Trial*, p. 79.

34. Hyman, *From Dreyfus to Vichy*, pp. 107, 110.

35. Quoted in Hyman, *From Dreyfus to Vichy*, pp. 305–306. See also Weinberg, *A Community on Trial*, pp. 101–117.

36. *Activité des organisations juives en France sous l'Occupation* (Paris: Editions du Centre, 1947), pp. 49–50.

37. Weinberg, *A Community on Trial*, pp. 213–217.

38. Yehuda Bauer, *My Brother's Keeper*, pp. 237–238.

39. Weinberg, *A Community on Trial*, pp. 205–207.

40. Ibid., p. 202.

41. Weinberg, *A Community on Trial*, pp. 219–220.

42. November 19, 1938, quoted by Rita Thalmann, in Emmanuel Feinerman, *La Nuit de Cristal* (Paris: Robert Laffont, 1972), p. 219.

43. Michel Bialod, "La Tragédie de Szbonszyn," *Les Nouveaux Cahiers*, 55 (Winter 1978–1979): 31–37; Bauer, *My Brother's Keeper*, pp. 249–250; Renée Neher-Bernheim, *Histoire juive de la Renaissance à nos jours* (Paris: Editions Klincksieck, 1974), 4: 552.

44. Neher-Bernheim, *Histoire juive*, 4: 264; Weinberg, *A Community on Trial*, pp. 228–231.

45. Weinberg, *A Community on Trial*, p. 247.

46. Ibid., pp. 252, 257; Schwarzfuchs, *Les Juifs de France*, p. 294.

47. Jacob Draenger, *Nahoum Goldmann* (Paris: Editions Météore, 1956), 2:292; Hyman, *From Dreyfus to Vichy*, p. 312.

48. Moshe Catane, *Des croisades à nos jours* (Paris: Albin Michel 1956).

49. Hyman, *From Dreyfus to Vichy*, pp. 231–267.

50. Quoted by Lucien Lazare, "Judaïsme français et sionisme," *Dispersion et Unité* 16 (1976): 238.

51. Lazare, "L'empreinte."

52. The periodicals *Samedi* and *Affirmation* are mentioned by Hyman, *From Dreyfus to Vichy*, p. 345.

53. Hyman, *From Dreyfus to Vichy*, p. 345.

54. On the disapproval aroused by the declaration in *Le Matin*, the reception of Jewish child refugees, and the creation of the *Comité de coordination de la jeunesse juive* see Joseph Weill, *Déjà! . . . Essai autobiographique* (n.p., n.d. [1983]), distribution limited to the author's relatives, pp. 162–165.

Chapter 3. The Uniqueness of Jewish Resistance

1. Henri Marrou, *L'Histoire et ses méthodes* (Paris: Editions du Seuil, 1961).

2. Yehuda Bauer, "Résistance et passivité juive face à l'Holocauste," in François Furet, ed., *L'Allemagne nazie et le génocide juif* (Paris: Gallimard-Le Seuil, 1985), p. 418.

3. Isaac Deutscher, *The Non-Jewish Jew and Other Essays* (London: Oxford University Press, 1968), p. 163.

4. In *Le Monde juif*, no. 118 (April–June 1985): 61–63.

5. Henri Michel, *Les Courants de pensée de la Résistance* (Paris: Presses Universitaires de France, 1962), passim.

6. Henri Michel, "La résistance juive dans la résistance européenne," *Le Monde Juif*, no. 52 (October–December 1968): 7–13.

7. Joseph Weill, *Contribution à l'histoire des camps d'internement dans l'Anti-France* (Paris: Editions du Centre, 1947).

8. David Knout, *Contribution à l'histoire de la résistance juive en France (1940–1944)* (Paris: Editions du Centre, 1947); Jacques Lazarus, *Juifs au combat* (Paris: Editions du Centre, 1947); Claude Vigée, *La Lune d'hiver* (Paris: Flammarion, 1970); René Nodot, *Les enfants ne partiront pas!* (Lyons: Imprimerie nouvelle lyonnaise, 1971); Abraham Lissner, *Un franc-tireur juif raconte . . .* (Paris: Self-published, 1977); Henri Bulawko, *Les Jeux de la mort et de l'espoir* (Paris: Montorgueil, 1980); Louis Gronowski-Brunot, *Le Dernier Grand Soir. Un Juif de Pologne* (Paris: Editions du Seuil, 1980); Léon Poliakov, *L'Auberge des musiciens. Mémoires* (Paris: Mazarine, 1981); Shmuel René Kapel, *Maavaq Yehudi be-Tsarfat Ha-Kvusha* (*The Jewish Struggle in Occupied France*, Hebrew) (Jerusalem: Yad Vashem, 1981); idem, *Un rabbin dans la tourmente (1940–1944)* (Paris: Editions du Centre, 1986); Robert Gamzon, *Les Eaux claires. Journal 1940–1944* (Paris: E.E.I.F., 1982); *L'Entraide temporaire. Sauvetage d'enfants juifs sous l'Occupation* (anonymous booklet by rescued children, Paris, 1985); Adam Rayski, *Nos illusions perdues* (Paris: Balland, 1985).

It would be too laborious to present a full list of articles, notably in *Le Monde juif*, *Les Nouveaux Cahiers*, and *Yad Vashem Studies*. Noteworthy is the special issue, "Il y a trente ans, le sursaut," *Les Nouveaux Cahiers* 37 (Summer 1974), with contributions by W. Rabi, A. Rayski, J. Jefroykin, and H. Bulawko.

9. Rachel Minc, *L'Enfer des innocents. Les enfants juifs dans la tourmente nazie* (Paris: Editions du Centurion, 1966); Anny Latour, *La Résistance juive en France (1940–1944)* (Paris, 1970); David Diamant, *Les Juifs dans la Résistance française (1940–1944)* (Paris: Roger Maria, Le Pavillon, 1971); Jacques Ravine, *La Résistance organisée des Juifs de France* (Paris: Julliard, 1973); Gérard Israël, *Heureux comme Dieu en France, 1940–1944* (Paris: Robert Laffont, 1975).

10. Adam Rayski, ed., *La Presse antiraciste sous l'occupation hitlérienne* (Paris: Centre de Documentation de l'U.J.R.E., 1953); Adam Rutkowski, *La Lutte des Juifs de France à l'époque de l'Occupation (1940–1944)* (Paris: Edition du Centre, 1975).

11. Among the collected papers from colloquia, see the contributions of François Delpech in De Montclos et al., eds., "La persécution des Juifs et l'Amitié chrétienne," in *Églises et chrétiens dans la Deuxième Guerre mondiale. La région Rhône-Alpes* (Grenoble, October 1976) (Lyons: Presses Universitaires de Lyon, 1978; that of Annie Kriegel, "Résistants communistes et juifs persécutés," in *La France et la question juive, 1940–1944* (Paris: C.D.J.C./ Sylvie Messinger, 1981); the acts of the colloquium held in Paris on October 7, 1984, sponsored by the RHICOJ, in *Les Juifs dans la Résistance et la Libération* (Paris: Bulletin du RHICOJ, no. 1, 1985); the acts of the round table held in Paris on December 9, 1984, sponsored by AMILAR, in *Le Monde juif*, no. 118 (April–June 1985).

12. Among the six studies that I have consulted, one was written in French, two in English, and three in Hebrew: Haïm Avni, *Ha-Hatsala Derekh Sfarad u-Portugal* (*Rescue Via Spain and Portugal*), (Masters Thesis, Hebrew University of Jerusalem, 1964); Hillel J. Kieval, "Legality and Resistance in Vichy France. The Rescue of Jewish Children,"

Proceedings of the American Philosophical Society 124: 5 (Philadelphia October 1980); Nili Keren-Patkin, "Hatsalat Ha-Yeladim Ha-Yehudiim Be-Tsarfat" ("The Rescue of Jewish Children in France"), *Yalkut Moreshet* 36 (1983); Alain Michel, *Les Éclaireurs israélites de France pendant la Second Guerre mondiale*; Jacques Adler, *The Jews of Paris and the Final Solution; Communal Response and Internal Conflicts* (New York: Oxford University Press, 1987); Fabienne Sadan, *Mahanot Ha-Hesger Bi-Drom Tsarfat* (*Detention Camps in Southern France*, Hebrew), (Masters Thesis, Hebrew University of Jerusalem, 1985).

Finally, it is worth noting a brief and interesting study connected with the methodology of research on Jewish resistance: Renée Poznanski, "La résistance juive en France," *Revue d'histoire de la Second Guerre mondiale*, no. 137 (1985): 2–32, and an indispensable essay by Annie Kriegel, "De la résistance juive," *Pardès*, 2 (1985): 191–209.

Studies of uneven value are collected in "Les Juifs de France et d'Algérie pendant la Seconde Guerre mondiale," *Yod* nos. 15–16 (1982), PAGE? and "Les Juifs pendant la Second Guerre mondiale," *Yod*, 19 (1984), PAGE?

13. Georges Wellers, "Quelques réflexions supplémentaires au sujet de la résistance juive," *Le Monde juif*, no. 118 (April–June 1985): 82.

14. Kieval, "Legality and Resistance," p. 340.

15. Jacques Adler, "L'historiographie de la résistance juive en France," *Le Monde juif*, no. 118 (April—June 1985): 40. This text reproduces a contribution by Adler to a round table held in Paris on December 9, 1984, sponsored by an organization of former Jewish resisters, AMILAR; in his contribution to the round table, Wellers expressed adhesion to the following narrow definition: "Jewish resistance had only a single, unique meaning: 'fraudulently' to save the Jewish population from deportation," p. 49.

16. *Le Monde juif*, no. 118 (April–June 1985): 50. Poznanski, "La résistance juive en France," p. 22.

17. *Le Monde Juif*, pp. 50–51 (Wellers's lecture at the AMILAR round table).

18. The main activities of the national resistance movement included intelligence and propaganda, the infiltration of the official administration and the intelligence service, the sabotage of war production and of recruitment of workers for the *Service du travail obligatoire* (STO), and military operations.

19. Rayski, *Nos illusions perdues*, pp. 130–135.

20. Léon Poliakov, "Les différentes formes de la résistance juive en France," in *Jewish Resistance during the Holocaust* (Jerusalem: Yad Vashem, 1971), p. 525.

21. Diamant, *Les Juifs dans la Résistance française*, p. 19.

22. David Douvette, "Une histoire controversée," in *Les Juifs dans la Résistance et la Libération*, p. 161.

23. Adam Rayski, "Diversité et unité de la résistance juive," in *Les Juifs dans la Résistance et la Libération*, pp. 165, 168.

24. Annie Kriegel, remarks during the round table of AMILAR, in *Le Monde juif*, no. 118 (April–June 1985): 53–55.

25. The AJDC never violated the regulations of the American Treasury Department, but nonetheless it assumed responsibility for financing Jewish resistance in France. See below, ch. 14. On the American governmental regulations and the action of the AJDC, see the comprehensive study by Yehuda Bauer, *American Jewry and the Holocaust* (Detroit, 1981).

26. Vidal-Naquet, *Les Juifs*, p. 88.

27. Ibid., p. 107.

28. Christopher R. Browning, "La décision concernant la solution finale," in Furet, ed., *L'Allemagne nazie et le génocide juif*, pp. 190–216. The author analyzes the respective

themes of the "intentionalists," who argue the continuity between Hitler's ideology and the Final Solution, and the "functionalists," who claim that the decisions were made on an ad hoc basis. Both schools admit that the order for extermination was issued in 1941. See also Saül Friedlander, "De l'antisémitisme à l'extermination," ibid., pp. 14–38 and Yehuda Bauer, ibid., p. 405.

29. Léon Poliakov, *Bréviaire de la haine* (Paris: Calmann-Lévy, 1971), pp. 265–266.

30. Werner Rings, *Life with the Enemy: Collaboration and Resistance in Hitler's Europe, 1939–1945* (New York, 1982), p. 75.

31. Poznanski, "La résistance juive en France," p. 9.

32. Poliakov, "Les différentes formes de la résistance," p. 527.

33. Michel, "La Resistance Juive."

34. Rayski, *Nos illusions perdues*, p. 168.

35. See the *Mémorial des héros de la résistance juive en France* at Yad Vashem in Jerusalem. It contains a personal dossier for each of the resisters who fell in the accomplishment of their missions.

Chapter 4. Jewish Assistance Organizations

1. Michel, *Les Éclaireurs israélites de France*, p. 136.

2. CDJC, LXXXIX, a10.

3. A. Rutkowski, *La Lutte des Juifs en France à l'époque de l'Occupation (1940–1944)* (Paris: Editions du Centre, 1975), pp. 10, 55.

4. L. Gronowski-Brunot, *Le Dernier Grand Soir. Un Juif de Pologne* (Paris: Editions du Seuil, 1980), p. 163. A. Rayski, *Nos illusions perdues*, p. 76.

5. YIVO, coll. 239, Notebooks of J. Bielinky, entry of October 25, 1940.

6. Ibid., entry of November 19, 1940.

7. J. Lubetzki, *La Condition des Juifs en France sous l'occupation allemande, 1940–1944* (Paris: Editions du Centre, 1945), p. 136: "Many Jews could have avoided declaring themselves to the authorities. They prefered to defy the enemy by declaring themselves Jews."

8. Jules [Dika] Jefroykin, "L'Organisation juive de combat. Le Refus," *Les Nouveaux Cahiers* 37 (Summer 1974): 18–24.

9. Marrus and Paxton, *Vichy France*, p. 10–11.

10. Determining the number of Jews detained from 1940 to 1942 is particularly difficult, notably because a large portion of the figures concerning the camps include Jews, Spaniards, Gypsies, Poles, etc. without distinction. Moreover, data is missing regarding the number of those who were able to leave the camps for an assigned place of residence, a possibility sometimes granted to those capable of showing they had sufficient resources for their subsistence. The author of a recent study of the camps in southern France emphasizes this factor in the mobility of the detained population, as well as frequent transfers from one camp to another. The study refrains from proposing an estimate for the total number of detainees. See F. Sadan, *Mahanot Ha-Hesger*. See also J. Weill, *Contribution à l'histoire des camps d'internement dans l'Anti-France*.

11. CDJC, B. 16390.

12. C. Malraux, *La Fin et le Commencement* (Paris, 1976), pp. 213, 227.

13. Adler, *The Jews of Paris*, pp. 27–28.

14. Arthur Koestler, *Scum of the Earth* (New York: MacMillan, 1941, rpt. 1968).

15. To our knowledge there exists no protocol of this meeting. It is described in an anonymous, undated manuscript report. The handwriting reveals that the author is Jacques Bielinky, a Jewish journalist born in Russia, deported on March 23, 1943, and gassed in Sobibor. The report reviews the activity of Rue Amelot from June 15, 1940 to September 1941. See YIVO, coll. 239, file Colonie scolaire. This account of the facts agrees with that of a more succinct report, written on August 30, 1945, by one of the leaders of Rue Amelot, J. Jacoubovitch, ibid., file 159, as well as that of *Activité des organisations juives en France sous l'Occupation* (Paris: Editions du Centre, 1947), pp. 189–195. See also YIVO, coll. 116, file 64; J. Jacoubovitch, *Rue Amelot. Hilf un Vidershtant* (Paris: Colonie Scolaire, 1948).

16. YIVO, coll. 239, file Colonie scolaire.

17. *La Mère et l'Enfant* served as a front for D. Rapoport and his colleagues in his dealings with other Jewish organizations and the government. The dispensary had belonged to the *Colonie scolaire* group, affiliated with the FSJF. This title emerged again after the liberation.

18. YV, p. 7–8 and O.9–11.3; YIVO, coll. 343, file 3 and 8. R. Cohen, *Ha-Hanhaga Ha-Yehudit be-Tsarfat be-Milhemet ha-Olam ha-Shniya* (Hebrew, *The Jewish Leadership in France During the Second World War*), Doctoral dissertation, Hebrew University of Jerusalem, 1981, p. 29; Adler, *The Jews of Paris*, pp. 37, 42, 48, 65.

19. YIVO, coll. 343, file 7.

20. Bulawko, *Les Jeux de la mort et de l'espoir*, pp. 38–41.

21. M. Uziel, "Miflagot La-Hayim ve-la-Mavet," ("Parties of Life and Death," Hebrew), *Maariv*, August 31, 1984.

22. *L'Un des trente-six* (Paris: Editions Kiyoum, 1946), textes by A. Alperine, R. Grinberg, H. Baruk, L. Chevalley-Sabatier, J. Jacoubovitch, M. Jarblum, E. Minkowski, S. Tern, R. Tsoutsoulkovski.

23. YIVO, coll. 239, file Colonie scolaire; coll. 343, file 7; coll. 116, file 64.

24. YIVO, coll. 343, file 416.

25. Ibid., file 7.

26. YIVO, coll. 239, file Colonie scolaire.

27. YIVO, coll. 343, file 2.

28. Ibid., file 5.

29. Bulawko, *Les Jeux de la mort et de l'espoir*, p. 36.

30. R. Grinberg, "Mon ami David," in *L'Un des trente-six*

31. YIVO, coll. 245, XII-France, file A.6 and A.7; see above, "The Rising Danger," p. 00.

32. Ibid., file A.12.

33. *Activité des organisations juives*, p. 92; Marrus and Paxton, *Vichy France*, pp. 161–164.

34. CDJC, CCXIX, 146, letter from Kapel, the Chief Rabbi of France, September 16, 1940; R. Kapel, "J'étais l'aumônier des camps du sud-ouest de la France (août 1940–décembre 1942)," *Le Monde juif*, no. 87 (July–September, 1977): 96–98.

35. Weill, *Contribution à l'histoire des camps d'internement dans l'Anti-France*, pp. 14–49.

36. Arch. Kapel, letter from Joseph Schwartz, European director of the AJDC, Marseilles, September 30, 1940.

37. CDJC, CCXIII, 46.

38. AJDC, coll. France, c° 607; YV, O.9 - 12a, 29.2 and 30: Cohen, *Ha-Hanhaga Ha-Yehudit*, pp. 39–45.

39. R. Sommer, *Le Grand Rabbin René Hirschler* (Strasbourg: Communauté israélite, 1962).

40. Lambert was the Secretary General of CAR, and in his *Carnet* he describes the shame of the camps only on July 7, 1941. R. R. Lambert, *Carnet d'un témoin. 1940–1943*, presented and annotated by R. Cohen (Paris: Fayard, 1985), pp. 113–115.

41. LB, coll. AR 3987, file I: Weill, *Contribution à l'histoire des camps d'internement dans l'Anti-France*, pp. 107–109.

42. Kapel, "J'étais l'aumônier," p. 98.

43. N. Gourfinkel, *L'Autre Patrie* (Paris: Editions du Seuil, 1953), p. 209.

44. Arch. de Lesage, telegram no. 93 of January 7, 1941: "Prefects of the free zone, please provide useful cooperation with M. Gilbert Lesage, charged with a mission by the Director General of the *Sûreté nationale* regarding assistance to foreigners lodged in reception centers and other foreigners superfluous to the national economy."

45. Testimony of G. Lesage, Jerusalem, May 24, 1985, in the author's possession.

Chapter 5. The Youth Movements.

1. Michel, *Les Éclaireurs israélites de France*, p. 67.

2. Bulawko, "Témoignage sur la résistance juive en France occupée," pp. 1, 5, and "Où commence (et où finit) la résistance juive en France?" *Le Monde juif*, no. 118 (April–June 1985): 56–57; see above, chap. 4.

3. YIVO, coll. 116, file 41; Bulawko, "Témoignage sur la résistance juive en France occupée," p. 7.

4. Michel, *Les Éclaireurs israélites de France*, pp. 135–137. Testimony of E. Lefschetz, Paris 1980, in the author's possession.

5. The archives consulted provide little information about the Jewish youth movements from June 1940 to June 1942. The EIF are an exception. Their national secretariat, 27, avenue de Ségur, Paris, conserves several unsorted and not numbered, containing correspondence, reports, and circulars from the years 1940–1944. A. Michel, *Les Éclaireurs israélites de France*, makes abundant use of them, and he enabled me to consult them. YV, O.9–32.a possesses two long reports dated respectively November 25, 1941 and March 15, 1941, as well as circulars and mimeographed courses, all regarding solely the southern zone. Another exception is the Yechouroun movement. After the Liberation, one of its leaders, Jacques Cohn, was able to obtain a copy of the reports of the interception of his mail and the tapping of his telephone conversations during the first six months of 1942 as well as a report of the *Service d'enquêtes et de recherches* (SEC) of June 28, 1943, all coming from the files of the CGQJ. These documents have been preserved by his widow, Margot Cohn, in Jerusalem, who allowed me to consult them. The other sources have been oral testimony, notably that gathered by Haim Avni of the French University, the Institute of Contemporary Judaism, the Oral Testimony section (ICJ-OT), coll. (1), 11 and 21 (P. Roitman, J. and M. Cohn) and by Anny Latour, CDJC, Paris, not numbered (M. Bernsohn, H. Bulawko, R. Cohn, T. Giniewski, M. Hausner, G. Loinger, I. Pougatch, E. and S. Simon, H. Wahl).

6. YV, O.9–3.4, "Récit d'un résistant (nom inconnu) sur l'activité du MJS et autres formations de résistance juive," n.d. [1945].

7. Vigée, *La Lune d'hiver*, p. 55.

8. Ibid., p. 56.

9. ICJ-OT (1) 11, 18, 67; Lefschetz, testimony.

10. I. Pougatch, *Un bâtisseur—Robert Gamzon* (Paris: Service technique pour l'Education - F.S.J.U., 1971), p. 82.

11. Ibid., p. 35 and passim.

12. R. Gamzon, *Tivliout* (Paris: Editions du Chant Nouveau, 1946).

13. Pougatch, *Un bâtisseur*, pp. 44–49; F. Ch. Hammel, *Souviens-toi d'Amalek* (Paris: C.L.K.H., 1982), pp. 326–327; Gamzon, *Les Eaux claires*, p. 8; L. Lazare, "Les éclaireurs israélites de France ont-ils transformé la communauté juive?" *Tribune juive*, no. 863 (March 22, 1985).

14. Gamzon, *Les Eaux claires*, p. 8; Hammel, *Souviens-toi d'Amalek*, p. 328.

15. Pougatch, *Un bâtisseur*, pp. 44–51; Hammel, *Souviens-toi d'Amalek*, p. 328; A. Michel, *Les Éclaireurs israélites de France*, p. 37.

16. Hammel, *Souviens-toi d'Amalek*, pp. 27, 43–44.

17. Gamzon, *Les Eaux claires*, p. 16.

18. Ibid.

19. Pougatch, *Un bâtisseur*, pp. 61–62; Hammel, *Souviens-toi d'Amalek*, p. 44.

20. Ibid.

21. Gamzon, *Les Eaux claires*, p. 17.

22. A. Michel, *Les Éclaireurs israélites de France*, p.60.

23. Hammel, *Souviens-toi d'Amalek*, pp. 278–312, 396–413.

24. Pougatch, *Un bâtisseur*, p. 41. Hasidism is a pietistic and spiritualistic movement that arose at the end of the eighteenth century in the persecuted and impoverished Jewish communities of eastern Poland.

25. Appointed by the Consistory as the General Chaplain for Jewish Youth, with Chief Rabbi René Hirschler, in May 1941, he constituted the *Conseil directeur de la jeunesse juive* (CDJJ). In September 1943, Sammy Klein was designated as the Adjunct Chief Rabbi of France.

26. Report by S. Klein, May 20, 1941, preserved in the EIF archives, quoted by A. Michel, *Les Éclaireurs israélites de France*, p. 65; Rachel Cohn archives, Jerusalem, containing mainly 150 manuscript pages of notes of the courses and lectures in Beauvallon; Pougatch, *Un bâtisseur*, pp. 72–73; Hammel, *Souviens-toi d'Amalek*, pp. 332–333.

27. A. Michel, *Les Éclaireurs israélites de France*, pp. 61–63. The lists of books in the circulating library, mimeographed courses, and circulars have been preserved by YV, 0.9–32a.

28. EIF archives, report of November 25, 1941, quoted by A. Michel, *Les Éclaireurs israélites de France*, pp. 67, 151. The number of members of the EIF does not include participants in the study circles.

29. Gamzon, *Les Eaux claires*, pp. 17–23.

30. Three of them wrote an account of their collective experience : I. Pougatch, *Charry, Vie d'une communauté de jeunesse* (Paris: Editions du Chant Nouveau, 1946); Gamzon, *Les Eaux claires*, pp. 32–96; Hammel, *Souviens-toi d'Amalek*, pp. 47–97, 190–194. The style of life of these communities survived their dispersal in the spring of 1944 and reconstituted itself in the rural partisan unit known as the Marc Haguenau Company, most of whose combatants had belonged to the rural groups of Lautrec, Taluyers, Charry, and Le Pusocq. The author experienced the life of these collectives directly, thanks to sojourns in Taluyers and Lautrec, and especially because of his membership in the Marc Haguenau Company.

31. *Lumière*, no. 1 (1935), quoted by A. Michel, *Les Éclaireurs israélites de France*, pp. 35–36.

32. Ibid., p. 37, quoting an article by Denise Gamzon in *Lumière*, no. 2 (1938–39). On the farm in Saumur, see also Weill, *Déjà!* . . . *Essai autobiographique*, p. 180.

33. See the introductory account by Gamzon of the meeting of commissioners held in Moissac, August 15–18, 1940, quoted by A. Michel, *Les Éclaireurs israélites de France*, p. 60.

34. Article by C. Guthmann, the regional commissioner of Lyons, in the *Journal des oeuvres*, February 1941, EIF archives, unnumbered; *Activité des organisations juives*, p. 62.

35. JTS, box 15, file 2.

36. EIF archives, quoted by A. Michel, *Les Éclaireurs israélites de France*, p. 84; Cohen, *Ha-Hanhaga Ha-Yehudit*, p. 19.

37. JTS, box 15, file 2. This text predates the Statute of the Jews, which eliminated the Jews from all public functions and other professions.

38. A. Michel, *Les Éclaireurs israélites de France*, p. 85. The anomaly of allocations paid to Jews by a regime practicing discrimination against the Jews was not limited to those disbursed to the rural worksites. Under the Vichy regime, the Jews benefited from the award for a first birth and from allowances paid to the families of prisoners, to refugees from Alsace-Lorraine, and to families of foreigners conscripted in the GTE. In the latter case, the prefectorial services demonstrated obstinate unwillingness to pay the allocations, doing so only after the repeated intervention of SSE officials.

39. Diamant, *Les Juifs dans la Résistance française*, p. 263.

40. W. Rabi, "Pour quoi ils ont combattu," *Les Nouveaux Cahiers*, 37 (summer 1974), pp. 1–9.

41. A. Michel, *Les Éclaireurs israélites de France*, pp. 105–109, reproduces the entire text of a letter sent by Gamzon in January 1942 to the leaders of the movement, explaining the circumstances and reasons for his joining the UGIF council.

42. Rabi, "Pour quoi ils ont combattu."

43. Hammel, *Souviens-toi d'Amalek*, p. 332.

44. Pougatch, *Charry, Vie d'une communauté de jeunesse*, p. 69.

45. Gamzon, *Les Eaux claires*, p. 45.

46. A. Michel, *Les Éclaireurs israélites de France*, p. 56.

47. Gamzon, *Les Eaux claires*, pp. 54–58.

48. EIF archives, unnumbered, quoted by A. Michel, *Les Éclaireurs israélites de France*, p. 104.

49. Gamzon, *Les Eaux claires*, p. 55.

50. Testimony of G. Lesage, Jerusalem, May 1985, in the author's possession. Gamzon, *Les Eaux claires*, p. 58. Pougatch, *Charry, Vie d'une communauté de jeunesse*, p. 75; A. Michel, *Les Éclaireurs israélites de France*, pp. 123–125.

51. The absence of archival material covering the Zionist youth movements during the first two years of the occupation presents a difficulty to the historian. See above, n. 7. The only contemporary documents uncovered regarding the unification congress held in Montpellier in May 1942 are: YV 0.9–22.3, and the papers preserved by Claude Vigée. The relative abundance of testimony that has been gathered partially compensates for this lack. Three books recounting personal stories are: Knout, *Contribution à l'histoire de la résistance juive en France (1940–1944)*; Vigée, *La Lune d'hiver*; and Bulawko, *Les Jeux de la mort et de l'espoir*. See the testimony gathered by H. Avni, ICJ-OT (1).11 (P. Roitman), 18 (A. Bok), and 67 (H. Pohorylès), by A. Latour, CDJC, unnumbered (T. Giniewski and J. D. Jefroykin), and by the author (T. Garyn, T. Giniewski, M. Hausner, P. Roitman, R. Kapel, H. Bulawko, O. Esseryk, and G. Schnek).

52. Bulawko, *Les Jeux de la mort et de l'espoir*, pp. 174–175.

53. Ibid., pp. 39, 42; testimony of O. Esseryk, Jerusalem, May 28, 1985, in the author's possession.

54. Testimony of Bulawko, CDJC, unnumbered.

55. Ibid.; Bulawko, *Les Jeux de la mort et de l'espoir*, pp. 40–41.

56. Bulawko, *Les Jeux de la mort et de l'espoir*, p. 41.

57. Hammel, *Souviens-toi d'Amalek*, pp. 422, 424.

58. YV, 0.9–22.3 and P.7–4.

59. YV, 0.9–22.3: "Programme d'activité des gdoudim pour l'année 1942–1943 défini à la réunion de Montpellier et l'École de cadres," par Simon [Lévitte], [Moissac], n.d.

60. Latour, *La Résistance juive en France (1940–1944)* p. 83.

61. Testimony of P. Roitman, Jerusalem, January 22, 1985, in the author's possession.

62. Testimony of E. Guinat (Giniewski), Jerusalem, November 10, 1985, in the author's possession.

63. *Activité des organisations juives*, pp. 182–183.

64. EIF archives, not numbered.

65. Scattered copies of these publications have been preserved in the EIF archives; YV, 0.9–22.3 and 3.4; YIVO, coll. 340, file 10; JTS, box 15, file 2.

66. YIVO, coll. 210, file XCII.108.

67. A. Michel, *Les Éclaireurs israélites de France*, p. 65.

68. YIVO, coll. 340, file 10.

69. Ibid. The price of a subscription for six months for a monthly course was 24 francs, for a bi-monthly course, 45 francs, for a weekly course, 85 francs.

70. Margot Cohn archives, Jerusalem.

71. Ibid., emphasis in the original document.

72. ICJ-OT (1), 21.

Chapter 6. From Social, Political, and Cultural Action to the Military Option.

1. Kieval, "Legality and Resistance," pp. 362, 366.

2. On the spontaneous and independent character of the German demands on the anti-Jewish policies of Vichy, see Marrus and Paxton, *Vichy France*, esp. pp. 3–21; J. Billig, *Le gouvernement de l'État français et la question juive* (n.c., n.d.) [Paris 1961]; the chief of Pétain's civilian cabinet from 1940 to 1942, H. du Moulin de Labarthète, *Le Temps des illusions. Souvenirs (juillet 1940–avril 1942)*, (Geneva s.d.) writes: "Germany was not at the origin of the anti-Jewish legislation of Vichy. That legislation was, if I dare say so, spontaneous, indigenous." See ibid., pp. 279–281; the Minister of the Interior of Pétain's government, discharged and arrested in July 1940, Ch. Pomaret, "Bordeaux 40," unpublished, p. 55, writes: "[Laval explained] that anti-Semitism was imposed by the victor upon the vanquished. . . . This is a lie." YV, P.7–19.

3. R. Sarraute and P. Tager, eds., *Les Juifs sous L'Occupation. Recueil des textes officiels français et allemands. 1940–1944* (Paris: Editions du Centre, 1945), pp. 18–19.

4. Marrus and Paxton, *Vichy France*, pp. 9–11, 69–71; Browning, "La décision concernant la solution finale," p. 194.

5. Marrus and Paxton, *Vichy France*, pp. 9–11, 69–71.

6. G. Wellers, "Birkenau, qu'est-ce que c'est?" *Le Monde juif* (October–December 1972): 25–36.

7. A. Rayski, "Contre la nuit et le brouillard," *Le Monde juif* (October–December 1967): 8–14.

8. G. Wellers, "Birkenau, qu'est-ce que c'est?"; Bulawko, *Les Jeux de la mort et de l'espoir*, p. 51–56.

9. Testimony of Professor Israel Guthmann, fighter in the Warsaw Ghetto, deported to Auschwitz, Jerusalem, February 19, 1986, in the author's possession.

10. *Unzer Wort*, 50 (November 20, 1942); *J'accuse* 7 (November 25, 1942).

11. Testimony of J. Weill, Besançon, March 15, 1984, in the author's possession; G. Lévy, "Souvenirs d'un médecin d'enfants à l'OSE en France occupée et en Suisse, 1940–1943," (Paris-Jerusalem, s.d.) unpublished, p. 8; A. Salomon Testimony, Jerusalem, January 15, 1984, in the author's possession.

12. L. E. Bitton Jackson, *Elli. Coming of Age in the Holocaust* (New York: Granada Publishing, 1980), p. 206.

13. H. Michel, "Jewish Resistance."

14. R. Kapel, *Maavaq Yehudi be-Tsarfat Ha-Kvusha*, p. 83; see also Weill, *Contribution à l'histoire des camps d'internement dans l'Anti-France*, pp. 177–178; Gourfinkel, *L'Autre Patrie*, p. 222.

15. Created by a law of March 29, 1941; Sarraute and Tager, eds., *Les Juifs sous l'Occupation*, p. 39.

16. Ibid., 102–103, 133. The complex story of the establishment of the UGIF and the resistance of the Consistory against its affiliation is studied by R. Y. Cohen, *Ha-Hanhaga Ha-Yehudit*.

17. Sarraute and Tager, eds., *Les Juifs sous l'Occupation*, pp. 19–21, 40–49, 52.

18. Ibid., pp. 18–19, 53. German ordinance of September 27, 1940 in the northern zone, law of June 2, 1941 in the southern zone and Algeria.

19. For an overall view of this subject see I. Trunk, *Judenrat, the Jewish Councils in Eastern Europe under Nazi Occupation* (New York: Scarborough Books, Stein and Day, 1977).

20. The history of the *Comité de coordination* of the UGIF is studied by Cohen, *Ha-Hanhaga Ha-Yehudit*, pp. 158, 207.

On negotiations related to the establishment of the UGIF, see ibid., pp. 46–71; YV, P.7–3,8 to 11, 13, 16. YIVO, coll. 210, file 597 and 608; JTS, coll. French Documents, Box 15; R. R. Lambert, *Carnet d'un témoin (1940–1943)*, pp. 33–41, 133–163; *Activité des organisations juives en France sous l'Occupation*, pp. 199–235.

21. Cohen, *Ha-Hanhaga Ha-Yehudit*, pp. 158, 207.

22. Ravine, *La Résistance organisée des Juifs de France*, p. 31.

23. CDJC, CCXIII 73.

24. YV, P.7–3.

25. YV, P.7–9.

26. YV, P.7–21.25.

27. YV, P.7–9.

28. All the foregoing quotations, from the appeal by Rapoport to the Chief Rabbi, are taken from the minutes of a secret meeting held in Paris on January 28, 1942. Baur, Musnik, Mme. Stern, Stora, and Professor Weill-Hallé, members of the council of the UGIF-North, as well as Dr. Minkowski and Rapoport participated in it. The document (YV, P.7–8) provides a long description of the relations between Rue Amelot, the Consistory of Paris, and the *Comité de coordination*.

29. YV, P.7–3; Cohen, *Ha-Hanhaga Ha-Yehudit*, pp. 6–11.

30. YIVO, coll. 245 XII-France, file A.28 and 33.

31. Ibid., file A.15.

32. Ibid., file A.13.

33. YIVO, ibid., file A.12.

34. Marrus and Paxton, *Vichy France*, p. 164.

35. For the definition of deportable Jews, see Sarraute and Tager, eds., *Les Juifs sous l'Occupation*, pp. 163–164.

36. YIVO, coll. 245-XII-France, file A.12.

37. Ibid., A. 15.

38. Sarraute and Tager, eds., *Les Juifs sous l'Occupation*, pp. 18–21, 25–30, 40–42, 49, 52.

39. YIVO, coll. 210, file I.20. The letters quoted bear dates between August 18 and 28, 1941.

40. Ibid.

41. Sarraute and Tager, eds., *Les Juifs sous l'Occupation*, pp. 18–19.

42. Rayski, *Nos illusions perdues*, pp. 76–78.

43. YIVO, coll. 343, file 8.

44. YIVO, coll. 239, ms. "Colonie scolaire," written by J. Bielinky, p. 17; Adler, *The Jews of Paris*, p. 55, writes that Dannecker accused Rapoport of being the source of leaflets attacking the *Comité de coordination* which in fact came from Solidarité. This version is not confirmed by Bielinky's text. Bielinky, an intimate associate of Rapoport and his colleagues, whose report is contemporary with the events, was arrested in March 1943 and deported. Furthermore, it is known from other sources that Dannecker knew what he was talking about regarding the authors of these leaflets, known and identified by the *Renseignements généraux*, who informed the Nazi SD in April 1941. CDJC, LXVII.7; quoted by A. Rayski, "Le Front invisible. Les groupes de résistance juive à Paris face à la répression policière," *Le Monde juif*, no. 53 (1969), pp. 18–24 and no. 55 (1969), pp. 11–20.

45. J. Bielinky, "Colonie scolaire," pp. 27–30; YIVO, coll. 343, file 31. One of the social workers, Marcelle Valensi, was charged with contacts between the detainees, their families, and the Jewish organizations, ibid.

46. Ibid., file 14, 22, 39–48.

47. Ibid., file 25.

48. Ibid., file 6, 9; on the subject of the sources of these budgets, see below, ch. 15..

49. Ibid., file 24–31; see below, ch. 7.

50. Testimony of O. Esseryk, Jerusalem, May 28, 1985, in the author's possession.

51. Bulawko, *Les Jeux de la mort et de l'espoir*, p. 39; idem, "Un anniversaire oublié. Les premiers internements juifs à la caserne des Tourelles," *Le Monde juif*, 97 (January–March, 1980): 36–37.

52. Adler, *The Jews of Paris*, p. 174.

53. YIVO, coll. 343, file 22, report by Mlle. Panas, delegate of the Red Cross, to M. Rapoport, April 3, 1941: "Among the Jews, many have escaped (almost a hundred from the beginning). There remain only 39 . . . mainly old people, including a rabbi and his wife, and several veterans."

54. Ibid., file 29.

55. Klarsfeld, *Memorial to the Jews*, convoys 2–6.

56. YV, P.7–9, note dated July 3, 1942.

57. YIVO, coll. 210, file XCII.108 and coll. 340, file 42–72; LB,coll. Konzentrationslager Frankreich, 1939–1944, file AR 3987, protocol of the Comité de Nîmes, session of April 15, 1942.

58. Kapel, *Maavaq Yehudi be-Tsarfat Ha-Kvusha*, p. 39. YIVO, coll. 221.

59. The Young Men's Christian Association, an American Protestant organization active in Western and Central Europe.

60. The CIMADE was led by Madeleine Barot and represented in the Nîmes Committee by Pastor Toureille, who took Lowrie's place as president of the committee during his stay in Switzerland from June to October, 1941. The AC was placed under the patronage of Cardinal Gerlier, the Primate of Gaules. Its most active militants were R. P. Chaillet, Father Glasberg, and Germaine Ribière.

61. Arch. LB, box AR 3987, file 1; Weill, *Contribution à l'histoire des camps d'interne-ment dans l'Anti-France*, pp. 86–96, 110–111, gives a complete list and a brief description of the affiliated organizations. See ibid., p. 116, the list of the committee's commissions.

62. Ibid., p. 175. According to Marrus and Paxton, *Vichy France*, p. 162, 170–171, the press in Switzerland, Great Britain, and the USA, which denounced the barbarity of the French camps, was informed by the Quakers.

63. Arch LB, box AR 3987, file 11.

64. Weill, *Contribution à l'histoire des camps d'internement dans l'Anti-France*, pp. 96–102, 107, 110.

65. Gourfinkel, *L'Autre Patrie*, p. 209.

66. Ibid., 210, 222, 225.

67. See the testimony of Glasberg in De Montclos et al., eds., *Églises et chrétiens dans la Seconde Guerre mondiale. La région Rhône-Alpes*, acts of the Colloquium of Grenoble, 1976 (Lyons: Presses Universitaires de Lyon, 1978), p. 203.

68. Weill, *Contribution à l'histoire des camps d'internement dans l'Anti-France*, pp. 177–178; René S. Kapel, *Un rabbin dans la tourmente* (1940–1944), p. 86: "We were too prone to respect a certain legality, in hopes of better serving the interests of the detainees. . . . We should have provided false identity papers to a larger number of detainees, and done everything to facilitate their escape."

69. That is to say, people provided with a visa issued by an overseas country.

70. Arch. LB, box AR 3987, file 11, protocol of the Nîmes Committee, session of October 7, 1941.

71. AN, AG^{II}27.

72. Weill, *Contribution à l'histoire des camps d'internement dans l'Anti-France*, pp. 21–22.

73. Marrus and Paxton, *Vichy France*, p. 162. These figures derive from estimates, made difficult by the fact that the official reports and those of the Nîmes Committee often provide numerical indications regarding all of the detainees, including Spaniards, Gypsies, Poles, and Czechs. This is not true of the GTE, for the Jews were conscripted into special units, sometimes known as Palestinian companies. A note of the CGQJ places the number of Jews in the GTE at 20,000.

74. Klarsfeld, *Memorial to the Jews*.

75. Marrus and Paxton, *Vichy France*, p. 159.

76. *Activité des organisations juives en France sous l'Occupation*, p. 36; Nodot, *Les enfants ne partiront pas!*, pp. 27–28.

77. R. Nodot, "Résistance non violente 1940–1944," n.d., unpublished (testimony delivered in 1978 before the Commission d'histoire de la Seconde Guerre mondiale), p. 26.

78. Archives G. Lesage, Direction de la police du territoire et des étrangers, circulaire aux préfets régionaux no. 76, Vichy, January 2, 1942, and note of the SSE, Vichy, February 27, 1942; see above, ch. 5, and below, ch. 12, pp. 000–000.

79. LB, box AR 3987, file 11, session of December 3, 1941.

80. François Delpech, "La persécution des Juifs et l'Amitié chrétienne," in *Églises et chrétiens dans la Second Guerre mondiale. La région Rhône-Alpes*, pp. 160–164; Jean-Marie Soutou, "Souvenirs des années noires," *Les Cahiers de l'Alliance israélite universelle* (October–November, 1979): 9–14.

81. Weill, *Contribution à l'histoire des camps d'internement dans l'Anti-France*, pp. 158–163; Gourfinkel, *L'Autre Patrie*, pp. 245–256: Latour, *La Résistance juive en France (1940–1944)*, pp. 52–53; Hammel, *Souviens-toi d'Amalek*, pp. 69–71; Schramm and Vormeir, *Vivre à Gurs*, pp. 151–153.

82. Hammel, *Souviens-toi d'Amalek*, pp. 69–71.

83. Delpech, "La persécution des Juifs et l'Amitié chrétienne," p. 178, reports that Glasberg was condemned to death in absentia in December 1942 for sabotaging the railroad track with the Franc-Tireur network.

84. YIVO, coll. 221; *Activité des organisations juives en France sous l'Occupation*, pp. 33–36.

85. Kapel, *Un rabbin dans la tourmente (1940–1944)*, p. 71.

86. Testimony of Y. Ansbacher, Jerusalem, April 25, 1960, ICJ-OT (1), 1; A. Salomon, Testimony, Paris, June 8, 1963, ibid., (1) 20.

87. We have drawn upon sources permitting us to trace the origin of the AJ in the private archives of Polonski and Lublin as well as YV, O.9–3.4; Lublin, Testimony, n.d., ICJ-OT (1), 66; Knout, *Contribution à l'histoire de la résistance juive en France*, pp. 129–148; Lazarus, *Juifs au combat*, pp. 28–31; Latour, *La Résistance juive en France (1940–1944)*, pp. 90–98; Vigée, *La Lune d'hiver*, pp. 49–72; 403–412.

The plan regarding the formation of a military force to support the demand for a Jewish state figures in the Lublin, Testimony, ICJ-OT (1), 66 and in the appended document cited by Vigée, *La Lune d'hiver*, pp. 408–409.

The Haganah was the Jewish armed force in Palestine, under the control of the World Zionist Organization (WZO).

88. Ibid., pp. 70–72. The manifesto is analyzed below.

89. Cited by J. Lazarus, *Juifs au combat*, pp. 14–15.

90. Marrus and Paxton, *Vichy France*, pp. 310–315.

91. [Kadmi-Cohen], *Massada*, n.c., n.d. [Paris 1942]. The leaflet was not found. Knout gives a brief analysis of it in *Contribution à l'histoire de la résistance juive en France*, pp. 142–143. Fragments of this text, corrected, were used by the AJ manifesto, reproduced by Vigée, *La Lune d'hiver*, pp. 403–412, see also pp. 70–72.

92. Knout, *Contribution à l'histoire de la résistance juive en France*, p. 144.

93. Lazarus, *Juifs au combat*, p. 29; Latour, *La Résistance juive en France (1940–1944)*, p. 92; for a portrait of the Knouts, see Vigée, *La Lune d'hiver*, pp. 51–52.

94. Knout, *Contribution à l'histoire de la résistance juive en France*, p. 140; Latour, *La Résistance juive en France (1940–1944)*, pp. 91–92; Cohen, *Ha-Hanhaga Ha-Yehudit*, p. 26.

95. A. Polonski, testimony, Paris, March 21, 1984, in the author's possession.

96. Jules [Dika] Jefroykin, "L'Organisation juive de combat. Le refus," *Les Nouveaux Cahiers* 37 (summer 1974): 18–24.

97. Lazarus, *Juifs au combat*, p. 30; Knout, *Contribution à l'histoire de la résistance juive en France*, p. 48; Vigée, *La Lune d'hiver*, p. 53.

98. Lublin, ICJ-OT (1), 66, p. 5; Vigée, *La Lune d'hiver*, p. 70.

99. Ibid., pp. 403–412.

100. Lublin archives, file 20; Polonski archives, file D.7,22.

101. Latour, *La Résistance juive en France (1940–1944)*, p. 90.

102. Polonski archives, file D.7.

103. Lublin, ICJ-OT (1), 66, p. 11.

104. Knout, *Contribution à l'histoire de la résistance juive en France*, p. 139.

105. H. Michel, *Les Courants de la pensée de la Résistance*. The text from which we have taken these quotations appeared in 1968.

Chapter 7. The Jewish Communist Organizations

1. Weinberg, *A Community on Trial*, pp. 55–60.

2. Rayski, *Nos illusions perdues*, p. 65; Gronowski-Brunot, *Le Dernier Grand Soir*, p. 117.

3. Rayski, *Nos illusions perdues*, p. 76.

4. Gronowski-Brunot, *Le Dernier Grand Soir*, p. 121.

5. YV, 0.9–3.4.

6. Diamant, *Les Juifs dans la Résistance française*, p. 54; Ravine, *La Résistance organisée des Juifs de France*, p. 121 et passim; Rayski, *Nos illusions perdues*, p. 76.

7. Only Raski and Gronowski-Brunot explicitly mention what Annie Kriegel has denounced as the "outrageous silences" of offical Communist historiography; see her *Réflexion sur les questions juives* (Paris: Hachette, 1984), p. 32.

We were not granted access to the PCF and MOI archives preserved by the Institut des études marxistes in Paris. The references to these archives in the studies of David Diamant and Roger Bourderon thus cannot be subjected to a critical test. J. Adler, *The Jews of Paris*, pp. 159–161 dates the distribution of the clandestine Jewish Communist newspaper and the renewal of their political activity to July 1940. Although he was permitted to consult the Communist archives (ibid., p. 13), he supports this chronology only by conversations with two leaders of Solidarité as well as a statement by Rayski that appeared in 1950 in Rayski, ed., *La Presse antiraciste sous l'occupation hitlérienne*, p. 15 but later revised by the same author. The chronology proposed by Adler cannot therefore be retained; see also R. Cohen, *Ha-Hanhaga Ha-Yehudit*, pp. 23–25. Just recently the restrictions upon access to the archives controlled by the French Communist Party were relaxed. In January 1995 I was able to consult the twelves boxes of documents in the David Diamant collection at the Institut des études marxistes de Paris, labelled: A_2, A_3, B_1, $B_{3(2)}$, $B_{4(1)}$, $B_{4(2)}$, C_2, $C_3C_{4(1)}$, $D_{1(1)}$, $D_{1(2)}$, D_2, and "Clandestinité FFI-FTP." In additon, I consulted the personal archives of David Diamant, donated to the CDJC in Paris by his wife in 1994. These archives were piled into boxes and have not been sorted. I found no document mentioning Communist Jewish activity before September 1940. There is no trace of an underground newspaper produced before that date.

8. Diamant, *Les Juifs dans la Résistance française*, p. 54; Ravine, *La Résistance organisée des Juifs de France*, pp. 28–31; Adler, *The Jews of Paris*, p. 167.

9. Ravine, *La Résistance organisée des Juifs de France*, pp. 29–34.

10. Rayski, *Nos illusions perdues*, p. 81.

11. Adler, *The Jews of Paris*, p. 167.

12. CDJC, LXVII.7; Diamant, *Les Juifs dans la Résistance française*, p. 53.

13. The archives of the Prefecture of Police for 1940 and 1941 are not yet available for consultation.

14. Kriegel, *Réflexion sur les questions juives*, pp. 32–38.

15. Rayski, *Nos illusions perdues*, pp. 79–80.

16. Israël, *Heureux comme Dieu en France*, pp. 93–94, 101.

17. Ravine, *La Résistance organisée des Juifs de France*, pp. 42–44; Rayski, *Nos illusions perdues*, p. 78; Diamant, *Les Juifs dans la Résistance française*, p. 55.

18. Kriegel, *Réflexion sur les questions juives*, p. 53; Ravine, *La Résistance organisée des Juifs de France*, pp. 84–85; Adler, *The Jews of Paris*, p. 174; Israël, *Heureux comme Dieu en France*, pp. 116–117.

19. Adler, *The Jews of Paris*, p. 55.

20. Ravine, *La Résistance organisée des Juifs de France*, p. 31.

21. CDJC, LXXV.238; YIVO, coll. 210, file 113; Ravine, *La Résistance organisée des Juifs de France*, p.173.

22. Ibid., p. 73; Diamant, *Les Juifs dans la Résistance française*, pp. 75–82; Adler, *The Jews of Paris*, pp. 172, 184.

23. Gronowski-Brunot, *Le Dernier Grand Soir*, p. 163.

24. Ravine, *La Résistance organisée des Juifs de France*, p. 85; Adler, *The Jews of Paris*, p. 174.

25. Diamant, *Les Juifs dans la Résistance française*, pp. 56, 82; Ravine, *La Résistance organisée des Juifs de France*, p. 78; Adler, *The Jews of Paris*, pp. 176–178; Bulawko, *Les Jeux de la mort et de l'espoir*, pp. 39–41.

26. YV,0.9–3.4; Diamant, *Les Juifs dans la Résistance française*, p. 80; Ravine, *La Résistance organisée des Juifs de France*, p. 80; Adler, *The Jews of Paris*, pp. 178–180; Bulawko, *Les Jeux de la mort et de l'espoir*, p. 40.

27. CDJC, CCCLXXXIV.68.

28. The demonstration was held at 88, rue de la Roquette, where there stands a monument "to the memory of Oriental Jewish volunteers who fell for France. 1914–1918." Hundreds of demonstrators marched in silence, each one placing flowers on the monument. The police did not arrive until after they had dispersed. See Rayski, ed., *La Presse antiraciste sous l'occupation hitlérienne*, p. 41; CDJC, CCXV.18.

29. Diamant, *Les Juifs dans la Résistance française*, p. 75; Ravine, *La Résistance organisée des Juifs de France*, p. 78.

30. *Notre parole* and *Unzer Wort*, September 1, 1941, reproduced in Rayski, ed., *La Presse antiraciste sous l'occupation hitlérienne*, pp. 31–32; and Rayski, Adam, ed., *Dos Vort fun Vidershant un Zieg* (Paris: Centre de documentation de l'UJRE, 1949), pp. 51–52.

31. Rayski, *Nos illusions perdues*, p. 130.

32. CDJC, LXXV.275, quoted by A. Rutkowski, *La Lutte des Juifs en France à l'époque de l'Occupation*, pp. 90–92; Rayski, *Nos illusions perdues*, p. 130; Ravine, *La Résistance organisée des Juifs de France*, p. 91.

33. Diamant, *Les Juifs dans la Résistance française*, p. 72.

34. H. Amouroux, *Le Peuple réveillé, juin 1940–février 1942* (Paris: Robert Laffont, 1979), p. 316.

35. Rayski, *Nos illusions perdues*, pp. 90–91.

36. Ravine, *La Résistance organisée des Juifs de France*, pp. 90–91.

37. Rayski, *Nos illusions perdues*, pp. 131–132.

38. Kriegel, *Réflexion sur les questions juives*, p. 52.

39. L. Poliakov, "Jewish Resistance in the West," in *Jewish Resistance During the Holocaust* (Jerusalem: Yad Vashem, 1971), pp. 284–290.

40. A. Rayski, "Les immigrés dans la Résistance," *Les Nouveaux Cahiers*, 37 (summer 1974), n. 1.

41. Patrick Jarreau and Edwy Plenel, "Les ombres de 1943," *Le Monde*, July 2, 1984; Charles Tillon, letter to the editor, *Le Monde*, July 25, 1985; see below, ch. 16, p. 000.

42. Kriegel, *Réflexion sur les questions juives*, p. 629.
43. Ibid.

Chapter 8. The Consistory and Other Religious Associations

1. F. Furet, *L'Atelier de l'histoire* (Paris: Flammarion, 1982), p. 277. The author takes note of the analysis of assimilation proposed by M. R. Marrus in *Les Juifs de France à l'époque de l'affaire Dreyfus* (Paris: Calmann-Lévy, 1972).
2. Rings, *Life with the Enemy: Collaboration and Resistance in Hitler's Europe*.
3. CDJC, XI.39–LXX.II.2; LXXII.90; XCXI.16; CCXII.28; CCXIV.8; CCXIX.14, 94, 104, 105; extracts of these documents are reproduced in Rutkowski, *La Lutte des Juifs en France à l'époque de l'Occupation*; see also Cohen, *Ha-Hanhaga Ha-Yehudit*, pp. 19–21.
4. Lambert, *Carnet d'un témoin (1940–1943)*, p. 133.
5. Ibid., introduction by R. Cohen, p. 32. Lambert chides himself for "dying on the field of honor," pp. 31, 101.
6. Marrus and Paxton, *Vichy France*, p. 87; according to Simon Schwarzfuchs, *Les Juifs de France*, p. 301, Heilbronner met with Pétain twenty-seven times in 1940–41.
7. Ibid., pp. 108, 114–117, 330–339.
8. YIVO, coll. 239, box 4, notebook of Jacques Bielinky, entries of July 19, 1940 through May 13, 1941, passim.
9. J. Kaplan, *Les Temps d'épreuve* (Paris: Editions de Minuit, 1952), pp. 81–140.
10. P. Pierrard, *Le Grand rabbin Kaplan. Justice pour la foi juive* (Paris: Edition du Centurion, 1977), p. 73; see the text of the letter of July 31, 1941, in Rutkowski, *La Lutte des Juifs en France à l'époque de l'Occupation*, pp. 55–57; J. Kaplan, *Le Vrai Visage du judaïsme* (Paris: Berger-Levrault, 1987), pp. 28–32.
11. J. Kaplan, *Les Temps d'épreuve*, pp. 105–111.
12. *Activité des organisations juives en France*, pp. 19–21.
13. JTS, French Documents, box 15, file Consistoire israélite; AJDC, coll. France, file 608.
14. YIVO, coll. 245, file XII. France A.33 and B.11; Lambert, *Carnet d'un témoin (1940–1943)*, pp. 42–43; 180, 182. Cohen (notes 75, p. 256 and 133, p. 279) would have wished to make use of other sources to confront Lambert's remarks on the refusal of the President of the Consistory to intervene in Vichy together with his colleague from the UGIF. The letters of Wladimir Schah (August 1942) and Raphaël Spanien (February 1943) of the HICEM, YIVO, coll. 245, file XII give a version identical to that of Lambert; see V. Szajkowski, "The French Central Jewish Consistory during the Second World War," *Yad Vashem Studies*, 3 (1959): 193, n. 5. The crisis was mentioned on October 18, 1942 during a meeting of the social commission of the Consistory chaplaincy of the camps, where Joseph Weill and Robert Gamzon urged Jacques Heilbronner to renounce the presidency: JTS, French Documents, box 13, file 1.
15. CDJC, CCXIII.15.
16. According to the "Livre de raison du docteur André Bernheim" (Lyons, n.d.), unpublished, pp. 36, 37, the protest was taken to Vichy by a delegation led by the Chief Rabbi of France, I. Schwartz. The same source reports that a mimeographed copy of that protest, signed by Schwartz and Heilbronner, was seized by the Gestapo in Marseilles on August 21, 1943 in the office of R. R. Lambert, who was arrested with his wife and four children. Dr. Bernheim writes that the document was "most probably sent to Berlin,

which gave the order directly to arrest the Chief Rabbi of France and President Heilbronner. Only the latter was deported" with his wife, October 23, 1943.

17. Pierrard, *Le Grand rabbin Kaplan. Justice pour la foi juive*, p. 101.

18. CDJC, CCCLXXXIV.68 and CDLXXII.90, in Rutkowski, *La Lutte des Juifs en France à l'époque de l'Occupation*, pp. 66–67, 94–95.

19. Pierrard, *Le Grand rabbin Kaplan. Justice pour la foi juive*, p. 70.

20. The Hebrew name of the Jewish Holiday of Lights, commemorating the fight of the Maccabees against the Hellenistic oppressor in the second century BCE. The *Menorah* is the nine-branched candelabrum used for the symbolic lighting of candles.

21. V. Samuel, "Comme des brebis . . ." s.d., unpublished.

22. The New Year and the Day of Atonement in the Jewish calendar.

23. Kapel, *Maavaq Yehudi be-Tsarfat Ha-Kvusha*, p. 46.

24. Ibid., 42, 43.

25. Pougatch, *Un bâtisseur*, p. 70.

26. Margon Cohn Archives, letter from S. Klein to Jacques Cohn, April 16, 1942.

27. Testimony of Samy Klein, reproduced in Hammel, *Souviens-toi d'Amalek*, pp. 401–404.

28. Personal memories of the author; Hammel, *Souviens-toi d'Amalek*, pp. 187, 218.

29. YIVO, coll. 340, file 10; JTS, French Documents, box 13, file 10.

30. CDJ, XXXI.19.

31. Mme. Matthieu Muller, Testimony, Jerusalem, September 25, in the author's possession.

32. A voluminous collection of the archives of the AIP was donated to YIVO by Z. Schneerson: collection 340; see also Poliakov, *L'Auberge des musiciens. Mémoires*, pp. 84–96. Poliakov was the secretary of the AIP from November 1941 to August 1942.

33. YIVO, coll. 340, file 63 and 81; see below, ch. 14.

34. YIVO, coll. 340, file 47 and 51. We have reproduced the extracts of these letters without changing them.

35. YIVO, coll. 343, file 48 and 65. The correspondence concerning the adoption of detainees, promoted by Chaplain Kapel and taken in charge by Simone Hirschler in 1941, has not, to our knowledge, been preserved.

Chapter 9. The Particular Case of Jewish Children

1. See H. Kieval, "Legality and Resistance in Vichy France," pp. 341–342; Anne Grynberg, "L'assistance aux enfants juifs internés dans les camps de la zone sud," *Yod*, 19 (1984), pp. 67–80; Weill, *Déjà! . . . Essai autobiographique*, pp. 198 and passim, 214 and passim; Keren-Patkin, "Hatsalat Ha-Yeladim Ha-Yehudiim Be-Tsarfat" in *Yalkut Moreshet*, no. 36 (1983): 3–50; L. Poliakov, "Jewish Resistance in France," *Yivo Annual of Jewish Social Science* 7 (1953): 257–259; A. Michel, *Les Éclaireurs israélites de France pendant la Seconde Guerre mondiale*, pp. 50–54; S. Friedlander, *Quand vient le souvenir* (Paris: Editions du Seuil, 1978), p. 47; E. Papenek, *Out of the Fire* (New York: William Morrow, 1975), pp. 49 and 168–182; *Activité des organisations juives*, pp. 58–118; Arch. CDJC, XXVII-8. The centers administered by the OSE sheltered 1,600 children, those of the EIF, 350 children.

2. The Comité central des réfugiés had authorized the admission of a few hundred

foreign Jewish children in the Parisian region. See Papenek, *Out of the Fire*, p. 45 and Kieval, "Legality and Resistance in Vichy France," p. 342.

3. A. Michel, *Les Éclaireurs israélites de France pendant la Seconde Guerre mondiale*, p. 50.

4. Samuel, "Comme des brebis . . ."

5. G. Israël, *Heureux comme Dieu en France*; see the Kurt Niedermayer, Testimony, p. 43.

6. Weill, *Déjà!* . . . *Essai autobiographique*, p. 198; Lévy, "Souvenirs d'un médecin d'enfants à l'OSE en France occupée et en Suisse, 1940–1943."

7. Weill, *Déjà!* . . . *Essai autobiographique*, pp. 218–219.

8. Israël, *Heureux comme Dieu en France*; Samuel, "Comme des brebis . . . "; Minc, *L'Enfer des innocents. Les enfants juifs dans la tourmente nazie*; Friedlander, *Quand vient le souvenir*, pp. 70–72.

9. L. Schwarz, "La Résistance-autrement ou Pédagogie dans les miroirs," n.d., unpublished. This MS also contains the testimony of the wards of the shelter in Chaumont, delivered between 1960 and 1970. Schwarz's parents took their own lives in June 1941, one week after the Nazis invaded the USSR.

10. Kieval, "Legality and Resistance in Vichy France," p. 354: "[The Jewish organizations] did not seem to understand the potential of Nazi racial anti-Semitism. What is more, they failed to comprehend the role that Vichy, herself, would play in this tragedy."

11. Z. Szajkowski, *The Analytical Franco-Jewish Gazetteer, 1939–1945* (New York: S. Frydman, 1966); Cohen, *Ha-Hanhaga Ha-Yehudit*, pp. 113–121.

12. Kieval, "Legality and Resistance in Vichy France," p. 366: "The accomplishments of child rescue in France were real and impressive in their own right. The tragedy is that they came at such great cost and that more might have been done."

13. P. Rassinier, *Le Véritable Procès Eichmann ou les Vainqueurs incorrigibles* (Paris: Les Sept Couleurs, 1962); idem, *Le Drame des Juifs européens* (Paris: La vieille Taupe, 1964); idem, *Le Mensonge d'Ulysse* (Paris: La Vieille Taupe, rpt. Paris: La Librairie Française, 1979); idem, *Ulysse trahi par les siens, complément au Mensonge d'Ulysse* (Paris: La Vieille Taupe, rpt. Paris: La Librairie Française, 1980); see the writings of R. Faurisson, *Mémoire en défense contre ceux qui m'accusent de falsifier l'histoire. La question des chambres à gaz* (Paris: La Vieille Taupe, 1980).

14. R. Hilberg, *The Destruction of the European Jews* (Chicago: Holmes and Meir, 1961); H. Arendt, *Eichmann in Jerusalem* (Harmondsworth, Middlesex: Penguin Books, 1976).

15. G. Wellers, *La Solution finale et la mythomanie néo-nazie* (Paris: B. & S. Klarsfeld, 1978); N. Fresco, "Les redresseurs de torts," *Les Temps modernes* (June 1980); P. Vidal-Naquet, "Un Eichmann de papier," *Esprit* (September 1980), pp. 8–56; see also Lucien Lazare, "De trois techniques pour occulter les Juifs de la scène de l'histoire," *Tribune juive*, no. 923 (June 6, 1986).

16. I. Trunk, *Judenrat: The Jewish Councils in Eastern Europe under Nazi Occupation* (New York: MacMillan, 1972); M. Rajsfus, *Des Juifs dans la collaboration. l'UGIF (1941–1944)* (Paris: Etudes et Documentation internationales, 1980).

17. Lettre from H. Arendt to G. Scholem, July 24, 1963, quoted by G. Scholem, *Fidélité et Utopie* (Paris: Calmann-Lévy, 1978), p. 225.

18. Ibid., pp. 216–218.

19. P. Vidal-Naquet, preface to M. R. Marrus, *Les Juifs de France à l'époque de l'affaire Dreyfus*.

20. Arch. YV, 09/32–3, report of J. Ratner; E. Masour-Ratner, *L'OSE en France* (unpublished).

21. YIVO, Coll. 343, file 116.

22. YIVO, coll. 239, manuscript journal of J. Bielinky, fourth notebook, entries of June 1, 1942; L. Lazare, "Juin 1942: les nazis ordonnent le port de 'l'étoile jaune'," *Tribune juive* no. 875 (June 14, 1985).

23. Klarsfeld, *Memorial to the Jews*.

24. C. Lévy and P. Tillard, *La Grande Rafle du Vel' d'hiv'* (Paris: Robert Laffont, 1967), pp. 29–36; Marrus and Paxton, *Vichy France and the Jews*, p. 251; Ravine, *La Résistance organisée des Juifs de France*, p. 105.

25. Lévy and Tillard, *La Grande Rafle*, pp. 100–107; Marrus and Paxton, *Vichy France and the Jews*, pp. 263–269; Klarsfeld, *Memorial to the Jews*.

26. YIVO, coll. 210, box XI, file 74.

27. Arrested and deported in 1944, Camille Ernst survived.

28. *Activité des organisations juives*, pp. 126, 131–132.

29. Arch. LB, AR 3987, file 1, protocol of the session of the Nîmes Committee of February 11–12, 1941. In his report J. Weill declares that the Rivesaltes camp is "improper for the reception of women and children."

30. Samuel, "Comme des brebis . . . "

31. Ibid.

32. Testimony recorded by H. Avni, June 8, 1963, ICJ-OT, coll. 1, no. 20.

33. Samuel, "Comme des brebis . . . "

34. Arch. LB, AR 3987, protocol of the session of December 10, 1940; Weill, *Déjà! . . . Essai autobiographique*, p. 153 et passim.

35. Arch. LB, AR 3987, protocol of the session of January 10, 1941 (pages 1–3 of the protocol are missing); Szajkowski, *The Analytical Franco-Jewish Gazetteer*, p. 34; Kieval, "Legality and Resistance in Vichy France," pp. 349–350.

36. *Activité des organisations juives*, p. 135; YIVO, coll. 340, file 343; letter from the OSE to the AIP, February 9, 1942: "have as many children as possible liberated."

37. YIVO, coll. 210, file XCVIII-1: 229 children placed with families, 246 in shelters of the EIF in Moissac and Beaulieu, 62 in the rural center of Charry and in vocational schools.

38. Arch. LB, AR 3987, file IV, annexes to the protocols of the sessions of the Nîmes Committee. From October 1941 to May 1942, the number of children in the camps fell from 2,700 to 848; ibid., file 1, protocol of the session of May 20, 1942: the delegate from Secours suisse points out that there remain "580 non-Jewish children" in the camps. The OSE delegate notes that the mothers, expecting to be liberated soon, do not wish to be separated from their children.

39. YIVO, coll. 210, file XCVIII-1.

40. Ibid., reports of the management of OSE-France in Montpellier dated May 12 and June 5, 1942. The first of these reports notes the release of 70 adolescents from eighteen to twenty years of age from the camp in Gurs; YIVO, coll. 340, file 49: the father of two children (fourteen and twelve), a widower, writes from Rivesaltes to the AIP on April 28, that his children refuse to be separated from him.

41. *Activité des organisations juives*, p. 132.

42. Uri (Carl) Landau, Testimony, February 4, 1984, Kibbutz Sheluhot, Israel, preserved by the author.

43. M. Landau met Miss Rech in 1983. She had received and kept the letter of July 21, 1941, of which she gave him a photocopy.

44. YIVO, coll. 210, file XCII, 96; see also twenty-seven written testimonies by survivors aged from eight to sixteen, YIVO, coll. 104, file 332.

45. Leo Baeck Archives, AR 3987, file II: report of the hygiene commission of the Nîmes Committee, September 1941: sixty (out of 140) infants had died in two and a half months in Rivesaltes.

46. YIVO, coll. 245, series XII-France, file B10.

47. YIVO, coll. 245, series II-France II file 197: letter from the OSE shelter in Montintin to HICEM-Marseilles.

48. Columbia University Libraries, Governor Lehman Papers, C 19/43, unsigned letter to H. Lehman, January 17, 1941 and letter from Troper, AJDC-Lisbon, June 7, 1941, to Mrs. Roosevelt.

49. YIVO, coll. 245, series XII-France, file A 15, report of HICEM-Marseilles, August 1941.

50. *Activité des organisations juives*, p. 137; Kieval, "Legality and Resistance in Vichy France," pp. 351–353; the author presents a minute analysis of the correspondence between OSE-France and OSE-New York in 1941, but he hardly mentions the failure of the efforts made by the E. Roosevelt Committee to enlarge the immigration quota. See also Cohen, *Ha-Hanhaga Ha-Yehudit*, pp. 13, 14.

51. Andrée Salomon, Testimony, Jerusalem, March 17, 1985, preserved by the author; Columbia University Libraries, Governor Lehman Papers, C 19/13, letter addressed to Mrs. Franklin D. Roosevelt, Washington, D.C. by Morris Troper, the AJDC delegate in Lisbon, June 7, 1941.

52. YIVO, coll. 343, file 30: the 433 *nomades* and 36 Spaniards of the Poitiers camp were not detained, unlike the 318 Jews, of whom 86 were children less than thirteen years old (September 11, 1941).

53. YIVO, coll. 343, file 48.1, manuscript, undated letter, addressed by Marcelle Valensi, from Poitiers to the La Mère et l'Enfant dispensary in Paris.

54. Marrus and Paxton, *Vichy France and the Jews*, pp. 9–12.

55. YIVO, coll. 343, file 15, 24, 30, 31: in February 1941, 104 Jewish children under fourteen years of age were counted in the Monts camp in Tours; in November 1941 there were 93 children under fourteen years of age or 86 children under thirteen in the Poitiers camp. We lack information regarding the camp in Mérignac, near Bordeaux. In the camp in Troyes, on April 3, 1941, thirty-nine Jews remained after the escape of around a hundred Jewish detainees.

56. *Activité des organisations juives*, p. 122.

57. YIVO, coll. 259, MS Colonie scolaire, n.d., unsigned (the author of this report is most probably Jacques Bielinky. The writing is identical to that in J. Bielink's *Carnet*, and was presented to YIVO by the widow of the *Carnet*'s author).

58. Ibid.

59. YIVO, coll. 343, file 48.1, manuscript letter from M. Valensi addressed from Poitiers to D. Rapoport in Paris.

60. YIVO, coll. 219, file XXXI.24, MS letter from Rabbi E. Bloch, addressed to the UGIF in Paris, March 2, 1942.

61. YIVO, coll. 343, file 10.

62. YIVO, coll. 210, file XXXI.24.

63. YIVO, coll. 343, file 31. The president of the SSAE, "a private, public service organization," Mme. Lucie Chevalley-Sabatier, played a role of the first order in numerous actions to rescue Jews, particularly children. See above, ch. 6 and below, ch. 11.

64. Doubtless they arrived by messenger, as indicated. In addition, Marcelle Valensi notes in one of her letters: "I am profiting by the opportunity of having a bearer to write

to you in haste." To entrust a letter to the mail exposed the sender and the recipient to a police inquiry if the censor's office, which supervised all correspondence during the war, judged the contents of the letter to be suspicious. Now Valensi expressed herself without any precaution, notably betraying the ambiguity of her situation as a pseudo-delegate of the Red Cross, working in the service of Rue Amelot. Her letters are rarely dated, sometimes written in a railroad station, while waiting for a late train, on little sheets detached from a notebook. They never indicate to whom they are addressed. When Valensi was expecting an answer or awaiting the dispatch of funds, she asked the recipient to write via Rabbi Bloch in Poitiers. See YIVO, coll. 343, file 24, 29, 30, 48.1.

65. The name of a religious holiday celebrated in synagogues, marking the end of the annual cycle of weekly readings from the Pentateuch as well as the beginning of the new cycle.

66. YIVO, coll. 343, file 30, letter of October 15, 1941 to D. Rapoport; L. Lazare, "Simhat Torah en 1941 au camp d'internement de Poitiers," *Tribune juive*, no. 841 (October 17, 1984).

67. YIVO, coll. 343, file29 and 48.1, undated letters addressed to D. Rapoport.

68. YV, 9-a/6977, letter of [April] 13, [1942] addressed to Rabbi Joseph Bloch, the father of E. Bloch.

69. YIVO, coll. 343, file 143. Remember that the population of the two camps of Loiret was composed of 4,000 Jewish male foreigners aged from eighteen to sixty, arrested in Paris, May 14, 1941.

70. YIVO, coll. 343, file 29.

71. YIVO, coll. 343, file 48.1.

72. Ibid.

73. YV, 0–9/6977, letters of M. Valensi, [April] 13, [1942] and November 12, [1942] to Rabbi J. Bloch in Clermont-Ferrand. No indication is given of the reasons and circumstances of Marcelle Valensi's passage from the northern zone to the southern zone. Her correspondence constitutes to some degree a chronicle of one part of the action of Rue Amelot which, for the period after her passage, is far more difficult to explore.

74. *L'Entraide temporaire. Sauvetage d'enfants juifs sous l'Occupation*, pp. 26–27, Robert Franck, Testimony; YIVO, coll. 210, file XXXI.24; see also below, ch. 11, p. 202.

75. Contrary to what occurred in the French Departments of Algeria, which were governed by Vichy, and where Jewish pupils were excluded from the public school system in 1941; see G. Amipaz-Silber, *Mahteret Yehudit be-Algeria, 1940–1942* (*Jewish Underground in Algeria*, Hebrew) (Jerusalem: Ministry of Defense Publishing House, 1983), p. 29; Michel Ansky, *Les Juifs d'Algérie du décret Crémieux à la Libération* (Paris: Editions du Centre, 1950), pp. 107–137; Michel Abitbol, *Les Juifs d'Afrique du Nord sous Vichy* (Paris: Maisonneuve et Larose, 1983), p. 108.

Chapter 10. The Establishment of Underground Networks

1. Klarsfeld, *Memorial to the Jews*, notice of convoy no. 1.

2. Ibid., notices to convoys no. 2 and 3.

3. Marrus and Paxton, *Vichy France and the Jews*, p. 226.

4. Ibid., pp. 204–206.

5. Adler, *The Jews of Paris*, p. 187; YIVO, coll. 239, MS notebook of J. Bielinky, entries of July 8 and 10, 1942.

6. YIVO, coll. 245, file XII-France A. 33; Lambert, *Carnet d'un témoin (1940–1943)*, pp. 178–179.

7. Lévy and Tillard, *La Grande Rafle*, pp. 23, 37–38; Marrus and Paxton, *Vichy France and the Jews*, pp. 232–233.

8. Quoted by Adam Rayski, "Paris face à la Grande Rafle. Comment plus de 12,000 Juifs ont pu échapper à la mort," *Le Monde juif*, 12 (April–June 1967): 27–29. The leaflet is reproduced in Rayski, ed., *Dos Vort fun Vidershtant un Zieg*, pp. 105–106.

9. Ravine, *La Résistance organisée des Juifs de France*, p. 98.

10. Lévy and Tillard, *La Grande Rafle*, pp. 29, 92, 202; Rayski, "Paris face à la Grande Rafle"; Marrus and Paxton, *Vichy France and the Jews*, p. 251.

11. YIVO, coll. 116, file 23: anonymous report entitled: "Situation au 25 août 1942." The English translation of this text appears in *Europe Speaks*, October 1, 1942, mimeographed publication of five pages produced in Cleveland by The League of Human Rights, YIVO, coll. 116, file 57.

12. YIVO, coll. 116, file 23, "Lettre de Paris," dated July 21, 1942, anonymous. "Wednesday night" is July 15, the eve of the launching of Operation Spring Wind in the northern zone.

13. Lévy and Tillard, *La Grande Rafle*, p. 29.

14. Ibid., pp. 29–36.

15. Rayski, *Nos illusions perdues*, pp. 93–95; Lévy and Tillard, *La Grande Rafle*, pp. 72–73.

16. In his preface to Lévy and Tillard, *La Grande Rafle*, p. 9.

17. Yehuda Jacoubovitch, *Rue Amelot, Hilf und Vidershtant* (Paris: Colonie Scolaire, 1948), pp. 96–96.

18. The Jewish Communist leaders had been individually "Aryanized" by the PC, separated from their families, which were forced to retain their legal status as Jews. See Rayski, *Nos illusions perdues*, pp. 82, 93. On the beginnings of the manufacture of false identity papers by the activists of Rue Amelot, see Bulawko, "Témoignage sur la résistance juive en France occupée," pp. 5, 11, 13, 14.

19. Lévy and Tillard, *La Grande Rafle*, pp. 32–32, 82.

20. Rayski, "Paris face à la Grande Rafle," p. 27.

21. Klarsfeld, *Memorial*, descriptions of convoys no. 7 and 39.

22. Adler, *The Jews of Paris*, p. 192.

23. Rayski, *Nos illusions perdues*, pp. 104–107.

24. Ibid., p. 132; Adler, *The Jews of Paris*, p. 193.

25. Rayski, *Nos illusions perdues*, p. 105.

26. Ibid., p. 126.

27. Rayski, ed., *La Presse antiraciste sous l'occupation hitlérienne*, pp. 301–328.

28. Rayski, "Paris face à la Grande Rafle," pp. 37 and 38.

29. Rayski, ed., *La Presse antiraciste sous l'occupation hitlérienne*, See: *Récit des traitements infligés aux familles juives dans la région parisienne à partir du 16 juillet 1942*, pp. 47–53; *Informations sur les atrocités nazies. Le Pogrom à blanc*, pp. 285–300.

30. Rayski, "Paris face à la Grande Rafle." The rescue of children is described below.

31. Undated report (written in October 1942 by Rapoport). YIVO, coll. 343, file 4 and 116. The four members of the directorate who were deported are named in this report: Kremer, Charavner, Shapiro, and Judkovski.

32. Ibid.

33. YIVO, coll. 343, file 4 and 116.

34. YIVO, coll. 343, file 16. The monthly allotments to individuals ranged from 200 to 1,000 francs, depending on the declarations of the beneficiaries and the evaluation of the social assistance agency. Compensation paid to foster families and institutions came to 600–700 francs per month per child.

35. Bulawko, "Témoignage sur la résistance juive en France occupée," pp. 13, 14.

36. Ibid.

37. Klarsfeld, *Vichy-Auschwitz. 1943–1944*, pp. 180, 184–187, 451–452, 484, 490.

38. Ibid., p. 187 and passim, convoys no. 1 and no. 45.

39. YIVO, coll. 343, file 36 (folder 43, 45, 46, 65, 99); Bulawko, *Les Jeux de la mort et de l'espoir*, p. 44.

40. YIVO, coll. 343, file 108, 158, 159; coll. 116, file 64; Bulawko, "Témoignage sur la résistance juive en France occupée," p. 25.

41. Ibid., pp. 12, 21–23.

42. Lefschetz, Testimony; Michel, *Les Éclaireurs israélites de France pendant la Seconde Guerre mondiale*, pp. 146–148; Hammel, *Souviens-toi d'Amalek*, pp. 246–247; see below, ch. 11.

43. Klarsfeld, *Vichy-Auschwitz. 1943–1944*, pp. 158–159, 393.

44. Ibid., pp. 148, 337–338.

45. Klarsfeld, *Vichy-Auschwitz. 1943–1944*, p. 393.

46. YIVO, coll. 245, file XII-France A.33; Lambert, *Carnet d'un témoin (1940–1943)*, p. 177.

47. YIVO, coll. 245, file XII-France A.33.

48. See the identical versions of Lambert, *Carnet d'un témoin* (1940–1943), p. 180 and of W. Schach, the director of HICEM-Marseilles in a letter written in August 1942 to HICEM-Lisbon: YIVO, coll. 245, file XII-France B.11; see also François Delpech, "La persécution des Juifs et l'Amitié chrétienne," in *Églises et chrétiens dans la Second Guerre mondiale. La région Rhône-Alpes*, p. 209. In his contribution to this colloquium, Father Glasberg reports that Heilbronner (the president of the Consistory) said in his presence: "Cardinal [Gerlier] should not intervene in behalf of foreigners. That could only make the situation worse."

49. Memorandum of August 10, 1942 of D. Lowrie, quoted by Klarsfeld, *Vichy-Auschwitz. 1943–1944*, pp. 324–327.

50. YIVO, coll. 245, file A.56: "Rapport sur la situation des Juifs en France," written in September 1942 by Spanien.

51. Klarsfeld, *Vichy-Auschwitz. 1943–1944*, p. 352.

52. Michel, *Les Éclaireurs israélites de France pendant la Seconde Guerre mondiale*, p. 123.

53. Ibid., p. 125; Joseph Weill, Testimony, Besançon, March 15, 1984, in the author's possession.

54. *Le Matin*, Paris, August 15, 1942, quoted by Klarsfeld, *Vichy-Auschwitz. 1943–1944*, p. 337.

55. YV, coll. 09, file 22.5; Soutou, "Souvenirs des années noires," p. 10.

56. Klarsfeld, *Vichy-Auschwitz. 1943–1944*, p. 295.

57. Jacob Kaplan, *N'oublie pas* (Paris: Stock, 1984), pp. 139–146.

58. Michel, *Les Éclaireurs israélites de France pendant la Seconde Guerre mondiale*, p.123.

59. Klarsfeld, *Vichy-Auschwitz. 1943–1944*, p. 360.

60. YIVO, coll. 116, file 23; Kapel, *Maavaq Yehudi be-Tsarfat Ha-Kvusha*, pp. 57, 77–80.

61. YIVO, coll. 343, file 33: "Instructions du chef du SSE."

62. See above, n. 61; Kapel, *Maavaq Yehudi be-Tsarfat Ha-Kvusha*, pp. 74–76; Pougatch, *Un bâtisseur*, p. 75; CDJC, CDLXXII.93, on the action in Haute-Savoie by Rabbi Meyers.

63. Kapel, *Maavaq Yehudi be-Tsarfat Ha-Kvusha*, p. 75.

64. Delpech, "La persécution des Juifs et l'Amitié chrétienne," p. 166; René Nodot, "Le pasteur Roland de Pury et les protestants de la région lyonnaise dans la Résistance," unpublished, Commission d'histoire de la Second Guerre mondiale, Lyons, n.d. [1982], p. 17; Klarsfeld, *Vichy-Auschwitz. 1943–1944*, p. 393.

65. AN, F Ic III.1193. The police report reproduced by Klarsfeld, *Vichy-Auschwitz. 1943–1944*, p. 393 bears the same date as the Angeli report, September 1, 1942, and indicates 595 (and not 545) deportees from Lyons. But the train that arrived in Drancy from Lyons on August 30 contained 544 Jews.

66. AN, F Ic III.1201 and 1156.

67. CDJC, XXVI.58; Kapel, *Maavaq Yehudi be-Tsarfat Ha-Kvusha*, p. 81.

68. Klarsfeld, *Vichy-Auschwitz. 1943–1944*, pp. 158–159, 394.

described below, ch. 11.

69. See above, n. 58.

70. Marrus and Paxton, *Vichy France and the Jews*, p. 203.

71. Ibid., p. 204.

72. Delpech, "La persécution des Juifs et l'Amitié chrétienne," p. 161.

73. The best study of the clandestine issues of *Témoignage chrétien* is that of Renée Bédarida, *Les Armes de l'esprit: Témoignage chrétien (1941–1944)* (Paris: Editions Ouvrières, 1977); see also François and Renée Bédarida, "Une résistance spirituelle: Aux origines du 'Témoignage chrétien' (1941–1942)," *Revue d'histoire de la Seconde Guerre mondiale*, 61 (Jan. 1966): 3–33.

74. Klarsfeld, *Vichy-Auschwitz. 1943–1944*, pp. 342, 344–345, 405.

75. Ibid., pp. 356–357.

76. Ibid., pp. 382–383.

77. See the selection of documents reproduced by Klarsfeld, *Vichy-Auschwitz. 1943–1944*, passim.

78. Ibid., 369–370.

79. Ibid., pp. 407–409. The protocol of the Laval-Oberg interview was written by SS officer Hagen.

80. Ibid., pp. 171, 181.

81. Marrus and Paxton, *Vichy France and the Jews*, pp. 261, 291.

82. Klarsfeld, *Vichy-Auschwitz. 1943–1944*, pp. 176–177.

83. Klarsfeld, *Vichy-Auschwitz. 1943–1944*, p. 393.

84. Sources are cited in the notes to ch. 11, below. Fichtenberg permitted me to consult and decipher these stupefying daybooks as well as his personal archives. A leader of the Chantiers de jeunesse, he had been excluded from it in July 1942 because he was Jewish. On the page of Tuesday, August 25 he wrote: "Was in Vichy. Saw Chamois [Henri Wahl] and Castor [Robert Gamzon] with Liliane [Klein] at the UGIF. Returned [to Lapalisse] by bicycle at 11 o'clock [p.m.]. Warned the I [Jews] sleeping in the house."

85. CDJC, unnumbered file containing testimony collected by Anny Latour. See also Latour, *La Résistance juive en France (1940–1944)*, pp. 109–115, 138–139, 237–239.

86. Denise Sikierski, Testimony, Jerusalem, November 18, 1984, in the author's possession.

87. Poliakov, *L'Auberge des musiciens*, passim; also CDJC, CCCLXXXIV.41.

88. Poliakov, *L'Auberge des musiciens*, p. 93.

89. Joseph Weill, Testimony, Montfaucon, March 15, 1984, in the author's possession.

90. Poliakov, *L'Auberge des musiciens*, p. 97.

91. See notably the collections of the CDJC (Paris), Yad Vashem (Jerusalem), and YIVO (New York): Lublin archives, file 30.

92. Personal memory. The author counterfeited dozens of documents using this method in the improvised workshop of the rural group of Taluyers (Rhône) during the autumn of 1942. The resisters had attached a little sign to the wall of the small alcove used for the workshop, stating sarcastically: "The counterfeiter is subject to forced labor."

93. Otto ("Toto") Ginat-Giniewski, Testimony, Jerusalem, November 10, 1985, in the author's possession; CDJC, CCX.3.

94. Personal archives of Roger Fichtenberg, Paris.

95. Michel, *Les Éclaireurs israélites de France pendant la Seconde Guerre mondiale*, p. 169; Poliakov, *L'Auberge des musiciens*, p. 134.

96. Gamzon, *Les Eaux claires*, pp. 76–77; CDJC, CCXVIII.94.

97. Created by a law promulgated on September 4, 1942.

98. Personal memory.

99. Personal archives of Roger Fichtenberg, Paris.

100. Latour, *La Résistance juive en France (1940–1944)*, p. 128.

101. Maison diocésaine de Paris, historical archives, 3 B (I), 4.

102. CDJC, CCXVIII.94. See above, n. 99, testimony of Josué Lifschitz.

103. Latour, *La Résistance juive en France (1940–1944)*, p. 132; Moussa Abadi, Testimony, Paris, April 3, 1984, preserved by the author; Marie-Rose Gineste, Testimony, Montauban, June 12, 1974, p. 38, preserved by the author.

104. An enterprise of the Third Reich created by the Minister of Armaments, Fritz Todt, and charged with equipment and fortifications projects.

105. Latour, *La Résistance juive en France (1940–1944)*, pp. 107, 108. See also Szajkowski, *Analytical Franco-Jewish Gazetteer*, p. 28.

106. CDJC, CCXV.16, reproduced by Rutkowski, *La Lutte des Juifs en France à l'époque de l'Occupation*, pp. 325–326.

107. Hammel, *Souviens-toi d'Amalek*, pp. 380–382.

108. Rutkowski, *La Lutte des Juifs en France à l'époque de l'Occupation*, pp. 261–263. Several sources refer to David Donoff as a Russian Jewish convert to Catholicism, doubtless because of an error of indeterminate origin. In 1945 Joseph Fischer reported the testimony of a nurse in Edouard-Herriot hospital, where Donoff had been transferred, according to which, before dying, he declared to a priest that, since he was Jewish, "he could not accept the help of a Christian priest," ibid.; see Delpech, "La persécution des Juifs et l'Amitié chrétienne," p. 178; François and Renée Bédarida, "Une résistance spirituelle: Aux origines du 'Témoignage chrétien' (1941–1942)," p. 9. Donoff, born in France, was neither Russian nor a convert. See the exchange of correspondence between Jacques Pulver and René Nodot in *Sens*, no. 88 (September–October 19): 233, quoting Nina Gourfinkel.

109. Latour, *La Résistance juive en France (1940–1944)*, pp. 126–127.

110. Hammel, *Souviens-toi d'Amalek*, p. 374; Poliakov, *L'Auberge des musiciens*, p. 138.

111. See the Polonski archives, D5.10: "We have a debt toward the nurse. There is no doubt, none," and D5.9: "I hope that the account has been settled with the nurse and her acquaintances." Nevertheless, after the Liberation, Bass helped her clear herself of the suspicions weighing upon her, whereas Poliakov, *L'Auberge des musiciens*, pp. 125–126, 135–141, 149 continued wondering "what was the true role played by that woman?"

Chapter 11. The Rescue of Jewish Children

1. G. Wellers, "La Tragédie des deux journées," *Le Monde juif*, nos. 28–29 (January–June 1962): 3–16; Lévy and Tillard, *La Grande Rafle*, pp. 37–49 and passim; S. Klarsfeld, *Memorial to the Jews Deported from France*.

2. Emmanuel Lefschetz, Testimony (addressed to F. Hammel), Savigny-sur-Orge, undated [1979 or 1980], in the author's possession: "In the Vélodrome d'hiver, we tried to enable the EI to escape, as well as others, but without success. The guard manned by the French police and gendarmerie was very effective in this circumstance." Notebook of Denise Lefschetz, unpaginated, in the author's possession, entries of Tuesday July 14 [1942], Wednesday 15, Thursday 16, Friday, Saturday, Sunday [July 29, 1942].

3. Marrus and Paxton, *Vichy France and the Jews*, p. 249. Regarding the 28,000 people figuring on the lists, Wellers, "La Tragédie des deux journées," states that a minimum of 22,000 arrests were expected, "taking account of the inevitable 'shortfall.'"

4. Ravine, *La Résistance organisée des Juifs de France*, p. 98; Marrus and Paxton, *Vichy France and the Jews*, p. 249; Adler, *The Jews of Paris*, p. 188. The chief of the anti-Jewish service of the Gestapo, Röthke, accused the police officials of corruption and suspected them of having warned "the rich Jews": Lévy and Tillard, *La Grande Rafle*, p. 92. But Kriegel, *Réflexion sur les questions juives*, p. 28, writes that these were "officials coming from the White Russian immigration who were in contact with members of the Jewish intelligentsia of Russian origin."

5. Ibid., pp. 28, 52; Ravine, *La Résistance organisée des Juifs de France*, pp. 104–106; Marrus and Paxton, *Vichy France and the Jews*; see above, ch. 10.

6. Marrus and Paxton, *Vichy France and the Jews*, pp. 263–269; Wellers, "La Tragédie des deux journées," pp. 6–10; Adler, *The Jews of Paris*, pp. 106–111; Klarsfeld, *Vichy-Auschwitz. 1943–1944*, pp. 108, 237, 244.

7. Lévy and Tillard, *La Grande Rafle*, pp. 37–49; Minc, *L'Enfer des innocents*.

8. YIVO, coll. 343, file 4, *Bulletin d'informations de l'UGIF*, no. 24, July 27, 1942; Emmanuel Lefschetz, Testimony: "many young people and children were not arrested with their families on July 16. Hence there was an appreciable number of abandoned children."

9. Because of confusion it has been written that these children were "snatched from the Vel' d'hiv." Hammel, *Souviens-toi d'Amalek*, pp. 242, 435; Michel, *Les Éclaireurs israélites de France pendant la Seconde Guerre mondiale*, p. 144. With the exception of an infinitesimal number of escapees, there were no child survivors among those who were thrown into the Vélodrome d'hiver. See above, n. 2.

10. Odette Meyers, Testimony, (Melszpajz), November 2, 1979, "The Oral History Committee, The Holocaust Library and Research Center of San Francisco, Ca." See also Lucien Lazare, *Le Livre des Justes* (Paris: J. Cl. Lattès, 1993), pp. 74–77; YV, M31/3125.

11. Adler, *The Jews of Paris*, pp. 111, 188.

12. Rayski, "Paris face à la Grande Rafle," pp. 1–13.

13. Notebook of Denise Lefschetz.

14. YIVO, coll. 210, file XLV.1 to 6; file XLVI.1 to 6; file XLVIII.1 to 5.

15. Klarsfeld, *Memorial to the Jews Deported from France*.

16. YIVO, coll. 210, file XI.13 and 74.

17. YIVO, coll. 210, file XI.78.

18. YIVO, coll. 210, file XXXII.3; Adler, *The Jews of Paris*, p. 113.

19. Ibid., p. 116.

20. YIVO, coll. 343, file 16: July 1942, 35,269 francs; January 1943, 290,560 francs. The monthly allowance came to an average of 600 francs per child.

21. Ibid., file 101–103; YV, M31/62 and 3980.

22. CDJC, CDLXIX.53, and above, n. 20; YV, M31/4599; Lazare, *Livre des Justes*, pp. 34–38.

23. *L'Entraide temporaire*, pp. 1–24 and passim.

24. YV, O-9/22.5; *L'Entraide temporaire*, p. 10.

25. Ibid., pp. 4–5; photocopies of the account book of Sauvetage de l'enfance, years 1916–1917, in the author's possession.

26. Ravine, *La Résistance organisée des Juifs de France*, p. 109; Adler, *The Jews of Paris*, p. 191; Bulawko, *Les Jeux de la mort et de l'espoir*, pp. 38–40; YIVO, coll. 116, file 12.

27. Ravine, *La Résistance organisée des Juifs de France*, p. 193; Diamant, *Les Juifs dans la Résistance française*, pp. 139–140; see also above, ch. 10.

28. Rajsfus, *Des Juifs dans la collaboration. l'UGIF (1941–1944)*, p. 338.

29. YV, M31/62, 3980 and 4392; CDJC, CDLXVIII.17: Testimony of Mlle. Guillemot, director of the charity of the Temple de l'Oratoire du Louvre; Gilles Perrault, *L'Orchestre rouge* (Paris: Fayard, 1971), pp. 500–501; Diamant, *Les Juifs dans la Résistance française*, p. 129; Ravine, *La Résistance organisée des Juifs de France*, pp. 111–112; Adler, *The Jews of Paris*, pp. 198–199 (on the MNCR, see ibid., p. 187); *L'Entraide temporaire*, pp. 10–11; Robert Debré, *L'Honneur de vivre* (Paris: Hermann et Stock, 1974), pp. 228–231.

30. Ravine, *La Résistance organisée des Juifs de France*, pp. 111–112.

31. *L'Entraide temporaire*, pp. 10–11.

32. See above, ch. 10.

33. *L'Entraide temporaire*, pp. 10–11.

34. Lefschetz, Testimony.

35. See above, the operations of la Clairière, p. 000; Adler, *The Jews of Paris*, p. 149.

36. YIVO, coll. 210, file XI.7 and XI.75: manuscript "discharges" of detainees in Drancy, placing their children in the care of the UGIF.

37. YIVO, coll. 210, file XXI.24. E. Bloch was also alerted by a letter sent on November 12, 1942 by Léo Israélowicz of the Service no. 14 of the UGIF. The latter calls his attention to the presence of approximately 60 children of French nationality in Angoulême, whose parents were deported: "Check with the police to see what you can do." Cf. YIVO, coll. 210, file XI.10.

38. *L'Entraide temporaire*, pp. 26–30; see also the odyssey of André Schwarz-Bart from Angoulême to the École de travail, Rue des Rosiers, with the help of Rabbi Elie Bloch and the center in Rue Lamarck, related by Francine Kaufmann, *Pour relire Le Dernier des Justes* (Paris: Méridien-Klincksieck, 1986), pp. 15–16.

39. YIVO, coll. 210, file XCVIII.1.

40. Lambert, *Carnet d'un témoin (1940–1943)*, pp. 177–189.

41. Sarraute and Tager, eds., *Les Juifs sous L'occupation. Recueil des textes officiels français et allemands. 1940–1944*, pp. 163–164.

42. AN, F 1, III, 1193.

43. YIVO, coll. 245, XII-France, file A.29, HICEM report, unsigned, September 20, 1942.

44. Ibid.

45. Israël, *Heureux comme Dieu en France*, pp. 137–150; Michel, *Les Éclaireurs israélites de France pendant la Seconde Guerre mondiale*, p. 125.

46. Testimony of Denise Lévy, an agent of the *Sixième*, Paris, April 2, 1984, in the author's possession; Testimony of Denise Caraco-Sikierski, an agent of the *Sixième* and of

Service André, Jerusalem, January 26, 1984, in the author's possession; Testimony of Itzhak Mikaëli, agent of the *Sixième*, Jerusalem, February 14, 1984, in the author's possession; Hammel, *Souviens-toi d'Amalek*, p. 184; Michel, *Les Éclaireurs israélites de France pendant la Seconde Guerre mondiale*, pp. 125–126; Gamzon, *Les Eaux claires*, p. 58; Latour, *La Résistance juive en France (1940–1944)*, p. 39.

47. Andrée Salomon, Testimony, 1963, ICJ-OT (1)20.

48. YV, O-9.32–3: Ratner-Masur report, p. 45; *Activité des organisations juives*, p. 154; E. Papanek, *Out of the Fire* (New York: William Morrow, 1975), p. 250; Kieval, "Legality and Resistance in Vichy France," p. 355; YV, M31/3195; Anne-Marie Im Hof-Piguet, *La Filière. En France occupée, 1942–1944* (Yverdon-les-Bains: Edition de la Thiele, 1985); Lucien Lazare, "Réseaux de sauvetage des enfants juifs en France (1938–1944)," in Shmuel Trigano, ed., *La Société Juive à travers l'Histoire* 4 vols. (Paris: Fayard, 1993), 4: 472–483.

49. Klarsfeld, *Memorial*, convoys no. 28, 29, 30, 31, 33; *Activité des organisations juives*, p. 151.

50. Weill, *Contribution à l'histoire des camps d'internement dans l'Anti-France*, p. 204.

51. *Activité des organisations juives*, p. 151–152.

52. Andrée Salomon, Testimony.

53. Ibid.; Sadan, *Mahanot Ha-Hesger*, p. 72.

54. Weill, *Contribution à l'histoire des camps d'internement dans l'Anti-France*, p. 199.

55. Lambert, *Carnet d'un témoin (1940–1943)*, pp. 183–185.

56. Ibid., p. 188.

57. Fanny Loinger-Nezer, Testimony, Ramat-Gan, February 9, 1984, in the author's possession.

58. Nodot, "Résistance non violente 1940–1944," p. 24.

59. Delpech, "La persécution des Juifs et l'Amitié chrétienne," p. 170.

60. Soutou, "Souvenirs des années noires," pp. 9–14.

61. Delpech, "La persécution des Juifs et l'Amitié chrétienne," p. 169.

62. G. Garel, Testimony, ICJ-OT, (1)64.

63. Delpech, "La persécution des Juifs et l'Amitié chrétienne," pp. 204–207; Jean-Marie Soutou, Testimony, Neuilly, December 12, 1986, preserved by the author.

64. AN, F 1c III, 1200.

65. In moving testimony taken by H. Kieval in Paris in July 1972, Garel describes the scenes he witnessed in Vénissieux. Recording in Kieval's possession. He, too, was a member of the screening committee in Vénissieux with the AC team.

66. Ibid.; J. Weill, Testimony, Besançon, March 15, 1984, in the author's possession. The Vénissieux affair is mentioned in a large number of sources, where variants appear on certain points. Our version results from the comparison of these sources and multiple verifications. In addition to the sources cited above, notes 68–75, see CDJC, CCXVIII.104; Elisabeth Hirsch, Testimony, ICJ-OT, (1)60; Renée Neher-Bernheim, Testimony, Jerusalem, February 14, 1984, in the author's possession; G. Lesage, Testimony, Jerusalem, May 22, 1985, in the author's possession; F. Hammel, Testimony, Jerusalem, February 22, 1984, in the author's possession; "Livre de raison du docteur André Bernheim," unpublished, n.d. [1964], pp. 37–38; Weill, *Contribution à l'histoire des camps d'internement dans l'Anti-France*, pp. 206–208; Kieval, "Legality and Resistance in Vichy France," pp. 144–145; Latour, *La Résistance juive en France (1940–1944)*, pp. 58–61; Hammel, *Souviens-toi d'Amalek*, p. 373; Nodot, *Les enfants ne partiront pas!*, pp.14–17; Ravine, *La Résistance organisée des Juifs de France*, pp. 125–126 (the latter version verges on fantasy); H. Noguères, *Histoire de la Résistance en France de 1940 à 1945*, (Paris: Robert Lafffont,

1969), 2: 540; Marrus and Paxton, *Vichy France and the Jews*, p. 272; Bauer, *American Jewry and the Holocaust*, pp. 246–247; Lucien Lazare, *L'Abbé Glasberg* (Paris: Cerf, 1990), pp. 11–18.

67. YV, M31/1807; *Activité des organisations juives*, pp. 156–158.

68. YIVO, coll. 343, file 33.

69. Dispatch 2765 P, telegram no. 12 393 and telegram no. 12 519, reproduced in Sarraute and Tager, eds., *Les Juifs sous l'Occupation*, pp. 163–164.

70. Report of Chief Commissioner Mortier, Vichy, October 5, 1942, preserved by Gilbert Lesage. Lesage was arrested on April 8, 1944, for "interference with government policy and the divulgation to those concerned of measures that were going to be taken against them." His agency was dissolved by a law of June 25, 1944.

71. Lesage, Testimony.

72. *Activité des organisations juives*, pp. 156–157; Kieval, "Legality and Resistance in Vichy France," p. 360.

73. See a list of these organizations in *Activité des organisations juives*, p. 160.

74. YIVO, coll. 343, file 113.4.

75. Transferred after the war by the CICR to the International Organization of Refugees in London, today these lists are preserved in the Archives nationales in Paris, numbered AJ 43 16, file 56.292.

76. YV, M31/5061; M. Abadi, Testimony, Paris, April 3, 1984, in the author's possession; Morvan Lebesque, "Les chasseurs d'enfants," *Carrefour*, nos. 218, 219, 220 (November 16, 23, December 1, 1948); *Activité des organisations juives*, p. 169–171.

77. On the structure of the Garel network, see *Activité des organisations juives*, pp. 156–166.

78. The border crossing operations are described below. See Eva Cohn-Mendelsohn, Testimony, London, November 15, 1983, in the author's possession. In October 1940 she was deported from Offenbourg to Gurs and then to Rivesaltes, taken in charge by an OSE shelter, returned to Rivesaltes by the French gendarmerie in August 1942, saved again by the OSE and put back in the same shelter. Finally she was escorted to Switzerland in 1943.

79. YIVO, coll. 242, XII-France, file a. 46.

80. R. Job and G. Garel, Testimony, taken by H. Kieval, Paris, July 27 and 30, 1972. Recordings in Kieval's possession.

81. *Activité des organisations juives*, pp. 171–179.

82. S. Klarsfeld, *Les Enfants d'Izieu, une tragédie juive* (Paris: Serge Klarsfeld, 1984), see esp. pp. 27–32.

83. Lambert, *Carnet d'un témoin (1940–1943)*, pp. 59, 244, 291–292; *Activité des organisations juives*, pp. 173–174.

84. Ibid.; Lévy, "Souvenirs d'un médecin d'enfants à l'OSE en France occupée et en Suisse, 1940–1943," p. 26.

85. *Activité des organisations juives*, p. 147.

86. CDJC, XXII.9. The action is described in an underground newspaper of the UJRE, *Notre voix*, no. 76 (July 15, 1944).

87. Lesage Archives, Circular no. 76 of the Police du territoire et des étrangers regarding the reception of foreign workers, January 2, 1942.

88. Ibid., Circular no. 337, May 26, 1942.

89. Arch. AJDC, coll. France, file 602.13, list of names; EIF archives, "Rapport sur les activités des EIF," July 30, 1942, unnumbered.

90. Denise Lévy, Testimony; Roger Fichtenberg, agent of the *Sixième*, Testimony, Paris, April 4, 1984, in the author's possession; Michel, *Les Éclaireurs israélites de France pendant la Seconde Guerre mondiale*, p. 125.

91. Until then, this directorate, the fourth, comprised five divisions: administration, scouting, youth movements, the work of young people, physical education. The "Sixth Division" appears in reports submitted to the UGIF following July 30, 1942. EIF archive, unnumbered.

92. Ibid.

93. On this decision see Michel, *Les Éclaireurs israélites de France pendant la Seconde Guerre mondiale*, pp. 128–132.

94. Lefschetz, Testimony; Michel, *Les Éclaireurs israélites de France pendant la Seconde Guerre mondiale*, p. 165; Latour, *La Résistance juive en France (1940–1944)*, p. 79.

95. CDJC, XXXVII.9, quoted by Rutkowski, *La Lutte des Juifs en France à l'époque de l'Occupation*, pp. 208–209.

96. Georges Schneck, Testimony, Brussels, April 30, 1984, in the author's possession.

97. Fichtenberg, Testimony; see also the "register" of La Grave, open and in code, preserved by Fichtenberg.

98. Arch. LB, AR 3987, 586 to 606: Extract from Radio-Bulletin no. 242, issued in Washington, October 15, 1942, as released by the American Embassy at Vichy, October 16, 1942; Conversation with Mr. Bousquet, Secretary-General of the Police, Vichy, October 16, signed: Donald A. Lowrie; Notes on Conferences at Vichy, October 16, 1942, regarding Children's Emigration, signed: Lindsley H. Noble; letter from D. A. Lowrie, Marseilles, October 17, 1942, to Fourcade, Vichy; Notes on Conferences at Marseille, October 19, 1942, regarding Children's Emigration; Diary of Emergency Emigration of Jewish Refugee Children, Marseille, Oct. 16 to Nov. 4, signed: L. H. Noble; Marrus and Paxton, *Vichy France and the Jews*, p. 239. The authors quote a source (Szajkowski, *Analytical Franco-Jewish Gazetteer*, p. 74) according to which, "350 children succeeded in emigrating secretly to the United States after that date." In our opinion this could only refer to cases of illegal crossing of the Spanish border by entire families, mostly prior to November 1942, but whose departure from Lisbon to the United States occurred after that date. The number indicated by that source seems too high. A convoy of twelve wards of the OSE, taken to Spain by the AJ in August 1944, later left for Palestine.

99. J. Weill, Testimony; E. Heymann, *Le Camp du bout du monde* (Lausanne: Pierre Marcel Favre, 1983).

100. I. Mikaëli, Testimony.

101. CDJC, XXXVII.2, police report dated October 20, 1942. The information possessed by the police was exact. Claude Gutman had directed the EIF in Lyons for two years. After the police uncovered his underground activity, he was transferred and became responsible for the *Sixième* in Nice. He was denounced and arrested by the Gestapo in September 1943 and died in deportation.

102. Jail book kept by the German border guard of people detained at the Hotel Pax in Annemasse, from September 1943 to August 1944, preserved by the Annemasse municipality.

103. Hammel, *Souviens-toi d'Amalek*, pp. 206, 449–551; Latour, *La Résistance juive en France (1940–1944)*, pp. 166–169; Michel, *Les Éclaireurs israélites de France pendant la Seconde Guerre mondiale*, pp. 161–163; Weill, *Déjà! . . . Essai autobiographique*, pp. 241–242; Nodot, "Résistance non violente 1940–1944," p. 46; [Jeanne Merle d'Aubigné], *Les Clandestins de Dieu* (Paris: Fayard, 1968), pp. 147–148 and 169–170. The poem writ-

ten in detention by Marianne Cohn, "Je trahirai demain," is reproduced in Latour, *La Résistance juive en France (1940–1944)*, p. 157.

104. AN, AJ 43 16 file 56.292.

105. This number refers to those under eighteen. The estimate includes children who remained in the UGIF centers in Paris until July 1944 but who escaped deportation. See below.

106. Klarsfeld, *Memorial*.

107. Ibid., list no. 74 and the following pages.

108. L. Poliakov, *L'Étoile jaune* (Paris: Editions du Centre, 1949), p. 41.

109. 2.5% of these had emigrated overseas. See YIVO, coll. 245, XII-France, file A.24.

110. Testimony of A. Akerberg, agent of the *Sixième*, Paris, November 18, 1985, in the author's possession; Rajsfus, *Des Juifs dans la collaboration. l'UGIF (1941–1944)*, pp. 258–260.

111. Ibid.; Adler, *The Jews of Paris*, p. 153; Cohen, *Ha-Hanhaga Ha-Yehudit*, p. 101.

112. CDJC, CCXVIII.7, CCXXI.26, 27; Adler, *The Jews of Paris*, p. 153. Although she had been left free, Marie Zalmanski, a school teacher from the center on L'Avenue Secrétan, left with her pupils for Drancy and then Auschwitz, where she was gassed. See Leah Raich, Testimony, Paris, February 24, 1986, in the author's possession.

113. Rajsfus, *Des Juifs dans la collaboration. l'UGIF (1941–1944)*, pp. 321–326; Adler, *The Jews of Paris*, p. 154. See the letter from Léo Cohn, written in Drancy, preserved in the Lublin archives, file 4.

114. Testimony of Darville and Wichène, as well as that of Georges Harden, quoted by Klarsfeld in his note regarding convoy no. 77, show that the UGIF children were isolated, unlike those deported with their parents. That is why it seems closer to the truth to set the number of UGIF wards included in this convoy at 250 rather than 300, the figure given by other authors such as Adler, *The Jews of Paris*, pp. 154; Rajsfus, *Des Juifs dans la collaboration. l'UGIF (1941–1944)*, pp. 321–326; Cohen, *Ha-Hanhaga Ha-Yehudit*, p. 101.

115. YV, P.7, 16: CRIF, jury d'honneur, session of January 14, 1945; Adler, *The Jews of Paris*, pp. 154–155.

116. CDJC, XXVIII.159, XCI.29, report dated May 18, 1943, quoted by Rutkowski, *La Lutte des Juifs en France à l'époque de l'Occupation*, pp. 172–174; Cohen, *Ha-Hanhaga Ha-Yehudit*, p. 95.

117. *Activité des organisations juives*, pp. 209–212.

118. CDJC, XXVIII.159, XCI.29.

119. YIVO, coll. 210, file IV.4, *L'un des trente-six*; *Activité des organisations juives*, pp. 212–213.

120. Cohen, *Ha-Hanhaga Ha-Yehudit*, p. 95. Adler mentions neither the Antignac report nor the arrests in rue de la Bienfaisance.

121. Leah Raich, "La Wizo sous l'Occupation," *La Terre retrouvée*, 4 (156), February 1, 1945; Joseph Ariel [Fischer], "Jewish Self-Defense and Resistance in France During World War II," *Yad Vashem Studies*, 6 (1967): 230; Rajsfus, *Des Juifs dans la collaboration. l'UGIF (1941–1944)*, pp. 321–326.

122. YV, 0.9, 32.3, Ratner-Masur report, p. 28; See "Comme des brebis . . . ," p. 89.

123. YIVO, coll. 210, file XI.75. The children had been placed in the Indre-et-Loire and Sarthe departments. The report of the investigation is dated November 5, 1942.

124. YIVO, coll. 343, file 113.4.

125. YV, coll. 343, file 113.4; A. Salomon, Testimony; Friedlander, *Quand vient le souvenir*, p. 72.

126. YIVO, coll. 340.3 and 170. There is no need to mention here the six children captured in August 1942 in the AIP center in Marseilles. They were handed over to the UGIF by the authorities and placed with the OSE.

127. Kieval, "Legality and Resistance in Vichy France," p. 366.

128. Cohen, *Ha-Hanhaga Ha-Yehudit*, p. 100.

129. YV, P.7, 16, CRIF, decision made on December 3, 1946.

130. YV, P.7, 9, Z. Lewin, the financial manager of the Fifth Direction, the Second Section of the UGIF (administering the charity organization of the dissolved FSJF) confirms his resignation from the general directorate of the UGIF on October 13, 1943.

131. YV, P.7, 3.2, clandestine press of the UJRE and the MNCR.

132. YV, P.7, 13, report by Jarblum entitled, "UGIF," written one year after the liberation.

133. YIVO, coll. 210, file XCII.2: in a letter of April 7, 1944 to Edinger, the president of the UGIF in Paris, Geissmann, at that time the director of UGIF-south, "recommends the closure of UGIF-south."

134. JTS, French Documents, box 15, protocol of the deliberations of the CRIF, July-August 1944.

135. YV, P17, 13.

136. YV, 0.9, 27 and 3.2, clandestine publication of the UJRE, February 15, 1944; Cohen, *Ha-Hanhaga Ha-Yehudit*, p. 137; Rayski, *Nos illusions perdues*, p. 134.

137. Denise Gamzon, Testimony, Jerusalem, April 17, 1985, preserved by the author; Michel, *Les Éclaireurs israélites de France pendant la Seconde Guerre mondiale*, p. 109.

138. Klarsfeld, *Vichy-Auschwitz*.

139. Cohen, *Ha-Hanhaga Ha-Yehudit*, p. 207.

140. Rayski, *Nos illusions perdues*, pp. 126–129.

141. Delpech, "La persécution des Juifs et l'Amitié chrétienne," p. 195, contribution by W. Rabi at the colloquium.

142. André Neher, *Jérusalem, vécu juif et message* (Monaco: Editions du Rocher, 1984), pp. 165–166, 173; Hammel, *Souviens-toi d'Amalek*, p. 30.

143. YIVO, coll. 239, *Carnet* of J. Bielinky, entry of November 19, 1940.

144. Ibid., entries of June 2–July 7, 1942; Marrus and Paxton, *Vichy France and the Jews*, p. 239, quoting the *Manchester Guardian* of August 4, 1942, a report that the symbol "J.U.I.F." worn by the students was that of a pretended "Jeunesse universitaire intellectuelle française"; Poliakov, *L'Étoile jaune*, pp. 78–86; Lazare, "Juin 1942: les nazis ordonnent le port de l'étoile jaune."

145. Several dozens of them paid for this courage with several weeks of detention in Drancy; Poliakov, *L'Étoile jaune*.

146. Maison diocésaine de Paris, Archives historiques, 3B 6 [1], 4. The circular calls the act committed "a flagrant violation of the laws of private or public morality." One of the priests, an auxiliary vicar, was relieved of his functions. The other was deprived of his title as first honorary vicar. We are grateful to Cardinal Lustiger, the Archbishop of Paris, for permitting us to consult this document.

147. YIVO, coll. 116, file 42. The author of this report, Spanien, frequently shuttled between Lisbon and Marseilles. See above.

148. Marrus and Paxton, *Vichy France and the Jews*, pp. 263–269; G. Wellers, *De Drancy à Auschwitz* (Paris: Editions du Centre, 1946), pp. 55–58; Klarsfeld, *Memorial*, convoys 20–25.

149. Report of Pastor Boegner before the general assembly of French Protestantism, October 24, 1945.

150. AN, F^lc III, file 1143–1204; Marrus and Paxton, *Vichy France and the Jews*, pp. 145, 270–279.

151. AN, F^lc III, file 1200. Lemoine, the Regional Prefect of Limoges, noted on September 6, 1942, after having described the deportation of a convoy of 446 people constituted in the Nexon camp: "Many Jews are still in the region, where they show themselves to be distinctly undesirable, grabbing alimentary products in scandalous proportions. Concentration measures would permit the limiting of this harmful activity."

152. Ibid.

153. Ibid., file 1204. On October 5, 1942, Cheneaux de Leyritz, the Prefect of Toulouse, describes a "profound reaction . . . following the sending of certain categories of foreign Jews to the occupied zone. . . . These operations fed the propaganda of the adversaries of the government."

154. *Gardes mobiles de réserve.*

155. AN, F^lc III, file 1201.

156. Ibid., file 1156.

157. *Les Cahiers du TC*, nos. 4 and 5, March 1942.

158. *Cahiers Paul Claudel 7. La figure d'Israël* (Paris: Gallimard, 1968), pp. 325–326. Copies of this letter even circulated in the Drancy camp. Informed, the police searched the poet's home. See ibid., pp. 164–165 and 327–333. I am grateful to Denise Gamzon for indicating this source.

159. Kriegel, *Réflexion sur les questions juives*, pp. 34–39. Kriegel emphasizes the ambivalences of the underground PC organization, which condemned anti-Semitism and wrote that the Nazis collaborated with Jewish capitalists.

160. *Franc-Tireur*, no. 121, (September 1942); *Combat*, no. 34 (September 1942); *Le Populaire*, no. 6 (October 15, 1942); *L'Insurgé*, no. 8 (October 1942); see also Kriegel, *Réflexion sur les questions juives*, pp. 34–39; H. R. Kedward, *Resistance in Vichy France* (Oxford: Oxford University Press, 1978), pp. 182–184.

161. AN, F^lc III, file 1154, 1203, reports of October 5, 1942.

162. Ibid., file 1143.

163. In the words of Jean Chelini, *L'Église sous Pie XII. La tourmente, 1939–1945* (Paris, 1983), p. 224.

164. J. Duquesne, *Les Catholiques français sous l'Occupation* (Paris: Grasset, 1966), p. 262.

165. AN, F^lc III, file 1143 and 1150 especially.

166. According to Henri Michel, "Awareness of the total wickedness of Nazism and the general movement of revolt that it provoked were born in many cases of the flate inflicted upon the Jews." See H. Michel, "Jewish Resistance and the European Resistance Movement." For an overall view of rescue of Jews by non-Jews, see Lazare, *Le Livre des justes.*

167. Cf. YIVO, coll. 343, file 67, 101–103 (file of cards containing the reports of the visiting social workers) and 113.4 (reports of the visits to 119 children placed in the Nièvre Department).

168. YIVO, coll. 343, file 60.

169. YIVO, coll. 104, file 332, 333.

170. A prudent estimate, taking into account that certain rescue operations were carried out jointly by two or more networks, each taking charge of the children who were saved. The allocation by network in the northern zone is as follows: WIZO and OSE: 2,000 children saved; Rue Amelot: 900; Solidarité: 500; *Sixième* and *Éducation physique*: 3,000.

Chapter 12. The Jewish Underground: Solidarity and Vitality

1. Lambert, *Carnet d'un témoin (1940–1943)*, p. 199.

2. Klarsfeld, *Vichy-Auschwitz*, pp. 186–187.

3. Lambert, *Carnet d'un témoin (1940–1943)*, p. 187; see above, ch. 11.

4. Émilienne Eychenne, *Les Portes de la liberté, le franchissement clandestin de la frontière espagnole dans les Pyrénées-Orientales* (Toulouse: Editions Privat, 1985), pp. 126, 134, 135. The measure was the object of a Vichy law dated January 20, 1943 and of a decree defining the boundaries of the reserved zone, presented on February 18. See Émilienne Eychenne, *Les Pyrénées de la liberté* (Paris: France-Empire, 1983), pp. 337–338.

5. Kapel, *Un rabbin dans la tourmente (1940–1944)*, pp. 91–96; Lambert, *Carnet d'un témoin (1940–1943)*, p. 205.

6. *Activité des organisations juives*, p. 209; Lambert, *Carnet d'un témoin (1940–1943)*, p. 201; Cohen, *Ha-Hanhaga Ha-Yehudit*, pp. 175–182.

7. Sarraute and Trager, eds., *Les Juifs sous l'Occupation*, p. 172.

8. Klarsfeld, *Vichy-Auschwitz*, p. 13.

9. CDJC, LIV. 41; EIF archives, unnumbered; Michel, *Les Éclaireurs israélites de France pendant la Seconde Guerre mondiale*, p. 129.

10. Klarsfeld, *Vichy-Auschwitz*, pp. 13, 15; below, p. 000.

11. Michel, *Les Éclaireurs israélites de France pendant la Seconde Guerre mondiale*, p. 132.

12. Kapel, *Un rabbin dans la tourmente (1940–1944)*, pp. 96–97; see also the summary of the report of the Chief Rabbi of France, Lyons, February 28, 1942, preserved by Kapel.

13. Klarsfeld, *Vichy-Auschwitz*, pp. 20–21.

14. See the report of the Chaplain General, Hirschler, ibid., pp. 206–211.

15. Ibid., p. 21.

16. YV, P7.9; CDJC, XLVI. A.; Klarsfeld, *Vichy-Auschwitz*, p. 26.

17. Ibid., pp. 24–25, 249–254. The police planned to arrest 7,317 Jews in Paris and the suburbs, but 5,748 of them had fled their homes.

18. Ibid., p. 150.

19. Ibid., p. 105.

20. Richard Cohen, introduction to Lambert, *Carnet d'un témoin (1940–1943)*, p. 50.

21. JTS box 13, file 1, letters from December 30, 1942, May 12 and 13, July 30, and August 2, 1943.

22. Richard Cohen, introduction, p. 51.

23. Ibid. Cohen also retains the hypothesis of hidden complicity between Lambert and the Resistance.

24. Dika Jefroykin, Testimony, CDJC, file of testimony gathered by Anny Latour, unnumbered [1969], p. 13; Michel, *Les Éclaireurs israélites de France pendant la Seconde Guerre mondiale*, pp.145–146.

25. Isaac Schneersohn, "Naissance du CDJC," *Le Monde juif*, no. 7 (1953), pp. 4–5; Lambert, *Carnet d'un témoin (1940–1943)*, p. 220, n. 1860; Poliakov, *L'Auberge des musiciens*, p. 164.

26. *Activité des organisations juives*, pp. 26–29; Pierrard, *Le Grand rabbin Kaplan. Justice pour la foi juive*, p. 76.

27. "Livre de raison du docteur André Bernheim," pp. 37–38. This text refers to the synagogue on quai Tilsitt in Lyons.

28. Ibid.; Pierrard, *Le Grand rabbin Kaplan. Justice pour la foi juive*, p. 76.

29. *Activité des organisations juives*, p. 28.

30. Pierrard, *Le Grand rabbin Kaplan. Justice pour la foi juive*, pp. 103, 105–106; Kaplan, *N'oublie pas*, p. 152.

31. Klarsfeld, *Vichy-Auschwitz*, pp. 170–171.

32. Ibid.

33. The members of their families met the same tragic fate.

34. Consistoire Central, *Mémorial en souvenir de nos rabbins et ministres-officiants victimes de la barbarie nazie* (Paris: J. Jacobs, 1947).

35. Kriegel, "De la résistance juive," p. 97.

36. In December 1942 the Chief Rabbi of France proposed disobeying the decree instituting the stamping of identity papers and ration cards with the word "juif." The majority of the Consistory rejected this proposition so as not to "expose ourselves to sanctions that could have the result of suppressing the Jewish religion in France." See Maurice Moch, unpublished MS. The fragment quoted here was made available to us by Chief Rabbi Kaplan.

37. Kapel, *Un rabbin dans la tourmente (1940–1944)*, p. 42.

38. YIVO, coll. 221 and coll. 340, file 33; Cohen, *Ha-Hanhaga Ha-Yehudit*, p. 190.

39. Léo Ansbacher, Testimony recorded by Haïm Avni, ICJ-OT, (1), Jerusalem 1962.

40. Ibid; Hammel, *Souviens-toi d'Amalek*, p. 205.

41. Jeanne Merle d'Aubigné in *Les Clandestins de Dieu*, pp. 86–91.

42. A letter of August 2, 1943 from Chief Rabbi Schwartz and from President Heilbronner to the head of the government protesting against the arrest of André Baur in Paris and against the regime of terror instituted in the Drancy camp by SS Brunner, as well as an appeal by Lambert to the president of the council on August 14 were the final Jewish addresses to high places. See JTS, box 13, file 1 and Lambert, *Carnet d'un témoin (1940–1943)*, p. 236.

43. Constituted in Rome after the fall of Mussolini, July 25, 1943.

44. Klarsfeld, *Vichy-Auschwitz*, pp. 13–15, 198.

45. Ibid., p. 199.

46. Ibid., pp. 38, 46; the letter in which Himmler asks Ribbentrop in January 1943 to intervene with the Duce is preserved in NA, "Alexandria," German Records, FM 4383 (2580642–3); Daniel Karpi, *Bein Shevet le-Hesed* (*Between Punishment and Mercy*, Hebrew), (Jerusalem: Zalman Shazar Center for Jewish History, 1993, pp. 135–136.

47. JTS, box 13, file 1, letter from President Heilbronner addressed on May 12, 1943 to Jardin, the director of Laval's cabinet. On the policies of the Italian, French, and German authorities in the Italian zone, see Léon Poliakov, *La Condition des Juifs en France sous l'occupation italienne* (Paris: Editions du Centre, 1946); Marrus and Paxton, *Vichy France and the Jews*, p. 315–320; Carpi, *Bein Shevet le-Hesed*, pp. 105–234; Klarsfeld, *Vichy-Auschwitz*, passim.

48. Ibid., pp. 31–36.

49. Eytan Guinat [Otto Giniewski], Testimony, Jerusalem, November 1985, in the author's possession.

50. Hammel, *Souviens-toi d'Amalek*, pp. 169 and 425.

51. YV, 09.22–3.

52. Henry Phorylès, Testimony, ICJ,OT (1) 67, Jerusalem [1962]; Poliakov, *L'Auberge des musiciens*, p. 127.

53. YV, 0.0.22–3; EIF archives, unnumbered; Hammel, *Souviens-toi d'Amalek*, p. 171.

54. Hammel, *Souviens-toi d'Amalek*, p. 170; Giniewski, Testimony.

55. YV, 09.22–3; CDJC, CCXX; Hammel, *Souviens-toi d'Amalek*, p. 115.

56. Fichtenberg archives, Paris.

57. YIVO, coll. 340, file 26; Poliakov, *L'Auberge des musiciens*, p. 115.

58. Marrus and Paxton, *Vichy France and the Jews*, p. 318; Klarsfeld, *Vichy-Auschwitz*, p. 309; Rutkowski, *La Lutte des Juifs en France à l'époque de l'Occupation*, pp. 320.

59. Ignace Fink, Testimony, Paris 1947, unpublished, p. 3.

60. CDJC, I.65 and CCXVIII.22, reproduced partially by Rutkowski, *La Lutte des Juifs en France à l'époque de l'Occupation*, pp. 318–323; Marrus and Paxton, *Vichy France and the Jews*, p. 319.

61. Ibid., p. 291; Henri Michel, "Les relations franco-italiennes (de l'armistice de juin 1940 à l'armistice de septembre 1943)" in *La Guerre en Méditerranée, 1939–1945*, acts of an international colloquium held in Paris, April 8–11, 1969 (Paris, 1971), pp. 503–504.

62. Klarsfeld, *Vichy-Auschwitz*, pp. 261–262.

63. YIVO, coll. 116, file 35; Fink, Testimony, pp. 7–8; Rutkowski, *La Lutte des Juifs en France à l'époque de l'Occupation*, pp. 319–320; Klarsfeld, *Vichy-Auschwitz*, pp. 49–50.

64. Ibid., pp. 51, 80; YIVO, coll. 116, file 25.

65. CDJC, CDLXXI; Fink, Testimony, p. 12.

66. CDJC, CCIV.20; Poliakov, *La Condition des Juifs en France sous l'occupation italienne*, p. 23; Marrus and Paxton, *Vichy France and the Jews*, p. 320; Alberto Cavaglion, *Nella Notte Straniera, Gli Ebrei Di S. Martin Vesubia* (Cuneo: L'Arciere, 1981), p. 30.

67. Lublin archives, file 5.1 and 9; David Blum, Testimony, Brussels, October 17, 1983, in the author's possession.

68. YIVO, coll. 116, file 25.

69. CDJC, CCXVIII.22; Léon Papeleux, "Le Vatican et le problème juif en 1943 (III)," *Revue d'histoire de la Second Guerre mondiale*, no. 115 (July 1979), pp. 60 ff.

70. YIVO, coll. 116, file 25.

71. CDJC, CCXVIII.22.

72. Fink, Testimony, p. 18; YIVO, coll. 104, file 732; Blum, Testimony; Louise Maury-Saba, Testimony, Toulouse, April 9, 1984, in the author's possession; Klarsfeld, *Vichy-Auschwitz*, pp. 113–114, 115–117. A report of the SEC in Nice to the director of the SEC in Vichy affirms that "the yacht Sarina, anchored in Cannes, left that city on September 6, for Corsica, with 1,000 on board. The price of the journey ranged between 30,000 and 50,000 francs." (See CDJC, XXVII.1). The contents of this report seem fanciful. Research conducted at the maritime register of Cannes and in the yacht's log as well as the testimony of Jews who were living in Cannes at that date have not brought to light the slightest trace of this supposed craft. I am grateful to Henri Grosmann for the research he conducted in Cannes.

73. Klarsfeld, *Vichy-Auschwitz*, p. 116; Fink, Testimony, p. 10; Rutkowski, *La Lutte des Juifs en France à l'époque de l'Occupation*, p. 321.

74. Cavaglion, *Nella Notte Straniera, Gli Ebrei Di S. Martin Vesubia*, pp. 98–106; Klarsfeld, *Memorial*, convoys of December 7 and 17, 1943.

75. Klarsfeld, *Vichy-Auschwitz*, pp. 117–120, 124; Poliakov, *L'Auberge des musiciens*, pp. 122–125; Mary Felstiner, "Alois Brunner," *Simon Wiesenthal Center Annual*, 3 (1986): 1–46.

76. Marrus and Paxton, *Vichy France and the Jews*, p. 320.

77. Klarsfeld, *Vichy-Auschwitz*, p. 125.

78. Fink, Testimony, p. 125; Rutkowski, *La Lutte des Juifs en France à l'époque de l'Occupation*, pp. 198–200.

79. Central Zionist Archives, S26.1545: Raymond Heymann, "Le groupe Maurice Cachoud né le 8 septembre 1943 à Nice," Nice, December 1945, unpublished; Fink, Testimony, p. 28; Lublin archives, file 5.3 and 5.

80. Poliakov, *L'Auberge des musiciens*, pp. 128–137.

81. Heymann, "Le groupe Maurice Cachoud." The following quotations are frequently taken from the same source.

82. Ibid., see below, ch. 14.

83. CDJC, CCXV, 16.

84. CDJC, XXXVII.9 and CCCLXVI.64; Polonski archives, D2.50; on the convoys to Switzerland, see above, ch. 11, pp. 000–000.

85. Lublin archives, file 5.2 and 3 and file 12; see below, ch 16.

86. These numbers are taken from the research of Serge Klarsfeld, *Vichy-Auschwitz*, pp. 117–120, 124, and passim, notices of convoys nos. 66–77.

87. Polonski archives, D5.8,9 and 10, letters from Weintrob and Appenzeller, detainees in Drancy; Lublin archives, file 20.8 and 16.

88. Ibid., and file 20.4

89. Claude Lanzmann, *Shoah* (Paris: Fayard, 1985), p. 186.

Chapter 13. The Primacy of Tendencies Toward Unity and the Dynamism of Spiritual Life

1. Adam Rayski, "L'impact du soulèvement du ghetto de Varsovie en France occupée," summary report of the round table of the CDJC held on April 17, 1983, *Le Monde juif*, no. 114 (April–June 1984): 63; Diamant, *Les Juifs dans la Résistance française*, p. 224; Adler, *The Jews of Paris*, p. 203.

2. Adam Rayski, "Gestapo contre résistants juifs, *Le Monde juif*, no. 55 (1969), pp. 11–20; idem, *Nos illusions perdues*, p. 144. Among the victims caught in this trap was Henri Krasucki, a leader of the UJJ.

3. Adam Rayski, "Les immigrés dans la Résistance," *Les Nouveaux Cahiers*, no. 37 (summer 1974): 16.

4. Rayski, *Nos illusions perdues*, p. 133.

5. Ibid.

6. Or of the Comintern, according to the version of Charles Tillon, who was then the head of the FTP and a member of the PC directorate. See *Le Monde*, July 25, 1985.

7. Rayski, *Nos illusions perdues*, p. 145; idem, "Les immigrés," p. 16; Stéphane Courtois, "Les scandales de l'affaire Manouchian," *Le Nouvel Observateur*, no. 1077 (June 28, 1985); Irène Allier, "Les vengeurs sublimes de la MOI," ibid. The same sources mention an action similar to that of Rayski's, attempted by Manouchian, who wanted to transfer his men "to Marseilles and Grenoble, where significant colonies of Armenians lived." His demand was also rejected.

8. Rayski, *Nos illusions perdues*, p. 147. But the fighters of the second detachment who escaped were sent in Paris itself to two new FTP units, commanded respectively by Manouchian and Marcel Rayman.

9. Henri Michel, *Histoire de la Résistance en France* (Paris: Presses Universitaires de France, 1975), p. 48.

10. Rayski, *Nos illusions perdues*, p. 233.

11. Diamant, *Les Juifs dans la Résistance française*, p. 233; Ravine, *La Résistance organisée des Juifs de France*, p. 154; Adler, *The Jews of Paris*, pp. 205–206; Adam Rayski, "Le Comité juif de défense: son rôle dans la résistance juive en France," *Le Monde juif*, no. 52 (October–December 1968): 22–35.

12. Adler, *The Jews of Paris*, p. 208 quotes the protocols of the unity committee in Paris, preserved by the Institut Maurice Thorez. Adler indicates that Toni Stern represented the UGIF in the unity committee. She was in fact the delegate of the youth networks. T. Stern resigned from the UGIF council "for reasons of health," and Dr. Didier Hesse replaced her. See YIVO, coll. 310, file XLIII.6.

13. Poliakov, *L'Auberge des musiciens*, p. 128. The author describes the arrest and execution of Georges Spolianski on pp. 140–144.

14. Rayski, "Le Comité," pp. 29–35.

15. Diamant, *Les Juifs dans la Résistance française*, p. 233 writes that the CGD distributed 4 million francs in assistance per month. According to the same source, a total sum of a million francs was allocated to the UJRE. *Activité des organisations juives*, pp. 85–88. A coded extract from this report cited on p. 86 reads: "150 adults and children have been placed in the sanatorium of Dr. Maro [Marc], 35 in that of Dr. Halévy." This means: 150 adults and children have secretly crossed the border to Switzerland (named "the sanatorium of Dr. Marc" after the President of the FSJF, Marc Jarblum, who had taken refuge in Geneva in March 1943), 35 in Spain ("Dr. Halévy" refers to the great Spanish Jewish poet of the twelfth century, Judah Halevy).

16. A copy of *Unzer Qempf* is preserved in the Lublin archives. See an analysis of this issue in Rayski, "Le Comité," pp. 29–35.

17. YIVO, coll. 116, file 8; Faivel Schrager, *Oifn Rund fun Tsvey Tqoufess* (Paris: self-published, 1976); Pinches Szmajer, "La Guerre, clandestinité et résistance," *Combat pour la Diaspora*, no. 4 (third trimester, 1980); Minc, *L'Enfer des innocents*.

18. But Jacoubovitch reached the southern zone in May 1943, a few days before Rapoport's arrest.

19. Adler, *The Jews of Paris*, p. 164. The discord between the Communists and Bundists continued to be manifest even after the formation of the GCD. See *Notre voix*, no. 70 (March 1944), which denounces the Bund's refusal to sign a motion of the CGD saluting the Red Army: YV 09–3.2.

20. *Unzer Wort*, May 15, 1943, quoted by Rayski, *Nos illusions perdues*, p. 137.

21. *Jeune Combat*, no. 4, Toulouse (November 5, 1944), preserved by YV, 09–3.1. On the crisis of Jewish consciousness among the chiefs of the UJRE, see Rayski, *Nos illusions perdues*, pp. 135–142. On the echo given to the Warsaw Ghetto Uprising by the UJRE and MNCR press, see Rayski, ed., *La Presse antiraciste sous l'occupation hitlérienne*; *Notre Voix* (May 15 and June 1, 1943), no. 71 (April 1944), pp. 87, 89, 179–180; *Droit et Liberté*, no. 4 (April 1944): 161, undated leaflets, pp. 183–189, 191–193; *J'accuse*, no. 14 (June 1943), pp. 311–312; Rayski, ed., *Dos Vort fun Vidershtant un Zieg*; *Unzer Wort*, no. 59 (June 15, 1943): 165–167, 176–176, 179–180, leaflets of May 1943 and April 1944, pp. 171–172, 251–253.

22. Polonski archives, file D5.25.

23. Ibid., and Lublin archives, file 6.

24. Sarraute and Tager, eds., *Les Juifs sous l'Occupation*, p. 72.

25. "Livre de raison du docteur André Bernheim," pp. 42–43.

26. Five copies of *Sois chic* are preserved by the author. On the subject of the KKL bulletin, see *Activité des organisations juives*, pp. 182–183.

27. YV, P7.4. On the subject of the Zionist socialist bulletins, see Rutkowski, *La Lutte des Juifs en France à l'époque de l'Occupation*, pp. 179, 187–188, 204–205.

28. The first issue of *Quand même* is reproduced in plates in Knout, *Contribution à l'histoire de la résistance juive en France*, pp. 96–97. Number 2 is preserved by BDIC, 4°P

363 Rés. To our knowledge, nothing remains of the other issues. See also, Latour, *La Résistance juive en France (1940–1944)*, p. 102.

29. Rayski, ed., *La Presse antiraciste sous l'occupation hitlérienne*; Rayski, ed., *Dos Vort fun Vidershtant un Zieg*; see above, ch. 10.

30. Adam Rayski, "Le front invisible. Les groupes de résistance juive à Paris face à la répression policière," pp. 18–24; see above, ch. IV,.

31. "Nobody should work for [the Germans] voluntarily; if you are forced to do so, sabotage production, work slowly," in Rayski, ed., *Dos Vort fun Vidershtant un Zieg*, p. 65.

32. Adler, *The Jews of Paris*, pp. 174, 179, 186.

33. Rayski, *Nos illusions perdues*, pp. 124–125.

34. Ibid., p. 123; idem, "L'impact," p. 61.

35. Rayski, *Nos illusions perdues*, p. 124.

36. Rayski, "L'impact," p. 62. A degree of incoherence in this report, inevitable in any event, bewildered the reader. Thus *Unzer Vort* and *Notre parole* wrote in 1944 that masses of Jews from the Baltic countries celebrated their liberation with enthusiasm and cheered the victorious Red Army. The editors themselves still retained illusions about the survival of the people whose extermination they had nevertheless reported.

37. Henri Michel, *Paris résistant*, cited by Rayski, *Nos illusions perdues*, p. 123.

38. CDJC roundtable, April 17, 1983, *Le Monde juif*, no. 114 (April–June 1984); see especially the contributions of Germaine Ribière and Jean-Pierre Lévy, the founder of the underground *Franc-Tireur*, pp. 70–76.

39. Adler, *The Jews of Paris*, pp. 170.

40. Klarsfeld, *Vichy-Auschwitz*, pp. 131, 133–134.

41. YIVO, coll. 116, file 6.

42. Klarsfeld, *Vichy-Auschwitz*, p. 148.

43. Ibid., p. 393.

44. Jacques Darville and Simon Wichené, *Drancy la Juive* (Cachan: Breger, 1945), pp. 49, 69.

45. Ibid., p. 72. The camp of Drancy was placed in a group of unfinished workers' flats built in the form of a U. It contained 22 staircases, which were the equivalents of blocks in other concentration camps.

46. Durin, Jacques, ed., *Drancy, 1941–1944* (Le Bourget, 1982), a collective work produced by the students of the Lycée Eugène-Delacroix of Drancy, under the direction of the principal, Jacques Durin; and the account of André Ullmo, pp. 68–70.

47. Ibid., p. 69.

48. Ibid., p. 68.

49. Darville and Wichené, *Drancy la Juive*, p. 86.

50. Ibid., p. 88; Durin, ed., *Drancy, 1941–1944*, p. 68; Klarsfeld, *Memorial*, convoy no. 62 of November 20, 1943. On the escape from the train, see CDJC, XXVc.249.

51. Darville and Wichené, *Drancy la Juive*, pp. 78–79. Letters from Drancy written by Juliette Weill, an EIF staff member arrested during the Gestapo raid of February 9, 1943 in Lyons, were preserved by her sister, Jacqueline Dreyfus, Jerusalem; Jacques Weintrob, MJS leader, arrested in Nice, September 25, 1943 and deported from Drancy on the following October 28, organized an MJS group in the camp; Léo Cohn, the chaplain of the rural worksites, was arrested in Toulouse, May 17, 1944 and spent only from July 6 to 31 in Drancy (convoy no. 77). He formed and led a youth chorus, gathered the EIF members interned in Drancy on July 22 and deported on the 31st; see his letter addressed to Gamzon from Drancy, preserved in the Lublin archives, file 4.

52. Darville and Wichené, *Drancy la Juive*, pp. 121–122.

53. Klarsfeld, *Vichy-Auschwitz 1943–1944*, pp. 154–155.

54. Ibid., pp. 167–170.

55. YIVO, coll. 210, file XXXI-25; Paul Roitman, Testimony, Jerusalem, January 22, 1984, preserved by the author; Latour, *La Résistance juive en France (1940–1944)*, pp. 77–78, 80–82.

56. A pejorative medieval Spanish term (meaning swine) for Jews who were converted to Catholicism by force at the end of the fourteenth century in Spain but secretly continued observing Jewish religious rituals.

57. The document is preserved by YV, 09.32a.

58. Ibid.

59. Latour, *La Résistance juive en France (1940–1944)*, pp. 77–78.

60. AJDC archives, file 602; EIF archives, "Rapport sur la 4e direction de l'UGIF, 1er novembre 1942," unnumbered; Hammel, *Souviens-toi d'Amalek*, p. 71.

61. EIF archives.

62. CDJC, Testimony of Roger Fichtenberg, taken by Anny Latour, unnumbered, pp. 7–10; Gamzon, *Les Eaux claires*, pp. 66–75; Hammel, *Souviens-toi d'Amalek*, p. 153.

63. Roger Fichtenberg, Testimony, Paris, April 4, 1984, in the author's possession; Fichtenberg archives.

64. Michel, *Histoire de la Résistance*, p. 183; Israël, *Heureux comme Dieu en France*, pp. 229–231, 271.

65. Ibid., pp. 271–276; Michel, *Histoire de la Résistance*, p. 183.

66. Hammel, *Souviens-toi d'Amalek*, pp. 187–188; Michel, *Histoire de la Résistance*, pp. 184–185.

67. YV, 09.32a, *Sois chic* [no. 9], May 1944; Gamzon, *Les Eaux claires*, pp.94–96.

68. Hammel, *Souviens-toi d'Amalek*, p. 190; Janine Lazare, "Le Seder de Pierre-Blanche," in *Le Temps qu'on n'oublie pas*, a collective work (Paris: Fondation Sefer, 1963), pp. 149–164.

69. Hammel, *Souviens-toi d'Amalek*, pp. 113–114.

70. Roitman, Testimony

71. Hammel, *Souviens-toi d'Amalek*, pp. 134–136.

72. Ibid., p. 203; on the subject of the spiritual efforts of the social workers, see also YIVO, coll. 343, file 113.4.

73. YIVO, coll. 210, file XLIII.16.

74. YV, file compiled for the award of the Medal of the Righteous to Marinette Guy and Juliette Vidal.

75. André Neher, *L'Existence juive* (Paris: Editions du Seuil, 1962), p. 11 (Nanteuil is called there "Mahanayim-en-Corrèze"); A. Neher, Testimony, Jerusalem, April 7, 1986, preserved by the author.

Chapter 14. The Budgets of the Jewish Resistance

1. AJDC archives, coll. France, file 600.

2. Ibid., Report of the auditor, Loeb and Troper, 1914–1973.

3. Ibid., coll. SM, file 33A; Bauer, *American Jewry and the Holocaust*, p. 480, n. 12 and p. 481, n. 14.

4. YIVO, coll. 245, file A26 and A46.

5. Herbert Katski, testimony, New York, June 5, 1984, in the author's possession.

6. Bauer, *American Jewry and the Holocaust*, passim.

7. AJDC archives, coll. SM, file 32 and 33.

8. Bauer, *American Jewry and the Holocaust*, p. 169.

9. Ibid. Bauer notes that the policy of the AJDC reflected the contradiction between the legalistic approach of the New York office, under the direction of Paul Baerwald, and the humanitarian approach of the director for Europe in Lisbon, Joseph Schwartz.

10. YIVO, coll. 343, file 148.1.

11. Ibid., file 59, 87, 131.

12. AJDC archives, coll. SM, file 32.

13. Jules Jefroykin, Testimony taken by Haïm Avni, Paris, July 1, 1963, ICJ, OT (1) 61, pp. 11–14; Bauer, *American Jewry and the Holocaust*, p. 256.

14. Ibid., pp. 402–404.

15. AJDC archives, coll. SM, file 33. This amount was later increased. Action taken by the AJDC to rescue Jews in Central Europe became more massive in 1944. The sum spent in France in 1943, $1,748,500, represented 21.3% of the total overseas operations ($8,220,200). In 1944 $1,657,223 were allocated to France, which was 11.3% of the total overseas expenditure ($14,613,391). AJDC archives, Report of the auditor, Loeb and Troper, 1914–1973.

16. AJDC archives, coll. SM, file 33. During 1943 and 1944 the Jewish resisters in France contracted loans to be reimbursed after the war at the rate of one dollar for an average of 100 francs (the loans were undertaken at rates ranging from 80 to 130 francs). In Switzerland in 1944, the dollar was traded for rates as high as 200 francs or even higher. On May 15, 1944, Saly Mayer indicated that the exchange rate for the dollar was 265 ff. See ibid. Similarly, Jarblum wrote from Geneva in March and April 1944 that the exchange rate for the dollar had passed 215 francs in December and 265 francs at the end of April. See the Lublin archives, file 15, letters of March 29 and April 17 and 29, 1944.

17. Ibid. On April 19, 1944 Mayer had demanded "the urgent dispatch of reserve funds because of the imminent debarcation." See also Bauer, *American Jewry and the Holocaust*, p. 481.

18. Ibid., p. 258; AJDC archives, coll. SM, file 33; Lublin archives, file 15; Central Zionist Archives, coll. S 26, file 1545.

19. YIVO, coll. 343, file 59.

20. Ibid., file 8.

21. YIVO, coll. 116, file 24, and coll. 210, file XCII. 114.

22. Central Zionist Archives, coll. S 26, file 1545.

23. Adler, *The Jews of Paris*, pp. 174, 186.

24. Diamant, *Les Juifs dans la Résistance française*, p. 103.

25. EIF archives, unnumbered.

26. R. Sarraute and P. Tager gathered the official French and German texts and the circulars of the banking institutions concerning the despoiling of the Jews for the CJDC. See Sarraute and Tager, eds., *Les Juifs sous l'Occupation*.

27. See for example the German ordinance of May 28, 1941, ibid., p. 48.

28. Jefroykin, "L'Organisation juive de combat. Le refus," pp. 20, 21.

29. AJDC archives, coll. SM, file 33 (April 24, 1944).

30. Ibid., file 33A.

31. Ibid.; Bauer, *American Jewry and the Holocaust*, pp. 159, 480, n. 12, and 481, n. 14; YIVO, coll. 116, file 24 and coll. 210, file XCII.10.

32. Bauer, *American Jewry and the Holocaust*, p. 177; Jefroykin, "L'Organisation juive de combat. Le refus," p. 20 (through a typographical error, "1942" is printed instead of "1943"); see Jefroykin, Testimony, ICJ-OT (1) 61, pp. 10, 11.

33. YV, P7–20.

34. Polonski archives, file D6–12.

35. Lublin archives, file 15; AJDC archives, coll. SM, file 32.

36. Weill, *Déjà! . . . Essai autobiographique*, pp. 283–284.

37. Pierre Brambilla.

38. Polonski archives, file D6–12.

39. Lucien Lublin, Testimony, La Bresse, March 12, 1984, in the author's possession.

40. Ibid.

Chapter 15. The Groundwork of the Postwar Community

1. The Board of Deputies represents all the Jewish communities of the United Kingdom. Unlike the CRIF, political bodies do not have delegates to it. As the spokesman for all the Jews of the country, nevertheless its mission is comparable to that of the CRIF in France.

2. Quoted by the "Rapport politique et d'organisation" addressed to the leadership of the PC by Rayski in December 1943. No copy of the leaflet, *Les Juifs et la guerre* have been preserved, to our knowledge. See the "Rapport," CDJC, CDLXXIII.93.

3. Adam Rayski, "Le Comité juif de défense: son rôle dans la résistance juive en France," *Le Monde juif*, no. 52 (October–December 1968): 29–35.

4. YV, *Jeune Combat*, no. 45 (September 4, 1943).

5. Ibid., *Notre voix*, no. 66 (January 1, 1944).

6. Reproduced in Rayski, ed., *La Presse antiraciste sous l'occupation hitlérienne*, pp. 125–127.

7. "Rapport."

8. YV, 09–3.3.

9. Kriegel, *Réflexion sur les questions juives*, p. 623.

10. Jean Lacouture, *Charles de Gaulle, 1. Le Rebelle* (Paris: Editions du Seuil, 1984), pp. 673, 677, 715, 716.

11. "Le CRIF a 40 ans," dossier established by Henri Bulawko with the assistance of Roger Berg (Paris: C.R.I.F., n.d. [1984]), passim.

12. Quoted by Rayski, *Nos illusions perdues*, p. 156.

13. Testament of Rabbi Samy Klein, in Edmond Fleg, *Anthologie juive* (Paris: Sulliver, 1951), p. 586.

14. Rayski, *Nos illusions perdues*, p. 154.

15. Pierrard, *Le Grand rabbin Kaplan. Justice pour la foi juive*, pp. 129–132.

16. "Le CRIF a 40 ans"; Pierrard, *Le Grand rabbin Kaplan. Justice pour la foi juive*, pp. 104–105.

17. Rayski, Adam, "La fondation du Conseil représentatif des juifs de France," *Le Monde juif*, no. 51 (July–September 1968): 32–37; Rayski, *Nos illusions perdues*, pp. 154, 155, 160.

18. Rayski, "La fondation," p. 34.

19. Rayski, *Nos illusions perdues*, pp. 156, 160–161.

20. Adler, *The Jews of Paris*, makes a distinction between the date of the foundation of the CRIF—late 1943 or January 1944) (see pp. 152, 209)—from that of the adoption of

its charter: May 1944 (see p. 225). He bases his case on archives preserved in the Institut des Etudes marxistes, to which we were denied access. According to JTS, French Documents, box 15 and the memories of Rayski, *Nos illusions perdues,* the charter was adopted in January 1944, which also marks the foundation of the CRIF.

21. Rayski, *Nos illusions perdues,* p. 162.

22. JTS, French Documents, box 15, protocol of the deliberations of the CRIF, July–August 1944.

Chapter 16. The Armed Struggle

1. Henri Michel, *La guerre de l'ombre* (Paris: Grasset, 1970), p. 191.

2. Ibid. On this subject, see the communications and testimony presented at the colloquium on "The Participation of the Jews in the Liberation of the National Territory," held in Paris, October 1984, in A.R.H.C.J., *Les Juifs dans la Résistance et la Libération,* pp. 23–86.

3. Georges Hertz, "Résistance des Juifs et résistance juive," *Information juive* (January 1985).

4. Daniel Mayer, "Socialiste, puis français et enfin juif," in A.R.H.C.J., *Les Juifs dans la Résistance et la Libération,* p. 53.

5. Léo Hamon, "Le témoignage hexagonal d'un Français de l'intérieur," ibid., pp. 50–52.

6. Marc Bloch, *L'Étrange Défaite* (Paris: Franc-Tireur, 1946), p. 193.

7. Béatrice Philippe, "Juifs dans la Résistance," *Yod,* nos. 15–16 (1982), p. 92.

8. Lucien Steinberg, *La Révolte des Justes* (Paris: Fayard, 1970), p. 146; see also W. Rabi, "Pour quoi ils ont combattu," pp. 1–9, who proposes a reflection on "Jewish honor, aligned with the honor of the gentiles," with respect to military resistance.

9. Jacques Adler, director of the staff of the UJRE in occupied Paris, testified that he held individual conversations with almost two hundred new recruits, almost all of whom spoke of vengeance after the deportation of their families (letter to the author, Melbourne, September 16, 1986).

10. Polonski archives, D1.7 to 10; Lublin archives, file 1.

11. Klarsfeld, *Vichy-Auschwitz,* pp. 370–383, convoys no. 66–71.

12. Poliakov, *L'Auberge des musiciens,* p. 112: "a very exact price list was established: 10 francs for a grenade, 400 francs for a revolver, 3,000 francs for a submachine gun."

13. Lublin archives, file 5 and 12; Polonski archives, D.2.1,50 and D7.19; CDJC, CDLXIX.38.

14. Klarsfeld, *Vichy-Auschwitz,* pp. 388, 389, convoys 72–77.

15. Lublin archives, file 1 and 12; Polonski archives, D.2.64 and D7.19; CDJC, XI.36; Testimony of Silvain Berman, Wezembek-Oppem (Belgium), June 12, 1983, in possession of Rachel Chegam, Paris.

16. CDJC, XI.27 and 36, CDLXXVI.6.

17. An anonymous manuscript preserved by the widow of Ernest Lambert, entitled, "Rapport sur la fusillade du 8 juillet 1944" (the author is probably a Gendarme, Lenoir, who himself buried all the bodies), describes the massacre of thirty hostages from Fort Montluc of Lyons, one of whom was Ernest Lambert, on July 8, in Portes-lès-Valence (Drôme Department), in reprisal for an attack against the railroad depot of that town. See below.

18. Diamant, *Les Juifs dans la Résistance française,* passim; Ravine, *La Résistance organisée des Juifs de France,* passim.

19. Rayski, *Nos illusions perdues*, pp. 130–131.

20. The story of the betrayals of Lucienne G. and Joseph D., ibid., pp. 116–120, 148–152.

21. These are the names of the ten heroes of the red poster: "Grzywacz: Polish Jew, two attacks. Elek: Hungarian Jew, 8 derailments. Wasjbrot: Polish Jew, 1 attack, 2 derailments. Witchitz: Hungarian Jew, 15 attacks. Fingerweig: Polish Jew, 3 attacks, 5 derailments. Boczov: Hungarian Jew, head derailler, 20 attacks. Fontanot: Italian Communist, 12 attacks. Alfonso: Spanish Red, 7 attacks. Rayman: Polish Jew, 13 attacks. Manouchian: Armenian, chief of the gang, 56 attacks, 150 dead, 600 wounded."

22. Rayski, *Nos illusions perdues*, pp. 142–152.

23. CDJC, CCXV. 15; Rayski, *Nos illusions perdues*, p. 135.

24. Maxime Steinberg, *Extermination, sauvetage et résistance des Juifs de Belgique*, vol. 4 (Brussels: Vie ouvrière, April 1979), p. 54 and idem, *Dossier Bruxelles Auschwitz* (Brussels: Comité belge de soutien à la partie civile dans le procès des officiers SS, 1980), pp. 115–125.

25. Raymond Aron, *Mémoires* (Paris: Julliard, 1983), p. 176; Georges Wellers, *L'Étoile jaune à l'heure de Vichy* (Paris: Fayard, 1973), p. 281; see also Rayski, *Nos illusions perdues*, p. 134.

26. Henri Michel, "Maquis et maquis," *Revue d'histoire de la Second Guerre mondiale*, no. 49 (January 1963), pp. 3 and 10; see also, idem, "Les maquis au-delà de la légende," *Le Monde* (December 30–31, 1984).

27. YV, 09–3.4.

28. Lublin archives, file 13 and 14.

29. Kapel, *Un rabbin dans la tourmente (1940–1944)*, p. 134.

30. Lublin archives, file 13 and 14; Polonski archives, DCVIII.5, DII bis 1.10 and V.3; Kapel, *Un rabbin dans la tourmente (1940–1944)*, pp. 125–184; Lazarus, *Juifs au combat*, pp. 100–105, 115–122; Jacques Delarue, *Trafics et crimes sous l'Occupation* (Paris: Fayard, 1979), pp. 138 ff.; Jean-François Chaigneau, *Le Dernier Wagon* (Paris: France Loisirs, 1981), passim.

31. ICJ-OT (1), Testimonies 1, 5, 12, 18, 29, 34, 60, 65, 66, and 67; Avni, *Ha-Hatsala Derekh Sfarad u-Portugal*; Eychenne, *Les Pyrénées de la liberté*; idem, *Les Montagnards de la Liberté, évasions par l'Ariège et la Haute-Garonne . . .* (Toulouse: Editions Milan, 1984); idem, *Les Portes de la Liberté, le franchissement clandestin de la frontière espagnole dans les Pyrénées-Orientales . . .* (Toulouse: Editions Privat, 1985); Polonski archives, D2.67, D5.29, D6.4, and D6VII.23; Lublin archives, file 2, 8, 13, and 20.

32. Ibid.; Polonski archives, D6VII.1, 2, and 5; [Roger Mompezat], *Le Corps franc de la Montagne Noire. Journal de marche (avril-septembre 1944)*, 3rd edition (Albi: Les Anciens du C.F.M.N., 1963); deposit of the municipal library of Toulouse, coll. Joseph-Georges Cohen (OJC).

33. Manuscript of the log of Lacado, preserved by his chief, Adrien Gensburger, Belfort; Jean Hirsch, "Les grandes manoeuvres," unpublished account reconstructing the log of the Malquière-Larroque platoon, which disappeared in the fire of Larroque, August 8, 1944; EIF archives, unnumbered documents; Gamzon, *Les Eaux claires*, pp. 97–160; Robinson, *Les Nouvelles Compagnies franches du Tarn* (Offenbourg: Carnet de Route du 12ème Dragons, 1946); André Maynadier, *8 août 1944 . . . maquis de Larroque* (Pratlong: unpublished, 1984); Pierre Dunoyer de Segonzac, *Le Vieux Chef, mémoires et pages choisies* (Paris: Editions du Seuil, 1971), pp. 141–152; idem, *Historique et anecdotes des maquis de Vabre* (Albi: unpublished, 1964).

34. CDJC, CDLXX. 1b, reproduced by Adam Rutkowski, *La Lutte des Juifs en France à l'époque de l'Occupation*, p. 126; Hammel, *Souviens-toi d'Amalek*, pp. 205–296; A. Michel, *Les Éclaireurs israélites de France pendant la Seconde Guerre mondiale*, p. 172; Avni, *Ha-Hatsala Derekh Sfarad u-Portugal*, p. 34; Georges Weill, Testimony, Jerusalem, July 9, 1986, in the author's possession. The captured escapees were Roger Picard and Samy Stourdzé, a rabbi and a noncommissioned officer in the reserves.

35. Avni, *Ha-Hatsala Derekh Sfarad u-Portugal*, p. 38.

36. Ibid., pp. 42–57.

37. Eychenne, *Les Portes*, p. 145; idem, *Les Pyrénées*, pp. 90–91.

38. Avni, *Ha-Hatsala Derekh Sfarad u-Portugal*, pp. 38–42; Eychenne, *Les Portes*, pp. 58–59. The author notes that the border-runners were secretive about the number of their clients so as not to reveal their income. She nevertheless indicates that "D. . . . boasted that in that month [September 1943] 350,000 francs a week by smuggling Jews across the border."

39. Avni, *Ha-Hatsala Derekh Sfarad u-Portugal*, pp. 148–158.

40. Lublin archives, file 2; Polonski archives, D5.15 and D6VII.23; Lazarus, *Juifs au combat*, pp. 24, 34, 38–40, 49–52, 65–69; Latour, *La Résistance juive en France (1940–1944)*, pp. 211–215.

41. Avni, *Ha-Hatsala Derekh Sfarad u-Portugal*, pp. 41–45, 193.

42. Posthumously awarded the Medal of the Righteous by the Yad Vashem National Memorial in Jerusalem; Avni, *Ha-Hatsala Derekh Sfarad u-Portugal*, pp. 195–196.

43. Testimony of Dély Técuciano, responsible for this escape route, Tel Aviv, April 20, 1987, in the author's possession.

44. Testimonies of Jacques Roitman and Henri Pohorylès, ICJ-OT, (1)34 and (1)67.

45. CDJC, XI.36 [written by Maurice Hausner]; Avni, *Ha-Hatsala Derekh Sfarad u-Portugal*, p. 65.

46. See the account by Jacques Samuel, a veteran of Taluyers, in Hammel, *Souviens-toi d'Amalek*, pp. 177–184; Avni, *Ha-Hatsala Derekh Sfarad u-Portugal*, pp. 198–199.

47. Ibid., pp. 199–200; Gamzon, *Les Eaux claires*, pp. 101–102.

48. Avni, *Ha-Hatsala Derekh Sfarad u-Portugal*, pp. 207–212; Lubin archives, file 20.

49. Polonski archives, D6.7; Kapel, *Un rabbin dans la tourmente (1940–1944)*, pp. 186–187.

50. ICJ-OT 1(20) (Andrée Salomon) and (1)60 (Élisabeth Hirsch); Avni, *Ha-Hatsala Derekh Sfarad u-Portugal*, pp. 203–207, 212.

51. Central Zionist Archives, collection S 26 file 1538 (report by Jefroykin, Barcelona, September 24, 1944); Avni, *Ha-Hatsala Derekh Sfarad u-Portugal*, p. 213 points out that estimates of the total number of escapes vary, depending on the sources, between a minimum of 270 and a maximum of 900.

52. See the works cited herein and in the bibliography of David Diamond, Jacques Ravine, Louis Gronowski-Brunot, Abraham Lisner, Alfred Grant, Claude Lévy. The same tendency emerges from the works of Adam Rayski following the period of his membership in the PC.

53. This is the case of the books of David Knout and Jacques Lazarus.

54. Rabi, "Pour quoi ils ont combattu," pp. 7–9.

55. The first specific research on rescuer-resisters was published in 1980 in the United States: Hillel J. Kieval, "Legality and Resistance in Vichy France."

56. An association for research in contemporary Jewish history.

57. A.R.H.C.J., *Les Juifs dans la Résistance et la Libération*, passim.

58. See for example the list of the names of members of the Marc Haguenau Company, EIF archives, unnumbered.

59. Letter from Gamzon to his wife, June 26, 1944. The author is grateful to Denise Gamzon for having placed at his disposition the letters received from her husband in May and June 1944.

60. Poliakov, *L'Auberge des musiciens*, pp. 107–109, 146–147; Philippe Boegner, *Ici on a aimé les juifs* (Paris: J. C. Lattès, 1981), passim.

61. Hirsch, "Les grandes manoeuvres," pp. 22–26; Mompezat, *Le Corps franc de la Montagne Noire*, p. 28. The remark made by Renée Poznanski, according to which the Jewish partisans were subject "to a double authority, that of the commanders delegated by the Armée secrète and that of the leaders of the Jewish organizations," does not correspond with reality. The latter placed military personnel at the disposition of the former. The authority was exercised in complementary fashion. See R. Poznanski, "La résistance juive en France," *Revue d'histoire de la Seconde Guerre Mondiale*, no. 137 (1985), p. 15.

62. Mompezat, *Le Corps franc de la Montagne Noire*, p. 44, entry of June 10, [1944].

63. Ibid., p. 34, entry of June 7.

64. Hirsch, "Les grandes manoeuvres," pp. 37–40, 55; Lacado, Log, entries of June 25, July 17, 29, August 6,7,8.

65. Poliakov, *L'Auberge des musiciens*, p. 146.

66. Lublin archives, file 2 (containing the log). Citations and croix de guerre awarded by the military governor of Lyons to Léon Avraham (documents preserved by Arlette Avraham, Jerusalem) and to Claude Spiero, hero of the combat waged on August 18 at Saint-Geneys (documents preserved by C. Spiero, Strasbourg).

67. Gérard Combes, *Haute-Loire 1940–1944* (Gap: Comité d'histoire de la Deuxième Guerre mondiale, 1967), p. 17.

68. Mompezat, *Le Corps franc de la Montagne Noire*, pp. 17–34; Pierre Loeb, unpublished autobiographical essay, Brussels, June 30, 1983, pp. 4–5 and annexes; lists of names of the "effectifs du 1er peloton du 4e escadron du CFMN."

69. Mompezat, *Le Corps franc de la Montagne Noire*, pp. 25–26, 29, 32–34.

70. Loeb, unpublished autobiographical essay, p. 7. In texts written after the liberation, the AJ unit of the CFMN is called "peloton Trumpeldor," named after the hero of the resistance of the Jewish pioneers of the Galilee against the raids of Arab commandos in 1919–1920.

71. Polonski archives, D6VII. 1,2 and 5.

72. Mompezat, *Le Corps franc de la Montagne Noire*, p. 65.

73. Ibid., p. 94; Loeb, unpublished autobiographical essay, p. 8.

74. Ibid., p. 7; Latour, *La Résistance juive en France (1940–1944)*, p. 222.

75. Michel, *Les Éclaireurs israélites de France pendant la Seconde Guerre mondiale*, n. 30; Mompezat, *Le Corps franc de la Montagne Noire*, pp. 221–232; see also Charles de Gaulle, *War Mémoirs* v. 3, *Unity* (London: Collins, 1959), pp. 269, 297, 303, 306, 308, 703, and 705; Jean Lacouture, *Charles de Gaulle, 1. Le Rebelle*, pp. 811–812.

76. Ministère des Armées, Service historique, no. 2392, letter of Pierre Dunoyer de Segonzac, Rabat, July 10, 1947; Michel Goubet, "La résistance toulousaine, structures, objectifs (printemps-été 1944)," *Revue d'histoire de la Seconde Guerre mondiale*, no. 99 (July 1975): 39, n. 3.

77. Mompezat, *Le Corps franc de la Montagne Noire*, pp. 106–139; Loeb, unpublished autobiographical essay, pp. 8–9.

78. Toulouse, February 24, 1945, preserved by the municipal library of Toulouse, coll. Joseph-Georges Cohen (OJC).

79. Ibid., entries of August 1, 2; Loeb, unpublished autobiographical essay, pp. 9–11; Polonski archives, D2.4.

80. Loeb, unpublished autobiographical essay, p. 11; Mompezat, *Le Corps franc de la Montagne Noire*, pp. 199–210.

81. The last clandestine escape to Spain carried out by SERE was a convoy of eight children, on September 10, 1944, thus after the liberation of Toulouse; see the testimony of Jo Fuchs, Tel Aviv, February 17, 1984, in the author's possession.

82. ICJ-OT (1)12 and (1)34.

83. Lublin archives, file 16.

84. Hirsch, "Les grandes manoeuvres," p. 9; Lacado, Log, entry of April 29.

85. Michel, *Les Éclaireurs israélites de France pendant la Seconde Guerre mondiale*, pp. 184–185.

86. Personal memory.

87. Segonzac, *Le Vieux Chef*, p. 143; see also Hirsch, "Les grandes manoeuvres," pp. 6–7.

88. Lacado, Log, entries of May 5, June 3; Hirsch, "Les grandes manoeuvres," pp. 13, 19 and passim; Gamzon, *Les Eaux claires*, pp. 99–100, 107.

89. Ibid., pp. 99–100.

90. See above, p. 000; Hirsch, "Les grandes manoeuvres," p. 26.

91. Ibid., pp. 28–31.

92. Maynadier, *8 Août 1944*, p. 3.

93. Hirsch, "Les grandes manoeuvres," pp. 35–36.

94. Ibid., pp. 37–40; Lacado, Log, entries of June 11 and 26.

95. Maynadier, *8 Août 1944*; see also Lacado, Log, entries of June 25, July 17, 29, August 6; Gamzon, *Les Eaux claires*, pp. 109–116.

96. Ibid., pp. 131–134; Lacado, Log, entries of May 28, June 16.

97. ibid., entries of July 7; Hirsch, "Les grandes manoeuvres," p. 43.

98. Segonzac, *Le Vieux Chef*, pp. 143–144.

99. Hirsch, "Les grandes manoeuvres," pp. 43–44.

100. Segonzac, *Le Vieux Chef*, pp. 79–110.

101. Hirsch, "Les grandes manoeuvres," pp. 46–47; see also Lacado, Log, entries of July 21 and 25.

102. Segonzac, *Le Vieux Chef*, pp. 144–145, 147.

103. Ibid., p. 157.

104. Maynadier, *8 Août 1944*, p. 4.

105. A brilliant student at the École Polytechnique, endowed with an ardent spirit, he had directed the rural worksite in Lautre. Bloch was the commander of the Larroque Platoon.

106. Hirsch, "Les grandes manoeuvres," pp. 55–59; Lacado, Log, entries of August 8, 9; Gamzon, *Les Eaux claires*, pp. 135–145.

107. Segonzac, *Le Vieux Chef*, p. 145.

108. Gamzon, *Les Eaux claires*, pp. 146–150.

109. Ibid., p. 149.

110. Ibid., p. 135.

111. Maynadier, *8 Août 1944*, passim.

112. Hirsch, "Les grandes manoeuvres," p. 62.

113. Ibid., p. 63.

114. Deuteronomy XX, 2–8, Jewish Publication Society of America translation; see also Hirsch, "Les grandes manoeuvres," p. 62; personal memory of the author.

115. Lacado, Log, entries of August 15, 17; Hirsch, "Les grandes manoeuvres," pp. 65–67.

116. Segonzac, *Le Vieux Chef*, p. 148.

117. Ibid., p. 149; see also Lacado, Log, entry of August 19; Hirsch, "Les grandes manoeuvres," pp. 69–70; Gamzon, *Les Eaux claires*, pp. 156–157.

118. T. E. Lawrence, quoted by H. Michel, *Les Maquis au-delà de la légende*.

119. Gamzon, *Les Eaux claires*, pp. 158–159.

120. Michel, *Les Éclaireurs israélites de France pendant la Seconde Guerre mondiale*, p. 191; Pougatch, *Un bâtisseur*, p. 22.

121. Hirsch, "Les grandes manoeuvres," pp. 71–80; Lacado, Log, entries of August 20, 21.

122. Léon Bergman, Testimony, Jerusalem, November 1985, in the author's possession.

123. Personal memory.

Conclusion

1. The non-Jewish rescuers of Jews have not been recognized as resisters for France and enjoyed the concomitant benefits. However the State of Israel has awarded them the Medal of the Righteous to those who have been identified. See Lazare, *Le Livre des Justes*.

2. Kriegel, "De la résistance juive," p. 195.

3. Ibid., pp. 201–202.

4. Rayski, *Nos illusions perdues*, p. 178.

5. Weill, *Contribution à l'histoire des camps d'internement dans l'Anti-France*, p. 207.

6. Lambert, *Carnet d'un témoin*, p. 184.

7. Pierre Vidal-Naquet, *Les Juifs, la mémoire et le présent*, p. 109.

8. Weill, *Contribution à l'histoire des camps d'internement dans l'Anti-France*, p. 207.

9. Vidal-Naquet, *Les Juifs*, p. 109.

10. Dominique Schnapper, *Juifs et Israélites* (Paris: Gallimard, 1980), pp. 69–70.

11. Ibid., pp. 141–144.

Bibliography

1. Books

Abitbol, Michel. *Les Juifs d'Afrique du Nord sous Vichy* Paris: Maisonneuve et Larose, 1983.

Activité des organisations juives en France sous l'Occupation. Paris: Editions du Centre, 1947. *Cahiers Paul Claudel 7. La figure d'Israël*. Paris: Gallimard, 1968.

Adler, Jacques. *The Jews of Paris and the Final Solution; Communal Response and Internal Conflicts*. New York: Oxford University Press, 1987.

Amipaz-Silber, G. *Mahteret Yehudit be-Algeria, 1940–1942 (Jewish Underground in Algeria*, Hebrew). Jerusalem: Ministry of Defense Publishing House, 1983.

Amouroux, H. *Le Peuple réveillé, juin 1940–février 1942*. Paris: Robert Laffont, 1979.

Ansky, Michel. *Les Juifs d'Algérie du décret Crémieux à la Libération*. Paris: Editions du Centre, 1950.

Arendt, H. *Eichmann in Jerusalem*. Harmondsworth, Middlesex: Penguin Books, 1976.

Aron, Raymond. *Mémoires*. Paris: Julliard, 1983.

Aschheim, Steven. *Brothers and Strangers: The Eastern European Jew in Germany and German Jewish Consciousness, 1800–1923*. Madison, 1983.

Avni, Haïm. *Ha-Hatsala Derekh Sfarad u-Portugal* (Hebrew, *Rescue Via Spain and Portugal*), Masters Thesis, Hebrew University of Jerusalem, 1964.

[d'Aubigné, Jeanne Merle]. *Les Clandestins de Dieu*. Paris: Fayard, 1968.

Bauer, Yehuda. *American Jewry and the Holocaust*. Detroit, 1981.

Bauer, Yehuda. *My Brother's Keeper: A History of the American Joint Distribution Committee*. Philadelphia: Jewish Publication Society of America, 1974.

Bédarida, Renée. *Les Armes de l'esprit: Témoignage chrétien (1941–1944)*. Paris: Editions Ouvrières, 1977.

Bensimon, Doris and Sergio Della Pergola. *La Population juive de France*. Jerusalem, 1984.

Bloch, Marc. *L'Étrange Défaite*. Paris: Franc-Tireur, 1946.

Boegner, Philippe. *Ici on a aimé les juifs*. Paris: J. C. Lattès, 1981.

Bulawko, Henri and Roger Berg. *Le CRIF a 40 ans*. Paris: C.R.I.F., n.d. [1984].

Bulawko, Henri. *Les Jeux de la mort et de l'espoir*. Paris: Montorgueil, 1980.

Cahiers Paul Claudel 7. La figure d'Israël. Paris: Gallimard, 1968.

Catane, Moshe. In *Encyclopaedia Hebraica*. Jerusalem: Encyclopaedia Publishing Company, 1976, 28: 961.

Catane, Moshe. *Des croisades à nos jours*. Paris: Albin Michel 1956.

Cavaglion, Alberto. *Nella Notte Straniera, Gli Ebrei Di S. Martin Vesubia*. Cuneo: L'Arciere, 1981.

Chaigneau, Jean-François. *Le Dernier Wagon*. Paris: France Loisirs, 1981.

Chelini, Jean. *L'Église sous Pie XII. La tourmente, 1939–1945*. Paris, 1983.

Chouraqui, André. *L'Amour fort comme la mort. Une autobiographie*. Paris: Robert Laffont, 1990.

Cohen, Richard Y. *Ha-Hanhaga Ha-Yehudit be-Tsarfat be-Milhemet ha-Olam ha-Shniya* (Hebrew, *The Jewish Leadership in France During the Second World War*), Doctoral dissertation, Hebrew University of Jerusalem, 1981. Expanded English version: *The Burden of Conscience: French Jewish Leadership During the Holocaust*. Bloomington: University of Indiana Press, 1987.

Combes, Gérard. *Haute-Loire 1940–1944*. Gap: Comité d'histoire de la Deuxième Guerre mondiale, 1967.

Consistoire Central. *Mémorial en souvenir de nos rabbins et ministres-officiants victimes de la barbarie nazie*. Paris: J. Jacobs, 1947.

Courtois, Stéphane, Denis Peschanski, and Adam Rayski. *Le Sang de l'étranger. Les immigrés de la MOI dans la Résistance*. Paris: Fayard, 1989.

Darville Jacques and Simon Wichené. *Drancy la Juive*. Cachan: Breger, 1945.

Debré, Robert. *L'Honneur de vivre*. Paris: Hermann et Stock, 1974.

Delarue, Jacques. *Trafics et crimes sous l'Occupation*. Paris: Fayard, 1979.

De Montclos, X., et al., eds. *Églises et chrétiens dans la Second Guerre mondiale. La région Rhône-Alpes*. Acts of the Colloquium of Grenoble, 1976. Lyons: Presses Universitaires de Lyon, 1978.

Deutscher, Isaac. *The Non-Jewish Jew and Other Essays*. London: Oxford University Press, 1968.

Diamant, David. *Les Juifs dans la Résistance française (1940–1944)*. Paris: Roger Maria, Le Pavillon, 1971.

Draenger, Jacob. *Nahoum Goldmann*. Paris: Editions Météore, 1956.

Duquesne, J. *Les Catholiques français sous l'Occupation*. Paris: Grasset, 1966.

Durin, Jacques, ed. *Drancy, 1941–1944*. Le Bourget, 1982. (A collective work produced by the students of the Lycée Eugène-Delacroix of Drancy, under the direction of the principal, Jacques Durin.)

Encrevé, André and Jacques Poujoul, eds. *Les protestants français pendant la Seconde Guerre Mondiale. Actes du colloque de Paris, 19–21 novembre 1992*. Paris: Société de l'Histoire du Protestantisme français, 1994.

L'Entraide temporaire. Sauvetage d'enfants juifs sous l'Occupation. Anonymous booklet by rescued children, Paris, 1985.

Eychenne, Émilienne. *Les Montagnards de la Liberté, évasions par l'Ariège et la Haute-Garonne.* Toulouse: Editions Milan, 1984.

Eychenne, Émilienne. *Les Portes de la Liberté, le franchissement clandestin de la frontière espagnole dans les Pyrénées-Orientales.* Toulouse: Editions Privat, 1985.

Eychenne, Émilienne. *Les Pyrénées de la liberté.* Paris: France-Empire, 1983.

Faurisson, R. *Mémoire en défense contre ceux qui m'accusent de falsifier l'histoire. La question des chambres à gaz.* Paris: La Vieille Taupe, 1980.

Feinerman, Emmanuel. *La Nuit de Cristal.* Paris: Robert Laffont, 1972. An English edition of this book exists: *Crystal Night: 9–10 November, 1938.* London, 1974.

Fleg, Edmond, ed. *Anthologie juive.* Paris: Sulliver, 1951.

Fontaine, André. *Le Camp d'étrangers des Milles, 1939–1943.* Aix-en-Provence: Edisud, 1989.

Friedländer, Saül. *Quand vient le souvenir.* Paris: Editions du Seuil, 1978. English translation: *When Memory Comes.* New York: Farrar, Straus, 1979.

Furet, François, ed. *L'Allemagne nazie et le génocide juif.* Paris: Gallimard-Le Seuil, 1985.

Furet, F. *L'Atelier de l'histoire.* Paris: Flammarion, 1982. Gamzon, Robert. *Les Eaux claires. Journal 1940–1944.* Paris: E.E.I.F., 1982.

Gamzon, R. *Tivliout.* Paris: Editions du Chant Nouveau, 1946.

Gartner, Lloyd. *The Jewish Immigrant in England, 1870–1914.* Detroit, 1960.

Goguel, François. *La Politique des partis sous la Troisième République.* Paris: Editions du Seuil, 1946.

Gordon, Milton. *Assimilation in American Life.* New York: Oxford University Press, 1964.

Gourfinkel, N. *L'Autre Patrie.* Paris: Editions du Seuil, 1953.

Gronowski-Brunot, Louis. *Le Dernier Grand Soir. Un Juif de Pologne.* Paris: Editions du Seuil, 1980.

Grynberg, Anne. *Les Camps de la honte. Les internés juifs des camps français, 1939–1944.* Paris: La Découverte, 1991.

La Guerre en Méditerranée, 1939–1945. Acts of an international colloquium held in Paris, April 8–11, 1969. Paris, 1971.

Hammel, F. Ch. *Souviens-toi d'Amalek.* Paris: C.L.K.H., 1982.

Heymann, E. *Le Camp du bout du monde.* Lausanne: Pierre Marcel Favre, 1983.

Hilberg, R. *The Destruction of the European Jews.* Chicago: Holmes and Meir, 1961.

Hyman, Paula. *From Dreyfus to Vichy: The Remaking of French Jewry, 1906–1939.* New York: Columbia University Press, 1979.

Im Hof-Piguet, Anne-Marie. *La Filière. En France occupée, 1942–1944.* Yverdon-les-Bains: Edition de la Thiele, 1985.

Israël, Gérard. *Heureux comme Dieu en France, 1940–1944.* Paris: Robert Laffont, 1975.

Jackson, L. E. Bitton. *Elli: Coming of Age in the Holocaust.* New York: Granada Publishing, 1980.

Jacoubovitch, J. *Rue Amelot. Hilf un Vidershtant.* Paris: Colonie Scolaire, 1948.

Les Juifs dans la Résistance et la Libération. Paris: Bulletin du RHICOJ, no. 1 (1985). Acts of colloquium held in Paris on October 7, 1984, sponsored by the RHICOJ.

Kapel, Shmuel René. *Maavaq Yehudi be-Tsarfat Ha-Kvusha (The Jewish Struggle in Occupied France,* Hebrew. Jerusalem: Yad Vashem, 1981).

Kapel, Shmuel René. *Un rabbin dans la tourmente (1940–1944).* Paris: Editions du Centre, 1986.

Kaplan, Jacob. *N'oublie pas.* Paris: Stock, 1984.

Kaplan, J. *Les Temps d'épreuve.* Paris: Editions de Minuit, 1952.

Kaplan, J. *Le Vrai Visage du judaïsme*. Paris: Berger-Levrault, 1987.

Karpi, Daniel. *Bein Shevet le-Hesed* (*Between Punishment and Mercy*, Hebrew). Jerusalem: Zalman Shazar Center for Jewish History, 1993.

Kaspi, André. *Les Juifs pendant l'Occupation*. Paris: Editions du Seuil, 1991.

Kaufmann, Francine. *Pour relire Le Dernier des Justes*. Paris: Méridien-Klincksieck, 1986.

Kedward, H. R. *Resistance in Vichy France*. Oxford: Oxford University Press, 1978.

Kieval, Hillel J. "Legality and Resistance in Vichy France. The Rescue of Jewish Children," *Proceedings of the American Philosophical Society* vol. 124, no. 5. Philadelphia October 1980.

Klarsfeld, S. *Les Enfants d'Izieu, une tragédie juive*. Paris: Serge Klarsfeld, 1984.

Klarsfeld, Serge. *Le Mémorial des Enfants Juifs déportés de France*. Paris: I.F.D.J.F. and the Beate Klarsfeld Foundation, 1994.

Klarsfeld, Serge. *Memorial to the Jews Deported from France, 1942–1944; Documentation of the Deportation of the Victims of the Final Solution in France*. New York: Beate Klarsfeld Foundation, 1983.

Klarsfeld, Serge. *Vichy-Auschwitz. 1943–1944*. Paris: Fayard, 1985.

Knout, David. *Contribution à l'histoire de la résistance juive en France (1940–1944)*. Paris: Editions du Centre, 1947.

Koestler, Arthur. *Scum of the Earth*. New York: MacMillan, 1941, rpt. 1968.

Kriegel, Annie. *Ce que j'ai cru comprendre*. Paris: Robert Laffont, 1991.

Kriegel, Annie. *Réflexion sur les questions juives*. Paris: Hachette, 1984.

Lacouture, Jean. *Charles de Gaulle, 1. Le Rebelle*. Paris: Editions du Seuil, 1984.

Lambert, R. R. *Carnet d'un témoin. 1940–1943*. Presented and annotated by R. Cohen. Paris: Fayard, 1985.

Lanzmann, Claude. *Shoah*. Paris: Fayard, 1985.

Latour, Anny. *La Résistance juive en France (1940–1944)*. Paris, 1970. English edition: *The Jewish Resistance in France (1940–1944)*. New York: Holocaust Library, 1982.

Lazare, Lucien. *L'Abbé Glasberg*. Paris: Cerf, 1990.

Lazare, Lucien. *Le Livre des Justes*. Paris: J. Cl. Lattès, 1993.

Lazarus, Jacques. *Juifs au combat*. Paris: Editions du Centre, 1947).

Lévy C. and P. Tillard. *La Grande Rafle du Vel' d'hiv'*. Paris: Robert Laffont, 1967

Lissner, Abraham. *Un franc-tireur juif raconte . . .* Paris: Self-published, 1977.

Lubetzki, J. *La Condition des Juifs en France sous l'occupation allemande, 1940–1944*. Paris: Editions du Centre, 1945.

Malraux, C. *La Fin et le Commencement*. Paris, 1976.

Mandel, Arnold. *Les Temps incertains*. Paris: Albin Michel, 1950.

Marrou, Henri. *L'Histoire et ses méthodes*. Paris: Editions du Seuil, 1961.

Marrus, M. R. *Les Juifs de France à l'époque de l'affaire Dreyfus*. Paris: Calmann-Lévy, 1972.

Marrus, Michael R. and Robert O. Paxton. *Vichy France and the Jews*. New York: Basic Books, 1982.

Michel, Alain. *Les Éclaireurs israélites de France pendant la Seconde Guerre mondiale*. Paris: Editions des E.I.F., 1984.

Michel, Henri. *Les Courants de pensée de la Résistance*. Paris: Presses Universitaires de France, 1962.

Michel, Henri. *La guerre de l'ombre*. Paris: Grasset, 1970. In English translation: *The Shadow War: Resistance in Europe 1939–1945*. London, 1972.

Michel, Henri. *Histoire de la Résistance en France*. Paris: Presses Universitaires de France, 1975.

Minc, Rachel. *L'Enfer des innocents. Les enfants juifs dans la tourmente nazie.* Paris: Editions du Centurion, 1966.

Moch, Maurice and Alain Michel. *L'Etoile et la Francisque. Les Institutions juives sous Vichy.* Paris: Cerf, 1990.

[Mompezat, Roger]. *Le Corps franc de la Montagne Noire. Journal de marche (avril-septembre 1944),* 3rd edition. Albi: Les Anciens du C.F.M.N., 1963.

Muller, Annette. *La Petite fille du Vél' d'Hiv.* Paris: Denoël, 1991.

Neher, André. *Jérusalem, vécu juif et message.* Monaco: Editions du Rocher, 1984.

Neher, André. *L'Existence juive.* Paris: Editions du Seuil, 1962.

Neher-Bernheim, Renée. *Histoire juive de la Renaissance à nos jours.* Paris: Editions Klincksieck, 1974.

Nodot, René. *Les enfants ne partiront pas!* Lyons: Imprimerie nouvelle lyonnaise, 1971.

Noguères, H. *Histoire de la Résistance en France de 1940 à 1945.* 2 vols. Paris: Robert Laffont, 1969.

Papenek, E. *Out of the Fire.* New York: William Morrow, 1975.

Perrault, Gilles. *L'Orchestre rouge.* Paris: Fayard, 1971.

Philippe, Béatrice. *Etre juif dans la société française.* Paris: Montalba-Pluriel, 1979.

Pierrard, P. *Le Grand rabbin Kaplan. Justice pour la foi juive.* Paris: Edition du Centurion, 1977.

Poliakov, Léon. *L'Auberge des musiciens. Mémoires.* Paris: Mazarine, 1981.

Poliakov, Léon. *Bréviaire de la haine.* Paris: Calmann-Lévy, 1971.

Poliakov, Léon. *La Condition des Juifs en France sous l'occupation italienne.* Paris: Editions du Centre, 1946.

Poliakov, Léon. *L'Étoile jaune.* Paris: Editions du Centre, 1949.

Poliakov, Léon. *Histoire de l'Antisémitisme.* Vol. 4, *L'Europe suicidaire, 1870–1933.* Paris: Calmann-Lévy, 1977. English translation: *The History of Anti-Semitism,* vol. 4, *Suicidal Europe, 1870–1933.* New York 1983.

Pougatch, I. *Un bâtisseur—Robert Gamzon.* Paris: Service technique pour l'Education - F.S.J.U., 1971.

Pougatch, I. *Charry, Vie d'une communauté de jeunesse.* Paris: Editions du Chant Nouveau, 1946.

Rajsfus, M. *Des Juifs dans la collaboration. l'UGIF (1941–1944).* Paris: Etudes et Documentation internationales, 1980.

Rassinier, P. *Le Drame des Juifs européens.* Paris: La Vieille Taupe, 1964.

Rassinier, P. *Le Mensonge d'Ulysse.* Paris: La Vieille Taupe, rpt. Paris: La Librairie Française, 1979.

Rassinier, P. *Ulysse trahi par les siens, complément au Mensonge d'Ulysse.* Paris: La Vieille Taupe, rpt. Paris: La Librairie Française, 1980.

Rassinier, P. *Le Véritable Procès Eichmann ou les Vainqueurs incorrigibles.* Paris: Les Sept Couleurs, 1962.

Ravine, Jacques. *La Résistance organisée des Juifs de France.* Paris: Julliard, 1973.

Rayski, Adam. *Nos illusions perdues.* Paris: Balland 1985.

Rayski, Adam, ed. *La Presse antiraciste sous l'occupation hitlérienne.* Paris: Centre de Documentation de l'U.J.R.E., 1953).

Rayski, Adam, ed. *Dos Vort fun Vidershant un Zieg.* Paris: Centre de documentation de l'UJRE, 1949.

Rings, Werner. *Life with the Enemy; Collaboration and Resistance in Hitler's Europe, 1939–1945.* New York, 1982.

Robinson. *Les Nouvelles Compagnies franches du Tarn*. Offenbourg: Carnet de Route du 12ème Dragons, 1946.

Roblin, Michel. *Les Juifs de Paris*. Paris: A. & J. Picard, 1952.

Roland, Charlotte. *Du ghetto à l'occident*. Paris: Editions de Minuit, 1962.

Rutkowski, Adam. *La Lutte des Juifs de France à l'époque de l'Occupation (1940–1944)*. Paris: Editions du Centre, 1975.

Sadan, Fabienne. *Mahanot Ha-Hesger Bi-Drom Tsarfat* (Hebrew, *Detention Camps in Southern France*, Hebrew), Masters Thesis, Hebrew University of Jerusalem, 1985.

Sarraute, R. and Tager, P. eds. *Les Juifs sous L'Occupation. Recueil des textes officiels français et allemands. 1940–1944*. Paris: Editions du Centre, 1945.

Scholem, G. *Fidélité et Utopie*. Paris: Calmann-Lévy, 1978.

Schrager, Faivel. *Oifn Rund fun Tsvey Tqoufess*. Paris: Self-Published.

Schramm, Hanna and Barbara Vormeir. *Vivre à Gurs*. Paris: François Maspero, 1979.

Schwarzfuchs, Simon. *Les Juifs de France*. Paris: Albin Michel, 1975.

Segonzac, Pierre Dunoyer de. *Le Vieux Chef, mémoires et pages choisies*. Paris: Editions du Seuil, 1971.

Sommer, R. *Le Grand Rabbin René Hirschler*. Strasbourg: Communauté israélite, 1962.

Steinberg, Lucien. *La Révolte des Justes*. Paris: Fayard, 1970.

Steinberg, Maxime. *Dossier Bruxelles Auschwitz*. Brussels: Comité belge de soutien à la partie civile dans le procès des officiers SS, 1980.

Steinberg, Maxime. *Extermination, sauvetage et résistance des Juifs de Belgique*, 4 vols. Brussels: Vie ouvrière, April 1979.

Szajkowski, Z. *The Analytical Franco-Jewish Gazetteer, 1939–1945*. New York: S. Frydman, 1966.

Trigano Shmuel, ed. *La Société Juive à travers l'Histoire*. 4 vols. Paris: Fayard, 1993.

Trunk, I. *Judenrat: The Jewish Councils in Eastern Europe under Nazi Occupation*. New York: Macmillan, 1972.

Vidal-Naquet, Pierre. *Les Juifs, la mémoire et le présent*. Paris: François Maspero, 1981.

Vigée, Claude. *La Lune d'hiver*. Paris: Flammarion, 1970.

Weill, Joseph. *Contribution à l'histoire des camps d'internement dans l'Anti-France*. Paris: Editions du Centre, 1947.

Weinberg, David H. *A Community on Trial: The Jews of Paris in the 1930s*. Chicago: University of Chicago Press, 1977.

Wellers, Georges. *De Drancy à Auschwitz*. Paris: Editions du Centre, 1946.

Wellers, Georges. *L'Étoile jaune à l'heure de Vichy*. Paris: Fayard, 1973.

Wellers, Georges. *La Solution finale et la mythomanie néo-nazie*. Paris: B. & S. Klarsfeld, 1978.

Wieviorka, Annette. *Ils étaient juifs, résistants, communistes*. Paris: Denoël, 1986.

Zeitoun, Sabine. *Ces enfants qu'il fallait sauver*. Paris: Albin Michel, 1989.

Zuccotti, Susan. *The Holocaust, the French, and the Jews*. New York: Basic Books, 1993.

2. Articles

Acts of the roundtable held in Paris on December 9, 1984, sponsored by AMILAR, in *Le Monde juif*, no. 118 (April–June 1985).

Adler, Jacques. "L'historiographie de la résistance juive en France." *Le Monde juif*, no. 118 (April–June 1985).

Ariel [Fischer], Joseph. "Jewish Self-Defense and Resistance in France During World War II." *Yad Vashem Studies* 6 (1967): 230.

Bartov, Hanokh. "Conformisme et sionisme du judaïsme anglais." *Dispersion et Unité* 10 (1970): 138–148.

Bédarida, François and Renée. "Une résistance spirituelle: Aux origines du 'Témoignage chrétien' (1941–1942)." *Revue d'histoire de la Seconde Guerre mondiale* 61 (Jan. 1966): 3–33.

Bialod, Michel. "La Tragédie de Szbonszyn." *Les Nouveaux Cahiers* 55 (Winter 1978–1979): 31–37.

Bulawko, Henri. "Un anniversaire oublié. Les premiers internements juifs à la caserne des Tourelles." *Le Monde juif* 97 (January–March 1980): 36–37.

Bulawko, Henri. "Où commence (et où finit) la résistance juive en France?" *Le Monde juif*, no. 118 (April–June 1985): 56–57

Caron, Vicki. "Prelude to Vichy: France and the Jewish Refugees in the Era of Appeasement." *Journal of Contemporary History* 20 (1988): 157–176.

Delpech, François. "La persécution des Juifs et l'Amitié chrétienne." *Églises et chrétiens dans la Deuxième Guerre mondiale. La région Rhône-Alpes* (Grenoble, October 1976). Lyons: Presses Universitaires de Lyon, 1978.

Douvette, David. "Une histoire controversée." *Le Monde juif* no. 118 (April–June 1985): 61–63.

Felstiner, Mary. "Alois Brunner." *Simon Wiesenthal Center Annual*, 3 (1986): 1–46.

Fresco, N. "Les redresseurs de torts." *Les Temps modernes* (June 1980).

Jefroykin, Jules [Dika]. "L'Organisation juive de combat. Le Refus." *Les Nouveaux Cahiers* 37 (summer 1974): 18–24.

"Les Juifs de France et d'Algérie pendant la Seconde Guerre mondiale." *Yod* nos. 15–16 (1982): 7–164 (collected articles).

"Les Juifs pendant la Second Guerre mondiale." *Yod* 19 (1984): 9–132 (collected articles).

Kapel, R. "J'étais l'aumônier des camps du sud-ouest de la France (août 1940–décembre 1942)." *Le Monde juif*, no, 87 (July–September 1977): 96–98.

Keren-Patkin, Nili. "Hatsalat Ha-Yeladim Ha-Yehudiim Be-Tsarfat" (Hebrew, "The Rescue of Jewish Children in France"), *Yalkut Moreshet* 36 (1983): 3–50.

Kriegel, Annie. "De la résistance juive." *Pardès*, 2 (1985): 191–209.

Kriegel, Annie. "Résistants communistes et juifs persécutés." in *La France et la question juive, 1940–1944*. Paris: C.D.J.C./ Sylvie Messinger, 1981).

Lazare, Janine. "Le Seder de Pierre-Blanche." in *Le Temps qu'on n'oublie pas*. Paris: Fondation Sefer, 1963.

Lazare, L. "Les éclaireurs israélites de France ont-ils transformé la communauté juive?" *Tribune juive*, no. 863 (March 22, 1985).

Lazare, Lucien. "L'empreinte fondatrice des Éclaireurs israélites de France." *Tribune juive*, no. 863 (March 22, 1985).

Lazare, Lucien. "Judaïsme français et sionisme." *Dispersion et Unité* 16 (1976).

Lazare, Lucien. "De trois techniques pour occulter les Juifs de la scène de l'histoire." *Tribune juive*, no. 923 (June 6, 1986).

Michel, Henri. "Maquis et maquis." *Revue d'histoire de la Seconde Guerre mondiale*, no. 49 (January 1963).

Michel, Henri. "Les maquis au-delà de la légende." *Le Monde* (December 30–31, 1984).

Michel, Henri. "La résistance juive dans la résistance européenne." *Le Monde Juif*, no. 52 (October-December 1968): 7–13. English translation in *Yad Vashem Studies*, 1971.

Nicault, Catherine and Anne Grynberg. "La résistance sioniste sous l'occupation." *Pardès*, 16. Paris: Cerf, 1992.

Philippe, Béatrice. "Juifs dans la Résistance." *Yod*, nos. 15–16 (1982).

Poliakov, Léon. "Les différentes formes de la résistance juive en France." in *Jewish Resistance During the Holocaust*. Jerusalem: Yad Vashem, 1971.

Poliakov, Léon. "Jewish Resistance in the West." in *Jewish Resistance during the Holocaust*. Jerusalem: Yad Vashem, 1971),: 284–290.

Poznanski, Renée. "La résistance juive en France." *Revue d'histoire de la Second Guerre mondiale*, no. 137 (1985): 2–32.

Rabi, W. "Pour quoi ils ont combattu." *Les Nouveaux Cahiers* 37 (summer 1974): 1–9.

Raich, Leah. "La Wizo sous l'Occupation." *La Terre retrouvée* 4 (156), February 1, 1945.

Rayski, Adam. "Contre la nuit et le brouillard." *Le Monde juif* 14 (48) (October–December 1967): 8–14.

Rayski, Adam. "La fondation du Conseil représentatif des juifs de France." *Le Monde juif*, no. 51 (July-September 1968): 32–37.

Rayski, A. "Le Front invisible. Les groupes de résistance juive à Paris face à la répression policière." *Le Monde juif*, no. 53 (1969): 18–24 and no. 55 (1969): 11–20.

Rayski, A. "Les immigrés dans la Résistance." *Les Nouveaux Cahiers* 37 (Summer 1974).

Scherr, Lilly. "Les Juifs de France à veille de la Second Guerre mondiale." *Yod* 15–16 (1982): 12–18.

Schneersohn, Isaac. "Naissance du CDJC." *Le Monde juif*, no. 7 (1953): 4–5

Sklare, Marshall. "Le judaïsme américain et la célébration du bicentenaire." *Dispersion et Unité* 16 (1976): 188–197.

Soutou, Jean-Marie. "Souvenirs des années noires." *Les Cahiers de l'Alliance israélite universelle* (October–November 1979): 9–14.

L'Un des trente-six. Paris: Editions Kiyoum, 1946.

Uziel, M. "Miflagot La-Hayim ve-la-Mavet." ("Parties of Life and Death." Hebrew), *Maariv*, August 31, 1984.

Vidal-Naquet, P. "Un Eichmann de papier." *Esprit* (September 1980): 8–56.

Wellers, G. "Birkenau, qu'est-ce que c'est?" *Le Monde juif* 68 (October–December 1972): 25–36.

Wellers, Georges. "Quelques réflexions supplémentaires au sujet de la résistance juive." *Le Monde juif*, no. 118 (April-June 1985).

Wellers, G. "La Tragédie des deux journées." *Le Monde juif*, nos. 28–29 (January–June) 1962: 3–16;

3. Unpublished Sources

Bernheim, André. "Livre de raison du docteur André Bernheim." Unpublished, n.d. [1964]

Bulawko, Henri. "Témoignage sur la résistance juive en France occupée." Paris, November 30, 1982, in the author's possession.

Hirsch, Jean. "Les grandes manoeuvres." Unpublished account reconstructing the log of the Malquière-Larroque Platoon, which disappeared in the fire of Larroque, August 8, 1944.

Lacado log. Manuscript preserved by its chief, Adrien Gensburger. Belfort.

Maynadier, André. *8 août 1944 . . . maquis de Larroque*. Pratlong: unpublished, 1984.

Segonzac, Pierre Dunoyer de. *Historique et anecdotes des maquis de Vabre*. Albi: unpublished, 1964.

Weill, Joseph. *Déjà! . . . Essai autobiographique*, pp. 162–165. (n.p., n.d. [1983]), distribution limited to the author's relatives.

4. Public Archives

American Joint Distribution Committee, New York (AJDC).

Archives Nationales de France, Paris (AN).

Bibliothèque de documentation internationale contemporaine, Nanterre, France (BDIC).

Bibliothèque marxiste de Paris.

Centre de documentation juive contemporaine, Paris (CDJC).

Columbia University, Library

Governor Lehman Papers, New York

Varian Fry Collection, New York.

EIF, Paris (unclassified).

Hebrew University, Institute for Contemporary Judaism, Oral Testimony Division, Jerusalem (ICJ-OT).

Holocaust Library and Research Center, San Francisco.

Jewish Theological Seminary, Archives, New York (JTS).

Leo Baeck Institute, Archives, New York (LB).

Maison diocésaine de Paris, Archives historiques, Paris.

Yad Vashem, Archives, Jerusalem (YV).

Yivo Institute for Jewish Research, Archives, New York (YIVO).

5. Private Archives

Jacques Cohn, Jerusalem.

Roger Fichtenberg, Paris.

Joseph Fischer, Jerusalem.

Gilbert Lesage, Paris.

Lucien Lublin, Paris.

Abraham Polonski, Paris-Tel Aviv.

Charles Wittenberg, Toronto.

Index

Hesse, Didier, 353n12
Heymann, Raymond, 233
HICEM: AJDC and, 266; Central Commission and, 48; child refugees and, 135; Consistory and, 80; emigrees assisted by, 47; finances of, 257; Immigration Ministry and, 19; National Security Office and, 156; Nîmes Committee and, 49, 91; on non-Jewish population, 210; SSE and, 160; U.S. State Department and, 199; see also General Union of French Jews subdivisions. Sixth Directorate
High Holidays, 121
Hilberg, Raul, 129
Himmler, Heinrich, 350n46
Hirsch, Berthe, 251
Hirsch, Sigismund, 60, 64, 250–51
Hirschler, René, 49; arrest of, 222, 224, 271; CDJJ founding and, 71; Central Commission post of, 48, 96; general chaplaincy of, 95, 96, 223; Kapel and, 47; Katzki and, 48; Klein and, 322n25; Lesage and, 50, 157, 190; Marseilles arrests and, 218; on warning system, 160
Hirschler, Simone, 90, 332n35
Hitler, Adolf: French anti-Bolshevism and, 6; "intentionalist"/"functionalist" interpretations of, 319n28; Kriegel on, 308; Munich conference and, 19; prophecy of, 159; Rayski on, 105, 107
Hitler regime, see Nazi Germany
Hitler-Stalin Pact (1939), see German-Soviet Nonaggression Pact (1939)
Home for Jewish Refugees, 45
Hotel Bompart (Marseilles), 185
Hotel Pax (Annemasse), 345n102
Hotel Versigny (Paris), 287
House of Jesuits, 234
L'Humanité (newspaper), 19, 107, 211
Hungarian Jews, 84, 110
Hyman, Paula, 14, 15, 21, 315n16

"The Ideas of a Madman" (play), 87
Igeret (newsletter), 242
Ile-de-France Department, 126
Immigrant Manual Labor (organization): archives of, 329n7; census order and, 36; Comintern and, 112; communists and, 17, 105; conscription call of, 20; FTP and, 110; German-Soviet pact and, 106; Rue Amelot Committee and, 42; Secours populaire and, 107; Solidarité and, 84; south-

ern relocation proposal and, 237; UGIF and, 81; see also Second FTP-MOI Detachment
Immigration Ministry, 19
Indre Department, 131
Indre-et-Loire Department, 346n123
Inexpensive Housing (organization), 179–80
Les Informations juives (periodical), 85, 117
Institute of Marxist Studies (Institut des études marxistes), 180–81, 329n7, 358n20
Institut Maurice Thorez, 261, 353n12
L'Insurgé (periodical), 211
Intelligence Service, 282, 283, 288
Intergovernmental Committee on Refugees, 202
Intermovement Commission for the Evacuees, 49; AC and, 93; AJDC and, 263; foreign Jews and, 162; Gurs counselors and, 63; Nîmes Committee and, 90, 327n60; SSAE and, 262; SSE and, 160
Internal Security Department, 245, 351n72
International Brigades, 8, 104
International Conference on Refugees (1938), 7, 19, 21
International League Against anti-Semitism: Consistory and, 16, 18; convention of, 19; EIF and, 17; immigrant Jews and, 13, 15, 22; MNCR and, 150
International Organization of Refugees, 344n75
International Red Cross, 178, 193, 258
"Interprofessional Group for the Distribution of Products Indispensable to Agriculture," 249–50
Irregular Corps of the Black Mountain, 284, 291–94, 299, 361n70
Isère Department: AIP in, 232; Kapel in, 218; partisans in, 293; shelters in, 196, 206, 227
Islamic countries, 311; see also Arabs
Israel, 24, 311, 363n1; see also Palestine
Israélowicz, Léo, 342n37
Istors, 252
Italian Fascists, 278
Italian forces: AIP and, 232; AJ and, 279; Jews detained by, 228; Nazis vs., 225, 230; in Nice, 193, 227, 239, 269; rescue network and, 165; retreat of, 231; in southern zone, 216; at Swiss border, 184, 194, 200, 202, 226
Italian Fourth Army, 228
Italian immigrants, 8
Italian Ministry of Foreign Affairs, 227, 228
Italian Ministry of Interior, 231

Italian zone, 224–30, 236; deportations from, 234; foreign Jews in, 217, 218; Nazi invasion of, 198–99; OSE shelters in, 194
Italy: escape route through, 229, 230–31; legislation of, 225, 227; surrender of, 193, 194, 229
Izieu shelter, 195, 206

Jabotinsky, Vladimir, 97
J'accuse (periodical), 150, 244
Jacob, Simone, 234
Jacoubovitch, J., 151, 153, 239, 320*n*15, 353*m*18
Jarblum, Marc: AJ and, 265, 295; colleagues of, 90; on exchange rate, 356*m*6; Gourfinkel and, 92; international organizations and, 260; Katzki and, 48; non-Jewish associations and, 209; OSE underground team and, 166; prestige of, 68; Rogowski and, 232; sanatorium named for, 353*m*5; strategy of, 81–82, 89; Swiss authorities and, 200; on UGIF, 207–8; Zionist policies of, 14–15; mentioned, 268
Jean-Faure, André, 93
Jefroykin, Jules (Dika): AJ and, 69, 102, 166, 220, 295; border-runners and, 287, 288; Brunner and, 235; "consulting committee" of, 263–64; financial responsibilities of, 257–58, 263; Jarblum and, 90; S. Lévitte and, 68; J. Schwartz and, 258–59
Jesuits, 234
Jeunesse Mizrahi (Mizrahi Youth), 51, 69
Jewish Action (organization), 101
Jewish Agency for Palestine, 98, 257, 260, 264, 266
Jewish Army, 30, 97–98, 193, 275; Action juive and, 101; ADJC loan records and, 263; anonymous member of, 53; "Dutch" members of, 170; finances of, 256, 295; Finkelstein and, 70; guerrilla training by, 252; hostages from, 248; irregular corps of, 278–79, 282–83; Jefroykin and, 69, 102, 166, 220, 295; D. Knout and, 99; Liberation and, 294; MF and, 102; Montpellier congress and, 69; oath of, 103; Palestine-bound escapes of, 30, 169, 252, 284–89, 308; "physiognomists" and, 234; Quand même, 242–43; Rabi on, 62; smuggling by, 200, 264, 265; Spanish border-crossing by, 170, 263; Toulouse origins of, 65, 68, 102; UGIF files and, 208, 221; Youth Unification Committee on, 269; Zionists and, 97, 268, 278, 295; see also Blue-White Squad;

Central Administrative Committee; Éclair corps; Irregular Corps of the Black Mountain; Jewish Combat Organization
Jewish Brigade, 30
Jewish Colonization Association, 47, 80, 135
Jewish Combat Organization, 26, 294; see also Jewish Army
Jewish Committee for Children from Germany and Central Europe, 126
Jewish Councils, 77–78, 129
Jewish Documentation Center, 220, 274, 329*n*7, 356*n*26
Jewish Fortress (organization), 100, 101, 102
Jewish Lycée of Limoges, 122–23
Jewish National Fund: AJDC and, 166, 258, 263; FSJF and, 90; Igeret, 242; MJS and, 69; pioneer farms and, 65; publications of, 70; SSE and, 197
"Jewish Religious Association of the Ashkenazi Rite, Nice," 229
Jewish Scouting Movement, see Éclaireurs israélites de France
Jewish Second Detachment, see Second FTP-MOI Detachment
Jewish Social Assistance Mission, 48, 165
Jewish Union for Resistance and Mutual Assistance: CGD and, 240, 261, 268, 269; children kidnapped by, 196; Consistory and, 272; CRIF charter and, 273; establishment of, 238; financial aid to, 257, 353*n*15; on Jewish unity, 271; militarization of, 278; multiple roles of, 276; "patriotic militias" of, 281; UGIF and, 207, 208, 221; see also Solidarité (organization)
Jewish Welfare Committee of Paris: attempted reactivation of, 44–45; German refugees and, 18; Immigration Ministry and, 19; relief work of, 84, 86; Rue Amelot and, 82
Jewish Women's Union, 238
The Jews and the War (leaflet), 269
Jews in the War Against Fascism (manifesto), 269
Joint Distribution Committee, see American Joint Distribution Committee
Joliot-Curie gymnasium, 246
Journal officiel, 169
Judenräte, 77–78, 129
Junior Jewish Seminary of Limoges, 122–23

Kapel, René: "adoption" network of, 90, 332*n*35; AJ and, 102; arrest of, 217, 283;